Volume Zero

X Protocol Reference Manual

---

*for Version 11 of the
X Window System*

Edited and with an Introduction by Adrian Nye

O'Reilly & Associates, Inc.

Revision and Printing History

July 1989:   First Printing

May 1990:   Second Printing. Release 4 changes incorporated.

Small Print

The X Window System

The books in the X Window System Series are based in part on the original MIT X Window System documentation, but are far more comprehensive, easy to use, and are loaded with examples, tutorials and helpful hints. Over 20 major computer vendors recommend or license volumes in the series. In short, these are the definitive guides to the X Window System.

Volume 0:
X Protocol Reference Manual

A complete programmer's reference to the X Network Protocol, the language of communication between the X server and the X clients. 498 pages. $30.00.

Volumes 1 and 2:
Xlib Programming Manual
Xlib Reference Manual

Revised for Release 4. Complete guide and reference to programming with the X library (Xlib), the lowest level of programming interface to X. 672 and 792 pages. $60.00 for the set, or $34.95 each.

Volume 3:
X Window System User's Guide

Revised and enlarged for X11 Release 4. Describes window system concepts and the most common client applications available for X11. Includes complete explanation of the new window manager, *twm*, and a chapter on Motif. For experienced users, later chapters explain customizing the X environment. Useful with either Release 3 or Release 4. 749 pages. $30.00.

Volumes 4 and 5:
X Toolkit Intrinsics Programming Manual
X Toolkit Intrinsics Reference Manual

Complete guides to programming with the X Toolkit. The *Programming Manual* provides concepts and examples for using widgets and for the more complex task of writing new widgets. The *Reference Manual* provides reference pages for Xt functions, and Xt and Athena widgets. 582 and 545 pages. $55.00 for the set, or $30.00 each.

Volume 7:
XView Programming Manual

XView is an easy-to-use toolkit that is not just for Sun developers. It is available on MIT's R4 tape and System V Release 4, as well as being a part of Sun's Open Windows package. This manual provides complete information on XView, from concepts to creating applications to reference pages. 566 pages. $30.00.

The X Window System in a Nutshell

For the experienced X programmer, contains essential information from other volumes of the series in a boiled-down, quick reference format that makes it easy to find the answers needed most often. 380 pages. $24.95.

For orders or a free catalog of all our books, please contact us.

O'Reilly & Associates, Inc.

Creators and Publishers of Nutshell Handbooks
632 Petaluma Avenue, Sebastopol, CA 95472
email: uunet!ora!nuts · 1-800-338-6887 · 1-707-829-0515 · FAX 1-707-829-0104

Table of Contents

Preface

About This Manual

This reference manual describes the X Network Protocol which underlies all software for Version 11 of the X Window System. The X protocol is the language in which computers communicate all the information between the X server and X clients, whether the server and clients are operating on different systems in the network or on the same system.

The C language X library, known as Xlib, is the lowest level of C programming interface to the X protocol. The Lisp library CLX is the lowest level library for Lisp. These libraries translate procedure calls into the X protocol described in this volume. Additional higher level software such as the X Toolkit, CLUE, XView, Andrew, and InterViews are written using these low-level libraries to make X application programming easier.

In general, application programmers do not need to know the details of the protocol. However, it can be helpful to have access to the protocol specification when things do not work the way you expect.

Summary of Contents

This manual is divided into three major parts. Part One provides a conceptual introduction to the X protocol. It describes the role of the server and client and demonstrates the network transactions that take place during a minimal client session. Part Two contains an extensive set of reference pages for each protocol request and event. Part Three consists of several appendices describing particular parts of the X protocol and also several reference aids.

The reference pages contain a reformatted version of the Release 4 version of the original X protocol specification. The original document was formatted as running text. The reference section in this document treats each protocol request or event on a separate alphabetical reference page. Introductory material from the original document is presented on two separate reference pages—one entitled "Introduction," which describes the format and syntax of the reference pages, and one entitled "Connection Setup." The encoding of requests and replies, presented as an appendix in the original document, have been placed on the reference pages with each request. Every word and sentence in the original document is present in this manual with as little editing as possible to reduce the chance of errors. Therefore, the only difference between the reference section in this book and the original document is the organization of the material (which is intended to provide greater ease of access).

The appendices in Part Three contain several miscellaneous topics from the original document and several reference tables:

Appendix A, *Connection Close*, describes the server's operations to clean up after a client connection terminates.

Appendix B, *Keysyms*, describes the keyboard key symbols.

Appendix C, *Errors*, describes the problems that cause the server to generate each type of error.

Appendix D, *Predefined Atoms*, lists the predefined atoms.

Appendix E, *Keyboards and Pointers*, describes the X Window System model of keyboard handling.

Appendix F, *Flow Control and Concurrency*, specifies the constraints on server implementations for multi-threaded computer architectures.

Appendix G, *Request Group Summary*, lists the protocol requests by function with a brief description of each.

Appendix H, *Alphabetical Listing of Requests*, lists the requests alphabetically with a brief description of each.

Appendix I, *Xlib Functions to Protocol Requests*, lists each Xlib function and the protocol request it generates. This table is useful because there is sometimes more than one Xlib function that calls a particular protocol request.

Appendix J, *Protocol Requests to Xlib Functions*, lists each protocol request and the Xlib function that calls it.

Appendix K, *Events Briefly Described*, summarizes the conditions that trigger each event type.

Appendix L, *Interclient Communication Conventions*, describes the conventions for interclient communication that have been accepted as an X Consortium standard. This appendix is a reprint of David Rosenthal's *Inter-Client Communication Conventions Manual*.

Appendix M, *Logical Font Description Conventions*, describes the X Consortium standard for font naming and font properties. This appendix is a reprint of the X Consortium document.

Glossary describes many of the terms used in the reference section. This glossary is unedited from the original protocol document.

How to Use This Manual

This manual is intended for server implementors and client-library programmers and for application programmers who want to increase their knowledge of the underlying principles of the X Window System. The tutorial section explains how the protocol works and some of the issues involved in implementing it. The reference section contains the true definition of the protocol.

For application programmers seeking a deeper understanding of how Xlib works, probably the most effective way to use the manual is to read the tutorial introduction and then turn to Appendix I, *Xlib Functions to Protocol Requests*. This appendix lists the protocol requests corresponding to a given Xlib call (though not every Xlib call generates a protocol request). From there, simply turn to the alphabetical reference page for the appropriate request. The "Introduction" reference page contains additional information (such as definitions of data types) necessary for a complete understanding of many of the reference pages.

The more serious student of the protocol should probably read the "Introduction" and "Connection Setup" reference pages thoroughly, before working systematically through the reference pages and appendices. Appendix H, *Alphabetical Listing of Requests*, provides a useful overview in the form of brief descriptions of each request.

Assumptions

The tutorial section is written for the experienced programmer familiar with the principles of raster graphics but who knows little about X. The reference section assumes a strong familiarity with X, but much of this information can be learned by reading the tutorial.

Font Conventions Used in This Manual

Italics is used for:

- UNIX pathnames, filenames, program names, user command names, and options for user commands.

- Text added to reference pages by the editor that was not part of the original protocol document written at MIT.

Helvetica Italics is used for:

- Titles of examples, figures, and tables.

`Typewriter Font` is used for:

- C language function calls such as Xlib functions and UNIX system calls.

Boldface is used for:

- Chapter and section headings.

- X protocol terms and defined constants.

Related Documents

This manual is Volume Zero of the X Window System series by O'Reilly & Associates, Inc. Other documents from O'Reilly & Associates, Inc.:

Volume One — *Xlib Programming Manual*
Volume Two — *Xlib Reference Manual*
Volume Three — *X Window System User's Guide*
Volume Four — *X Toolkit Intrinsics Programming Manual*
Volume Five — *X Toolkit Intrinsics Reference Manual*
Volume Six — *X Toolkit Widget Reference Manual* (available summer 1990)
Volume Seven — *XView Programming Manual*

Request for Comments

Please write to tell us about any flaws you find in this manual or how you think it could be improved, to help us provide you with the best documentation possible.

Our U.S. mail address, e-mail address, and telephone number are as follows:

Ordering

O'Reilly & Associates, Inc.
632 Petaluma Avenue
Sebastopol, CA 95472
(800) 338-6887

Internet: nuts@ora.com
UUCP: uunet!ora!nuts

Editorial (Adrian Nye)

O'Reilly & Associates, Inc.
90 Sherman Street
Cambridge, MA 02140
(617) 354-5800

Internet: adrian@ora.com
UUCP: uunet!ora!adrian

Bulk Sales Information

This manual is being resold by many workstation manufacturers as their official X Window System documentation. For information on volume discounts for bulk purchase, call O'Reilly and Associates, Inc. at (800) 338-6887 (in CA 800-533-6887) or send e-mail to linda@ora.com (uunet!ora!linda).

For companies requiring extensive customization of the book, source licensing terms are also available.

Acknowledgements

The information contained in this manual is based in large part on the *X Window System Protocol, Version 11* (with many contributors). The X Window System software and the protocol document were written under the auspices of the Laboratory for Computer Science at MIT and are now controlled by the X Consortium.

The tutorial introduction has benefited from the review and suggestions of several people, including Jim Fulton of the X Consortium, Dave Striker of Convex Computer Corp., Pat Wood of Pipeline Associates, and Tim O'Reilly. Any errors that remain are my own.

— Adrian Nye

Part One:

Introduction to the X Protocol

Part One consists of a lengthy introduction to the concepts embodied in the X protocol, the tradeoffs involved in its design, and the techniques used in the implementation of servers and client libraries. It also describes the network interaction that takes place during a minimal client session.

Introduction to the X Protocol

The X Window System (or simply X) provides a hierarchy of resizable windows and supports high performance device-independent graphics (see Figure 1-1). Unlike most other window systems for UNIX that have a built-in user interface, X is a substrate on which almost any style of user interface can be built. But what is most unusual about X is that it is based on an asynchronous network protocol rather than on procedure or system calls. This protocol basis has a number of advantages:

- Both local and network connections can be operated in the same way using the protocol, making the network transparent both from the user's point of view and from the application programmer's point of view.

- The X protocol can be implemented using a wide variety of languages and operating systems.

- The X protocol can be used over any reliable byte stream (through local interprocess communication or over a network), several of which are standard and available on most architectures.

- For most applications, the X protocol has little performance penalty. Performance is limited more by the time required to draw graphics than by the overhead in the protocol.

It makes sense that networks and window systems should be used together. Since the window makes no distinction between local and network connections, the applications automatically provide a user interface to the network. The window system lets users get the benefit of access to remote computing abstractions using the same commands they use for running programs locally.

The protocol basis and concomitant portability of the X Window System is especially important today, when it is common to have several makes of machines in a single network. Until X, there was no common window system, and the common graphics languages that did exist did little to hide the differences between operating systems and graphics hardware. On the other hand, code that implements X is freely available and has shown itself to be extremely portable. Implementations exist for machines ranging from personal computers to supercomputers. The system is so hardware and operating system independent that properly written application software will compile and run on any system.

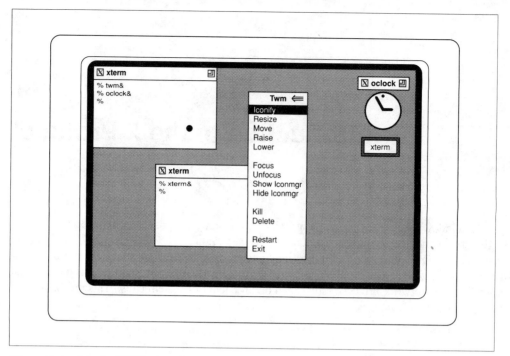

Figure 1-1. A typical X Window System display

1.1 The Server and Client*

The use of the terms *server* and *client* in X may at first seem different from their use in other computing contexts. To X, the *server* is the software that manages one display, keyboard, and mouse. One user is controlling the keyboard and mouse and looking at the display controlled by a server. The *client* is a program displaying on the screen and taking input from that keyboard and mouse. A client sends drawing requests and information requests to the server, and the server sends back to the client user input, replies to information requests, and error reports. The client may be running on the same machine as the server or on a different machine over the network.

You are probably familiar with the concept of a "file server," which is a remote machine with a disk drive from which several machines can read and write files. But in X, the server is the local system, whose abstractions the (perhaps remote) client programs are accessing. Figure 1-2 shows a server and client and their relationship to the network.

The X Window System is not limited to a single client interacting with a single server. There may be several clients interacting with a single server, which is the case when several applications are displaying on a single screen. Also, a single client can communicate with several servers, which would happen when an announcement program is displaying the same thing on several people's screens.

---

*If you have already programmed X applications or used the X Window System extensively, feel free to skip the sections early in this chapter that cover familiar topics.

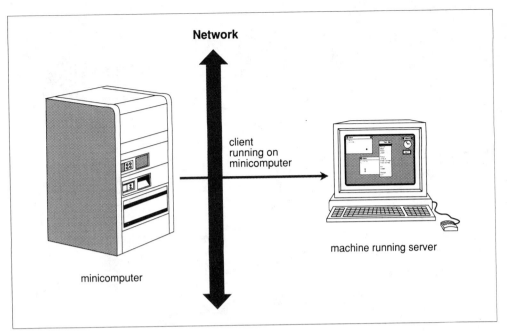

Figure 1-2. The server and client

A client may be running on the same machine as the server if that machine supports multi-tasking, or the client may run on a different machine connected over the network. On multitasking UNIX workstations, it is normal to have some clients running locally and others operating over the network. Naturally, other users will probably have clients running on their own system and perhaps on yours as well, but most will be displayed only on their own screens. With servers running on single-tasking systems such as IBM or compatible PC and AT class computers, all clients must run on other systems over the network. The same is true of specialized X terminals that have the server software built into ROM, and have an integral Ethernet™ network interface. Figure 1-3 shows a network with two servers, in which clients can run on any node and display on either server.

The *window manager* is a client that has authority over the layout of windows on the screen. Certain X protocol features are used only by the window manager to enforce this authority. Otherwise, the window manager is just like any other client.

X clients are programmed using various client programming libraries in C and Lisp. The C libraries are the most widely used. They include a low level procedural interface to the X protocol called Xlib and a higher level toolkit written in object-oriented style called the Xt Intrinsics. The Intrinsics are used to build user interface components called widgets. Several widget sets that implement certain user interface conventions are available from various vendors. The one supplied by MIT is called the Athena widgets. Figure 1-4 shows how the various programming interfaces for C are combined to write clients that utilize the X protocol to communicate with the server.

Xlib and the Xt Intrinsics were developed at MIT. Several other toolkit layers that use Xlib to interface to the protocol have been developed outside of MIT, some written in C and some in C++. These include Andrew, InterViews, and XView.

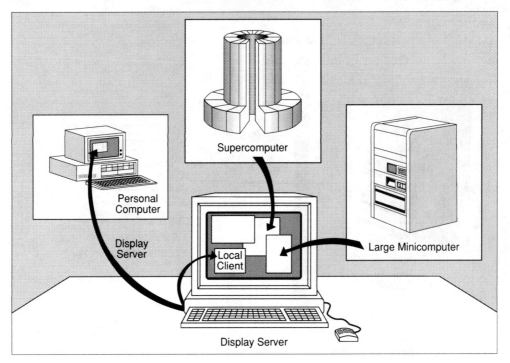

Figure 1-3. A distributed X environment

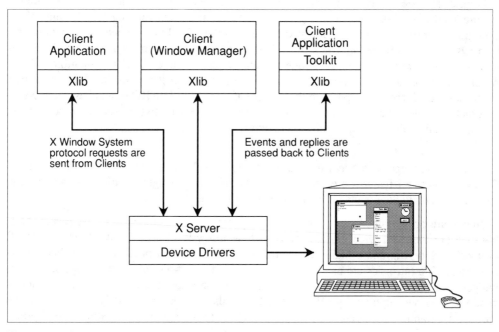

Figure 1-4. The client programming libraries in C

1.2 The X Protocol

The X protocol is the true definition of the X Window System, and any code in any language that implements it is a true implementation of X. It is designed to communicate all the information necessary to operate a window system over a single asynchronous bidirectional stream of 8-bit bytes.

Below the X protocol, any lower layer of network can be used, as long as it is bidirectional and delivers bytes in sequence and unduplicated between a server process and a client process. When the client and server are on the same machine, the connection is based on local interprocess communication (IPC) channels, shared memory, or UNIX domain sockets. However, even local connections use the X protocol.

The protocol is designed to be operated asynchronously because this allows much higher performance. Synchronous operating speed is limited by the time required to make a round trip, which on most currently available local area networks is between 5 and 50 milliseconds. This speed is usually much less than the speed of the network in requests without replies. The server also sends events asynchronously, because this allows local polling for applications that must poll continuously for input. An example of such an application would be a game where the display is changing continuously but user input is still sought. Otherwise, applications that must poll for input during continuous drawing would actually be forced to operate synchronously.

Numerous window systems under UNIX use file or channel descriptors to represent windows. This has several disadvantages compared to X's approach of multiplexing all the windows on a single network connection. There is often a limit to the number of such descriptors, and they cannot be shared by clients on different machines and sometimes even on the same machine. Finally, the time order of communications through each descriptor is difficult to guarantee. The multiplexing of requests affecting different windows on the same stream allows the client to control the time order of updates, and similarly, the multiplexing of events on one stream also guarantees that the correct order is preserved.

Normally, clients implement the X protocol using a programming library that interfaces to a single underlying network protocol, typically TCP/IP or DECnet. The sample implementation provided by MIT of the C language client programming library called Xlib uses *sockets* on systems based on Berkeley UNIX.* MIT does not provide a routine for handling networking on systems based on AT&T's System V Release 3 UNIX. AT&T, in its proprietary implementation of Xlib, uses the System V native *streams*, where a protocol module supporting any underlying network protocol can be "pushed" onto a stream, allowing Xlib to use any underlying protocol for which a streams module exists. Some vendors have implemented shared memory to speed communication between the server and clients running on the same machine.

---

*The *interfaces* defined in MIT's implementation of Xlib are standard, but the code is not. In other words, hardware vendors are allowed to change and optimize the library code for their systems as long as it provides exactly the programming interface defined in the Xlib specification document. The same is true of the server, the Xt Intrinsics, and all other X code controlled by an X Consortium standard.

Servers often understand more than one underlying protocol so that they can communicate with clients on more than one type of network at once. For example, the DECwindows server accepts connections from clients using TCP/IP or from clients using DECnet. Currently, these are the only two network protocols commonly supported in X servers.

1.2.1 Message Types

The X protocol specifies four types of messages that can be transferred over the network. Requests are sent from the client to the server, and replies, events, and errors are sent from the server to the client.

- A *request* is generated by the client and sent to the server. A protocol request can carry a wide variety of information, such as a specification for drawing a line or changing the color value in a cell in a colormap or an inquiry about the current size of a window. A protocol request can be any multiple of 4 bytes in length.

- A *reply* is sent from the server to the client in response to certain requests. Not all requests are answered by replies—only the ones that ask for information. Requests that specify drawing, for example, do not generate replies, but requests that inquire about the current size of a window do. Protocol replies can be any multiple of 4 bytes in length, with a minimum of 32 bytes.

- An *event* is sent from the server to the client and contains information about a device action or about a side effect of a previous request. The data contained in events is quite varied because it is the principal method by which clients get information. All events are stored in a 32-byte structure to simplify queueing and handling them.

- An *error* is like an event, but it is handled differently by clients. Errors are sent to an error-handling routine by the client-side programming library. Error messages are the same size as events, to simplify handling them.

A protocol request that requires a reply is called a *round-trip request*. Round-trip requests have to be minimized in client programs because they lower performance when there are network delays. This will be discussed in more detail in the section on client library implementation.

You will notice that all the X protocol message types are designed to have a length in multiples of 4 bytes. This is to simplify implementation of the protocol on architectures that require alignment of values on 16- or 32-bit boundaries. As we will see, 16- and 32-bit values within the messages are always placed on 16- and 32-bit boundaries respectively.

We will define the contents of each of these protocol message types in more detail a little later.

1.2.2 Division of Responsibilities

In the process of designing the X protocol, much thought went into the division of capability between the server and the client, since this determines what information has to be passed back and forth through requests, replies, and events. An excellent source of information about the rationale behind certain choices made in designing the protocol is the article *The X Window System*, by Robert W. Scheifler and Jim Gettys, published in the Association of Computing Machinery journal *Transactions on Graphics*, Vol. 5, No. 2, April 1987. The decisions ultimately reached were based on portability of client programs, ease of client programming, and performance.

First, the server is designed, as much as possible, to hide differences in the underlying hardware from client applications. The server manages windows, does all drawing, and interfaces to the device drivers to get keyboard and pointer input. The server also manages off-screen memory, windows, fonts, cursors, and colormaps. The sample server code written at MIT contains a device-independent part and a device-dependent part. The device-dependent part must be customized for each hardware configuration, and it is here that the characteristics of the hardware are translated into the abstractions used by X such as "colormap."

Having the server responsible for managing the hierarchy and overlapping of windows has few, if any, disadvantages. It would seem quite possible for the client to waste network time by requesting graphics to a window that is not visible, since the client knows nothing of the window position or stacking order. (Such a request would have no effect since X does not preserve the contents of obscured windows.) However, this situation is dealt with by having clients draw only in response to an **Expose** event that announces when an area of a window has become exposed. In X, it is the client's responsibility to send the appropriate requests needed to redraw the contents of the rectangle of a window specified in the **Expose** event. For the rare clients where this responsibility leads to a severe performance penalty, X servers may (but are not required to) have a backing store feature that lets the server maintain window contents regardless of visibility.

There are certain hardware variations that are impossible or unwise to hide in the server. The X server could attempt to insulate the client from screen variations such as screen size, color vs. monochrome, number of colors, etc., but each of these would come at some cost. Hiding the screen size would make it easier to program applications that require graphics of a consistent size independent of the screen resolution, but it would make it harder to identify and manipulate single pixels, and it would add a burden to the server code. Hiding whether the screen is color or monochrome and the number of planes would lessen the load on the client program for simple color use, but it would be harder to manipulate the colormap in powerful ways, or use tricks in color such as overlays. A decision was made to make client programming more complicated in order to make it more powerful, since the goal was to hide this complexity in toolkit libraries anyway.

The server takes steps to make keyboard handling as uniform as possible on different machines, but it cannot completely hide variations in what symbols are actually embossed on the caps of the keys. For example, not all keyboards have Control and Meta keys. X handles this by providing several ways of handling the keyboard at different levels of abstraction. Each physical key has a code assigned by the server's device-dependent layer, which is reported in each key event. The server implementation also provides a table of key combinations and a resulting symbol which is the meaning of that key combination. For example, if the "a" key was pressed while the "Shift" key was being held, the key symbol in the table would represent "A". This table is managed by the server so that it applies to all clients, but the client library often maintains a copy of it so that the client can interpret events locally (quickly). The server does not use the table to interpret events before sending them to the client, which allows the client to interpret the keys in different languages or to use other event-handling techniques if desired (a client might want to treat the keyboard as a musical instrument rather than for text, for example). X supplies a request (**ChangeKeyboardMapping**) for changing the key symbol table, which results in an **MappingNotify** event to be sent to all clients. Clients other than the one that called **ChangeKeyboardMapping** respond to this event by sending a (**GetKeyboardMapping**) request, which gets the updated table.

Some decisions were made purely to simplify (or enhance) client programming. For example, coordinates in drawing requests are interpreted relative to the window being drawn into rather than to the entire screen. This provides a virtual drawing surface or "window" and makes client programming easier because the client does not need to continually track the window position and calculate where to draw based on this position. This gives the server the burden of determining where to actually draw graphics on the screen based on window positions. This, in turn, allows the server to support the window hierarchy without necessarily having to report all changes back to the client.

In other cases, decisions were made to increase performance. An example of this is the graphics context. The X *graphics context* (GC) allows the server to cache information about how graphics requests are to be interpreted, so this information need not be sent over the network from the client with every graphics request. This reduction in network traffic results in improved performance, particularly when the network is slow. Also, servers can be designed to cache GCs so that switching between them is fast and efficient. Finally, it is a happy coincidence that the GC usually makes client programming easier, because it reduces the number of parameters needed in drawing calls.

The GC is one of several abstractions X maintains in the server; the most important others are the Window, Pixmap (an off-screen virtual drawing surface that must be copied into a window to become visible), Colormap, and Font. The client refers to each abstraction in protocol requests using a unique integer ID assigned by the server. This ID is a 29-bit integer (high bits are unused to simplify implementation on architectures that employ garbage collection). IDs are chosen by the client-side libraries, but using a specific subrange specified by the server at connection time that guarantees that the IDs will be unique from all other IDs that can be created by other clients using the same server. The fact that IDs are not assigned by the server means that creating an abstraction does not require a reply by the server. This is very important in reducing the startup time of applications because creating each abstraction would otherwise waste at least one round-trip time.

The Window abstraction lets the server manage which parts of the screen are displaying which parts of which window, and lets the server take care of applying the window attributes (such things as the border and background) to each window. The X protocol includes requests that get information about abstractions, so that the client is not completely in the dark. However, not every detail of each abstraction is necessarily accessible from the client side, since some information of limited usefulness was left out of query replies to allow more flexibility in server code design. One example of this is that some of the window attributes cannot be queried (such as bit gravity, which is for redrawing optimization). Another is that the values in GCs cannot be queried at all. Neither the window attributes that cannot be queried nor the GC values are changed by any client other than the one that created them. Therefore, it does not add much burden to clients to require them to keep track of their own parameter settings if they need the information later. Furthermore, programming the server to be able to provide this information places constraints on the server that could affect performance.

1.3 A Sample Session

The following sections describe what happens over the network during a minimal application that creates a window, allocates a color, waits for events, draws into the window, and quits. This example uses three of the four types of X network messages as they would occur in an application. The fourth is the error, which we hope will not occur during the normal operation of an application. How errors are generated and handled and what the network message for an error looks like will be explained after successful operation is described.

Here are the network events that will take place during a successful client session:

- Client opens connection to the server and sends information describing itself.

- Server sends back to client data describing the server or refusing the connection request.

- Client makes a request to create a window. Note that this request has no reply.

- Client makes a request to allocate a color.

- Server sends back a reply describing the allocated color.

- Client makes a request to create a graphics context, for using in later drawing requests.

- Client makes a request identifying the types of events it requires. In this case, **Expose** and **ButtonPress** events.

- Client makes a request to map (display on the screen) the created window.

- Client waits for an **Expose** event before continuing. This sends the accumulated requests to the server.

- Server sends to client an **Expose** event indicating that the window has been displayed.

- Client makes a request to draw a graphic, using graphics context.

- Loop back to wait for an **Expose** event.

We note in this session description that client requests are queued up by the client library before being sent to the server and that the client reading events triggers the sending. This is not actually a required characteristic of client libraries, but it improves performance greatly because it takes advantage of the asynchronous design of the protocol. Xlib works this way. This behavior allows the client to continue running without having to stop to wait for network access, until it would have to wait for an event anyway.

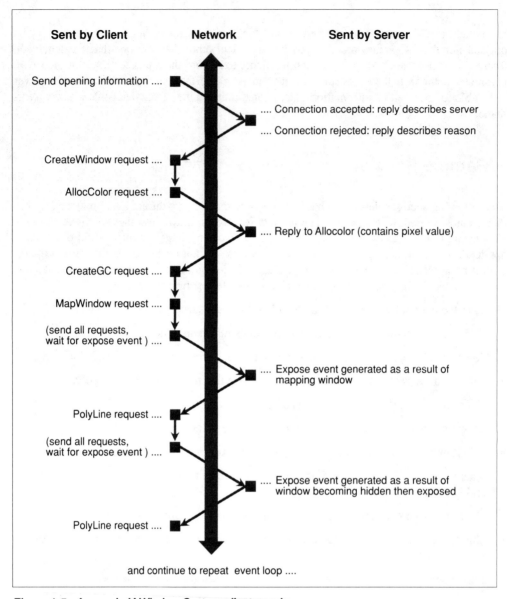

Sent by Client **Network** **Sent by Server**

Send opening information ....

.... Connection accepted: reply describes server

.... Connection rejected: reply describes reason

CreateWindow request ....

AllocColor request ....

.... Reply to Allocolor (contains pixel value)

CreateGC request ....

MapWindow request ....

(send all requests,
wait for expose event) ....

.... Expose event generated as a result of
mapping window

PolyLine request ....

(send all requests,
wait for expose event) ....

.... Expose event generated as a result of
window becoming hidden then exposed

PolyLine request ....

and continue to repeat event loop ....

Figure 1-5. A sample X Window System client session.

Note that many of the actions taken by the client in the session must be done in the order shown for the application to work properly. For example, **Expose** events must be selected before the window is mapped, because otherwise no event would arrive to notify the client when to draw. This becomes even more important when a window manager is managing the screen. Many window managers let the user decide on the size and position of a window before allowing it to be mapped, introducing a sizeable delay between the time the client requests mapping the window and when the window actually appears on the screen ready to be drawn into. Only the **Expose** event tells the client when it is time to draw.

Colors are allocated very early in the session before creating the graphics context to optimize the usage of protocol requests. To allocate a color, the client tells the server what color is desired, and the server responds by giving the client a "pixel value," which is a number that identifies the cell in the colormap containing the closest color available (the exact color may not be physically possible on the screen, or all colormap entries may already be in use by other clients). When creating the graphics context, this pixel value can be used to set the foreground color to be used for drawing. It is also possible to create a default graphics context before allocating the color, but then setting the foreground value in the existing graphics context would require an additional, unnecessary request.*

1.3.1 Opening the Connection

The client allows the user to identify the server it wants to connect to by specifying a host and display number. The display number is zero on personal workstations, because there is only one keyboard, pointer, and display connected to a single host, and hence only one server. Multi-user workstations and timesharing systems that support graphics terminals are rare today, but X leaves open the possibility that a single host could support two or more servers by having two or more sets of display, keyboard, and mouse.

The client-side library should provide an easy-to-use method for the user to specify which server to connect to. Under UNIX, Xlib reads the environment variable DISPLAY. The user specifies the server by setting DISPLAY to the host name and server number separated by a colon, for example, *ghost:0*. The networking utilities under Berkeley UNIX translate host names into network addresses using the file */etc/hosts* (or on some systems, the yellow pages daemon).

For TCP connections, displays on a given host are numbered starting from zero, and the server for display N listens and accepts connections on port 6000+N. For DECnet connections, displays on a given host are numbered starting from zero, and the server for display N listens and accepts connections on the object name obtained by concatenating "X$X" with the decimal representation for N, e.g., X$X0 and X$X1.

Once the proper address is known, the client begins sending bytes that describe itself. Then the server sends back information describing itself if the connection is acceptable or describing what went wrong if the connection is refused.

Table 1-1 specifies the data that the client sends. Throughout this chapter, when the type for a certain piece of data is not defined by the protocol, it is not critical and is not shown.

---

*For more information about of the order of operations for most effective client programming, see Volume One, *Xlib Programming Manual*.

Table 1-1. Byte Stream Sent by Client to Open Connection

# of Bytes	Type	Values	Description
1		102 (MSB first) 154 (LSB first)	byte-order
1			unused
2	unsigned integer		protocol-major-version
2	unsigned integer		protocol-minor-version
2		n	length of authorization-protocol-name
2		d	length of authorization-protocol-data
2			unused
n	list of unsigned integers		authorization-protocol-name
p			unused, p=pad(n)
d	list of unsigned integers		authorization-protocol-data
q			unused, q=pad(d)

The first byte of data identifies the byte order employed on the client's machine. The value 102 (ASCII upper case B) means values are transmitted most significant byte first, and the value 154 (ASCII lower case l) means values are transmitted least significant byte first. All 16-bit and 32-bit quantities, except those involving image data, are transferred in both directions using this byte order specified by the client. Image data is an exception and is described at the end of this section.

Next, the client tells the server the version of the protocol it expects the server to implement. The major version is currently 11 and the minor version is 0 (this is true for Release 1 through Release 4 of X Version 11). The version numbers are an escape hatch in case future revisions of the protocol are necessary. In general, the major version would increment for incompatible changes, and the minor version would increment for small upward-compatible changes. The server returns the protocol version numbers it actually supports, which might not equal the version sent by the client. The server can (but need not) refuse connections frpm clients that offer a different version than the server supports. A server can (but need not) support more than one version simultaneously.

The authorization name indicates what authorization protocol the client expects the server to use, and the data is specific to that protocol. Specification of valid authorization mechanisms is not part of the core X protocol. (See Section 1.4.5.)

The padding and unused bytes are required because each network message generated by X always has a length that is a multiple of 4 bytes, and all 16- and 32-bit quantities are placed in the message such that they are on 16- or 32-bit boundaries. This is done to make implementation of the protocol easier on architectures that require data to be aligned on 16- or 32-bit boundaries. Consequently, lengths of data in the X protocol are always specified in units of 4 bytes.

The server sends back the information shown in Table 1-2 if connection is refused.

Table 1-2. Byte Stream Returned by Server on Failed Connection

# of Bytes	Type	Values	Description
1		0	failed
1		n	length of reason in bytes
2	unsigned integer		protocol-major-version
2	unsigned integer		protocol-minor-version
2		(n+p)/4	length in 4-byte units of "additional data"
n	list of unsigned integers		reason
p			unused, p=pad(n)

The value of the first element is 1 if the connection succeeded or 0 if it failed. The protocol version elements describe the protocol version preferred (or the only one accepted) by the server. (This may be the reason for connection failure if the client expected a different version.) The reason element describes why connection failed. Current servers do not use standard codes for reasons.

Table 1-3 shows the stream of data returned when the connection is successful. The Xlib client programming library stores this information in the `Display` structure, and the pointer to this structure is passed as an argument to most Xlib routines. The routines then access this information internally when necessary. Xlib also provides macros (and function equivalents) for accessing a few of the more frequently used items, so that client programs do not depend on the particular implementation of the structure that contains this information.

You need to know that an X server can support multiple screens to understand the returned connection information. An X server shows information to a single user but perhaps through more than one physical or logical screen. An example of a use for two physical screens would be to be able to debug an application on a color screen and on a monochrome screen at the same time. Both screens are controlled by a single server. The sample server on Sun color systems currently provides two logical screens on a single physical screen, one with the screen acting as monochrome (which is currently much faster), and the other with the screen acting in color. The user switches between the screens by moving the pointer off either side of the screen. No geometry of the screens is defined by the protocol, and how the mouse moves between the various screens depends on the server implementation.

The connection information describes each of the attached screens separately. Since there can be any number of attached screens, there is a section of the connection information that is repeated for each screen. Moreover, each screen can sometimes be used in a variety of ways. For example, a color screen can also be used to display windows in black and white. X calls the attributes describing a particular way of using a screen a *visual*. For each screen, there is information describing the one or more ways that screen can be used.

The concept of the visual has a number of advantages. If you know a certain window is going to be used in black and white even on a color screen (for example, a terminal emulator window), it is much more efficient to treat it that way because it requires handling only 1 bit per pixel instead of up to 24. Some servers can take advantage of this to improve performance dramatically.

As we will see in the **CreateWindow** request, a window is created with a particular visual, and this is a permanent aspect of the created window. Since there may be several different ways of using color on a certain screen, the block of data that describes a visual may be repeated several times for each screen. Each screen description includes the width-in-pixels, height-in-pixels, width-in-millimeters, and height-in-millimeters of the root window (which cannot be changed). This information can be used to tailor client operation according to the screen size and aspect ratio.

Each screen also has a default colormap which contains at least two permanently allocated entries called BlackPixel and WhitePixel, which can be used in implementing a monochrome application on monochrome or color screens. The actual RGB values of BlackPixel and WhitePixel may be settable on some screens and, in any case, may not actually be black and white. The names are intended to convey the expected relative intensity of the colors.

Table 1-3. Byte Stream Returned by Server on Successful Connection

# of Bytes	Type	Values	Description
1		1	success
1			unused
2	unsigned integer		protocol-major-version
2	unsigned integer		protocol-minor-version
2		$8+2n+(v+p+m)/4$	length in 4-byte units of "additional data"
4	unsigned integer		release-number
4	unsigned integer		resource-id-base
4	unsigned integer		resource-id-mask
4	unsigned integer		motion-buffer-size
2		v	length of vendor
2	unsigned integer		maximum-request-length
1	unsigned integer		number of SCREENs in roots
1		n	number for FORMATs in pixmap-formats
1		0 (LSBFirst) 1 (MSBFirst)	image-byte-order
1		0 (LeastSignificant) 1 (MostSignificant)	bitmap-format-bit-order

# of Bytes	Type	Values	Description
1	unsigned integer		bitmap-format-scanline-unit
1	unsigned integer		bitmap-format-scanline-pad
1	KEYCODE (unsigned integer)		min-keycode
1	KEYCODE (unsigned integer)		max-keycode
4			unused
v	list of unsigned integers		vendor
p			unused, p=pad(v)
8n	LISTofFORMAT		pixmap-formats
m	LISTofSCREEN		roots (m is always a multiple of 4)
FORMAT			
1	unsigned integer		depth
1	unsigned integer		bits-per-pixel
1	unsigned integer		scanline-pad
5			unused
SCREEN			
4	WINDOW		root
4	COLORMAP		default-colormap
4	unsigned integer		white-pixel
4	unsigned integer		black-pixel
4	SETofEVENT		current-input-masks
2	unsigned integer		width-in-pixels
2	unsigned integer		height-in-pixels
2	unsigned integer		width-in-millimeters
2	unsigned integer		height-in-millimeters
2	unsigned integer		min-installed-maps
2	unsigned integer		max-installed-maps
4	VISUALID		root-visual
1		0 (Never) 1 (WhenMapped) 2 (Always)	backing-stores
1	BOOL		save-unders
1	unsigned integer		root-depth
1	unsigned integer		number of DEPTHs in allowed-depths

# of Bytes	Type	Values	Description
n	LISTofDEPTH		allowed-depths (n is always a multiple of 4)
DEPTH			
1	unsigned integer		depth
1			unused
2		n	number of VISUAL-TYPES in visuals
4			unused
24n	LISTofVISUALTYPE		visuals
VISUALTYPE			
4	VISUALID		visual-id
1		0 (StaticGray) 1 (GrayScale) 2 (StaticColor) 3 (PseudoColor) 4 (TrueColor) 5 (DirectColor)	class
1	unsigned integer		bits-per-rgb-value
2	unsigned integer		colormap-entries
4	unsigned integer		red-mask
4	unsigned integer		green-mask
4	unsigned integer		blue-mask
4			unused

All this information describes the server in painstaking detail. It is impossible to describe all of it in detail here, but we will touch on some of the more interesting parts.

The resource-id-mask and resource-id-base elements provide the information necessary for the client to generate IDs that are unique within the client but also unique from IDs generated in other clients. An ID must be unique with respect to the IDs of all other abstractions created by all clients, not just other abstractions of the same type and by the same client, because the server manages them all. The resource-id-mask is a 32-bit value with at least 18 bits set. The client allocates an abstract ID* by choosing a value with some subset of these bits set and ORing it with resource-id-base. To allocate the next ID, normally the client increments its value that is a subset of resource-id-mask. This local allocation of IDs is important because it eliminates the need for round-trip requests when creating abstractions, which speeds the startup time of clients.

---

*In this book, we use the term "abstract" instead of the term "resource" because resource has another meaning in programming contexts (the resource database).

Maximum-request-length specifies the maximum length of a request, in 4-byte units, accepted by the server. This limit might depend on the amount of available memory in the server. This is the maximum value that can appear in the length field of a request. Requests larger than this generate a **BadLength** error, and the server will read and simply discard the entire request. Maximum-request-length will always be at least 4096 (that is, requests of length up to and including 16384 bytes will be accepted by all servers).

X servers are required to swap the bytes of data from machines with different native byte order, in all cases except in image processing. The first byte in the message that opens the connection between the client and the server, sent from the client library, indicates to the server which byte order is native on the host running the client.

Image data is always sent to the server and received from the server using the server's byte order. This is because image data is likely to be voluminous and byte-swapping it expensive. The client is told the server's byte order in the information returned after connecting to the server. The client may then be able to store and operate on the image in the correct format for the server, eliminating the need to swap bytes.

1.3.2 Creating a Window

Once the connection to the server is successfully opened, the first thing most applications do is create one or more windows.

The **CreateWindow** request is more complicated than most X protocol requests, but all requests have the same structure; a block of data consisting of an opcode, some number of fixed length parameters, and sometimes a variable-length parameter. Every request begins with an 8-bit major opcode, followed by a 16-bit length field expressed in units of 4 bytes. The length field defines the total length of the request, including the opcode and length field and must equal the minimum length required to contain the request, or an error is generated. Unused bytes in a request are not required to be zero.

Major opcodes 128 through 255 are reserved for extensions. Each extension is intended to contain multiple requests; all requests within a particular extension would use the same major opcode. Therefore, extension requests typically have an additional minor opcode encoded in the data byte immediately following the length field.

We will describe the fixed- and variable-length components of **CreateWindow** after you have seen the data sent in this request. Table 1-4 shows the byte stream sent by a client to the server to create a window. (Do not be put off by its complexity; most requests are much simpler than this one.)

Table 1-4. The CreateWindow *Request*

# of Bytes	Type	Values	Description
1	1		opcode of request
1	unsigned integer		depth
2	8+n		request length
4	WINDOW		client selected ID for window
4	WINDOW		parent's ID
2	signed integer		x (position)
2	signed integer		y
2	unsigned integer		width (size, inside border)
2	unsigned integer		height
2	unsigned integer		border-width
2		0 (CopyFromParent) 1 (InputOutput) 2 (InputOnly)	class
4	VISUALID	(id) 0 (CopyFromParent)	visual
4	BITMASK		value-mask (has n 1-bits) for attributes
	#x00000001	background-pixmap	
	#x00000002	background-pixel	
	#x00000004	border-pixmap	
	#x00000008	border-pixel	
	#x00000010	bit-gravity	
	#x00000020	win-gravity	
	#x00000040	backing-store	
	#x00000080	backing-planes	
	#x00000100	backing-pixel	
	#x00000200	override-redirect	
	#x00000400	save-under	
	#x00000800	event-mask	
	#x00001000	do-not-propagate-mask	
	#x00002000	colormap	
	#x00004000	cursor	
4n	LISTofVALUE		value-list
VALUES			
4	PIXMAP	(pixmap) 0 (None) 1 (ParentRelative)	background-pixmap

Table 1-4. The CreateWindow *Request (continued)*

# of Bytes	Type	Values	Description
4	unsigned integer		background-pixel
4	PIXMAP	(pixmap) 0 (**CopyFromParent**)	border-pixmap
4	unsigned integer		border-pixel
1	BITGRAVITY		bit-gravity
1	WINGRAVITY		win-gravity
1		0 (**NotUseful**) 1 (**WhenMapped**) 2 (**Always**)	backing-store
4	unsigned integer		backing-planes
4	unsigned integer		backing-pixel
1	BOOL		override-redirect
1	BOOL		save-under
4	SETofEVENT		event-mask
4	SETofDEVICEEVENT	do-not-propagate-mask	
4	COLORMAP	(colormap) 0 (**CopyFromParent**)	colormap
4	CURSOR	(cursor) 0 (**None**)	cursor

The most interesting aspect of **CreateWindow** is that it varies in length according to how much information needs to be transferred. The fixed-length components of **CreateWindow** include the ID of the parent window; the ID the client has chosen for this window; the window size, position, and border width; the window class (**InputOutput** or **InputOnly**); and the window's visual (ID of a server-created abstraction which describes how color should be used in the window). The final component of the fixed-length portion of **Create-Window** is a bitmask which describes which of the optional components are present. Optional components are always bits of information for which the server has a reasonable default for the ones not specified. The bitmask tells the server which items are going to be present in the remainder of the request.

The optional components in **CreateWindow** are the window attributes. The window attributes control:

- The background and border colors or patterns.

- Whether the contents of a window are saved when the window is resized and where the old contents are placed (bit gravity).

- Whether and how subwindows should be automatically moved when the parent is resized (window gravity).

- Whether the window contents should be preserved by the server (backing store).

- Whether the server should save under a temporary window to speed redrawing when this window is unmapped (save under).

- The events that should be delivered to the client when they occur in this window (event mask).

- Events that should not propagate to higher windows in the hierarchy (do-not-propagate-mask).

- Whether the window should be immune to window manager intervention (override-redirect).

- Which colormap should be used to translate pixel values into colors for this window (colormap).

- What cursor should be used in this window (cursor).

1.3.2.1 Selecting Events

The only attribute that every client sets is the event mask.

The server is capable of sending many types of events to the client, each of which contains information about a different user action or side effect of a request. But the client is not always interested in every type of event, and it is wasteful to send them over simply to be thrown away. Therefore, each window has an attribute that controls which events are sent over when they occur in that window.

The event mask can be set in **CreateWindow** or as part of a somewhat simpler request called **ChangeWindowAttributes**. However, if the correct event mask is known when the window is created, it is more efficient to set the event mask at that window creation time rather than with a separate request. Note that the time delay between window creation and setting of the event mask when done in separate requests is not a problem, because events cannot occur in this window yet because it is not yet displayed. Windows do not appear on the screen until they are mapped, which is discussed in Section 1.3.5.

For this sample session, we will select **Expose** and **ButtonPress** events. The **Expose** events are necessary to tell us when our window appears on the screen so we can draw on it, and the **ButtonPress** event will allow us to escape from the closed event handling loop.

1.3.3 A Request with Reply

Some requests require an immediate reply from the server, because the client cannot continue without the information. Most of these requests get information about server abstractions such as windows, fonts, and properties. Others report success or failure of a request whose effects must take place before the client can safely continue. Some requests require replies for both these reasons. Either a particular request has a reply or it does not; there are no requests that sometimes have replies and other times do not. Replies are always immediate.

As an example, we demonstrate here a request that allocates a color. To describe color handling in X completely would take considerable space, and it is unnecessary for a conceptual understanding of the protocol. But you can understand the request and the reply if you understand just a little about color. The client specifies a color by specifying the index of a cell in a server-maintained colormap. This index is called a pixel value. The client has to request from the server the pixel value that represents a certain color, because only the server knows what color is in each cell. The X server is capable of maintaining multiple virtual colormaps, and it can install one or more of them depending on the hardware. Each of these colormaps has an ID and can be read-only or read/write. Read-only colormaps contain cells with preset color values, and these cells can be shared because no client can change them, but often clients will not find the exact color they need in the colormap. Read/write colormaps can have colorcells that are private to a single application and others that are shared among applications. X specifies colors in red, green, and blue values that are each 16-bit numbers.

The **AllocColor** request allocates a read-only color from a colormap. Therefore, it works on any kind of colormap. However, the exact color the client asks for might not be available, so the server has to supply the pixel value of the closest color that exists in the map. At one extreme, if the colormap happened to be monochrome, the closest color allocated will always be either black or white. The reply to **AllocColor** tells the client the pixel value of the closest color available, and the red, green, and blue values of the color stored in that cell. The client can decide whether the red, green, and blue values of the cell are close enough to the requested color to be adequate.

Table 1-5. The AllocColor *Request*

# of Bytes	Type	Values	Description
1		84	opcode
1			unused
2		4	request length
4	COLORMAP		colormap ID
2	unsigned integer		red
2	unsigned integer		green
2	unsigned integer		blue
2			unused

The **AllocColor** request specifies which colormap the client wants to use, and the red, green, and blue values for the desired color. The server replies with the ID of the read-only cell in the colormap that comes closest to the color desired, and the actual red, green, and blue values in that cell.

The reply opcode is always 1; this member in errors is 0 and in core (non-extension) events ranges from 2 to 34. The sequence number is a count kept by the server of the last request processed before sending this information. Everything that the server sends to the client (replies, events, and errors) contains a sequence number field.

Notice that replies, like requests, contain a length field even when they are of fixed length. This makes it easier to write client library code to process the requests and replies correctly because there is no need to look up the length in a table based on the opcode. This is a trade-off that simplifies the client library code in exchange for transferring a few unnecessary bytes over the network.

Table 1-6. Server Reply to AllocColor

# of Bytes	Type	Values	Description
1		1	reply opcode
1			unused
2	unsigned integer		sequence number
4		0	reply length
2	unsigned integer		red
2	unsigned integer		green
2	unsigned integer		blue
2			unused
4	unsigned integer		pixel value
12			unused

As in requests, the length field is expressed in units of 4 bytes. Unused bytes within a reply are not guaranteed to be zero.

The unused field right after the blue field is present to align the pixel field, which is a 32-bit value, with a 32-bit boundary for easier handling on architectures that require either 16- or 32-bit alignment.

Table 1-7 lists all X requests that generate replies. From this table, you should get an idea of the types of requests that require replies. Each of these requests is briefly described in Appendix H, *Alphabetical Listing of Requests*.

Table 1-7. Requests that have Replies

AllocColor	GetSelectionOwner	QueryBestSize
GetAtomName	GetWindowAttributes	QueryColors
GetGeometry	GrabKeyboard	QueryExtension
GetImage	GrabPointer	QueryFont
GetKeyboardControl	InternAtom	QueryKeymap
GetKeyboardMapping	ListExtensions	QueryPointer
GetModifierMapping	ListFonts	QueryTextExtents
GetMotionEvents	ListHosts	QueryTree
GetPointerControl	ListInstalledColormaps	SetModifierMapping
GetPointerMapping	ListProperties	SetPointerMapping
GetProperty	LookupColor	TranslateCoordinates
GetScreenSaver		

1.3.4 Creating a Graphics Context

A graphics context (GC) is an abstraction that controls the server's interpretation of graphics requests. The GC controls line width, how lines connect, how they end, what colors are used, what planes of the display are affected, how the existing contents of the screen are factored into the calculation, and how areas are filled or patterned.

GCs should be created early and set once (if possible) to speed up the loop that responds to user events.

The **CreateGC** request is very similar to the **CreateWindow** request, in that one member of the request is a bitmask, which defines the length and composition of the remainder of the request. Only the members of the GC that are being set to values other than the default take up space in the request.

Since **CreateGC** shows nothing new, we will not show you the detailed contents of the request here.

1.3.5 Mapping a Window

Mapping makes a window eligible for display on the screen. In the simplest case, when the application is alone on the screen, mapping does actually display the window. But more generally, whether the window appears depends on the following:

1. The window must be mapped with **MapWindow**.

2. All of the window's ancestors must be mapped.

3. The window must in a position so that it is not obscured by visible sibling windows or their ancestors. If sibling windows are overlapping, whether or not a window is obscured depends on the stacking order. The stacking order can be manipulated with **Configure-Window**.

4. The client-library request buffer must be flushed. More information on this topic is provided in Section 1.4.1.

5. The initial mapping of a top-level window is a special case, since the window's visibility may be delayed by the window manager. For complicated reasons, a client must wait for the first **Expose** event before assuming that its window is visible and drawing into it.

Table 1-8 shows the request that maps a window, **MapWindow**.

Table 1-8. The MapWindow *Request*

# of Bytes	Type	Values	Description
1		8	opcode of request
1			unused
2		2	request length
4	WINDOW		window

That's a refreshing sight after the connection information and **CreateWindow**! The **MapWindow** request simply sends the ID of the window that is to be marked for display, so that it will be visible when the conditions listed above are met.

1.3.6 The Expose event

From the client's point of view, the only true indication that a window is visible is when the server generates an **Expose** event for it. Only after receiving this **Expose** event can the client begin drawing into the window. The server generates one or more **Expose** events for a window when it meets all the criteria listed above. There may be more than one **Expose** event because each one describes an exposed rectangle, and it may take several such rectangles to describe the areas of a window not covered by overlapping windows.

Table 1-9 shows what the server sends to the client to represent an **Expose** event. Note that all events are exactly 32 bytes long.

Table 1-9. The Expose *Event, as Sent from Server*

# of Bytes	Type	Values	Description
1		12	code
1			unused
2	unsigned integer		sequence number
4	WINDOW		window
2	unsigned integer		x
2	unsigned integer		y
2	unsigned integer		width
2	unsigned integer		height
2	unsigned integer		count
14			unused

The code indicates which type of event this is. The sequence number is the number assigned by the server for the most recently processed request; it is used in tracking errors. The window field specifies which window was exposed, and the x, y, width, and height fields specify the area within that window that was exposed. The count specifies how many more **Expose** events follow that were generated as the result of the same protocol request.

Figure 1-6 shows a window arrangement in which, if window E were raised, four **Expose** events would be generated, to report that the four corners of window E have now become visible.

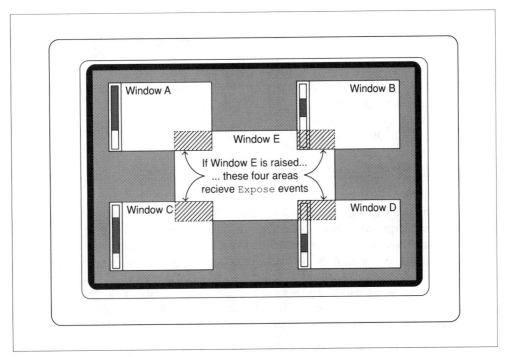

Figure 1-6. Expose events generated when window E is raised.

The X protocol specifies that all the **Expose** events resulting from a single protocol request (in this case, **ConfigureWindow** raising window E) must be contiguous.

In client programs, events are gathered and processed one at a time in a closed loop. **Expose** events will always be processed in these loops (unless the client has no windows). Clients may but need not provide any way to exit, since a separate client (called *xkill* in the standard X distribution) is normally available to kill running programs.

1.3.7 Drawing a Graphic

The **Expose** event says to the client, in effect, "go ahead and draw now." This applies not only to the first time the window is displayed on the screen but also to any later time when the window becomes obscured and then exposed. It applies to redrawing as well as to first-time drawing.

Now let's take a look at the request to draw some lines. The protocol request to draw connected lines is **PolyLine**, shown in Table 1-10.

Table 1-10. The PolyLine *Request*

# of Bytes	Type	Values	Description
1		65	opcode
1			coordinate-mode
		0 (**Origin**)	
		1 (**Previous**)	
2		3+n	request length
4	DRAWABLE		drawable
4	GCONTEXT		gc
4n	LISTofPOINT (pair of signed integers)		points

The opcode indicates that this is a **PolyLine** request. The coordinate-mode specifies whether points are to be interpreted relative to the **Origin** of the window or relative to the **Previous** point in the list. Then comes the request length, which specifies how many points are in the list. Next are the ID of the drawable (window or pixmap) in which the lines are to be drawn and the ID of the graphics context to be used in interpreting the request. Finally, there is the list of points. A point is a pair of 16-bit signed integers, since 8 bits would not be enough to cover the number of pixels on the screen (usually around 1000) and an unsigned value would not allow the x and y values to be outside the drawable, which is quite valid.

By now you should be seeing the pattern that all the requests and events that are likely to be issued during the loop that processes events are normally short, while the requests to setup things before this loop are long. Response to user actions is kept fast by spending the time necessary to setup before the event loop is started.

1.3.8 Closing the Connection

You may have noticed that there seems to be no way to exit this session! Some X clients are actually written this way. They can only be killed by a separate X client (called *xkill*) or by finding the process ID and killing the process from the UNIX shell. Other clients supply a button or command for exiting. Outside termination is acceptable because the client need not do anything to terminate the session properly. There is no request that the client sends to the server that means ''I'm about to quit.'' It is the server's responsibility to be able to clean up after the client dies.

The client library closes the session simply by closing the network connection (with `close` on BSD systems). This is also done automatically by the operating system when the client dies abnormally. The application program itself needs only to free any local structures that may have been created. The server then cleans up after the client by destroying the abstractions the client created.

The X protocol does, however, provide the **SetCloseDownMode** request to modify this behavior so that abstractions created by a client are not immediately destroyed when the client exits. This allows a new invocation of the client to attempt to recover from fatal errors such as a broken network connection that caused an earlier invocation to die before valuable information stored in the server could be saved to disk. A companion to this request is **KillClient**, which is used to kill the preserved abstractions when they are no longer needed.

1.3.9 Errors

We have described how requests, replies, and events operate during a successful client session. But what happens when a parameter does not meet the server's specifications for a given request, or the server cannot allocate enough memory to complete the request? An error message is generated and sent to the client.

Usually errors indicate a client programming error, but they can also occur when the server is unable to allocate enough memory or in other similar situations. Therefore, all clients must be able to handle errors. The definition of ''wrong'' depends on the particular request. The server does range checking to make sure that the arguments sent with each request are valid, and it also makes sure that each request sent from the client is the length it says it is. The client library does not do range checking because it does not have access to all the information necessary to check ranges (like window depths) and, secondly, because it makes more sense to have the server do it than to have multiple copies of this code in every client.

Although an error message looks much like an event, it is handled differently by the client. Unlike events, which are queued by the client library to be read later, errors are dispatched immediately upon arrival to a routine that processes the error. This routine may be a general routine that simply reports the error before exiting, or it may attempt to recover from the error by correcting the mistake in the request. However, recovery is normally difficult because of the delay between the time when a request is invoked by the application program and when the mistake is detected by the server and the error message is sent to the client. Often a number of other requests will have already been made in the intervening time, and the server will continue to act on these requests even after sending the error to the client. There is no way to ''take back'' the requests that have already been processed since the error. In any case, the X protocol specifies that the client is not allowed to respond to an error by making requests to the server, such as drawing to the screen, because this might cause a cycle of errors. For these reasons, the normal response to an error is for the client library to print an error message and then exit the client process.

Another form of error occurs when any sort of system call error occurs, such as the connection with a server dying due to a machine crash. These types of errors are detected on the client side, and the client library normally contains a routine for handling them. There is no alternative in this case but to report the error and exit the client process.

Let's continue our client session, but this time make an illegal request and see what happens.

- Client queues a illegal request for the server (just so we can see what happens).

- Client sends the illegal request to the server.

- Server processes the queued requests and sends an error report back to the client. Client processes the error and recovers somehow if the error is not fatal or exits.

As an example, lets say the client sends a request to draw a line to the server but gets the window and GC arguments reversed. The server will return a **BadWindow** error report, as shown in Table 1-11.

Table 1-11. The Error Message, as Sent from Server

# of Bytes	Type	Values	Description
1		0	error (always zero for errors)
1		3	code (**BadWindow**)
2	unsigned integer		sequence number
4	unsigned integer		bad resource id
2	unsigned integer		minor opcode
1	unsigned integer		major opcode
21			unused

Error reports are sent from the server to the client in a package identical to that used for events. This is because errors are so rare that they do not justify separate handling, even though this could save a small amount of network time (21 bytes are sent but not used by every error). They are basically treated just like events all the way to the routine in the client library that receives them. It is at this point that they are sent to the error-handling routine instead of being queued.

The first field is the one used to identify the various event types and is zero for all errors. The code field identifies the type of error that occurred. Error codes 128 through 255 are reserved for extensions. The sequence number, as in events, gives the last request successfully processed just before the error. The sequence number can be used to determine exactly which protocol request caused the error, which, as we will see after discussing how the client library is actually implemented, becomes quite important. The bad-resource-id field gives the value that was unacceptable for all the errors that are caused by invalid values and is unused by the other errors. The major and minor opcodes identify the type of request that caused the error. In the core protocol, the major opcode identifies which protocol request contained the error, and the minor opcode is unused. But for extensions, typically the entire extension will use a particular major opcode, and the minor opcode will identify each request within that extension.

Unused bytes within an error are not guaranteed to be zero.

1.4 Implementing the X Protocol

MIT includes on its distribution tape of the X Window System implementations of the X protocol in a "sample server" for several different machines and in two client side libraries, one for C and the other for Lisp.

This section discusses several issues that come up in porting this code to new machines.

1.4.1 Client Library Implementation

The client programming library that implements the protocol can do several things to improve performance. This section describes how Xlib, the lowest level C language interface to X, handles the network to improve performance.* If you can gain access to the source code for Xlib, you can look at how it handles the network by inspecting the files *XConnDis.c* and *XlibInt.c*.

Xlib buffers most requests instead of sending them to the server immediately, so that the client program can continue running instead of waiting to gain access to the network. This is possible for several reasons:

- Because most requests are drawing requests that do not require immediate action or reply.

- Because the network stream is reliable, and therefore no confirmation message from the server is necessary to indicate that the request was received.

This grouping of requests by the client before sending them over the network increases the performance of most networks, because it makes the network transactions longer and less numerous, reducing the total overhead involved.

Xlib triggers the sending of the buffer full of requests to the server under four conditions. The most common is when an application calls a blocking Xlib routine to get an event, but no matching event is currently available on Xlib's queue. Because the application must wait for an appropriate event anyway, it makes sense to flush the request buffer. This says to the server, "I'm waiting for a certain kind of event, so I'll check if you have already sent the event over to me. If not, please act on these requests immediately and then I'll be waiting for an event from you."

Secondly, some of the requests get information from the server, requiring an immediate reply. In this case, all the requests in the buffer are sent before waiting for the reply. This says to the server, "I need some information; act on these requests and then give it to me right away." This also means that requests that require replies are only buffered for the time it takes to get network access and send the existing buffer full of requests.

The client can also flush the request buffer explicitly (in Xlib with a call to **Xflush**) in situations where no user events are expected. Note that flushing the request buffer does not generate a protocol request, because it is a local instruction to Xlib. This third situation says

---

*Some implementations of Xlib may optimize communication differently than described here for local connections or when using certain graphics hardware.

to the server, "I don't need any information from you now, but I need you to act on these requests immediately." Normally, this is not used because there are enough of the first two types of calls in the client to make the flushes frequent enough.

Xlib also flushes the request buffer when it fills up.

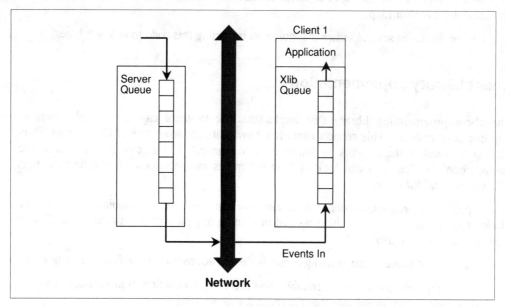

Figure 1-7. The server's event queue and each client's event queue

Client-library buffering of requests has important implications for errors. When the client makes an erroneous request, it will not be sent to the server immediately unless the flushing criteria listed above are met. Therefore, the client will continue, queueing additional requests until the flushing criteria are met. Then these requests are sent together to the server. The server then processes each request in turn and detects the error when it attempts to process the bad request, at which point the server sends an error report to the client. The client sends the library error report directly to one of the error-handling routines that reports the error to the user.

In other words, the error does not come to the user's attention until the request buffer is sent, the server processes the requests up to the one containing the error, the server sends the error report to the client, and the client error-handling routine processes it. This delay makes it more difficult to discover which request actually contained the error.

To allow the possibility of the client recovering from the error, the server does not stop itself or disconnect the client after the error. The server goes on processing requests. Therefore, after sending the error, the screen may reflect actions that take place after the error occurred. That is why error reports contain both the sequence number of the last request processed by the server and the opcode of the protocol request that caused the error.

The client library can also make programming easier by providing convenience routines that perform common tasks while hiding the complications in the actual protocol request to be issued. For example, in Xlib, XSetForeground sets the foreground color for drawing in a graphics context. XSetForeground really issues a **ChangeGC** request to the server, but it allows the client to ignore all the other aspects of the GC.

Convenience routines may seem like an invitation for inefficient programming. What if the client sets three different GC values using three convenience routines? This could lead to three round-trip protocol requests when only one would suffice. The solution to this problem is for the library to take advantage of the fact that requests are queued by combining all these similar requests into a single one before sending them to the server. Xlib actually does this: it provides convenience routines for setting all elements of a GC and combines these calls into a single protocol request that is sent just before it is needed by the next drawing call that uses that GC.

1.4.2 Server Implementation

As described earlier, a true X server is any server that accepts X protocol requests and generates replies, errors, and events according to the specifications in the X protocol document. The servers supplied by MIT are known as "sample servers" because no claim is made that they do everything in the best possible way for all machines and cases. In fact, some of the sample servers suffer from poor performance in color because few optimizations were attempted. Building reliability has been the main goal in the first three releases of X Version 11. Some performance enhancements have been made in the Release 4 sample servers.

The essential tasks of the server are to demultiplex the requests coming in from each client and execute them on the display, and to multiplex keyboard and mouse input back onto the network to the clients. On single-threaded architectures, the server is typically implemented as a single sequential process, using round-robin scheduling among the clients. Although the server might be placed in the kernel of the operating system in an attempt to increase performance, this makes the server much more difficult to maintain and debug. Performance under UNIX does not seem to suffer by having the server run as a process. The number of operating system calls in the server (and the client library) are minimized to improve performance.

The server is typically made up of a device-independent layer and a device-dependent layer. The device-independent layer includes code that is valid for all machines. Even this portion has not been highly tuned even though practically all current servers are based on it. It is primarily designed to be extremely portable between machines. Some improvements can be made by optimizing this code for each machine it is to run on, but the device-dependent layer is where most of the performance improvement can be had. Of course this code will be different for almost every model by every manufacturer.

The server must be designed so that it never trusts clients to provide correct data. It also must be designed so that if it ever has to wait for a response from a client, it must be possible to continue servicing other clients. Without this property, a bad client or a network failure could easily cause the entire display to hang.

The server normally has a buffering mechanism similar to Xlib's for sending data back to clients. According to the protocol specification, all events and errors generated by a single request must be sent contiguously. When the server is processing a request, it queues up all of the events and errors that the request generates (for example, unmapping a window could generate a lot of little exposures) and then tries to send them all. Furthermore, any events caused by executing a request from a given client must be sent to the client before any reply or error is sent.

If the client is a little slow at reading data from the network (usually because the application is doing something complicated, such as garbage collection in Common Lisp), the server can get an error telling it that the network was unable to transmit all of the data. In Release 2 and before, the sample servers would assume that the client was hung and would drop the connection. In Release 3 and later, they keep track of what needs to be sent and wait for the client to be ready for more data (in BSD UNIX, this is taken care of by the "writable" mask argument to the `select` system call). This is called delayed writing.

1.4.3 Reducing Network Traffic

X uses several techniques to reduce network traffic. One major technique is to have the server maintain abstractions such as windows, fonts, and graphics contexts and allocate an integer ID number for each one as a nickname to be used by clients. Whenever an operation is to be performed on an abstraction, the ID of the abstraction is specified in the request. This means that instead of an entire structure or string being sent over the network with a request, only a single integer is sent. Remember that since the client and the server may be on separate machines, pointers cannot be used to refer to server-maintained structures (moreover, not all languages allow use of pointers).

The caveat of the abstraction approach is that the client must query the server when it needs information about them, which, as mentioned above, leads to network delays. As it turns out, clients normally do not need to query the server very often, and abstractions greatly simplify programs.

1.4.4 Implementation on Multi-Threaded Architectures

There is nothing in the definition of the X protocol that prevents either the server or the client programming library from using multi-threaded features of the hardware.

For the server, there are obvious opportunities for separating elements of its task among separate processors. One could handle events and another do drawing, as a primitive example. Or perhaps each processor could handle different clients. The task of drawing can also be divided up to increase performance, perhaps along the lines of how the GC separates patterning from selecting pixels and planes to be drawn (which we have not described here).

For clients, the opportunities depend more on the particular characteristics of each application. Depending on the tools that are available on a particular system, the compiler may automatically look for parallelisms to exploit or the application programmer may be able to give the compiler hints.

1.4.5 Security

The connection information sent by the client to the server includes space for an authorization name and associated data. The X Consortium has developed a simple authorization mechanism with the name MIT-MAGIC-COOKIE-1.* A magic cookie is basically a long, randomly generated binary password that the client library must know in order to be able to connect to the server. The magic cookies change each time a server is reset. Under this mechanism, the server reads a file containing a list of magic cookies and only accepts connections from clients that know one of these magic cookies. Each user has a file in their home directory (*.Xauthority*) which contains the magic cookie for each server they have access to. When the user starts an application, the client library reads the user's *.Xauthority* file and sends an appropriate magic cookie to the server. The *xdm* display manager normally takes care of adding the appropriate magic cookie to the user's *.Xauthority* file after the user logs in. The *xauth* application can also be used to copy magic cookies from the server file to the user files; the system manager on the server system uses it to grant access to users.

Most servers also use a host access list file (*/etc/X0.hosts* on most UNIX-based systems) to determine whether to grant access. If the client is running on a host that is on the server's host access list, the connection is granted (even if the authorization data is wrong). The host access list will be empty if an authorization mechanism is in use.

X does not provide any protection from unauthorized access to individual windows, pixmaps, or other abstractions, once a connection has been made. For example, if an application gets (or guesses) the abstract ID of a window it did not create, using the **QueryTree** request, it can manipulate or even destroy the window. This property was necessary so that window managers could be written independently of the window system. It is a matter of courtesy that applications other than window managers do not attempt this sort of antisocial behavior.

1.4.6 Interclient Communication

The server must provide a means whereby clients operating on the same server can communicate, because the clients may not necessarily be running on the same machine. Otherwise, clients would not be able to communicate directly except by opening a separate network connection between them. This would introduce a operating system dependency in client programs, which is to be avoided.

X calls the base communication mechanism *properties*. Each property has a name and an ID (atom). The name is used by client programs to determine the ID and implies the meaning of the data by convention. For example, the WM_COMMAND atom by convention identifies a property that contains a string describing the command line that invoked an application. The format of the data is not necessarily implied by the property name, but for most of the properties for which conventions currently exist, the type is implied. Colors are an example of a property that might have more than one format. A particular color could be expressed as a string name such as "purple" or as a set of red, green, and blue values. Client applications

---

*The MIT-MAGIC-COOKIE-1 authorization scheme is implemented beginning in Release 4. Vendors may use other authorization schemes before or after Release 4.

that wished to set and read this property would have to agree on a code that distinguished the two formats.

Properties are attached to windows. In other words, window A may have the data "blurb" for property USELESS, while window B has data "flub" for the same property. Therefore, a window ID and a property ID uniquely identify a particular piece of data. Protocol requests are defined to set and get the values of this data.

The maximum size of a property is not limited by the maximum protocol request size accepted by the server. The requests that read and write properties provide ways to read and write them in chunks of the maximum request size. Since the length field is a 16-bit value and is in units of 4 bytes, the maximum request size is 262144 bytes. However, the maximum property size is server-dependent and usually depends on the amount of memory available.

There is also a higher level communication procedure called *selections* that uses properties but allows the two parties to communicate back and forth about the format of the data in a particular property. As for the example above for color, selections allow the client that wants to get the property (the requestor) to specify which of the two formats it desires. Then the client that sets the property (the owner) can set it according to the desired format, before indicating to the requestor that the property is ready to be read. There is, of course, also a way to respond when the owner is unable to translate the data into the required format.

1.5 Future Directions

X was meticulously designed not to be limiting in the near future. The extension mechanism allows new features to be built into the server that work at the same performance level as the core X protocol. In practice, extensions are being used by system manufacturers to take advantage of the unique features of their hardware and by the X Consortium to implement and standardize features such as 3-D graphics.

Now that X Version 11 has become widely accepted, development work on it has actually accelerated rather than subsided. The X Consortium at MIT is now very well funded and has a long agenda of improvements and additions that will be made to X. Among the work currently in progress are extensions to support multiple and various input devices, X for Japanese use, multi-buffering and stereo, and PHIGS (3-D graphics).

The lowest levels of X are stable and unlikely to change in incompatible ways. However, there are improvements in performance that can still be made even though the programming interfaces will remain the same.

Part Two:

Protocol Request and Event Reference

Part Two consists of reference pages to each protocol request and event, arranged alphabetically. Each reference page specifies the contents of the request and its reply, if any, the errors that may be generated, a description of what the request does, and the X protocol encoding for the request and reply. Each event reference page is analogous, but includes no reply or error sections.

ClearArea	FillPoly	GrabKey
ClientMessage	FocusIn	GrabKeyboard
CloseFont	FousOut	GrabPointer
GrabServer	OpenFont	SelectionRequest
GraphicsExpose	PolyArc	SendEvent
GravityNotify	PolyFillArc	SetAccessControl
ImageText16	PolyFillRectangle	SetClipRectangles
ImageText8	PolyLine	SetCloseDownMode
InstallColormap	PolyPoint	SetDashes
InternAtom	PolyRectangle	SetFontPath
KeyPress	PolySegment	SetInputFocus
KeyRelease	PolyText16	SetModifierMapping
KeymapNotify	PolyText8	SetPointerMapping
KillClient	PropertyNotify	SetScreenSaver
LeaveNotify	PutImage	SetSelectionOwner
ListExtensions	QueryBestSize	StoreColors
ListFonts	QueryColors	StoreNamedColor
ListFontsWithInfo	QueryExtension	TranslateCoordinates
ListHosts	QueryFont	UngrabButton
ListInstalledColormaps	QueryKeymap	UngrabKey
ListProperties	QueryPointer	UngrabKeyboard
LookupColor	QueryTextExtension	UngrabPointer
MapNotify	QueryTree	UngrabServer
MapRequest	RecolorCursor	UninstallColorMap
MapSubwindows	ReparentNotify	UnmapNotify
MapWindow	ReparentWindow	UnmapSubwindow
MappingNotify	ResizeRequest	UnmapWindow
MotionNotify	RotatePropertiies	VisibilityNotify
NoExpose	SelectionClear	WarpPointer
NoOperation	SelectionNotify	

Name

Introduction — guide to contents of reference pages

Request Contents

This section describes the contents of the request packet sent from the client to the server.

Requests are described in the following format:

> **RequestName**
> > *arg1*: type1
> >
> > . . .
> >
> > *argN*: typeN

Each piece of information is listed as a name/type pair. For example, *window*: WINDOW.

This entry identifies what window the request is to apply to, and the information is of type WINDOW. The type WINDOW and all other types represented by capitalized words are described in the Description section of this reference page.

The Request Contents section of the reference pages in the reference section of this document uses the following syntactic conventions:

- The syntax { . . . } encloses a set of alternatives.

- The syntax [. . .] encloses a set of structure components.

- In general, TYPEs are in upper case and **AlternativeValues** use initial capitals and are in bold font.

Reply Contents

If the request has a reply, then this section is present. This section is in the same format as the Request Contents section, but it describes the information sent back from the server to the client in response to this request.

Replies in the Reply Contents sections on the reference pages are described in the following format:

> result1: type1
>
> . . .
>
> resultM: typeM

A request with no reply may still report errors.

Event Contents

If the page is describing an event, then this section is present instead of Request Contents and Reply Contents. It describes the contents of the event sent from the server to the client, using the notation described under Request Contents.

Event Contents are described in the following format:

> **EventName**
>> *value1*: type1
>>
>> ...
>>
>> *valueN*: typeN

Errors

This section lists the errors that may be generated by this request. For example, **Window**. The errors themselves are described in Appendix F, *Errors*. The Description section of request reference pages may also mention what scenario causes each error.

Description

This section describes what the request does and what its reply contains. In the case of events, it describes what information the event contains and when the event is generated. For requests, this section also describes what events may be generated as a side effect.

Types

The reference pages use symbols to represent certain types of data.

A type name of the form LISTofFOO means a counted list of elements of type FOO. The size of the length field may vary (it is not necessarily the same size as a FOO), and in some cases, it may be implicit. It is fully specified in the Encoding portion of each reference page. Except where explicitly noted, zero-length lists are legal.

The types BITMASK and LISTofVALUE are somewhat special. Various requests contain arguments of the form:

> *value-mask*: BITMASK
> *value-list*: LISTofVALUE

These are used to allow the client to specify a subset of a heterogeneous collection of optional arguments. The value-mask specifies which arguments are to be provided; each such argument is assigned a unique bit position. The representation of the BITMASK will typically contain more bits than there are defined arguments. The unused bits in the value-mask must be zero (or the server generates a **Value** error). The value-list contains one value for each bit set to 1 in the mask, from least-significant to most-significant bit in the mask. Each value is represented with four bytes, but the actual value occupies only the least-significant bytes as required. The values of the unused bytes do not matter.

The type OR is of the form "T1 or ... or Tn" meaning the union of the indicated types. A single-element type is given as the element without enclosing braces.

WINDOW:	32-bit value (top three bits guaranteed to be zero)
PIXMAP:	32-bit value (top three bits guaranteed to be zero)
CURSOR:	32-bit value (top three bits guaranteed to be zero)
FONT:	32-bit value (top three bits guaranteed to be zero)
GCONTEXT:	32-bit value (top three bits guaranteed to be zero)

COLORMAP:	32-bit value (top three bits guaranteed to be zero)
DRAWABLE:	WINDOW or PIXMAP
FONTABLE:	FONT or GCONTEXT
ATOM:	32-bit value (top three bits guaranteed to be zero)
VISUALID:	32-bit value (top three bits guaranteed to be zero)
VALUE:	32-bit quantity (used only in LISTofVALUE)
BYTE:	8-bit value
INT8:	8-bit signed integer
INT16:	16-bit signed integer
INT32:	32-bit signed integer
CARD8:	8-bit unsigned integer
CARD16:	16-bit unsigned integer
CARD32:	32-bit unsigned integer
TIMESTAMP:	CARD32
BITGRAVITY:	{Forget, Static, NorthWest, North, NorthEast, West, Center, East, SouthWest, South, SouthEast}
WINGRAVITY:	{Unmap, Static, NorthWest, North, NorthEast, West, Center, East, SouthWest, South, SouthEast}
BOOL:	{True, False}
EVENT:	{KeyPress, KeyRelease, OwnerGrabButton, ButtonPress, ButtonRelease, EnterWindow, LeaveWindow, PointerMotion, PointerMotionHint, Button1Motion, Button2Motion, Button3Motion, Button4Motion, Button5Motion, ButtonMotion, Exposure, VisibilityChange, StructureNotify, ResizeRedirect, SubstructureNotify, SubstructureRedirect, FocusChange, PropertyChange, ColormapChange, KeymapState}
POINTEREVENT:	{ButtonPress, ButtonRelease, EnterWindow, LeaveWindow, PointerMotion, PointerMotionHint, Button1Motion, Button2Motion, Button3Motion, Button4Motion, Button5Motion, ButtonMotion, KeymapState}
DEVICEEVENT:	{KeyPress, KeyRelease, ButtonPress, ButtonRelease, PointerMotion, Button1Motion, Button2Motion, Button3Motion, Button4Motion, Button5Motion, ButtonMotion}
KEYSYM:	32-bit value (top three bits guaranteed to be zero)

KEYCODE:	CARD8
BUTTON:	CARD8
KEYMASK:	{**Shift**, **Lock**, **Control**, **Mod1**, **Mod2**, **Mod3**, **Mod4**, **Mod5**}
BUTMASK:	{**Button1**, **Button2**, **Button3**, **Button4**, **Button5**}
KEYBUTMASK:	KEYMASK or BUTMASK
STRING8:	LISTofCARD8
STRING16:	LISTofCHAR2B
CHAR2B:	[byte1, byte2: CARD8]
POINT:	[x, y: INT16]
RECTANGLE:	[x, y: INT16, width, height: CARD16]
ARC:	[x, y: INT16, width, height: CARD16, angle1, angle2: INT16]
HOST:	[family: {**Internet**, **DECnet**, **Chaos**} address: LISTofBYTE]

The [x,y] coordinates of a RECTANGLE specify the upper-left corner.

The primary interpretation of large characters in a STRING16 is that they are composed of two bytes used to index a 2-D matrix; hence, the use of CHAR2B rather than CARD16. This corresponds to the JIS/ISO method of indexing 2-byte characters. It is expected that most large fonts will be defined with 2-byte matrix indexing. For large fonts constructed with linear indexing, a CHAR2B can be interpreted as a 16-bit number by treating byte1 as the most-significant byte. This means that clients should always transmit such 16-bit character values most-significant byte first, as the server will never byte-swap CHAR2B quantities.

The length, format, and interpretation of a HOST address are specific to the family (see **ChangeHosts** request).

Encoding

The encoding section lists the detailed series of bytes that should be sent to represent the request, or that is sent back from the server in the case of replies, and events.

The following four sections describe the protocol format for requests, replies, errors, and events.

Request Format

Every request contains an 8-bit major opcode and a 16-bit length field expressed in units of four bytes. Every request consists of four bytes of a header (containing the major opcode, the length field, and a data byte) followed by zero or more additional bytes of data. The length field defines the total length of the request, including the header. The length field in a request must equal the minimum length required to contain the request. If the specified length is smaller or larger than the required length, an error is generated. Unused bytes in a request are not required to be zero. Major opcodes 128 through 255 are reserved for extensions. Extensions are intended to contain multiple requests, so extension requests typically have an additional minor opcode encoded in the "spare" data byte in the request header. However, the placement and interpretation of this minor opcode and of all other fields in extension requests are not defined by the core protocol. Every request on a given connection is implicitly assigned a sequence number, starting with 1, that is used in replies, errors, and events.

Defined constants are in bold face type in the description column, immediately after their real value in the Value column. For example, the **WarpPointer** request:

# of Bytes	Value	Description
1	41	opcode
1		unused
2	6	request length
4	WINDOW	src-window:
	0	**None**
4	WINDOW	dst-window:
	0	**None**
2	INT16	src-x
2	INT16	src-y
2	CARD16	src-width
2	CARD16	src-height
2	INT16	dst-x
2	INT16	dst-y

Reply Format

Every reply contains a 32-bit length field expressed in units of four bytes. Every reply consists of 32 bytes followed by zero or more additional bytes of data, as specified in the length field. Unused bytes within a reply are not guaranteed to be zero. Every reply also contains the least-significant 16 bits of the sequence number of the corresponding request.

Event Format

Events are 32 bytes long. Unused bytes within an event are not guaranteed to be zero. Every event contains an 8-bit type code. The most-significant bit in this code is set if the event was generated from a **SendEvent** request. Event codes 64 through 127 are reserved for extensions, although the core protocol does not define a mechanism for selecting interest in such events. Every core event (with the exception of **KeymapNotify**) also contains the least-significant 16 bits of the sequence number of the last request issued by the client that was (or is currently being) processed by the server.

Error Format

Error reports are 32 bytes long. Every error includes an 8-bit error code. Error codes 128 through 255 are reserved for extensions. Every error also includes the major and minor opcodes of the failed request and the least-significant 16 bits of the sequence number of the request. For the following errors, the failing resource ID is also returned: **Colormap**, **Cursor**, **Drawable**, **Font**, **GContext**, **IDChoice**, **Pixmap**, and **Window**. For **Atom** errors, the failing atom is returned. For **Value** errors, the failing value is returned. Other core errors return no additional data. Unused bytes within an error are not guaranteed to be zero.

Encoding of Types

In this document, the LISTof notation strictly means some number of repetitions of the FOO encoding; the actual length of the list is encoded elsewhere.

The SETof notation is always represented by a bitmask, with a 1-bit indicating presence in the set.

BITMASK: CARD32

WINDOW: CARD32

PIXMAP: CARD32

CURSOR: CARD32

FONT: CARD32

GCONTEXT: CARD32

COLORMAP: CARD32

DRAWABLE: CARD32

FONTABLE: CARD32

ATOM: CARD32

VISUALID: CARD32

BYTE: 8-bit value

INT8: 8-bit signed integer

INT16: 16-bit signed integer

INT32: 32-bit signed integer

CARD8: 8-bit unsigned integer

CARD16: 16-bit unsigned integer

CARD32: 32-bit unsigned integer

TIMESTAMP: CARD32

BITGRAVITY

0	**Forget**
1	**NorthWest**
2	**North**
3	**NorthEast**
4	**West**
5	**Center**
6	**East**

7	**SouthWest**
8	**South**
9	**SouthEast**
10	**Static**

WINGRAVITY

0	**Unmap**
1	**NorthWest**
2	**North**
3	**NorthEast**
4	**West**
5	**Center**
6	**East**
7	**SouthWest**
8	**South**
9	**SouthEast**
10	**Static**

BOOL

0	**False**
1	**True**

SETofEVENT

#x00000001	**KeyPress**
#x00000002	**KeyRelease**
#x00000004	**ButtonPress**
#x00000008	**ButtonRelease**
#x00000010	**EnterWindow**
#x00000020	**LeaveWindow**
#x00000040	**PointerMotion**
#x00000080	**PointerMotionHint**
#x00000100	**Button1Motion**
#x00000200	**Button2Motion**
#x00000400	**Button3Motion**
#x00000800	**Button4Motion**
#x00001000	**Button5Motion**
#x00002000	**ButtonMotion**
#x00004000	**KeymapState**
#x00008000	**Exposure**
#x00010000	**VisibilityChange**
#x00020000	**StructureNotify**
#x00040000	**ResizeRedirect**
#x00080000	**SubstructureNotify**
#x00100000	**SubstructureRedirect**
#x00200000	**FocusChange**
#x00400000	**PropertyChange**
#x00800000	**ColormapChange**

#x01000000	**OwnerGrabButton**
#xfe000000	unused but must be zero

SETofPOINTEREVENT

encodings are the same as for SETofEVENT, except with

#xffff8003	unused but must be zero

SETofDEVICEEVENT

encodings are the same as for SETofEVENT, except with

#xffffc0b0	unused but must be zero

KEYSYM: CARD32

KEYCODE: CARD8

BUTTON: CARD8

SETofKEYBUTMASK

#x0001	**Shift**
#x0002	**Lock**
#x0004	**Control**
#x0008	**Mod1**
#x0010	**Mod2**
#x0020	**Mod3**
#x0040	**Mod4**
#x0080	**Mod5**
#x0100	**Button1**
#x0200	**Button2**
#x0400	**Button3**
#x0800	**Button4**
#x1000	**Button5**
#xe000	unused but must be zero

SETofKEYMASK

encodings are the same as for SETofKEYBUTMASK, except with

#xff00	unused but must be zero

STRING8: LISTofCARD8

STRING16: LISTofCHAR2B

CHAR2B

1	CARD8	byte1
1	CARD8	byte2

POINT

2	INT16	x
2	INT16	y

RECTANGLE

2	INT16	x
2	INT16	y

2	CARD16	width	
2	CARD16	height	

ARC

2	INT16	x	
2	INT16	y	
2	CARD16	width	
2	CARD16	height	
2	INT16	angle1	
2	INT16	angle2	

HOST

1			family
	0	**Internet**	
	1	**DECnet**	
	2	**Chaos**	
1			unused
2	n		length of address
n	LISTofBYTE		address
p			unused, p=pad(n)

STR

1	n		length of name in bytes
n	STRING8		name

Encoding Syntax

The Encoding section of the reference pages is in table form, with the contents using the following syntax conventions.

All numbers are in decimal, unless prefixed with #x, in which case they are in hexadecimal (base 16).

For components described in the request, reply, or event contents as:

    name: TYPE

the encode-form is:

    N   TYPE   name

N is the number of bytes occupied in the data stream, and TYPE is the interpretation of those bytes. For example:

    depth: CARD8

becomes:

    1   CARD8 depth

For components with a static numeric value the encode-form is:

    N   value   name

The value is always interpreted as an N-byte unsigned integer. For example, the first two bytes of a **Window** error are always zero (indicating an error in general) and three (indicating the **Window** error in particular):

1	0	Error
1	3	code

For components described in the request, reply, or event contents as:

    name: {**Name1**,..., **NameI**}

the encode-form is:

    N   name
          value1 Name1
          ...
          valueI NameI

The value is always interpreted as an N-byte unsigned integer. Note that the size of N is sometimes larger than that strictly required to encode the values. For example:

    class: {**InputOutput**, **InputOnly**, **CopyFromParent**}

becomes:

    2   class
          0   **CopyFromParent**
          1   **InputOutput**
          2   **InputOnly**

For components described in the request, reply, or event contents as:

    NAME: TYPE or **Alternative1** ... or **AlternativeI**

the encode-form is:

    N   TYPE   NAME
          value1 **Alternative1**
          ...
          valueI **AlternativeI**

The alternative values are guaranteed not to conflict with the encoding of TYPE. For example:

    destination: WINDOW or **PointerWindow** or **InputFocus**

becomes:

    4   WINDOW   destination
          0   **PointerWindow**
          1   **InputFocus**

For components described in the request, reply, or event contents as:

    value-mask: BITMASK

the encode-form is:

N	BITMASK	value-mask
	mask1 mask-name1	
	...	
	maskI mask-nameI	

The individual bits in the mask are specified and named, and N is 2 or 4. The most-significant bit in a BITMASK is reserved for use in defining chained (multi-word) bitmasks, as extensions augment existing core requests. The precise interpretation of this bit is not yet defined here, although a probable mechanism is that a 1-bit indicates that another N bytes of bitmask follows, with bits within the overall mask still interpreted from least-significant to most-significant with an N-byte unit, with N-byte units interpreted in stream order, and with the overall mask being byte-swapped in individual N-byte units.

For LISTofVALUE encodings, the request is followed by a table listing an encode-form for each VALUE. The NAME in each encode-form keys to the corresponding BITMASK bit. The encoding of a VALUE always occupies four bytes, but the number of bytes specified in the encoding-form indicates how many of the least-significant bytes are actually used; the remaining bytes are unused and their values do not matter.

In various cases, the number of bytes occupied by a component will be specified by a lower case single-letter variable name instead of a specific numeric value, and often some other component will have its value specified as a simple numeric expression involving these variables. Components specified with such expressions are always interpreted as unsigned integers. The scope of such variables is always just the enclosing request, reply, error, event, or compound type structure. For example:

2	3+n	request length
4n	LISTofPOINT	points

For unused bytes (the values of the bytes are undefined and do no matter), the encode-form is:

N	unused

If the number of unused bytes is variable, the encode-form typically is:

p	unused, p=pad(E)

where E is some expression, and pad(E) is the number of bytes needed to round E up to a multiple of four.

$$pad(E) = (4 - (E \bmod 4)) \bmod 4$$

Name

Connection Setup

Description

Connection setup opens the connection between a client and a server, over which subsequent requests, replies, events, and errors can be sent.

The client must send an initial byte of data to identify the byte order to be employed. The value of the byte must be octal 102 or 154. The value 102 (ASCII upper case B) means values are transmitted most-significant byte first, and value 154 (ASCII lower case l) means values are transmitted least-significant byte first. Except where explicitly noted in the protocol, all 16-bit and 32-bit quantities sent by the client must be transmitted with this byte order, and all 16-bit and 32-bit quantities returned by the server will be transmitted with this byte order.

Following the byte-order byte, the client sends the following information at connection setup:

> protocol-major-version: CARD16
> protocol-minor-version: CARD16
> authorization-protocol-name: STRING8
> authorization-protocol-data: STRING8

The version numbers indicate what version of the protocol the client expects the server to implement.

The authorization name indicates what authorization protocol the client expects the server to use, and the data is specific to that protocol. Specification of valid authorization mechanisms is not part of the core X protocol. A server that implements a different protocol than the client expects or that only implements the host-based mechanism may simply ignore this information. If both name and data strings are empty, this is to be interpreted as "no explicit authorization."

The client receives the following information at connection setup:

> success: BOOL
> protocol-major-version: CARD16
> protocol-minor-version: CARD16
> length: CARD16

Length is the amount of additional data to follow, in units of four bytes. The version numbers are an escape hatch in case future revisions of the protocol are necessary. In general, the major version would increment for incompatible changes, and the minor version would increment for small upward compatible changes. Barring changes, the major version will be 11 and the minor version will be 0. The protocol version numbers returned indicate the protocol the server actually supports. This might not equal the version sent by the client. The server can (but need not) refuse connections from clients that offer a different version than the server supports. A server can (but need not) support more than one version simultaneously.

The client receives the following additional data if authorization fails:

    reason: STRING8

The client receives the following additional data if authorization is accepted:

    vendor: STRING8
    release-number: CARD32
    resource-id-base, resource-id-mask: CARD32
    image-byte-order: {**LSBFirst**, **MSBFirst**}
    bitmap-scanline-unit: {8, 16, 32}
    bitmap-scanline-pad: {8, 16, 32}
    bitmap-bit-order: {**LeastSignificant**, **MostSignificant**}
    pixmap-formats: LISTofFORMAT
    roots: LISTofSCREEN
    motion-buffer-size: CARD32
    maximum-request-length: CARD16
    min-keycode, max-keycode: KEYCODE

    where:

        FORMAT: [depth: CARD8,
                        bits-per-pixel: {1, 4, 8, 16, 24, 32}
                        scanline-pad: {8, 16, 32}]

        SCREEN: [root: WINDOW
                        width-in-pixels, height-in-pixels: CARD16
                        width-in-millimeters, height-in-millimeters: CARD16
                        allowed-depths: LISTofDEPTH
                        root-depth: CARD8
                        root-visual: VISUALID
                        default-colormap: COLORMAP
                        white-pixel, black-pixel: CARD32
                        min-installed-maps, max-installed-maps: CARD16
                        backing-stores: {**Never**, **WhenMapped**, **Always**}
                        save-unders: BOOL
                        current-input-masks: SETofEVENT]

        DEPTH: [depth: CARD8
                        visuals: LISTofVISUALTYPE]

> VISUALTYPE: [visual-id: VISUALID
>   class: { **StaticGray**, **StaticColor**, **TrueColor**, **GrayScale**,
>   **PseudoColor**, **DirectColor** }
>   red-mask, green-mask, blue-mask: CARD32
>   bits-per-rgb-value: CARD8
>   colormap-entries: CARD16]

The information that is global to the server is:

- The vendor string gives some identification of the owner of the server implementation. The vendor controls the semantics of the release number.

- The resource-id-mask contains a single contiguous set of bits (at least 18). The client allocates resource IDs for types WINDOW, PIXMAP, CURSOR, FONT, GCONTEXT, and COLORMAP by choosing a value with only some subset of these bits set and ORing it with resource-id-base. Only values constructed in this way can be used to name newly created resources over this connection. Resource IDs never have the top three bits set. The client is not restricted to linear or contiguous allocation of resource IDs. Once an ID has been freed, it can be reused, but this should not be necessary. An ID must be unique with respect to the IDs of all other resources, not just other resources of the same type. However, note that the value spaces of resource identifiers, atoms, visualids, and keysyms are distinguished by context and, as such, are not required to be disjoint; for example, a given numeric value might be both a valid window ID, a valid atom, and a valid keysym.

- Although the server is in general responsible for byte-swapping data to match the client, images are always transmitted and received in formats (including byte order) specified by the server. The byte order for images is given by image-byte-order and applies to each scanline unit in XY format (bitmap format) and to each pixel value in Z format.

- A bitmap is represented in scanline order. Each scanline is padded to a multiple of bits as given by bitmap-scanline-pad. The pad bits are of arbitrary value. The scanline is quantized in multiples of bits as given by bitmap-scanline-unit. The bitmap-scanline-unit is always less than or equal to the bitmap-scanline-pad. Within each unit, the leftmost bit in the bitmap is either the least-significant or the most-significant bit in the unit, as given by bitmap-bit-order. If a pixmap is represented in XY format, each plane is represented as a bitmap, and the planes appear from most-significant to least-significant in bit order with no padding between planes.

- Pixmap-formats contains one entry for each depth value. The entry describes the Z format used to represent images of that depth. An entry for a depth is included if any screen supports that depth, and all screens supporting that depth must support only that Z format for that depth. In Z format, the pixels are in scanline order, left to right within a scanline. The number of bits used to hold each pixel is given by bits-per-pixel. Bits-per-pixel may be larger than strictly required by the depth, in which case the least-significant bits are used to hold the pixmap data, and the values of the unused high-order bits are undefined. When the bits-per-pixel is 4, the order of nibbles in the byte is the same as the image byte-order. When the bits-per-pixel is 1, the format is identical for bitmap format. Each scanline is padded to a multiple of bits as given by scanline-pad. When bits-per-pixel is 1, this will be identical to bitmap-scanline-pad.

- How a pointing device roams the screens is up to the server implementation and is transparent to the protocol. No geometry is defined among screens.

- The server may retain the recent history of pointer motion and do so to a finer granularity than is reported by **MotionNotify** events. The **GetMotionEvents** request makes such history available. The motion-buffer-size gives the approximate size of the history buffer.

- Maximum-request-length specifies the maximum length of a request accepted by the server, in 4-byte units; that is, length is the maximum value that can appear in the length field of a request. Requests larger than this maximum generate a **Length** error, and the server will read and simply discard the entire request. Maximum-request-length will always be at least 4096 (that is, requests of length up to and including 16384 bytes will be accepted by all servers).

- Min-keycode and max-keycode specify the smallest and largest keycode values transmitted by the server. Min-keycode is never less than 8, and max-keycode is never greater than 255. Not all keycodes in this range are required to have corresponding keys.

The information that applies per screen is:

- The allowed-depths specifies what pixmap and window depths are supported. Pixmaps are supported for each depth listed, and windows of that depth are supported if at least one visual type is listed for the depth. A pixmap depth of one is always supported and listed, but windows of depth one might not be supported. A depth of zero is never listed, but zero-depth **InputOnly** windows are always supported.

- Root-depth and root-visual specify the depth and visual type of the root window. Width-in-pixels and height-in-pixels specify the size of the root window (which cannot be changed). The class of the root window is always **InputOutput**. Width-in-millimeters and height-in-millimeters can be used to determine the physical size and the aspect ratio.

- The default-colormap is the one initially associated with the root window. Clients with minimal color requirements creating windows of the same depth as the root may want to allocate from this map by default.

- Black-pixel and white-pixel can be used in implementing a monochrome application. These pixel values are for permanently allocated entries in the default-colormap. The actual RGB values may be settable on some screens and, in any case, may not actually be black and white. The names are intended to convey the expected relative intensity of the colors.

- The border of the root window is initially a pixmap filled with the black-pixel. The initial background of the root window is a pixmap filled with some unspecified two-color pattern using black-pixel and white-pixel.

- Min-installed-maps specifies the number of maps that can be guaranteed to be installed simultaneously (with **InstallColormap**), regardless of the number of entries allocated in each map. Max-installed-maps specifies the maximum number of maps that might possibly be installed simultaneously, depending on their allocations. Multiple static-visual colormaps with identical contents but differing in resource ID should be considered as a single map for the purposes of this number. For the typical case of a single hardware colormap, both values will be 1.

- Backing-stores indicates when the server supports backing stores for this screen, although it may be storage limited in the number of windows it can support at once. If save-unders is **True**, the server can support the save-under mode in **CreateWindow** and **ChangeWindowAttributes**, although again it may be storage limited.

- The current-input-events is what **GetWindowAttributes** would return for the all-event-masks for the root window.

The information that applies per visual-type is:

- A given visual type might be listed for more than one depth or for more than one screen.

- For **PseudoColor**, a pixel value indexes a colormap to produce independent RGB values; the RGB values can be changed dynamically. **GrayScale** is treated in the same way as **PseudoColor** except which primary drives the screen is undefined; thus, the client should always store the same value for red, green, and blue in colormaps. For **DirectColor**, a pixel value is decomposed into separate RGB subfields, and each subfield separately indexes the colormap for the corresponding value. The RGB values can be changed dynamically. **TrueColor** is treated in the same way as **DirectColor** except the colormap has predefined read-only RGB values. These values are server-dependent but provide linear or near-linear increasing ramps in each primary. **StaticColor** is treated in the same way as **PseudoColor** except the colormap has predefined read-only RGB values, which are server-dependent. **StaticGray** is treated in the same way as **StaticColor** except the red, green, and blue values are equal for any single pixel value, resulting in shades of gray. **StaticGray** with a two-entry colormap can be thought of as monochrome.

- The red-mask, green-mask, and blue-mask are only defined for **DirectColor** and **TrueColor**. Each has one contiguous set of bits set to 1 with no intersections. Usually each mask has the same number of bits set to 1.

- The bits-per-rgb-value specifies the log base 2 of the number of distinct color intensity values (individually) of red, green, and blue. This number need not bear any relation to the number of colormap entries. Actual RGB values are always passed in the protocol within a 16-bit spectrum, with 0 being minimum intensity and 65535 being the maximum intensity. On hardware that provides a linear zero-based intensity ramp, the following relationship exists:

```
hw-intensity = protocol-intensity / (65536 / total-hw-intensities)
```

- Colormap entries are indexed from 0. The colormap-entries defines the number of available colormap entries in a newly created colormap. For **DirectColor** and **TrueColor**, this will usually be 2 to the power of the maximum number of bits set to 1 in red-mask, green-mask, and blue-mask.

Encoding

For TCP connections, displays on a given host are numbered starting from 0, and the server for display N listens and accepts connections on port 6000+N. For DECnet connections, displays on a given host are numbered starting from 0, and the server for display N listens and accepts connections on the object name obtained by concatenating "X$X" with the decimal representation of N; for example, X$X0 and X$X1.

Information sent by the client at connection setup:

# Bytes	Value	Description
1		byte-order:
	#x42	MSB first
	#x6C	LSB first
1		unused
2	CARD16	protocol-major-version
2	CARD16	protocol-minor-version
2	n	length of authorization-protocol-name
2	d	length of authorization-protocol-data
2		unused
n	STRING8	authorization-protocol-name
p		unused, p=pad(n)
d	STRING8	authorization-protocol-data
q		unused, q=pad(d)

Except where explicitly noted in the protocol, all 16-bit and 32-bit quantities sent by the client must be transmitted with the specified byte order, and all 16-bit and 32-bit quantities returned by the server will be transmitted with this byte order.

Information received by the client if authorization fails:

# Bytes	Value	Description
1	0	failed
1	n	length of reason in bytes
2	CARD16	protocol-major-version
2	CARD16	protocol-minor-version
2	(n+p)/4	length in 4-byte units of "additional data"
n	STRING8	reason
p		unused, p=pad(n)

Information received by the client if authorization is accepted:

# Bytes	Value	Description
1	1	success
1		unused
2	CARD16	protocol-major-version
2	CARD16	protocol-minor-version
2	8+2n+(v+p+m)/4	length in 4-byte units of ''additional data''
4	CARD32	release-number
4	CARD32	resource-id-base
4	CARD32	resource-id-mask
4	CARD32	motion-buffer-size
2	v	length of vendor
2	CARD16	maximum-request-length
1	CARD8	number of SCREENs in roots
1	n	number for FORMATs in pixmap-formats
1		image-byte-order:
	0	LSBFirst
	1	MSBFirst
1		bitmap-format-bit-order:
	0	LeastSignificant
	1	MostSignificant
1	CARD8	bitmap-format-scanline-unit
1	CARD8	bitmap-format-scanline-pad
1	KEYCODE	min-keycode
1	KEYCODE	max-keycode
4		unused
v	STRING8	vendor
p		unused, p=pad(v)
8n	LISTofFORMAT	pixmap-formats
m	LISTofSCREEN	roots
		(m is always a multiple of 4)

LISTofFORMAT is n repetitions of the encoding for FORMAT shown in the table below:

# Bytes	Value	Description
1	CARD8	depth
1	CARD8	bits-per-pixel
1	CARD8	scanline-pad
5		unused

LISTofSCREEN is *n* repetitions of the encoding for SCREEN shown in the table below:

# Bytes	Value	Description
4	WINDOW	root
4	COLORMAP	default-colormap
4	CARD32	white-pixel
4	CARD32	black-pixel
4	SETofEVENT	current-input-masks
2	CARD16	width-in-pixels
2	CARD16	height-in-pixels
2	CARD16	width-in-millimeters
2	CARD16	height-in-millimeters
2	CARD16	min-installed-maps
2	CARD16	max-installed-maps
4	VISUALID	root-visual
1		backing-stores:
	0	Never
	1	WhenMapped
	2	Always
1	BOOL	save-unders
1	CARD8	root-depth
1	CARD8	number of DEPTHs in allowed-depths
n	LISTofDEPTH	allowed-depths
		(n is always a multiple of 4)

LISTofDEPTH is *n* repetitions of the encoding for DEPTH shown in the table below:

# Bytes	Value	Description
1	CARD8	depth
1		unused
2	n	number of VISUALTYPES in visuals
4		unused
24n	LISTofVISUALTYPE	visuals

LISTofVISUALTYPE is *n* repetitions of the encoding for VISUALTYPE shown in the table below:

# Bytes	Value	Description
4	VISUALID	visual-id
1		class:
	0	StaticGray
	1	GrayScale
	2	StaticColor
	3	PseudoColor

# Bytes	Value	Description
	4	TrueColor
	5	DirectColor
1	CARD8	bits-per-rgb-value
2	CARD16	colormap-entries
4	CARD32	red-mask
4	CARD32	green-mask
4	CARD32	blue-mask
4		unused

Name
AllocColor

Request Contents
cmap: COLORMAP
red, green, blue: CARD16

Reply Contents
pixel: CARD32
red, green, blue: CARD16

Errors
Colormap, Alloc

Description
This request allocates a read-only colormap entry corresponding to the closest RGB values provided by the hardware. It also returns the pixel and the RGB values actually used. Multiple clients requesting the same effective RGB values can be assigned the same read-only entry, allowing entries to be shared.

Request Encoding

# of Bytes	Value	Description
1	84	opcode
1		unused
2	4	request length
4	COLORMAP	cmap
2	CARD16	red
2	CARD16	green
2	CARD16	blue
2		unused

Reply Encoding

# of Bytes	Value	Description
1	1	reply
1		unused
2	CARD16	sequence number
4	0	reply length
2	CARD16	red
2	CARD16	green
2	CARD16	blue
2		unused

# of Bytes	Value	Description
4	CARD32	pixel
12		unused

AllocColorCells

Name
AllocColorCells

Request Contents
cmap: COLORMAP
colors, planes: CARD16
contiguous: BOOL

Reply Contents
pixels, masks: LISTofCARD32

Errors
Colormap, **Value**, **Alloc**

Description
The number of colors must be positive, and the number of planes must be nonnegative (or a **Value** error results). If C colors and P planes are requested, then C pixels and P masks are returned. No mask will have any bits in common with any other mask or with any of the pixels. By ORing together masks and pixels, $C*2^P$ distinct pixels can be produced; all of these are allocated writable by the request. For **GrayScale** or **PseudoColor**, each mask will have exactly one bit set to 1; for **DirectColor**, each will have exactly three bits set to 1. If contiguous is **True** and if all masks are ORed together, a single contiguous set of bits will be formed for **GrayScale** or **PseudoColor**, and three contiguous sets of bits (one within each pixel subfield) for **DirectColor**. The RGB values of the allocated entries are undefined.

Request Encoding

# of Bytes	Value	Description
1	86	opcode
1	BOOL	contiguous
2	3	request length
4	COLORMAP	cmap
2	CARD16	colors
2	CARD16	planes

Reply Encoding

# of Bytes	Value	Description
1	1	reply
1		unused
2	CARD16	sequence number
4	n+m	reply length

# of Bytes	Value	Description
2	n	number of CARD32s in pixels
2	m	number of CARD32s in masks
20		unused
4n	LISTofCARD32	pixels
4m	LISTofCARD32	masks

AllocColorPlanes

Name

AllocColorPlanes

Request Contents

cmap: COLORMAP
colors, reds, greens, blues: CARD16
contiguous: BOOL

Reply Contents

pixels: LISTofCARD32
red-mask, green-mask, blue-mask: CARD32

Errors

Colormap, **Value**, **Alloc**

Description

The number of colors must be positive, and the reds, greens, and blues must be nonnegative (or a **Value** error results). If C colors, R reds, G greens, and B blues are requested, then C pixels are returned, and the masks have R, G, and B bits set, respectively. If contiguous is **True**, then each mask will have a contiguous set of bits. No mask will have any bits in common with any other mask or with any of the pixels. For **DirectColor**, each mask will lie within the corresponding pixel subfield. By ORing together subsets of masks with pixels, $C*2^{R+G+B}$ distinct pixels can be produced; all of these are allocated by the request. The initial RGB values of the allocated entries are undefined. In the colormap, there are only $C*2^{R}$ independent red entries, $C*2^{G}$ independent green entries, and $C*2^{B}$ independent blue entries. This is true even for **PseudoColor**. When the colormap entry for a pixel value is changed using **StoreColors** or **StoreNamedColor**, the pixel is decomposed according to the masks, and the corresponding independent entries are updated.

Request Encoding

# of Bytes	Value	Description
1	87	opcode
1	BOOL	contiguous
2	4	request length
4	COLORMAP	cmap
2	CARD16	colors
2	CARD16	reds
2	CARD16	greens
2	CARD16	blues

Reply Encoding

# of Bytes	Value	Description
1	1	reply
1		unused
2	CARD16	sequence number
4	n	reply length
2	n	number of CARD32s in pixels
2		unused
4	CARD32	red-mask
4	CARD32	green-mask
4	CARD32	blue-mask
8		unused
4n	LISTofCARD32	pixels

AllocNamedColor

Name
AllocNamedColor

Request Contents
cmap: COLORMAP
name: STRING8

Reply Contents
pixel: CARD32
exact-red, exact-green, exact-blue: CARD16
visual-red, visual-green, visual-blue: CARD16

Errors
Colormap, **Name**, **Alloc**

Description
This request looks up the named color with respect to the screen associated with the colormap. Then, it does an **AllocColor** on cmap. The name should use the ISO Latin-1 encoding, and upper case and lower case do not matter. The exact RGB values specify the true values for the color, and the visual values specify the values actually used in the colormap.

Request Encoding

# of Bytes	Value	Description
1	85	opcode
1		unused
2	3+(n+p)/4	request length
4	COLORMAP	cmap
2	n	length of name
2		unused
n	STRING8	name
p		unused, p=pad(n)

Reply Encoding

# of Bytes	Value	Description
1	1	reply
1		unused
2	CARD16	sequence number
4	0	reply length
4	CARD32	pixel
2	CARD16	exact-red
2	CARD16	exact-green

# of Bytes	Value	Description
2	CARD16	exact-blue
2	CARD16	visual-red
2	CARD16	visual-green
2	CARD16	visual-blue
8		unused

Name

AllowEvents

Request Contents

mode: { AsyncPointer, SyncPointer, ReplayPointer, AsyncKeyboard, SyncKeyboard,
ReplayKeyboard , AsyncBoth, SyncBoth }
time: TIMESTAMP or **CurrentTime**

Errors

Value

Description

This request releases some queued events if the client has caused a device to freeze. The
request has no effect if the specified time is earlier than the last-grab time of the most recent
active grab for the client or if the specified time is later than the current server time.

For **AsyncPointer**, if the pointer is frozen by the client, pointer event processing continues
normally. If the pointer is frozen twice by the client on behalf of two separate grabs, **Async-
Pointer** thaws for both. **AsyncPointer** has no effect if the pointer is not frozen by the client,
but the pointer need not be grabbed by the client.

For **SyncPointer**, if the pointer is frozen and actively grabbed by the client, pointer event processing continues normally until the next **ButtonPress** or **ButtonRelease** event is reported to
the client, at which time the pointer again appears to freeze. However, if the reported event
causes the pointer grab to be released, then the pointer does not freeze. **SyncPointer** has no
effect if the pointer is not frozen by the client or if the pointer is not grabbed by the client.

For **ReplayPointer**, if the pointer is actively grabbed by the client and is frozen as the result of
an event having been sent to the client (either from the activation of a **GrabButton** or from a
previous **AllowEvents** with mode **SyncPointer** but not from a **GrabPointer**), then the pointer
grab is released and that event is completely reprocessed, this time ignoring any passive grabs
at or above (towards the root) the grab-window of the grab just released. The request has no
effect if the pointer is not grabbed by the client or if the pointer is not frozen as the result of an
event.

For **AsyncKeyboard**, if the keyboard is frozen by the client, keyboard event processing continues normally. If the keyboard is frozen twice by the client on behalf of two separate grabs,
AsyncKeyboard thaws for both. **AsyncKeyboard** has no effect if the keyboard is not frozen
by the client, but the keyboard need not be grabbed by the client.

For **SyncKeyboard**, if the keyboard is frozen and actively grabbed by the client, keyboard
event processing continues normally until the next **KeyPress** or **KeyRelease** event is reported
to the client, at which time the keyboard again appears to freeze. However, if the reported
event causes the keyboard grab to be released, then the keyboard does not freeze. **Sync-
Keyboard** has no effect if the keyboard is not frozen by the client or if the keyboard is not
grabbed by the client.

For **ReplayKeyboard**, if the keyboard is actively grabbed by the client and is frozen as the result of an event having been sent to the client (either from the activation of a **GrabKey** or from a previous **AllowEvents** with mode **SyncKeyboard** but not from a **GrabKeyboard**), then the keyboard grab is released and that event is completely reprocessed, this time ignoring any passive grabs at or above (towards the root) the grab-window of the grab just released. The request has no effect if the keyboard is not grabbed by the client or if the keyboard is not frozen as the result of an event.

For **SyncBoth**, if both pointer and keyboard are frozen by the client, event processing (for both devices) continues normally until the next **ButtonPress**, **ButtonRelease**, **KeyPress**, or **Key-Release** event is reported to the client for a grabbed device (button event for the pointer, key event for the keyboard), at which time the devices again appear to freeze. However, if the reported event causes the grab to be released, then the devices do not freeze (but if the other device is still grabbed, then a subsequent event for it will still cause both devices to freeze). **SyncBoth** has no effect unless both pointer and keyboard are frozen by the client. If the pointer or keyboard is frozen twice by the client on behalf of two separate grabs, **SyncBoth** thaws for both (but a subsequent freeze for **SyncBoth** will only freeze each device once).

For **AsyncBoth**, if the pointer and the keyboard are frozen by the client, event processing for both devices continues normally. If a device is frozen twice by the client on behalf of two separate grabs, **AsyncBoth** thaws for both. **AsyncBoth** has no effect unless both pointer and keyboard are frozen by the client.

AsyncPointer, **SyncPointer**, and **ReplayPointer** have no effect on processing of keyboard events. **AsyncKeyboard**, **SyncKeyboard**, and **ReplayKeyboard** have no effect on processing of pointer events.

It is possible for both a pointer grab and a keyboard grab to be active simultaneously (by the same or different clients). When a device is frozen on behalf of either grab, no event processing is performed for the device. It is possible for a single device to be frozen because of both grabs. In this case, the freeze must be released on behalf of both grabs before events can again be processed. If a device is frozen twice by a single client, then a single **AllowEvents** releases both.

Request Encoding

# of Bytes	Value	Description
1	35	opcode
1		mode:
	0	**AsyncPointer**
	1	**SyncPointer**
	2	**ReplayPointer**
	3	**AsyncKeyboard**
	4	**SyncKeyboard**
	5	**ReplayKeyboard**
	6	**AsyncBoth**
	7	**SyncBoth**

# of Bytes	Value	Description
2	2	request length
4	TIMESTAMP	time:
	0	**CurrentTime**

Bell

Name
Bell

Request Contents
percent: INT8

Errors
Value

Description
This request rings the bell on the keyboard at a volume relative to the base volume for the keyboard, if possible. Percent can range from −100 to 100 inclusive (or a **Value** error results). The volume at which the bell is rung when percent is nonnegative is:

```
base - [(base * percent) / 100] + percent
```

When percent is negative, it is:

```
base + [(base * percent) / 100]
```

Request Encoding

# of Bytes	Value	Description
1	104	opcode
1	INT8	percent
2	1	request length

Name

ButtonPress

Event Contents

root, event : WINDOW
child : WINDOW or **None**
same-screen : BOOL
root-x, root-y, event-x, event-y : INT16
detail : (See Description.)
state : SETofKEYBUTMASK
time : TIMESTAMP

(Same contents as **MotionNotify**.)

Description

ButtonPress events are sent by the server to the client when the user presses a pointer button. Only clients selecting **ButtonPress** events will receive them. The window member of this event depends on which window the pointer is in when the button is pressed and on the values of the event-mask and do-not-propagate field for that window and its ancestors.

For more information, see **MotionNotify**.

Request Encoding

# of Bytes	Value	Description
1	4	code
1	BUTTON	detail
2	CARD16	sequence number
4	TIMESTAMP	time
4	WINDOW	root
4	WINDOW	event
4	WINDOW	child:
	0	**None**
2	INT16	root-x
2	INT16	root-y
2	INT16	event-x
2	INT16	event-y
2	SETofKEYBUTMASK	state
1	BOOL	same-screen
1		unused

ButtonRelease

Name

ButtonRelease

Event Contents

root, *event*: WINDOW
child: WINDOW or **None**
same-screen: BOOL
root-x, *root-y*, *event-x*, *event-y*: INT16
detail: (See Description.)
state: SETofKEYBUTMASK
time: TIMESTAMP

(Same contents as **MotionNotify**.)

Description

ButtonRelease events are sent by the server to the client when the user presses a pointer button. Only clients selecting **ButtonRelease** events will receive them. The window member of this event depends on which window the pointer is in when the button is pressed and on the values of the event-mask and do-not-propagate field for that window and its ancestors.

For more information, see **MotionNotify**.

Request Encoding

# of Bytes	Value	Description
1	5	code
1	BUTTON	detail
2	CARD16	sequence number
4	TIMESTAMP	time
4	WINDOW	root
4	WINDOW	event
4	WINDOW	child:
	0	**None**
2	INT16	root-x
2	INT16	root-y
2	INT16	event-x
2	INT16	event-y
2	SETofKEYBUTMASK	state
1	BOOL	same-screen
1		unused

Name

ChangeActivePointerGrab

Request Contents

event-mask: SETofPOINTEREVENT
cursor: CURSOR or **None**
time: TIMESTAMP or **CurrentTime**

Errors

Cursor, **Value**

Description

This request changes the specified dynamic parameters if the pointer is actively grabbed by the client and the specified time is no earlier than the last-pointer-grab time and no later than the current server time. The interpretation of event-mask and cursor are the same as in **Grab-Pointer**. This request has no effect on the parameters of any passive grabs established with **GrabButton**.

Request Encoding

# of Bytes	Value	Description
1	30	opcode
1		unused
2	4	request length
4	CURSOR	cursor:
	0	**None**
4	TIMESTAMP	time:
	0	**CurrentTime**
2	SETofPOINTEREVENT	event-mask
2		unused

ChangeGC

Name

ChangeGC

Request Contents

gc: GCONTEXT
value-mask: BITMASK
value-list: LISTofVALUE

Errors

GContext, Pixmap, Font, Match, Value, Alloc

Description

This request changes components in gc. The value-mask and value-list specify which components are to be changed. The values and restrictions are the same as for **CreateGC**.

Changing the clip-mask also overrides any previous **SetClipRectangles** request on the context. Changing dash-offset or dashes overrides any previous **SetDashes** request on the context.

The order in which components are verified and altered is server-dependent. If an error is generated, a subset of the components may have been altered.

Request Encoding

# of Bytes	Value	Description
1	56	opcode
1		unused
2	3+n	request length
4	GCONTEXT	gc
4	BITMASK	value-mask (has n bits set to 1)
		(Encodings are the same as for **CreateGC**.)
4n	LISTofVALUE	value-list
		(Encodings are the same as for **CreateGC**.)

ChangeHosts

Name
ChangeHosts

Request Contents
mode: {**Insert, Delete**}
host: HOST

Errors
Access, Value

Description
This request adds or removes the specified host from the access control list. When the access control mechanism is enabled and a host attempts to establish a connection to the server, the host must be in this list, or the server will refuse the connection.

The client must reside on the same host as the server and/or have been granted permission by a server-dependent method to execute this request (or an **Access** error results).

An initial access control list can usually be specified, typically by naming a file that the server reads at startup and reset.

The following address families are defined. A server is not required to support these families and may support families not listed here. Use of an unsupported family, an improper address format, or an improper address length within a supported family results in a **Value** error.

For the Internet family, the address must be four bytes long. The address bytes are in standard order; the server performs no automatic swapping on the address bytes. For a Class A address, the network number is the first byte in the address and the host number is the remaining three bytes, most-significant byte first. For a Class B address, the network number is the first two bytes and the host number is the last two bytes, each most-significant byte first. For a Class C address, the network number is the first three bytes, most-significant byte first, and the last byte is the host number.

For the DECnet family, the server performs no automatic swapping on the address bytes. A Phase IV address is two bytes long: the first byte contains the least-significant eight bits of the node number, and the second byte contains the most-significant two bits of the node number in the least-significant two bits of the byte and the area in the most significant six bits of the byte.

For the Chaos family, the address must be two bytes long. The host number is always the first byte in the address, and the subnet number is always the second byte. The server performs no automatic swapping on the address bytes.

Request Encoding

# of Bytes	Value	Description
1	109	opcode
1		mode:
	0	**Insert**
	1	**Delete**
2	2+(n+p)/4	request length
1		family:
	0	**Internet**
	1	**DECnet**
	2	**Chaos**
1		unused
2	n	length of address
n	LISTofCARD8	address
p		unused, p=pad(n)

Name

ChangeKeyboardControl

Request Contents

value-mask: BITMASK
value-list: LISTofVALUE

Errors

Match, **Value**

Description

This request controls various aspects of the keyboard. The value-mask and value-list specify which controls are to be changed. The possible values are:

Control	Type
key-click-percent	INT8
bell-percent	INT8
bell-pitch	INT16
bell-duration	INT16
led	CARD8
led-mode	{**On**, **Off**}
key	KEYCODE
auto-repeat-mode	{**On**, **Off**, **Default**}

The key-click-percent sets the volume for key clicks between 0 (off) and 100 (loud) inclusive, if possible. Setting to –1 restores the default. Other negative values generate a **Value** error.

The bell-percent sets the base volume for the bell between 0 (off) and 100 (loud) inclusive, if possible. Setting to –1 restores the default. Other negative values generate a **Value** error.

The bell-pitch sets the pitch (specified in Hz) of the bell, if possible. Setting to –1 restores the default. Other negative values generate a **Value** error.

The bell-duration sets the duration of the bell (specified in milliseconds), if possible. Setting to –1 restores the default. Other negative values generate a **Value** error.

If both led-mode and led are specified, then the state of that LED is changed, if possible. If only led-mode is specified, then the state of all LEDs are changed, if possible. At most 32 LEDs, numbered from one, are supported. No standard interpretation of LEDs is defined. It is a **Match** error if an led is specified without an led-mode.

If both auto-repeat-mode and key are specified, then the auto-repeat mode of that key is changed, if possible. If only auto-repeat-mode is specified, then the global auto-repeat mode for the entire keyboard is changed, if possible, without affecting the per-key settings. It is a

Match error if a key is specified without an auto-repeat-mode. Each key has an individual mode of whether or not it should auto-repeat and a default setting for that mode. In addition, there is a global mode of whether auto-repeat should be enabled or not and a default setting for that mode. When the global mode is **On**, keys should obey their individual auto-repeat modes. When the global mode is **Off**, no keys should auto-repeat. An auto-repeating key generates alternating **KeyPress** and **KeyRelease** events. When a key is used as a modifier, it is desirable for the key not to auto-repeat, regardless of the auto-repeat setting for that key.

A bell generator connected with the console but not directly on the keyboard is treated as if it were part of the keyboard.

The order in which controls are verified and altered is server-dependent. If an error is generated, a subset of the controls may have been altered.

Request Encoding

# of Bytes	Value	Description
1	102	opcode
1		unused
2	2+n	request length
4	BITMASK	value-mask (has n bits set to 1):
	#x0001	key-click-percent
	#x0002	bell-percent
	#x0004	bell-pitch
	#x0008	bell-duration
	#x0010	led
	#x0020	led-mode
	#x0040	key
	#x0080	auto-repeat-mode
4n	LISTofVALUE	value-list

LISTofVALUE is *n* repetitions of the encoding for VALUE shown in the table below:

# of Bytes	Value	Description
1	INT8	key-click-percent
1	INT8	bell-percent
2	INT16	bell-pitch
2	INT16	bell-duration
1	CARD8	led
1		led-mode:
	0	**Off**
	1	**On**

# of Bytes	Value	Description
1	KEYCODE	key
1		auto-repeat-mode:
	0	**Off**
	1	**On**
	2	**Default**

ChangeKeyboardMapping

Name

ChangeKeyboardMapping

Request Contents

first-keycode: KEYCODE
keysyms-per-keycode: CARD8
keysyms: LISTofKEYSYM

Errors

Value, **Alloc**

Description

This request defines the symbols for the specified number of keycodes, starting with the specified keycode. The symbols for keycodes outside this range remained unchanged. The number of elements in the keysyms list must be a multiple of keysyms-per-keycode (or a **Length** error results). The first-keycode must be greater than or equal to min-keycode as returned in the connection setup (or a **Value** error results) and:

```
first-keycode + (keysyms-length / keysyms-per-keycode) - 1
```

must be less than or equal to max-keycode as returned in the connection setup (or a **Value** error results). KEYSYM number N (counting from zero) for keycode K has an index (counting from zero) of:

```
(K - first-keycode) * keysyms-per-keycode + N
```

in keysyms. The keysyms-per-keycode can be chosen arbitrarily by the client to be large enough to hold all desired symbols. A special KEYSYM value of **NoSymbol** should be used to fill in unused elements for individual keycodes. It is legal for **NoSymbol** to appear in nontrailing positions of the effective list for a keycode.

This request generates a **MappingNotify** event.

There is no requirement that the server interpret this mapping; it is merely stored for reading and writing by clients (see Appendix E, *Keyboards and Pointers*).

Request Encoding

# of Bytes	Value	Description
1	100	opcode
1	n	keycode-count
2	2+nm	request length
1	KEYCODE	first-keycode
1	m	keysyms-per-keycode
2		unused
4nm	LISTofKEYSYM	keysyms

ChangePointerControl

Name

ChangePointerControl

Request Contents

do-acceleration, *do-threshold*: BOOL
acceleration-numerator, *acceleration-denominator* : INT16
threshold: INT16

Errors

Value

Description

This request defines how the pointer moves. The acceleration is a multiplier for movement expressed as a fraction. For example, specifying 3/1 means the pointer moves three times as fast as normal. The fraction can be rounded arbitrarily by the server. Acceleration only takes effect if the pointer moves more than threshold number of pixels at once and only applies to the amount beyond the threshold. Setting a value to –1 restores the default. Other negative values generate a **Value** error, as does a zero value for acceleration-denominator.

Request Encoding

# of Bytes	Value	Description
1	105	opcode
1		unused
2	3	request length
2	INT16	acceleration-numerator
2	INT16	acceleration-denominator
2	INT16	threshold
1	BOOL	do-acceleration
1	BOOL	do-threshold

ChangeProperty

Name

ChangeProperty

Request Contents

window: WINDOW
property, *type*: ATOM
format: {8, 16, 32}
mode: {**Replace**, **Prepend**, **Append**}
data: LISTofINT8 or LISTofINT16 or LISTofINT32

Errors

Window, **Atom**, **Value**, **Match**, **Alloc**

Description

This request alters the property for the specified window. The type is uninterpreted by the server. The format specifies whether the data should be viewed as a list of 8-bit, 16-bit, or 32-bit quantities so that the server can correctly byte-swap as necessary.

If the mode is **Replace**, the previous property value is discarded. If the mode is **Prepend** or **Append**, then the type and format must match the existing property value (or a **Match** error results). If the property is undefined, it is treated as defined with the correct type and format with zero-length data. For **Prepend**, the data is tacked on to the beginning of the existing data, and for **Append**, it is tacked on to the end of the existing data.

This request generates a **PropertyNotify** event on the window.

The lifetime of a property is not tied to the storing client. Properties remain until explicitly deleted, until the window is destroyed, or until server reset (see Appendix A, *Connection Close*).

The maximum size of a property is server-dependent and may vary dynamically.

Request Encoding

# of Bytes	Value	Description
1	18	opcode
1		mode:
	0	**Replace**
	1	**Prepend**
	2	**Append**
2	6+(n+p)/4	request length
4	WINDOW	window
4	ATOM	property
4	ATOM	type
1	CARD8	format
3		unused

# of Bytes	Value	Description
4	CARD32	length of data in format units (= n for format = 8) (= n/2 for format = 16) (= n/4 for format = 32)
n	LISTofBYTE	data (n is a multiple of 2 for format = 16) (n is a multiple of 4 for format = 32)
p		unused, p=pad(n)

ChangeSaveSet

Name
ChangeSaveSet

Request Contents
window: WINDOW
mode: {**Insert**, **Delete**}

Errors
Window, **Match**, **Value**

Description
This request adds or removes the specified window from the client's save-set. The window must have been created by some other client (or a **Match** error results). For further information about the use of the save-set, see Appendix A, *Connection Close*.

When windows are destroyed, the server automatically removes them from the save-set.

Request Encoding

# of Bytes	Value	Description
1	6	opcode
1		mode:
	0	**Insert**
	1	**Delete**
2	2	request length
4	WINDOW	window

ChangeWindowAttributes

Name
ChangeWindowAttributes

Request Contents
window: WINDOW
value-mask: BITMASK
value-list: LISTofVALUE

Errors
Window, **Pixmap**, **Colormap**, **Cursor**, **Match**, **Value**, **Access**

Description
The value-mask and value-list specify which attributes are to be changed. The values and restrictions are the same as for **CreateWindow**.

Setting a new background, whether by background-pixmap or background-pixel, overrides any previous background. Setting a new border, whether by border-pixel or border-pixmap, overrides any previous border.

Changing the background does not cause the window contents to be changed. Drawing into the pixmap that was set as the background pixmap attribute has an undefined effect on the window background. The server may or may not make a copy of the pixmap. Setting the border or changing the background such that the border tile origin changes causes the border to be repainted. Changing the background of a root window to **None** or **ParentRelative** restores the default background pixmap. Changing the border of a root window to **CopyFromParent** restores the default border pixmap.

Changing the win-gravity does not affect the current position of the window.

Changing the backing-store of an obscured window to **WhenMapped** or **Always** or changing the backing-planes, backing-pixel, or save-under of a mapped window may have no immediate effect.

Multiple clients can select input on the same window; their event-masks are disjoint. When an event is generated, it will be reported to all interested clients. However, only one client at a time can select for **SubstructureRedirect**, only one client at a time can select for **Resize-Redirect**, and only one client at a time can select for **ButtonPress**. An attempt to violate these restrictions results in an **Access** error.

There is only one do-not-propagate-mask for a window, not one per client.

Changing the colormap of a window (by defining a new map, not by changing the contents of the existing map) generates a **ColormapNotify** event. Changing the colormap of a visible window might have no immediate effect on the screen (see **InstallColormap** request).

Changing the cursor of a root window to **None** restores the default cursor.

The order in which attributes are verified and altered is server-dependent. If an error is generated, a subset of the attributes may have been altered.

Request Encoding

# of Bytes	Value	Description
1	2	opcode
1		unused
2	3+n	request length
4	WINDOW	window
4	BITMASK	value-mask (has n bits set to 1)
		(Encodings are the same as for **CreateWindow**.)
4n	LISTofVALUE	value-list
		(Encodings are the same as for **CreateWindow**.)

CirculateNotify

Name

CirculateNotify

Event Contents

event, *window*: WINDOW
place: { **Top**, **Bottom** }

Description

This event is reported to clients selecting **StructureNotify** on the window and to clients selecting **SubstructureNotify** on the parent. It is generated when the window is actually restacked
from a **CirculateWindow** request. The event is the window on which the event was generated,
and the window is the window that is restacked. If place is **Top**, the window is now on top of
all siblings. Otherwise, it is below all siblings.

Request Encoding

# of Bytes	Value	Description
1	26	code
1		unused
2	CARD16	sequence number
4	WINDOW	event
4	WINDOW	window
4	WINDOW	unused
1		place:
	0	**Top**
	1	**Bottom**
15		unused

CirculateRequest

Name

CirculateRequest

Event Contents

parent, *window*: WINDOW
place: { **Top**, **Bottom** }

Description

This event is reported to the client selecting **StructureRedirect** on the parent and is generated when a **CirculateWindow** request is issued on the parent and a window actually needs to be restacked. The window specifies the window to be restacked, and the place specifies what the new position in the stacking order should be.

Request Encoding

# of Bytes	Value	Description
1	27	code
1		unused
2	CARD16	sequence number
4	WINDOW	parent
4	WINDOW	window
4		unused
1		place:
	0	**Top**
	1	**Bottom**
15		unused

CirculateWindow

Name

CirculateWindow

Request Contents

window: WINDOW
direction: { **RaiseLowest**, **LowerHighest** }

Errors

Window, **Value**

Description

If some other client has selected **Substructure** Redirect on the window, then a **CirculateRequest** event is generated, and no further processing is performed. Otherwise, the following is performed, and then a **CirculateNotify** event is generated if the window is actually restacked.

For **RaiseLowest**, **CirculateWindow** raises the lowest mapped child (if any) that is occluded by another child to the top of the stack. For **LowerHighest**, **CirculateWindow** lowers the highest mapped child (if any) that occludes another child to the bottom of the stack. Exposure processing is performed on formerly obscured windows.

Request Encoding

# of Bytes	Value	Description
1	13	opcode
1		direction:
	0	**RaiseLowest**
	1	**LowerHighest**
2	2	request length
4	WINDOW	window

Name
ClearArea

Request Contents
window: WINDOW
x, y: INT16
width, height: CARD16
exposures: BOOL

Errors
Window, Value, Match

Description
The x and y coordinates are relative to the window's origin and specify the upper-left corner of the rectangle. If width is zero, it is replaced with the current width of the window minus x. If height is zero, it is replaced with the current height of the window minus y. If the window has a defined background tile, the rectangle is tiled with a plane-mask of all ones and function of **Copy** and a subwindow-mode of **ClipByChildren**. If the window has background **None**, the contents of the window are not changed. In either case, if exposures is **True**, then one or more exposure events are generated for regions of the rectangle that are either visible or being retained in a backing store.

It is a **Match** error to use an **InputOnly** window in this request.

Request Encoding

# of Bytes	Value	Description
1	61	opcode
1	BOOL	exposures
2	4	request length
4	WINDOW	window
2	INT16	x
2	INT16	y
2	CARD16	width
2	CARD16	height

ClientMessage

Name

ClientMessage

Event Contents

window: WINDOW
type: ATOM
format: {8, 16, 32}
data: LISTofINT8 or LISTofINT16 or LISTofINT32

Description

This event is only generated by clients using **SendEvent**. The type specifies how the data is to be interpreted by the receiving client; the server places no interpretation on the type or the data. The format specifies whether the data should be viewed as a list of 8-bit, 16-bit, or 32-bit quantities, so that the server can correctly byte-swap, as necessary. The data always consists of either 20 8-bit values or 10 16-bit values or 5 32-bit values, although particular message types might not make use of all of these values.

Request Encoding

# of Bytes	Value	Description
1	33	code
1	CARD8	format
2	CARD16	sequence number
4	WINDOW	window
4	ATOM	type
20		data

CloseFont

Name

CloseFont

Request Contents

font: FONT

Errors

Font

Description

This request deletes the association between the resource ID and the font. The font itself will be freed when no other resource references it.

Request Encoding

# of Bytes	Value	Description
1	46	opcode
1		unused
2	2	request length
4	FONT	font

ColormapNotify

Name
ColormapNotify

Event Contents
window: WINDOW
colormap: COLORMAP or **None**
new: BOOL
state: { **Installed**, **Uninstalled** }

Description
This event is reported to clients selecting **ColormapChange** on the window. It is generated with value **True** for new when the colormap attribute of the window is changed and is generated with value **False** for new when the colormap of a window is installed or uninstalled. In either case, the state indicates whether the colormap is currently installed.

Request Encoding

# of Bytes	Value	Description
1	32	code
1		unused
2	CARD16	sequence number
4	WINDOW	window
4	COLORMAP	colormap:
	0	**None**
1	BOOL	new
1		state:
	0	**Uninstalled**
	1	**Installed**
18		unused

ConfigureNotify

Name

ConfigureNotify

Event Contents

event, *window*: WINDOW
x, y: INT16
width, height, border-width: CARD16
above-sibling: WINDOW or **None**
override-redirect: BOOL

Description

This event is reported to clients selecting **StructureNotify** on the window and to clients selecting **SubstructureNotify** on the parent. It is generated when a **ConfigureWindow** request
actually changes the state of the window. The event is the window on which the event was generated, and the window is the window that is changed. The x and y coordinates are relative to
the new parent's origin and specify the position of the upper-left outer corner of the window.
The width and height specify the inside size, not including the border. If above-sibling is
None, then the window is on the bottom of the stack with respect to siblings. Otherwise, the
window is immediately on top of the specified sibling. The override-redirect flag is from the
window's attribute.

Request Encoding

# of Bytes	Value	Description
1	22	code
1		unused
2	CARD16	sequence number
4	WINDOW	event
4	WINDOW	window
4	WINDOW	above-sibling:
	0	**None**
2	INT16	x
2	INT16	y
2	CARD16	width
2	CARD16	height
2	CARD16	border-width
1	BOOL	override-redirect
5		unused

ConfigureRequest

Name

ConfigureRequest

Event Contents

parent, window: WINDOW
x, y: INT16
width, height, border-width: CARD16
sibling: WINDOW or **None**
stack-mode: {**Above, Below, TopIf, BottomIf, Opposite**}
value-mask: BITMASK

Description

This event is reported to the client selecting **SubstructureRedirect** on the parent and is generated when a **ConfigureWindow** request is issued on the window by some other client. The value-mask indicates which components were specified in the request. The value-mask and the corresponding values are reported as given in the request. The remaining values are filled in from the current geometry of the window, except in the case of sibling and stack-mode, which are reported as **None** and **Above** (respectively) if not given in the request.

Request Encoding

# of Bytes	Value	Description
1	23	code
1		stack-mode:
	0	**Above**
	1	**Below**
	2	**TopIf**
	3	**BottomIf**
	4	**Opposite**
2	CARD16	sequence number
4	WINDOW	parent
4	WINDOW	window
4	WINDOW	sibling:
	0	**None**
2	INT16	x
2	INT16	y
2	CARD16	width
2	CARD16	height
2	CARD16	border-width
2	BITMASK	value-mask:
	#x0001	x
	#x0002	y
	#x0004	width
	#x0008	height

# of Bytes	Value	Description
	#x0010	border-width
	#x0020	sibling
	#x0040	stack-mode
4		unused

Name
ConfigureWindow

Request Contents
window: WINDOW
value-mask: BITMASK
value-list: LISTofVALUE

Errors
Window, **Match**, **Value**

Description
This request changes the configuration of the window. The value-mask and value-list specify which values are to be given. The possible values are:

Attribute	Type
x	INT16
y	INT16
width	CARD16
height	CARD16
border-width	CARD16
sibling	WINDOW
stack-mode	{**Above**, **Below**, **TopIf**, **BottomIf**, **Opposite**}

The x and y coordinates are relative to the parent's origin and specify the position of the upper-left outer corner of the window. The width and height specify the inside size, not including the border, and must be nonzero (or a **Value** error results). Those values not specified are taken from the existing geometry of the window. Note that changing just the border-width leaves the outer-left corner of the window in a fixed position but moves the absolute position of the window's origin. It is a **Match** error to attempt to make the border-width of an **InputOnly** window nonzero.

If the override-redirect attribute of the window is **False** and some other client has selected **SubstructureRedirect** on the parent, a **ConfigureRequest** event is generated, and no further processing is performed. Otherwise, the following is performed.

If some other client has selected **ResizeRedirect** on the window and the inside width or height of the window is being changed, a **ResizeRequest** event is generated, and the current inside width and height are used instead. Note that the override-redirect attribute of the window has no effect on **ResizeRedirect** and that **SubstructureRedirect** on the parent has precedence over **ResizeRedirect** on the window.

The geometry of the window is changed as specified, the window is restacked among siblings, and a **ConfigureNotify** event is generated if the state of the window actually changes. If the inside width or height of the window has actually changed, then children of the window are affected, according to their win-gravity. Exposure processing is performed on formerly obscured windows (including the window itself and its inferiors if regions of them were obscured but now are not). Exposure processing is also performed on any new regions of the window (as a result of increasing the width or height) and on any regions where window contents are lost.

If the inside width or height of a window is not changed but the window is moved or its border is changed, then the contents of the window are not lost but move with the window. Changing the inside width or height of the window causes its contents to be moved or lost, depending on the bit-gravity of the window. It also causes children to be reconfigured, depending on their win-gravity. For a change of width and height of W and H, we define the [x,y] pairs as:

Direction	Deltas
NorthWest	[0, 0]
North	[W/2, 0]
NorthEast	[W, 0]
West	[0, H/2]
Center	[W/2, H/2]
East	[W, H/2]
SouthWest	[0, H]
South	[W/2, H]
SouthEast	[W, H]

When a window with one of these bit-gravities is resized, the corresponding pair defines the change in position of each pixel in the window. When a window with one of these win-gravities has its parent window resized, the corresponding pair defines the change in position of the window within the parent. This repositioning generates a **GravityNotify** event. **GravityNotify** events are generated after the **ConfigureNotify** event is generated.

A gravity of **Static** indicates that the contents or origin should not move relative to the origin of the root window. If the change in size of the window is coupled with a change in position of [X,Y], then for bit-gravity, the change in position of each pixel is [–X,–Y] and, for win-gravity, the change in position of a child when its parent is so resized is [–X,–Y]. Note that **Static** gravity still only takes effect when the width or height of the window is changed, not when the window is simply moved.

A bit-gravity of **Forget** indicates that the window contents are always discarded after a size change, even if backing-store or save-under has been requested. The window is tiled with its background (except, if no background is defined, the existing screen contents are not altered), and zero or more exposure events are generated.

The contents and borders of inferiors are not affected by their parent's bit-gravity. A server is permitted to ignore the specified bit-gravity and use **Forget** instead.

A win-gravity of **Unmap** is like **NorthWest**, but the child is also unmapped when the parent is resized, and an **UnmapNotify** event is generated. **UnmapNotify** events are generated after the **ConfigureNotify** event is generated.

If a sibling and a stack-mode are specified, the window is restacked as follows:

Above   The window is placed just above the sibling.

Below   The window is placed just below the sibling.

TopIf   If the sibling occludes the window, then the window is placed at the top of the stack.

BottomIf   If the window occludes the sibling, then the window is placed at the bottom of the stack.

Opposite   If the sibling occludes the window, then the window is placed at the top of the stack. Otherwise, if the window occludes the sibling, then the window is placed at the bottom of the stack.

If a stack-mode is specified but no sibling is specified, the window is restacked as follows:

Above   The window is placed at the top of the stack.

Below   The window is placed at the bottom of the stack.

TopIf   If any sibling occludes the window, then the window is placed at the top of the stack.

BottomIf   If the window occludes any sibling, then the window is placed at the bottom of the stack.

Opposite   If any sibling occludes the window, then the window is placed at the top of the stack. Otherwise, if the window occludes any sibling, then the window is placed at the bottom of the stack.

It is a **Match** error if a sibling is specified without a stack-mode or if the window is not actually a sibling.

Note that the computations for **BottomIf**, **TopIf**, and **Opposite** are performed with respect to the window's final geometry (as controlled by the other arguments to the request), not to its initial geometry.

Attempts to configure a root window have no effect.

Request Encoding

# of Bytes	Value	Description
1	12	opcode
1		unused
2	3+n	request length
4	WINDOW	window
2	BITMASK	value-mask (has n bits set to 1):
	#x0001	x
	#x0002	y

# of Bytes	Value	Description
	#x0004	width
	#x0008	height
	#x0010	border-width
	#x0020	sibling
	#x0040	stack-mode
2		unused
4n	LISTofVALUE	value-list

LISTofVALUE is *n* repetitions of the encoding for VALUE shown in the table below:

# of Bytes	Value	Description
2	INT16	x
2	INT16	y
2	CARD16	width
2	CARD16	height
2	CARD16	border-width
4	WINDOW	sibling
1		stack-mode:
	0	**Above**
	1	**Below**
	2	**TopIf**
	3	**BottomIf**
	4	**Opposite**

Name
ConvertSelection

Request Contents
selection, *target*: ATOM
property: ATOM or **None**
requestor: WINDOW
time: TIMESTAMP or **CurrentTime**

Errors
Atom, **Window**

Description
If the specified selection has an owner, the server sends a **SelectionRequest** event to that owner. If no owner for the specified selection exists, the server generates a **SelectionNotify** event to the requestor with property **None**. The arguments are passed on unchanged in either event.

Request Encoding

# of Bytes	Value	Description
1	24	opcode
1		unused
2	6	request length
4	WINDOW	requestor
4	ATOM	selection
4	ATOM	target
4	ATOM	property:
	0	**None**
4	TIMESTAMP	time:
	0	**CurrentTime**

CopyArea

Name

CopyArea

Request Contents

src-drawable, *dst-drawable*: DRAWABLE
gc: GCONTEXT
src-x, *src-y*: INT16
width, *height*: CARD16
dst-x, *dst-y*: INT16

Errors

Drawable, **GContext**, **Match**

Description

This request combines the specified rectangle of src-drawable with the specified rectangle of dst-drawable. The src-x and src-y coordinates are relative to src-drawable's origin. The dst-x and dst-y are relative to dst-drawable's origin, each pair specifying the upper-left corner of the rectangle. The src-drawable must have the same root and the same depth as dst-drawable (or a **Match** error results).

If regions of the source rectangle are obscured and have not been retained in backing store or if regions outside the boundaries of the source drawable are specified, then those regions are not copied, but the following occurs on all corresponding destination regions that are either visible or retained in backing-store. If the dst-drawable is a window with a background other than **None**, these corresponding destination regions are tiled (with plane-mask of all ones and function **Copy**) with that background. Regardless of tiling and whether the destination is a window or a pixmap, if graphics-exposures in gc is **True**, then **GraphicsExpose** events for all corresponding destination regions are generated.

If graphics-exposures is **True** but no **GraphicsExpose** events are generated, then a **NoExpose** event is generated.

GC components: function, plane-mask, subwindow-mode, graphics-exposures, clip-x-origin, clip-y-origin, clip-mask.

Request Encoding

# of Bytes	Value	Description
1	62	opcode
1		unused
2	7	request length
4	DRAWABLE	src-drawable
4	DRAWABLE	dst-drawable
4	GCONTEXT	gc
2	INT16	src-x
2	INT16	src-y

# of Bytes	Value	Description
2	INT16	dst-x
2	INT16	dst-y
2	CARD16	width
2	CARD16	height

CopyColormapAndFree

Name
CopyColormapAndFree

Request Contents
mid, src-cmap: COLORMAP

Errors
IDChoice, **Colormap**, **Alloc**

Description
This request creates a colormap of the same visual type and for the same screen as src-cmap, and it associates identifier mid with it. It also moves all of the client's existing allocations from src-cmap to the new colormap with their color values intact and their read-only or writable characteristics intact, and it frees those entries in src-cmap. Color values in other entries in the new colormap are undefined. If src-cmap was created by the client with alloc **All** (see **CreateColormap** request), then the new colormap is also created with alloc **All**, all color values for all entries are copied from src-cmap, and then all entries in src-cmap are freed. If src-cmap was not created by the client with alloc **All**, then the allocations to be moved are all those pixels and planes that have been allocated by the client using either **AllocColor**, **Alloc-NamedColor**, **AllocColorCells**, or **AllocColorPlanes** and that have not been freed since they were allocated.

Request Encoding

# of Bytes	Value	Description
1	80	opcode
1		unused
2	3	request length
4	COLORMAP	mid
4	COLORMAP	src-cmap

Name

CopyGC

Request Contents

src-gc, dst-gc: GCONTEXT
value-mask: BITMASK

Errors

GContext, Value, Match, Alloc

Description

This request copies components from src-gc to dst-gc. The value-mask specifies which components to copy, as for **CreateGC**. The two gcontexts must have the same root and the same depth (or a **Match** error results).

Request Encoding

# of Bytes	Value	Description
1	57	opcode
1		unused
2	4	request length
4	GCONTEXT	src-gc
4	GCONTEXT	dst-gc
4	BITMASK	value-mask
		(Encodings are the same as for **CreateGC**.)

CopyPlane

Name

CopyPlane

Request Contents

src-drawable, *dst-drawable*: DRAWABLE
gc: GCONTEXT
src-x, *src-y*: INT16
width, *height*: CARD16
dst-x, *dst-y*: INT16
bit-plane: CARD32

Errors

Drawable, **GContext**, **Value**, **Match**

Description

The src-drawable must have the same root as dst-drawable (or a **Match** error results), but it need not have the same depth. The bit-plane must have exactly one bit set to 1, and the value of bit-plane must be less than 2^n, where n is the depth of src-drawable (or a **Value** error results). Effectively, a pixmap of the same depth as dst-drawable and with size specified by the source region is formed using the foreground/background pixels in gc (foreground everywhere the bit-plane in src-drawable contains a bit set to 1, background everywhere the bit-plane contains a bit set to 0), and the equivalent of a **CopyArea** is performed, with all the same exposure semantics. This can also be thought of as using the specified region of the source bit-plane as a stipple with a fill-style of **OpaqueStippled** for filling a rectangular area of the destination.

GC components: function, plane-mask, foreground, background, subwindow-mode, graphics-exposures, clip-x-origin, clip-y-origin, clip-mask

Request Encoding

# of Bytes	Value	Description
1	63	opcode
1		unused
2	8	request length
4	DRAWABLE	src-drawable
4	DRAWABLE	dst-drawable
4	GCONTEXT	gc
2	INT16	src-x
2	INT16	src-y
2	INT16	dst-x
2	INT16	dst-y

# of Bytes	Value	Description
2	CARD16	width
2	CARD16	height
4	CARD32	bit-plane

CreateColormap

Name

CreateColormap

Request Contents

mid: COLORMAP
visual: VISUALID
window: WINDOW
alloc: {**None**, **All**}

Errors

IDChoice, **Window**, **Value**, **Match**, **Alloc**

Description

This request creates a colormap of the specified visual type for the screen on which the window resides and associates the identifier mid with it. The visual type must be one supported by the screen (or a **Match** error results). The initial values of the colormap entries are undefined for classes **GrayScale**, **PseudoColor**, and **DirectColor**. For **StaticGray**, **StaticColor**, and **TrueColor**, the entries will have defined values, but those values are specific to the visual and are not defined by the core protocol. For **StaticGray**, **StaticColor**, and **TrueColor**, alloc must be specified as **None** (or a **Match** error results). For the other classes, if alloc is **None**, the colormap initially has no allocated entries, and clients can allocate entries.

If alloc is **All**, then the entire colormap is "allocated" writable. The initial values of all allocated entries are undefined. For **GrayScale** and **PseudoColor**, the effect is as if an **Alloc-ColorCells** request returned all pixel values from zero to N–1, where N is the colormap-entries value in the specified visual. For **DirectColor**, the effect is as if an **AllocColorPlanes** request returned a pixel value of zero and red-mask, green-mask, and blue-mask values containing the same bits as the corresponding masks in the specified visual. However, in all cases, none of these entries can be freed with **FreeColors**.

Request Encoding

# of Bytes	Value	Description
1	78	opcode
1		alloc:
	0	**None**
	1	**All**
2	4	request length
4	COLORMAP	mid
4	WINDOW	window
4	VISUALID	visual

Name

CreateCursor

Request Contents

cid: CURSOR
source: PIXMAP
mask: PIXMAP or **None**
fore-red, fore-green, fore-blue: CARD16
back-red, back-green, back-blue: CARD16
x, y: CARD16

Errors

IDChoice, **Pixmap**, **Match**, **Alloc**

Description

This request creates a cursor and associates identifier cid with it. The foreground and background RGB values must be specified, even if the server only has a **StaticGray** or **GrayScale** screen. The foreground is used for the bits set to 1 in the source, and the background is used for the bits set to 0. Both source and mask (if specified) must have depth one (or a **Match** error results), but they can have any root. The mask pixmap defines the shape of the cursor. That is, the bits set to 1 in the mask define which source pixels will be displayed, and where the mask has bits set to 0, the corresponding bits of the source pixmap are ignored. If no mask is given, all pixels of the source are displayed. The mask, if present, must be the same size as the source (or a **Match** error results). The x and y coordinates define the hotspot relative to the source's origin and must be a point within the source (or a **Match** error results).

The components of the cursor may be transformed arbitrarily to meet display limitations.

The pixmaps can be freed immediately if no further explicit references to them are to be made.

Subsequent drawing in the source or mask pixmap has an undefined effect on the cursor. The server might or might not make a copy of the pixmap.

Request Encoding

# of Bytes	Value	Description
1	93	opcode
1		unused
2	8	request length
4	CURSOR	cid
4	PIXMAP	source
4	PIXMAP	mask:
	0	**None**
2	CARD16	fore-red
2	CARD16	fore-green
2	CARD16	fore-blue

# of Bytes	Value	Description
2	CARD16	back-red
2	CARD16	back-green
2	CARD16	back-blue
2	CARD16	x
2	CARD16	y

Name
CreateGC

Request Contents
cid: GCONTEXT
drawable: DRAWABLE
value-mask: BITMASK
value-list: LISTofVALUE

Errors
IDChoice, **Drawable**, **Pixmap**, **Font**, **Match**, **Value**, **Alloc**

Description
This request creates a graphics context and assigns the identifier cid to it. The gcontext can be used with any destination drawable having the same root and depth as the specified drawable; use with other drawables results in a **Match** error.

The value-mask and value-list specify which components are to be explicitly initialized. The context components are:

Component	Type
function	{ Clear, And, AndReverse, Copy, AndInverted, NoOp, Xor, Or, Nor, Equiv, Invert, OrReverse, CopyInverted, OrInverted, Nand, Set }
plane-mask	CARD32
foreground	CARD32
background	CARD32
line-width	CARD16
line-style	{ Solid, OnOffDash, DoubleDash }
cap-style	{ NotLast, Butt, Round, Projecting }
join-style	{ Miter, Round, Bevel }
fill-style	{ Solid, Tiled, OpaqueStippled, Stippled }
fill-rule	{ EvenOdd, Winding }
arc-mode	{ Chord, PieSlice }
tile	PIXMAP
stipple	PIXMAP
tile-stipple-x-origin	INT16
tile-stipple-y-origin	INT16
font	FONT
subwindow-mode	{ ClipByChildren, IncludeInferiors }
graphics-exposures	BOOL
clip-x-origin	INT16
clip-y-origin	INT16

Component	Type
clip-mask	PIXMAP or **None**
dash-offset	CARD16
dashes	CARD8

In graphics operations, given a source and destination pixel, the result is computed bitwise on corresponding bits of the pixels; that is, a Boolean operation is performed in each bit plane. The plane-mask restricts the operation to a subset of planes, so the result is:

```
((src FUNC dst) AND plane-mask) OR (dst AND (NOT plane-mask))
```

Range checking is not performed on the values for foreground, background, or plane-mask. They are simply truncated to the appropriate number of bits.

The meanings of the functions are:

Function	Operation
Clear	0
And	src AND dst
AndReverse	src AND (NOT dst)
Copy	src
AndInverted	(NOT src) AND dst
NoOp	dst
Xor	src XOR dst
Or	src OR dst
Nor	(NOT src) AND (NOT dst)
Equiv	(NOT src) XOR dst
Invert	NOT dst
OrReverse	src OR (NOT dst)
CopyInverted	NOT src
OrInverted	(NOT src) OR dst
Nand	(NOT src) OR (NOT dst)
Set	1

The line-width is measured in pixels and can be greater than or equal to one, a wide line, or to the special value zero, a thin line.

Wide lines are drawn centered on the path described by the graphics request. Unless otherwise specified by the join or cap style, the bounding box of a wide line with endpoints [x1,y1], [x2,y2] and width w is a rectangle with vertices at the following real coordinates:

```
[x1-(w*sn/2),y1+(w*cs/2)], [x1+(w*sn/2),y1-(w*cs/2)],
[x2-(w*sn/2),y2+(w*cs/2)], [x2+(w*sn/2),y2-(w*cs/2)]
```

The sn is the sine of the angle of the line and cs is the cosine of the angle of the line. A pixel is part of the line (and hence drawn) if the center of the pixel is fully inside the bounding box, which is viewed as having infinitely thin edges. If the center of the pixel is exactly on the bounding box, it is part of the line if and only if the interior is immediately to its right (x increasing direction). Pixels with centers on a horizontal edge are a special case and are part of the line if and only if the interior or the boundary is immediately below (y increasing direction) and if the interior or the boundary is immediately to the right (x increasing direction). Note that this description is a mathematical model describing the pixels that are drawn for a wide line and does not imply that trigonometry is required to implement such a model. Real or fixed point arithmetic is recommended for computing the corners of the line endpoints for lines greater than one pixel in width.

Thin lines (zero line-width) are "one pixel wide" lines drawn using an unspecified, device-dependent algorithm. There are only two constraints on this algorithm. First, if a line is drawn unclipped from [x1,y1] to [x2,y2] and another line is drawn unclipped from [x1+dx,y1+dy] to [x2+dx,y2+dy], then a point [x,y] is touched by drawing the first line if and only if the point [x+dx,y+dy] is touched by drawing the second line. Second, the effective set of points comprising a line cannot be affected by clipping. Thus, a point is touched in a clipped line if and only if the point lies inside the clipping region and the point would be touched by the line when drawn unclipped.

Note that a wide line drawn from [x1,y1] to [x2,y2] always draws the same pixels as a wide line drawn from [x2,y2] to [x1,y1], not counting cap-style and join-style. Implementors are encouraged to make this property true for thin lines, but it is not required. A line-width of zero may differ from a line-width of one in which pixels are drawn. In general, drawing a thin line will be faster than drawing a wide line of width one, but thin lines may not mix well aesthetically with wide lines because of the different drawing algorithms. If it is desirable to obtain precise and uniform results across all displays, a client should always use a line-width of one, rather than a line-width of zero.

The line-style defines which sections of a line are drawn:

Solid   The full path of the line is drawn.

DoubleDash   The full path of the line is drawn but the even dashes are filled differently than the odd dashes (see fill-style), with Butt cap-style used where even and odd dashes meet.

OnOffDash   Only the even dashes are drawn, and cap-style applies to all internal ends of the individual dashes (except **NotLast** is treated as **Butt**).

The cap-style defines how the endpoints of a path are drawn:

NotLast   The result is equivalent to **Butt**, except that for a line-width of zero the final endpoint is not drawn.

Butt   The result is square at the endpoint (perpendicular to the slope of the line) with no projection beyond.

Round   The result is a circular arc with its diameter equal to the line-width, centered on the endpoint; it is equivalent to **Butt** for line-width zero.

Projecting   The result is square at the end but the path continues beyond the endpoint for a distance equal to half the line-width; it is equivalent to **Butt** for line-width zero.

The join-style defines how corners are drawn for wide lines:

Miter   The outer edges of the two lines extend to meet at an angle. However, if the angle is less than 11 degrees, a **Bevel** join-style is used instead.

Round   The result is a circular arc with a diameter equal to the line-width, centered on the joinpoint.

Bevel   The result is **Butt** endpoint styles, and then the triangular "notch" is filled.

For a line with coincident endpoints (x1=x2,y1=y2), when the cap-style is applied to both endpoints, the semantics depends on the line-width and the cap-style:

NotLast   thin   This is device-dependent, but the desired effect is that nothing is drawn.

Butt   thin   This is device-dependent, but the desired effect is that a single pixel is drawn.

Round   thin   This is the same as **Butt**/thin.

Projecting   thin   This is the same as **Butt**/thin.

Butt   wide   Nothing is drawn.

Round   wide   The closed path is a circle, centered at the endpoint and with a diameter equal to the line-width.

Projecting   wide   The closed path is a square, aligned with the coordinate axes, centered at the endpoint and with sides equal to the line-width.

For a line with coincident endpoints (x1=x2,y1=y2), when the join-style is applied at one or both endpoints, the effect is as if the line was removed from the overall path. However, if the total path consists of (or is reduced to) a single point joined with itself, the effect is the same as when the cap-style is applied at both endpoints.

The tile/stipple and clip origins are interpreted relative to the origin of whatever destination drawable is specified in a graphics request.

The tile pixmap must have the same root and depth as the gcontext (or a **Match** error results). The stipple pixmap must have depth one and must have the same root as the gcontext (or a **Match** error results). For fill-style **Stippled** (but not fill-style **OpaqueStippled**), the stipple pattern is tiled in a single plane and acts as an additional clip mask to be ANDed with the clipmask. Any size pixmap can be used for tiling or stippling, although some sizes may be faster to use than others.

The fill-style defines the contents of the source for line, text, and fill requests. For all text and fill requests (for example, **PolyText8**, **PolyText16**, **PolyFillRectangle**, **FillPoly**, and

PolyFillArc) as well as for line requests with line-style **Solid**, (for example, **PolyLine**, **PolySegment**, **PolyRectangle**, **PolyArc**) and for the even dashes for line requests with line-style **OnOffDash** or **DoubleDash**:

Solid	Foreground.
Tiled	Tile.
OpaqueStippled	A tile with the same width and height as stipple but with background everywhere stipple has a zero and with foreground everywhere stipple has a one.
Stippled	Foreground masked by stipple.

For the odd dashes for line requests with line-style **DoubleDash**:

Solid	Background.
Tiled	Same as for even dashes.
OpaqueStippled	Same as for even dashes.
Stippled	Background masked by stipple.

The dashes value allowed here is actually a simplified form of the more general patterns that can be set with **SetDashes**. Specifying a value of N here is equivalent to specifying the two element list [N,N] in **SetDashes**. The value must be nonzero (or a **Value** error results). The meaning of dash-offset and dashes are explained in the **SetDashes** request.

The clip-mask restricts writes to the destination drawable. Only pixels where the clip-mask has bits set to 1 are drawn. Pixels are not drawn outside the area covered by the clip-mask or where the clip-mask has bits set to 0. The clip-mask affects all graphics requests, but it does not clip sources. The clip-mask origin is interpreted relative to the origin of whatever destination drawable is specified in a graphics request. If a pixmap is specified as the clip-mask, it must have depth 1 and have the same root as the gcontext (or a **Match** error results). If clip-mask is **None**, then pixels are always drawn, regardless of the clip origin. The clip-mask can also be set with the **SetClipRectangles** request.

For **ClipByChildren**, both source and destination windows are additionally clipped by all viewable **InputOutput** children. For **IncludeInferiors**, neither source nor destination window is clipped by inferiors. This will result in including subwindow contents in the source and drawing through subwindow boundaries of the destination. The use of **IncludeInferiors** with a source or destination window of one depth with mapped inferiors of differing depth is not illegal, but the semantics is undefined by the core protocol.

The fill-rule defines what pixels are inside (that is, are drawn) for paths given in **FillPoly** requests. **EvenOdd** means a point is inside if an infinite ray with the point as origin crosses the path an odd number of times. For **Winding**, a point is inside if an infinite ray with the point as origin crosses an unequal number of clockwise- and counterclockwise-directed path segments. A clockwise-directed path segment is one that crosses the ray from left to right as observed from the point. A counter-clockwise segment is one that crosses the ray from right to left as observed from the point. The case where a directed line segment is coincident with the ray is uninteresting because one can simply choose a different ray that is not coincident with a segment.

For both fill rules, a point is infinitely small and the path is an infinitely thin line. A pixel is inside if the center point of the pixel is inside and the center point is not on the boundary. If the center point is on the boundary, the pixel is inside if and only if the polygon interior is immediately to its right (x increasing direction). Pixels with centers along a horizontal edge are a special case and are inside if and only if the polygon interior is immediately below (y increasing direction).

The arc-mode controls filling in the **PolyFillArc** request.

The graphics-exposures flag controls **GraphicsExpose** event generation for **CopyArea** and **CopyPlane** requests (and any similar requests defined by extensions).

The default component values are:

Component	Default
function	**Copy**
plane-mask	All ones
foreground	0
background	1
line-width	0
line-style	**Solid**
cap-style	**Butt**
join-style	**Miter**
fill-style	**Solid**
fill-rule	**EvenOdd**
arc-mode	**PieSlice**
tile	Pixmap of unspecified size filled with foreground pixel (that is, client specified pixel if any, else 0) (subsequent changes to foreground do not affect this pixmap)
stipple	Pixmap of unspecified size filled with ones
tile-stipple-x-origin	0
tile-stipple-y-origin	0
font	Server-dependent font
subwindow-mode	**ClipByChildren**
graphics-exposures	**True**
clip-x-origin	0
clip-y-origin	0
clip-mask	**None**
dash-offset	0
dashes	4 (that is, the list [4,4])

Storing a pixmap in a gcontext might or might not result in a copy being made. If the pixmap is later used as the destination for a graphics request, the change might or might not be reflected in the gcontext. If the pixmap is used simultaneously in a graphics request as both a destination and a tile or stipple, the results are not defined.

It is quite likely that some amount of gcontext information will be cached in display hardware and that such hardware can only cache a small number of gcontexts. Given the number and complexity of components, clients should view switching between gcontexts with nearly identical state as significantly more expensive than making minor changes to a single gcontext.

Request Encoding

# of Bytes	Value	Description
1	55	opcode
1		unused
2	4+n	request length
4	GCONTEXT	cid
4	DRAWABLE	drawable
4	BITMASK	value-mask (has n bits set to 1):
	#x00000001	function
	#x00000002	plane-mask
	#x00000004	foreground
	#x00000008	background
	#x00000010	line-width
	#x00000020	line-style
	#x00000040	cap-style
	#x00000080	join-style
	#x00000100	fill-style
	#x00000200	fill-rule
	#x00000400	tile
	#x00000800	stipple
	#x00001000	tile-stipple-x-origin
	#x00002000	tile-stipple-y-origin
	#x00004000	font
	#x00008000	subwindow-mode
	#x00010000	graphics-exposures
	#x00020000	clip-x-origin
	#x00040000	clip-y-origin
	#x00080000	clip-mask
	#x00100000	dash-offset
	#x00200000	dashes
	#x00400000	arc-mode
4n	LISTofVALUE	value-list

LISTofVALUE is *n* repetitions of the encoding for VALUE shown in the table below:

# of Bytes	Value	Description
1		function:
	0	**Clear**
	1	**And**
	2	**AndReverse**
	3	**Copy**
	4	**AndInverted**
	5	**NoOp**
	6	**Xor**
	7	**Or**
	8	**Nor**
	9	**Equiv**
	10	**Invert**
	11	**OrReverse**
	12	**CopyInverted**
	13	**OrInverted**
	14	**Nand**
	15	**Set**
4	CARD32	plane-mask
4	CARD32	foreground
4	CARD32	background
2	CARD16	line-width
1		line-style:
	0	**Solid**
	1	**OnOffDash**
	2	**DoubleDash**
1		cap-style:
	0	**NotLast**
	1	**Butt**
	2	**Round**
	3	**Projecting**
1		join-style:
	0	**Miter**
	1	**Round**
	2	**Bevel**
1		fill-style:
	0	**Solid**
	1	**Tiled**
	2	**Stippled**
	3	**OpaqueStippled**

# of Bytes	Value	Description
1		fill-rule:
	0	**EvenOdd**
	1	**Winding**
4	PIXMAP	tile
4	PIXMAP	stipple
2	INT16	tile-stipple-x-origin
2	INT16	tile-stipple-y-origin
4	FONT	font
1		subwindow-mode:
	0	**ClipByChildren**
	1	**IncludeInferiors**
1	BOOL	graphics-exposures
2	INT16	clip-x-origin
2	INT16	clip-y-origin
4	PIXMAP	clip-mask:
	0	**None**
2	CARD16	dash-offset
1	CARD8	dashes
1		arc-mode:
	0	**Chord**
	1	**PieSlice**

CreateGlyphCursor

Name
CreateGlyphCursor

Request Contents
cid: CURSOR
source-font: FONT
mask-font: FONT or **None**
source-char, *mask-char*: CARD16
fore-red, *fore-green*, *fore-blue*: CARD16
back-red, *back-green*, *back-blue*: CARD16

Errors
IDChoice, **Font**, **Value**, **Alloc**

Description
This request is similar to **CreateCursor**, except the source and mask bitmaps are obtained from the specified font glyphs. The source-char must be a defined glyph in source-font, and if mask-font is given, mask-char must be a defined glyph in mask-font (or a **Value** error results). The mask font and character are optional. The origins of the source and mask (if it is defined) glyphs are positioned coincidently and define the hotspot. The source and mask need not have the same bounding box metrics, and there is no restriction on the placement of the hotspot relative to the bounding boxes. If no mask is given, all pixels of the source are displayed. Note that source-char and mask-char are CARD16, not CHAR2B. For 2-byte matrix fonts, the 16-bit value should be formed with byte1 in the most-significant byte and byte2 in the least-significant byte.

The components of the cursor may be transformed arbitrarily to meet display limitations.

The fonts can be freed immediately if no further explicit references to them are to be made.

Request Encoding

# of Bytes	Value	Description
1	94	opcode
1		unused
2	8	request length
4	CURSOR	cid
4	FONT	source-font
4	FONT	mask-font:
	0	**None**
2	CARD16	source-char
2	CARD16	mask-char
2	CARD16	fore-red
2	CARD16	fore-green
2	CARD16	fore-blue

# of Bytes	Value	Description
2	CARD16	back-red
2	CARD16	back-green
2	CARD16	back-blue

CreateNotify

Name

CreateNotify

Event Contents

parent, window: WINDOW
x, y: INT16
width, height, border-width: CARD16
override-redirect: BOOL

Description

This event is reported to clients selecting **SubstructureNotify** on the parent and is generated when the window is created. The arguments are as in the **CreateWindow** request.

Request Encoding

# of Bytes	Value	Description
1	16	code
1		unused
2	CARD16	sequence number
4	WINDOW	parent
4	WINDOW	window
2	INT16	x
2	INT16	y
2	CARD16	width
2	CARD16	height
2	CARD16	border-width
1	BOOL	override-redirect
9		unused

Name

CreatePixmap

Request Contents

pid: PIXMAP
drawable: DRAWABLE
depth: CARD8
width, *height*: CARD16

Errors

IDChoice, **Drawable**, **Value**, **Alloc**

Description

This request creates a pixmap and assigns the identifier pid to it. The width and height must be nonzero (or a **Value** error results). The depth must be one of the depths supported by the root of the specified drawable (or a **Value** error results). The initial contents of the pixmap are undefined.

It is legal to pass an **InputOnly** window as a drawable to this request.

Request Encoding

# of Bytes	Value	Description
1	53	opcode
1	CARD8	depth
2	4	request length
4	PIXMAP	pid
4	DRAWABLE	drawable
2	CARD16	width
2	CARD16	height

CreateWindow

Name
CreateWindow

Request Contents
wid, parent: WINDOW
class: {**InputOutput, InputOnly, CopyFromParent**}
depth: CARD8
visual: VISUALID or **CopyFromParent**
x, y: INT16
width, height, border-width: CARD16
value-mask: BITMASK
value-list: LISTofVALUE

Errors
IDChoice, Window, Pixmap, Colormap, Cursor, Match, Value, Alloc

Description
This request creates an unmapped window and assigns the identifier wid to it.

A class of **CopyFromParent** means the class is taken from the parent. A depth of zero for class **InputOutput** or **CopyFromParent** means the depth is taken from the parent. A visual of **CopyFromParent** means the visual type is taken from the parent. For class **InputOutput**, the visual type and depth must be a combination supported for the screen (or a **Match** error results). The depth need not be the same as the parent, but the parent must not be of class **InputOnly** (or a **Match** error results). For class **InputOnly**, the depth must be zero (or a **Match** error results), and the visual must be one supported for the screen (or a **Match** error results). However, the parent can have any depth and class.

The server essentially acts as if **InputOnly** windows do not exist for the purposes of graphics requests, exposure processing, and **VisibilityNotify** events. An **InputOnly** window cannot be used as a drawable (as a source or destination for graphics requests). **InputOnly** and **Input-Output** windows act identically in other respects—properties, grabs, input control, and so on.

The window is placed on top in the stacking order with respect to siblings. The x and y coordinates are relative to the parent's origin and specify the position of the upper-left outer corner of the window (not the origin). The width and height specify the inside size (not including the border) and must be nonzero (or a **Value** error results). The border-width for an **InputOnly** window must be zero (or a **Match** error results).

The value-mask and value-list specify attributes of the window that are to be explicitly initialized. The possible values are:

Attribute	Type
background-pixmap	PIXMAP or **None** or **ParentRelative**
background-pixel	CARD32
border-pixmap	PIXMAP or **CopyFromParent**
border-pixel	CARD32
bit-gravity	BITGRAVITY
win-gravity	WINGRAVITY
backing-store	{ **NotUseful**, **WhenMapped**, **Always** }
backing-planes	CARD32
backing-pixel	CARD32
save-under	BOOL
event-mask	SETofEVENT
do-not-propagate-mask	SETofDEVICEEVENT
override-redirect	BOOL
colormap	COLORMAP or **CopyFromParent**
cursor	CURSOR or **None**

The default values when attributes are not explicitly initialized are:

Attribute	Default
background-pixmap	**None**
border-pixmap	**CopyFromParent**
bit-gravity	**Forget**
win-gravity	**NorthWest**
backing-store	**NotUseful**
backing-planes	All ones
backing-pixel	Zero
save-under	**False**
event-mask	{} (empty set)
do-not-propagate-mask	{} (empty set)
override-redirect	**False**
colormap	**CopyFromParent**
cursor	**None**

Only the following attributes are defined for **InputOnly** windows:

- win-gravity
- event-mask
- do-not-propagate-mask

- override-redirect

- cursor

It is a **Match** error to specify any other attributes for **InputOnly** windows.

If background-pixmap is given, it overrides the default background-pixmap. The background pixmap and the window must have the same root and the same depth (or a **Match** error results). Any size pixmap can be used, although some sizes may be faster than others. If background **None** is specified, the window has no defined background. If background **ParentRelative** is specified, the parent's background is used, but the window must have the same depth as the parent (or a **Match** error results). If the parent has background **None**, then the window will also have background **None**. A copy of the parent's background is not made. The parent's background is reexamined each time the window background is required. If background-pixel is given, it overrides the default background-pixmap and any background-pixmap given explicitly, and a pixmap of undefined size filled with background-pixel is used for the background. Range checking is not performed on the background-pixel value; it is simply truncated to the appropriate number of bits. For a **ParentRelative** background, the background tile origin always aligns with the parent's background tile origin. Otherwise, the background tile origin is always the window origin.

When no valid contents are available for regions of a window and either the regions are visible or the server is maintaining backing store, the server automatically tiles the regions with the window's background unless the window has a background of **None**. If the background is **None**, the previous screen contents from other windows of the same depth as the window are simply left in place if the contents come from the parent of the window or an inferior of the parent; otherwise, the initial contents of the exposed regions are undefined. Exposure events are then generated for the regions, even if the background is **None**.

The border tile origin is always the same as the background tile origin. If border-pixmap is given, it overrides the default border-pixmap. The border pixmap and the window must have the same root and the same depth (or a **Match** error results). Any size pixmap can be used, although some sizes may be faster than others. If **CopyFromParent** is given, the parent's border pixmap is copied (subsequent changes to the parent's border attribute do not affect the child), but the window must have the same depth as the parent (or a **Match** error results). The pixmap might be copied by sharing the same pixmap object between the child and parent or by making a complete copy of the pixmap contents. If border-pixel is given, it overrides the default border-pixmap and any border-pixmap given explicitly, and a pixmap of undefined size filled with border-pixel is used for the border. Range checking is not performed on the border-pixel value; it is simply truncated to the appropriate number of bits.

Output to a window is always clipped to the inside of the window, so that the border is never affected.

The bit-gravity defines which region of the window should be retained if the window is resized, and win-gravity defines how the window should be repositioned if the parent is resized (see **ConfigureWindow** request).

A backing-store of **WhenMapped** advises the server that maintaining contents of obscured regions when the window is mapped would be beneficial. A backing-store of **Always** advises the server that maintaining contents even when the window is unmapped would be beneficial. In this case, the server may generate an exposure event when the window is created. A value of **NotUseful** advises the server that maintaining contents is unnecessary, although a server may still choose to maintain contents while the window is mapped. Note that if the server maintains contents, then the server should maintain complete contents, not just the region within the parent boundaries, even if the window is larger than its parent. While the server maintains contents, exposure events will not normally be generated, but the server may stop maintaining contents at any time.

If save-under is **True**, the server is advised that when this window is mapped, saving the contents of windows it obscures would be beneficial.

When the contents of obscured regions of a window are being maintained, regions obscured by noninferior windows are included in the destination (and source, when the window is the source) of graphics requests, but regions obscured by inferior windows are not included.

The backing-planes indicates (with bits set to 1) which bit planes of the window hold dynamic data that must be preserved in backing-stores and during save-unders. The backing-pixel specifies what value to use in planes not covered by backing-planes. The server is free to save only the specified bit planes in the backing-store or save-under and regenerate the remaining planes with the specified pixel value. Any bits beyond the specified depth of the window in these values are simply ignored.

The event-mask defines which events the client is interested in for this window (or for some event types, inferiors of the window). The do-not-propagate-mask defines which events should not be propagated to ancestor windows when no client has the event type selected in this window.

The override-redirect specifies whether map and configure requests on this window should override a **SubstructureRedirect** on the parent, typically to inform a window manager not to tamper with the window.

The colormap specifies the colormap that best reflects the true colors of the window. Servers capable of supporting multiple hardware colormaps may use this information, and window managers may use it for **InstallColormap** requests. The colormap must have the same visual type as the window (or a **Match** error results). If **CopyFromParent** is specified, the parent's colormap is copied (subsequent changes to the parent's colormap attribute do not affect the child). However, the window must have the same visual type as the parent (or a **Match** error results), and the parent must not have a colormap of **None** (or a **Match** error results). For an explanation of **None**, see **FreeColormap** request. The colormap is copied by sharing the colormap object between the child and the parent, not by making a complete copy of the colormap contents.

If a cursor is specified, it will be used whenever the pointer is in the window. If **None** is specified, the parent's cursor will be used when the pointer is in the window, and any change in the parent's cursor will cause an immediate change in the displayed cursor.

This request generates a **CreateNotify** event.

The background and border pixmaps and the cursor may be freed immediately if no further explicit references to them are to be made.

Subsequent drawing into the background or border pixmap has an undefined effect on the window state. The server might or might not make a copy of the pixmap.

Request Encoding

# of Bytes	Value	Description
1	1	opcode
1	CARD8	depth
2	8+n	request length
4	WINDOW	wid
4	WINDOW	parent
2	INT16	x
2	INT16	y
2	CARD16	width
2	CARD16	height
2	CARD16	border-width
2		class:
	0	**CopyFromParent**
	1	**InputOutput**
	2	**InputOnly**
4	VISUALID	visual:
	0	**CopyFromParent**
4	BITMASK	value-mask (has n bits set to 1):
	#x00000001	background-pixmap
	#x00000002	background-pixel
	#x00000004	border-pixmap
	#x00000008	border-pixel
	#x00000010	bit-gravity
	#x00000020	win-gravity
	#x00000040	backing-store
	#x00000080	backing-planes
	#x00000100	backing-pixel
	#x00000200	override-redirect
	#x00000400	save-under
	#x00000800	event-mask
	#x00001000	do-not-propagate-mask
	#x00002000	colormap
	#x00004000	cursor
4n	LISTofVALUE	value-list

LISTofVALUE is *n* repetitions of the encoding for VALUE shown in the table below:

# of Bytes	Value	Description
4	PIXMAP	background-pixmap:
	0	**None**
	1	**ParentRelative**
4	CARD32	background-pixel
4	PIXMAP	border-pixmap:
	0	**CopyFromParent**
4	CARD32	border-pixel
1	BITGRAVITY	bit-gravity
1	WINGRAVITY	win-gravity
1		backing-store:
	0	**NotUseful**
	1	**WhenMapped**
	2	**Always**
4	CARD32	backing-planes
4	CARD32	backing-pixel
1	BOOL	override-redirect
1	BOOL	save-under
4	SETofEVENT	event-mask
4	SETofDEVICEEVENT	do-not-propagate-mask
4	COLORMAP	colormap:
	0	**CopyFromParent**
4	CURSOR	cursor:
	0	**None**

DeleteProperty

Name

DeleteProperty

Request Contents

window: WINDOW
property: ATOM

Errors

Window, Atom

Description

This request deletes the property from the specified window if the property exists and generates a **PropertyNotify** event on the window unless the property does not exist.

Request Encoding

# of Bytes	Value	Description
1	19	opcode
1		unused
2	3	request length
4	WINDOW	window
4	ATOM	property

DestroyNotify

Name

DestroyNotify

Event Contents

event, window: WINDOW

Description

This event is reported to clients selecting **StructureNotify** on the window and to clients select-ing **SubstructureNotify** on the parent. It is generated when the window is destroyed. The event is the window on which the event was generated, and the window is the window that is destroyed.

The ordering of the **DestroyNotify** events is such that, for any given window, **DestroyNotify** is generated on all inferiors of the window before being generated on the window itself. The ordering among siblings and across subhierarchies is not otherwise constrained.

Request Encoding

# of Bytes	Value	Description
1	17	code
1		unused
2	CARD16	sequence number
4	WINDOW	event
4	WINDOW	window
20		unused

DestroySubwindows

Name

DestroySubwindows

Request Contents

window : WINDOW

Errors

Window

Description

This request performs a **DestroyWindow** request on all children of the window, in bottom-to-top stacking order.

Request Encoding

# of Bytes	Value	Description
1	5	opcode
1		unused
2	2	request length
4	WINDOW	window

DestroyWindow

Name
DestroyWindow

Request Contents
window: WINDOW

Errors
Window

Description
If the argument window is mapped, an **UnmapWindow** request is performed automatically. The window and all inferiors are then destroyed, and a **DestroyNotify** event is generated for each window. The ordering of the **DestroyNotify** events is such that, for any given window, **DestroyNotify** is generated on all inferiors of the window before being generated on the window itself. The ordering among siblings and across subhierarchies is not otherwise constrained.

Normal exposure processing on formerly obscured windows is performed.

If the window is a root window, this request has no effect.

Request Encoding

# of Bytes	Value	Description
1	4	opcode
1		unused
2	2	request length
4	WINDOW	window

EnterNotify

Name

EnterNotify

Event Contents

root, *event*: WINDOW
child: WINDOW or **None**
same-screen: BOOL
root-x, *root-y*, *event-x*, *event-y*: INT16
mode: {**Normal**, **Grab**, **Ungrab**}
detail: {**Ancestor**, **Virtual**, **Inferior**, **Nonlinear**, **NonlinearVirtual**}
focus: BOOL
state: SETofKEYBUTMASK
time: TIMESTAMP

(Same contents as **LeaveNotify**.)

Description

EnterNotify events are sent from the server to the client when the user moves the pointer into a window.

For more information, see **LeaveNotify**.

Request Encoding

# of Bytes	Value	Description
1	7	code
1		detail:
	0	**Ancestor**
	1	**Virtual**
	2	**Inferior**
	3	**Nonlinear**
	4	**NonlinearVirtual**
2	CARD16	sequence number
4	TIMESTAMP	time
4	WINDOW	root
4	WINDOW	event
4	WINDOW	child:
	0	**None**
2	INT16	root-x
2	INT16	root-y
2	INT16	event-x
2	INT16	event-y
2	SETofKEYBUTMASK	state

# of Bytes	Value	Description
1		mode:
	0	**Normal**
	1	**Grab**
	2	**Ungrab**
1		same-screen, focus:
	#x01	focus (1 is True, 0 is False)
	#x02	same-screen (1 is True, 0 is False)
	#xfc	unused

Expose

Name
Expose

Event Contents
window: WINDOW
x, y, width, height: CARD16
count: CARD16

Description

This event is reported to clients selecting **Exposure** on the window. It is generated when no valid contents are available for regions of a window, and either the regions are visible, the regions are viewable and the server is (perhaps newly) maintaining backing store on the window, or the window is not viewable but the server is (perhaps newly) honoring window's backing-store attribute of **Always** or **WhenMapped**. The regions are decomposed into an arbitrary set of rectangles, and an **Expose** event is generated for each rectangle.

For a given action causing exposure events, the set of events for a given window are guaranteed to be reported contiguously. If count is zero, then no more **Expose** events for this window follow. If count is nonzero, then at least that many more **Expose** events for this window follow (and possibly more).

The x and y coordinates are relative to window's origin and specify the upper-left corner of a rectangle. The width and height specify the extent of the rectangle.

Expose events are never generated on **InputOnly** windows.

All **Expose** events caused by a hierarchy change are generated after any hierarchy event caused by that change (for example, **UnmapNotify**, **MapNotify**, **ConfigureNotify**, **Gravity-Notify**, **CirculateNotify**). All **Expose** events on a given window are generated after any **VisibilityNotify** event on that window, but it is not required that all **Expose** events on all windows be generated after all **Visibility** events on all windows. The ordering of **Expose** events with respect to **FocusOut**, **EnterNotify**, and **LeaveNotify** events is not constrained.

Request Encoding

# of Bytes	Value	Description
1	12	code
1		unused
2	CARD16	sequence number
4	WINDOW	window
2	CARD16	x
2	CARD16	y
2	CARD16	width
2	CARD16	height

# of Bytes	Value	Description
2	CARD16	count
14		unused

Name
FillPoly

Request Contents
drawable: DRAWABLE
gc: GCONTEXT
shape: {**Complex**, **Nonconvex**, **Convex**}
coordinate-mode: {**Origin**, **Previous**}
points: LISTofPOINT

Errors
Drawable, **GContext**, **Match**, **Value**

Description
This request fills the region closed by the specified path. The path is closed automatically if the last point in the list does not coincide with the first point. No pixel of the region is drawn more than once.

The first point is always relative to the drawable's origin. The rest are relative either to that origin or to the previous point, depending on the coordinate-mode.

The shape parameter may be used by the server to improve performance. **Complex** means the path may self-intersect. Contiguous coincident points in the path are not treated as self-intersection.

Nonconvex means the path does not self-intersect but the shape is not wholly convex. If known by the client, specifying **Nonconvex** over **Complex** may improve performance. If **Nonconvex** is specified for a self-intersecting path, the graphics results are undefined.

Convex means that for every pair of points inside the polygon, the line segment connecting them does not intersect the path. If known by the client, specifying **Convex** can improve performance. If **Convex** is specified for a path that is not convex, the graphics results are undefined.

GC components: function, plane-mask, fill-style, fill-rule, subwindow-mode, clip-x-origin, clip-y-origin, clip-mask

GC mode-dependent components: foreground, background, tile, stipple, tile-stipple-x-origin, tile-stipple-y-origin

Request Encoding

# of Bytes	Value	Description
1	69	opcode
1		unused
2	4+n	request length
4	DRAWABLE	drawable
4	GCONTEXT	gc

# of Bytes	Value	Description
1		shape:
	0	**Complex**
	1	**Nonconvex**
	2	**Convex**
1		coordinate-mode:
	0	**Origin**
	1	**Previous**
2		unused
4n	LISTofPOINT	points

FocusIn

Name
FocusIn

Event Contents
event: WINDOW
mode: {**Normal**, **WhileGrabbed**, **Grab**, **Ungrab**}
detail: {**Ancestor**, **Virtual**, **Inferior**, **Nonlinear**, **NonlinearVirtual**, **Pointer**, **PointerRoot**, **None**}

(Same contents as **FocusOut**.)

Description
FocusIn events are sent from the server to the client when the keyboard focus is transferred from one window to another. The window field in **FocusIn** events specifies the window that gained the keyboard focus.

For more information, see **FocusOut**.

Request Encoding

# of Bytes	Value	Description
1	9	code
1		detail:
	0	**Ancestor**
	1	**Virtual**
	2	**Inferior**
	3	**Nonlinear**
	4	**NonlinearVirtual**
	5	**Pointer**
	6	**PointerRoot**
	7	**None**
2	CARD16	sequence number
4	WINDOW	event
1		mode:
	0	**Normal**
	1	**Grab**
	2	**Ungrab**
	3	**WhileGrabbed**
23		unused

Name

FocusOut

Event Contents

event: WINDOW
mode: {**Normal**, **WhileGrabbed**, **Grab**, **Ungrab**}
detail: {**Ancestor**, **Virtual**, **Inferior**, **Nonlinear**, **NonlinearVirtual**, **Pointer**,
PointerRoot, **None**}

Description

FocusIn and FocusOut events are generated when the keyboard focus window changes and are reported to clients selecting **FocusChange** on the window. Events generated by **SetInput-Focus** when the keyboard is not grabbed have mode **Normal**. Events generated by **SetInput-Focus** when the keyboard is grabbed have mode **WhileGrabbed**. Events generated when a keyboard grab activates have mode **Grab**, and events generated when a keyboard grab deactivates have mode **Ungrab**.

All **FocusOut** events caused by a window unmap are generated after any **UnmapNotify** event, but the ordering of **FocusOut** with respect to generated **EnterNotify**, **LeaveNotify**, **VisibilityNotify**, and **Expose** events is not constrained.

Normal and **WhileGrabbed** events are generated as follows.

When the focus moves from window A to window B, A is an inferior of B, and the pointer is in window P:

- **FocusOut** with detail **Ancestor** is generated on A.

- **FocusOut** with detail **Virtual** is generated on each window between A and B exclusive (in order).

- **FocusIn** with detail **Inferior** is generated on B.

- If P is an inferior of B but P is not A or an inferior of A or an ancestor of A, **FocusIn** with detail **Pointer** is generated on each window below B down to and including P (in order).

When the focus moves from window A to window B, B is an inferior of A, and the pointer is in window P:

- If P is an inferior of A but P is not an inferior of B or an ancestor of B, **FocusOut** with detail **Pointer** is generated on each window from P up to but not including A (in order).

- **FocusOut** with detail **Inferior** is generated on A.

- **FocusIn** with detail **Virtual** is generated on each window between A and B exclusive (in order).

- **FocusIn** with detail **Ancestor** is generated on B.

When the focus moves from window A to window B, window C is their least common ancestor, and the pointer is in window P:

- If P is an inferior of A, **FocusOut** with detail **Pointer** is generated on each window from P up to but not including A (in order).

- **FocusOut** with detail **Nonlinear** is generated on A.

- **FocusOut** with detail **NonlinearVirtual** is generated on each window between A and C exclusive (in order).

- **FocusIn** with detail **NonlinearVirtual** is generated on each window between C and B exclusive (in order).

- **FocusIn** with detail **Nonlinear** is generated on B.

- If P is an inferior of B, **FocusIn** with detail **Pointer** is generated on each window below B down to and including P (in order).

When the focus moves from window A to window B on different screens and the pointer is in window P:

- If P is an inferior of A, **FocusOut** with detail **Pointer** is generated on each window from P up to but not including A (in order).

- **FocusOut** with detail **Nonlinear** is generated on A.

- If A is not a root window, **FocusOut** with detail **NonlinearVirtual** is generated on each window above A up to and including its root (in order).

- If B is not a root window, **FocusIn** with detail **NonlinearVirtual** is generated on each window from B's root down to but not including B (in order).

- **FocusIn** with detail **Nonlinear** is generated on B.

- If P is an inferior of B, **FocusIn** with detail **Pointer** is generated on each window below B down to and including P (in order).

When the focus moves from window A to **PointerRoot** (or **None**) and the pointer is in window P:

- If P is an inferior of A, **FocusOut** with detail **Pointer** is generated on each window from P up to but not including A (in order).

- **FocusOut** with detail **Nonlinear** is generated on A.

- If A is not a root window, **FocusOut** with detail **NonlinearVirtual** is generated on each window above A up to and including its root (in order).

- **FocusIn** with detail **PointerRoot** (or **None**) is generated on all root windows.

- If the new focus is **PointerRoot**, **FocusIn** with detail **Pointer** is generated on each window from P's root down to and including P (in order).

When the focus moves from **PointerRoot** (or **None**) to window A and the pointer is in window P:

- If the old focus is **PointerRoot**, **FocusOut** with detail **Pointer** is generated on each window from P up to and including P's root (in order).

- **FocusOut** with detail **PointerRoot** (or **None**) is generated on all root windows.

- If A is not a root window, **FocusIn** with detail **NonlinearVirtual** is generated on each window from A's root down to but not including A (in order).

- **FocusIn** with detail **Nonlinear** is generated on A.

- If P is an inferior of A, **FocusIn** with detail **Pointer** is generated on each window below A down to and including P (in order).

When the focus moves from **PointerRoot** to **None** (or vice versa) and the pointer is in window P:

- If the old focus is **PointerRoot**, **FocusOut** with detail **Pointer** is generated on each window from P up to and including P's root (in order).

- **FocusOut** with detail **PointerRoot** (or **None**) is generated on all root windows.

- **FocusIn** with detail **None** (or **PointerRoot**) is generated on all root windows.

- If the new focus is **PointerRoot**, **FocusIn** with detail **Pointer** is generated on each window from P's root down to and including P (in order).

When a keyboard grab activates (but before generating any actual **KeyPress** event that activates the grab), G is the grab-window for the grab, and F is the current focus:

- **FocusIn** and **FocusOut** events with mode **Grab** are generated (as for **Normal** above) as if the focus were to change from F to G.

When a keyboard grab deactivates (but after generating any actual **KeyRelease** event that deactivates the grab), G is the grab-window for the grab, and F is the current focus:

- **FocusIn** and **FocusOut** events with mode **Ungrab** are generated (as for **Normal** above) as if the focus were to change from G to F.

Request Encoding

# of Bytes	Value	Description
1	10	code
1		detail:
	0	**Ancestor**
	1	**Virtual**
	2	**Inferior**
	3	**Nonlinear**
	4	**NonlinearVirtual**
	5	**Pointer**

# of Bytes	Value	Description
	6	**PointerRoot**
	7	**None**
2	CARD16	sequence number
4	WINDOW	event
1		mode:
	0	**Normal**
	1	**Grab**
	2	**Ungrab**
	3	**WhileGrabbed**
23		unused

ForceScreenSaver

Name

ForceScreenSaver

Request Contents

mode : { **Activate** , **Reset** }

Errors

Value

Description

If the mode is **Activate** and screen-saver is currently deactivated, then screen-saver is activated (even if screen-saver has been disabled with a timeout value of zero). If the mode is **Reset** and screen-saver is currently enabled, then screen-saver is deactivated (if it was activated), and the activation timer is reset to its initial state as if device input had just been received.

Request Encoding

# of Bytes	Value	Description
1	115	opcode
1		mode:
	0	**Reset**
	1	**Activate**
2	1	request length

Name

FreeColormap

Request Contents

cmap: COLORMAP

Errors

Colormap

Description

This request deletes the association between the resource ID and the colormap and frees the colormap storage. If the colormap is an installed map for a screen, it is uninstalled (see **UninstallColormap** request). If the colormap is defined as the colormap for a window (by means of **CreateWindow** or **ChangeWindowAttributes**), the colormap for the window is changed to **None**, and a **ColormapNotify** event is generated. The protocol does not define the colors displayed for a window with a colormap of **None**.

This request has no effect on a default colormap for a screen.

Request Encoding

# of Bytes	Value	Description
1	79	opcode
1		unused
2	2	request length
4	COLORMAP	cmap

FreeColors

Name
FreeColors

Request Contents
cmap: COLORMAP
pixels: LISTofCARD32
plane-mask: CARD32

Errors
Colormap, **Access**, **Value**

Description
The plane-mask should not have any bits in common with any of the pixels. The set of all pixels is produced by ORing together subsets of plane-mask with the pixels. The request frees all of these pixels that were allocated by the client (using **AllocColor**, **AllocNamedColor**, **Alloc-ColorCells**, and **AllocColorPlanes**). Note that freeing an individual pixel obtained from **AllocColorPlanes** may not actually allow it to be reused until all of its related pixels are also freed. Similarly, a read-only entry is not actually freed until it has been freed by all clients, and if a client allocates the same read-only entry multiple times, it must free the entry that many times before the entry is actually freed.

All specified pixels that are allocated by the client in cmap are freed, even if one or more pixels produce an error. A **Value** error is generated if a specified pixel is not a valid index into cmap, and an **Access** error is generated if a specified pixel is not allocated by the client (that is, is unallocated or is only allocated by another client). If more than one pixel is in error, it is arbitrary as to which pixel is reported.

Request Encoding

# of Bytes	Value	Description
1	88	opcode
1		unused
2	3+n	request length
4	COLORMAP	cmap
4	CARD32	plane-mask
4n	LISTofCARD32	pixels

FreeCursor

Name
FreeCursor

Request Contents
cursor: CURSOR

Errors
Cursor

Description
This request deletes the association between the resource ID and the cursor. The cursor storage will be freed when no other resource references it.

Request Encoding

# of Bytes	Value	Description
1	95	opcode
1		unused
2	2	request length
4	CURSOR	cursor

Name
FreeGC

Request Contents
gc: GCONTEXT

Errors
GContext

Description
This request deletes the association between the resource ID and the gcontext and destroys the gcontext.

Request Encoding

# of Bytes	Value	Description
1	60	opcode
1		unused
2	2	request length
4	GCONTEXT	gc

FreePixmap

Name

FreePixmap

Request Contents

pixmap: PIXMAP

Errors

Pixmap

Description

This request deletes the association between the resource ID and the pixmap. The pixmap storage will be freed when no other resource references it.

Request Encoding

# of Bytes	Value	Description
1	54	opcode
1		unused
2	2	request length
4	PIXMAP	pixmap

Name
GetAtomName

Request Contents
atom: ATOM

Reply Contents
name: STRING8

Errors
Atom

Description
This request returns the name for the given atom.

Request Encoding

# of Bytes	Value	Description
1	17	opcode
1		unused
2	2	request length
4	ATOM	atom

Reply Encoding

# of Bytes	Value	Description
1	1	reply
1		unused
2	CARD16	sequence number
4	(n+p)/4	reply length
2	n	length of name
22		unused
n	STRING8	name
p		unused, p=pad(n)

GetFontPath

Name

GetFontPath

Request Contents

Opcode and request length only.

Reply Contents

path: LISTofSTRING8

Errors

This request generates no errors.

Description

This request returns the current search path for fonts.

Request Encoding

# of Bytes	Value	Description
1	52	opcode
1		unused
2	1	request list

Reply Encoding

# of Bytes	Value	Description
1	1	reply
1		unused
2	CARD16	sequence number
4	(n+p)/4	reply length
2	CARD16	number of STRs in path
22		unused
n	LISTofSTR	path
p		unused, p=pad(n)

GetGeometry

Name
GetGeometry

Request Contents
drawable: DRAWABLE

Reply Contents
root: WINDOW
depth: CARD8
x, y: INT16
width, height, border-width: CARD16

Errors
Drawable

Description
This request returns the root and current geometry of the drawable. The depth is the number of bits per pixel for the object. The x, y, and border-width will always be zero for pixmaps. For a window, the x and y coordinates specify the upper-left outer corner of the window relative to its parent's origin, and the width and height specify the inside size, not including the border.

It is legal to pass an **InputOnly** window as a drawable to this request.

Request Encoding

# of Bytes	Value	Description
1	14	opcode
1		unused
2	2	request length
4	DRAWABLE	drawable

Reply Encoding

# of Bytes	Value	Description
1	1	reply
1	CARD8	depth
2	CARD16	sequence number
4	0	reply length
4	WINDOW	root
2	INT16	x
2	INT16	y

# of Bytes	Value	Description
2	CARD16	width
2	CARD16	height
2	CARD16	border-width
10		unused

Name

GetImage

Request Contents

drawable: DRAWABLE
x, y: INT16
width, height: CARD16
plane-mask: CARD32
format: {**XYPixmap**, **ZPixmap**}

Reply Contents

depth: CARD8
visual: VISUALID or **None**
data: LISTofBYTE

Errors

Drawable, Value, Match

Description

This request returns the contents of the given rectangle of the drawable in the given format. The x and y coordinates are relative to the drawable's origin and define the upper-left corner of the rectangle. If **XYPixmap** is specified, only the bit planes specified in plane-mask are transmitted, with the planes appearing from most-significant to least-significant in bit order. If **ZPixmap** is specified, then bits in all planes not specified in plane-mask are transmitted as zero. Range checking is not performed on plane-mask; extraneous bits are simply ignored. The returned depth is as specified when the drawable was created and is the same as a depth component in a FORMAT structure (in the connection setup), not a bits-per-pixel component. If the drawable is a window, its visual type is returned. If the drawable is a pixmap, the visual is **None**.

If the drawable is a pixmap, then the given rectangle must be wholly contained within the pixmap (or a **Match** error results). If the drawable is a window, the window must be viewable, and it must be the case that, if there were no inferiors or overlapping windows, the specified rectangle of the window would be fully visible on the screen and wholly contained within the outside edges of the window (or a **Match** error results). Note that the borders of the window can be included and read with this request. If the window has a backing store, then the backing-store contents are returned for regions of the window that are obscured by noninferior windows; otherwise, the returned contents of such obscured regions are undefined. Also undefined are the returned contents of visible regions of inferiors of different depth than the specified window. The pointer cursor image is not included in the contents returned.

This request is not general-purpose in the same sense as other graphics-related requests. It is intended specifically for rudimentary hardcopy support.

Request Encoding

# of Bytes	Value	Description
1	73	opcode
1		format:
	1	**XYPixmap**
	2	**ZPixmap**
2	5	request length
4	DRAWABLE	drawable
2	INT16	x
2	INT16	y
2	CARD16	width
2	CARD16	height
4	CARD32	plane-mask

Reply Encoding

# of Bytes	Value	Description
1	1	reply
1	CARD8	depth
2	CARD16	sequence number
4	(n+p)/4	reply length
4	VISUALID	visual:
	0	**None**
20		unused
n	LISTofBYTE	data
p		unused, p=pad(n)

GetInputFocus

Name

GetInputFocus

Request Contents

Opcode and request length only.

Reply Contents

focus: WINDOW or **PointerRoot** or **None**
revert-to: {**Parent**, **PointerRoot**, **None**}

Errors

This request generates no errors.

Description

This request returns the current focus state.

Request Encoding

# of Bytes	Value	Description
1	43	opcode
1		unused
2	1	request length

Reply Encoding

# of Bytes	Value	Description
1	1	reply
1		revert-to:
	0	**None**
	1	**PointerRoot**
	2	**Parent**
2	CARD16	sequence number
4	0	reply length
4	WINDOW	focus:
	0	**None**
	1	**PointerRoot**
20		unused

GetKeyboardControl

Name

GetKeyboardControl

Request Contents

Opcode and request length only.

Reply Contents

key-click-percent: CARD8
bell-percent: CARD8
bell-pitch: CARD16
bell-duration: CARD16
led-mask: CARD32
global-auto-repeat: {**On**, **Off**}
auto-repeats: LISTofCARD8

Errors

This request generates no errors.

Description

This request returns the current control values for the keyboard. For the LEDs, the least-significant bit of led-mask corresponds to LED one, and each one bit in led-mask indicates an LED that is lit. The auto-repeats is a bit vector; each one bit indicates that auto-repeat is enabled for the corresponding key. The vector is represented as 32 bytes. Byte N (from 0) contains the bits for keys 8N to 8N+7, with the least-significant bit in the byte representing key 8N.

Request Encoding

# of Bytes	Value	Description
1	103	opcode
1		unused
2	1	request length

Reply Encoding

# of Bytes	Value	Description
1	1	reply
1		global-auto-repeat:
	0	**Off**
	1	**On**
2	CARD16	sequence number
4	5	reply length
4	CARD32	led-mask

# of Bytes	Value	Description
1	CARD8	key-click-percent
1	CARD8	bell-percent
2	CARD16	bell-pitch
2	CARD16	bell-duration
2		unused
32	LISTofCARD8	auto-repeats

GetKeyboardMapping

Name
GetKeyboardMapping

Request Contents
first-keycode : KEYCODE
count : CARD8

Reply Contents
keysyms-per-keycode: CARD8
keysyms: LISTofKEYSYM

Errors
Value

Description
This request returns the symbols for the specified number of keycodes, starting with the specified keycode. The first-keycode must be greater than or equal to min-keycode as returned in the connection setup (or a **Value** error results), and:

```
first-keycode + count - 1
```

must be less than or equal to max-keycode as returned in the connection setup (or a **Value** error results). The number of elements in the keysyms list is:

```
count * keysyms-per-keycode
```

and KEYSYM number N (counting from zero) for keycode K has an index (counting from zero) of:

```
(K - first-keycode) * keysyms-per-keycode + N
```

in keysyms. The keysyms-per-keycode value is chosen arbitrarily by the server to be large enough to report all requested symbols. A special KEYSYM value of **NoSymbol** is used to fill in unused elements for individual keycodes.

Request Encoding

# of Bytes	Value	Description
1	101	opcode
1		unused
2	2	request length
1	KEYCODE	first-keycode
1	m	count
2		unused

Reply Encoding

# of Bytes	Value	Description
1	1	reply
1	n	keysyms-per-keycode
2	CARD16	sequence number
4	nm	reply length
		(m = count field from the request)
24		unused
4nm	LISTofKEYSYM	keysyms

GetModifierMapping

Name

GetModifierMapping

Request Contents

Opcode and request length only.

Reply Contents

keycodes-per-modifier: CARD8
keycodes: LISTofKEYCODE

Errors

This request generates no errors.

Description

This request returns the keycodes of the keys being used as modifiers. The number of keycodes in the list is 8*keycodes-per-modifier. The keycodes are divided into eight sets, with each set containing keycodes-per-modifier elements. The sets are assigned to the modifiers **Shift**, **Lock**, **Control**, **Mod1**, **Mod2**, **Mod3**, **Mod4**, and **Mod5**, in order. The keycodes-per-modifier value is chosen arbitrarily by the server; zeros are used to fill in unused elements within each set. If only zero values are given in a set, the use of the corresponding modifier has been disabled. The order of keycodes within each set is chosen arbitrarily by the server.

Request Encoding

# of Bytes	Value	Description
1	119	opcode
1		unused
2	1	request length

Reply Encoding

# of Bytes	Value	Description
1	1	reply
1	n	keycodes-per-modifier
2	CARD16	sequence number
4	2n	reply length
24		unused
8n	LISTofKEYCODE	keycodes

Name

GetMotionEvents

Request Contents

start, stop: TIMESTAMP or **CurrentTime**
window: WINDOW

Reply Contents

events: LISTofTIMECOORD

where:

TIMECOORD: [x, y: INT16
                      time: TIMESTAMP]

Errors

Window

Description

This request returns all events in the motion history buffer that fall between the specified start and stop times (inclusive) and that have coordinates that lie within (including borders) the specified window at its present placement. The x and y coordinates are reported relative to the origin of the window.

If the start time is later than the stop time or if the start time is in the future, no events are returned. If the stop time is in the future, it is equivalent to specifying **CurrentTime**.

Request Encoding

# of Bytes	Value	Description
1	39	opcode
1		unused
2	4	request length
4	WINDOW	window
4	TIMESTAMP	start:
	0	**CurrentTime**
4	TIMESTAMP	stop:
	0	**CurrentTime**

Reply Encoding

# of Bytes	Value	Description
1	1	reply
1		unused
2	CARD16	sequence number
4	2n	reply length
4	n	number of TIMECOORDs in events
20		unused
8n	LISTofTIMECOORD	events

LISTofTIMECOORD is *n* repetitions of the encoding for TIMECOORD shown in the table below:

# of Bytes	Value	Description
4	TIMESTAMP	time
2	CARD16	x
2	CARD16	y

GetPointerControl

Name
GetPointerControl

Request Contents
Opcode and request length only.

Reply Contents
acceleration-numerator, acceleration-denominator: CARD16
threshold: CARD16

Errors
This request generates no errors.

Description
This request returns the current acceleration and threshold for the pointer.

Request Encoding

# of Bytes	Value	Description
1	106	opcode
1		unused
2	1	request length

Reply Encoding

# of Bytes	Value	Description
1	1	reply
1		unused
2	CARD16	sequence number
4	0	reply length
2	CARD16	acceleration-numerator
2	CARD16	acceleration-denominator
2	CARD16	threshold
18		unused

GetPointerMapping

Name

GetPointerMapping

Request Contents

Opcode and request length only.

Reply Contents

map: LISTofCARD8

Errors

This request generates no errors.

Description

This request returns the current mapping of the pointer. Elements of the list are indexed starting from one. The length of the list indicates the number of physical buttons.

The nominal mapping for a pointer is the identity mapping:

```
map[i] = i
```

Request Encoding

# of Bytes	Value	Description
1	117	opcode
1		unused
2	1	request length

Reply Encoding

# of Bytes	Value	Description
1	1	reply
1	n	length of map
2	CARD16	sequence number
4	(n+p)/4	reply length
24		unused
n	LISTofCARD8	map
p		unused, p=pad(n)

Name

GetProperty

Request Contents

window: WINDOW
property: ATOM
type: ATOM or **AnyPropertyType**
long-offset, *long-length*: CARD32
delete: BOOL

Reply Contents

type: ATOM or **None**
format: {0, 8, 16, 32}
bytes-after: CARD32
value: LISTofINT8 or LISTofINT16 or LISTofINT32

Errors

Window, **Atom**, **Value**

Description

If the specified property does not exist for the specified window, then the return type is **None**, the format and bytes-after are zero, and the value is empty. The delete argument is ignored in this case. If the specified property exists but its type does not match the specified type, then the return type is the actual type of the property, the format is the actual format of the property (never zero), the bytes-after is the length of the property in bytes (even if the format is 16 or 32), and the value is empty. The delete argument is ignored in this case. If the specified property exists and either **AnyPropertyType** is specified or the specified type matches the actual type of the property, then the return type is the actual type of the property, the format is the actual format of the property (never zero), and the bytes-after and value are as follows, given:

N   =   actual length of the stored property in bytes
        (even if the format is 16 or 32)
I   =   4 * long-offset
T   =   N − I
L   =   MINIMUM (T, 4 * long-length)
A   =   N − (I + L)

The returned value starts at byte index I in the property (indexing from 0), and its length in bytes is L. However, it is a **Value** error if long-offset is given such that L is negative. The value of bytes-after is A, giving the number of trailing unread bytes in the stored property. If delete is **True** and the bytes-after is zero, the property is also deleted from the window, and a **PropertyNotify** event is generated on the window.

Request Encoding

# of Bytes	Value	Description
1	20	opcode
1	BOOL	delete
2	6	request length
4	WINDOW	window
4	ATOM	property
4	ATOM	type:
	0	**AnyPropertyType**
4	CARD32	long-offset
4	CARD32	long-length

Reply Encoding

# of Bytes	Value	Description
1	1	reply
1	CARD8	format
2	CARD16	sequence number
4	(n+p)/4	reply length
4	ATOM	type:
	0	**None**
4	CARD32	bytes-after
4	CARD32	length of value in format units
		(= 0 for format = 0)
		(= n for format = 8)
		(= n/2 for format = 16)
		(= n/4 for format = 32)
12		unused
n	LISTofBYTE	value
		(n is zero for format = 0)
		(n is a multiple of 2 for format = 16)
		(n is a multiple of 4 for format = 32)
p		unused, p=pad(n)

GetScreenSaver

Name

GetScreenSaver

Request Contents

Opcode and request length only.

Reply Contents

timeout, interval: CARD16
prefer-blanking: {**Yes**, **No**}
allow-exposures: {**Yes**, **No**}

Errors

This request generates no errors.

Description

This request returns the current screen-saver control values.

Request Encoding

# of Bytes	Value	Description
1	108	opcode
1		unused
2	1	request length

Reply Encoding

# of Bytes	Value	Description
1	1	reply
1		unused
2	CARD16	sequence number
4	0	reply length
2	CARD16	timeout
2	CARD16	interval
1		prefer-blanking:
	0	**No**
	1	**Yes**
1		allow-exposures:
	0	**No**
	1	**Yes**
18		unused

GetSelectionOwner

Name
GetSelectionOwner

Request Contents
selection: ATOM

Reply Contents
owner: WINDOW or **None**

Errors
Atom

Description
This request returns the current owner window of the specified selection, if any. If **None** is returned, then there is no owner for the selection.

Request Encoding

# of Bytes	Value	Description
1	23	opcode
1		unused
2	2	request length
4	ATOM	selection

Reply Encoding

# of Bytes	Value	Description
1	1	reply
1		unused
2	CARD16	sequence number
4	0	reply length
4	WINDOW	owner:
	0	**None**
20		unused

Name
GetWindowAttributes

Request Contents
window: WINDOW

Reply Contents
visual: VISUALID
class: {**InputOutput, InputOnly**}
bit-gravity: BITGRAVITY
win-gravity: WINGRAVITY
backing-store: {**NotUseful, WhenMapped, Always**}
backing-planes: CARD32
backing-pixel: CARD32
save-under: BOOL
colormap: COLORMAP or **None**
map-is-installed: BOOL
map-state: {**Unmapped, Unviewable, Viewable**}
all-event-masks, your-event-mask: SETofEVENT
do-not-propagate-mask: SETofDEVICEEVENT
override-redirect: BOOL

Errors
Window

Description
This request returns the current attributes of the window. A window is **Unviewable** if it is mapped but some ancestor is unmapped. All-event-masks is the inclusive-OR of all event masks selected on the window by clients. Your-event-mask is the event mask selected by the querying client.

Request Encoding

# of Bytes	Value	Description
1	3	opcode
1		unused
2	2	request length
4	WINDOW	window

Reply Encoding

# of Bytes	Value	Description
1	1	reply
1		backing-store:
	0	**NotUseful**
	1	**WhenMapped**
	2	**Always**
2	CARD16	sequence number
4	3	reply length
4	VISUALID	visual
2		class:
	1	**InputOutput**
	2	**InputOnly**
1	BITGRAVITY	bit-gravity
1	WINGRAVITY	win-gravity
4	CARD32	backing-planes
4	CARD32	backing-pixel
1	BOOL	save-under
1	BOOL	map-is-installed
1		map-state:
	0	**Unmapped**
	1	**Unviewable**
	2	**Viewable**
1	BOOL	override-redirect
4	COLORMAP	colormap:
	0	**None**
4	SETofEVENT	all-event-masks
4	SETofEVENT	your-event-mask
2	SETofDEVICEEVENT	do-not-propagate-mask
2		unused

GrabButton

Name
GrabButton

Request Contents
modifiers: SETofKEYMASK or **AnyModifier**
button: BUTTON or **AnyButton**
grab-window: WINDOW
owner-events: BOOL
event-mask: SETofPOINTEREVENT
pointer-mode, *keyboard-mode*: {**Synchronous, Asynchronous**}
confine-to: WINDOW or **None**
cursor: CURSOR or **None**

Errors
Cursor, Window, Value, Access

Description
This request establishes a passive grab. In the future, the pointer is actively grabbed as described in **GrabPointer**, the last-pointer-grab time is set to the time at which the button was pressed (as transmitted in the **ButtonPress** event), and the **ButtonPress** event is reported if all of the following conditions are true:

- The pointer is not grabbed and the specified button is logically pressed when the specified modifier keys are logically down, and no other buttons or modifier keys are logically down.

- The grab-window contains the pointer.

- The confine-to window (if any) is viewable.

- A passive grab on the same button/key combination does not exist on any ancestor of grab-window.

The interpretation of the remaining arguments is the same as for **GrabPointer**. The active grab is terminated automatically when the logical state of the pointer has all buttons released, independent of the logical state of modifier keys. Note that the logical state of a device (as seen by means of the protocol) may lag the physical state if device event processing is frozen.

This request overrides all previous passive grabs by the same client on the same button/key combinations on the same window. A modifier of **AnyModifier** is equivalent to issuing the request for all possible modifier combinations (including the combination of no modifiers). It is not required that all specified modifiers have currently assigned keycodes. A button of **Any-Button** is equivalent to issuing the request for all possible buttons. Otherwise, it is not required that the button specified currently be assigned to a physical button.

An **Access** error is generated if some other client has already issued a **GrabButton** request with the same button/key combination on the same window. When using **AnyModifier** or

AnyButton, the request fails completely (no grabs are established), and an **Access** error is generated if there is a conflicting grab for any combination. The request has no effect on an active grab.

Request Encoding

# of Bytes	Value	Description
1	28	opcode
1	BOOL	owner-events
2	6	request length
4	WINDOW	grab-window
2	SETofPOINTEREVENT	event-mask
1		pointer-mode:
	0	**Synchronous**
	1	**Asynchronous**
1		keyboard-mode:
	0	**Synchronous**
	1	**Asynchronous**
4	WINDOW	confine-to:
	0	**None**
4	CURSOR	cursor:
	0	**None**
1	BUTTON	button:
	0	**AnyButton**
1		unused
2	SETofKEYMASK	modifiers:
	#x8000	**AnyModifier**

Name
GrabKey

Request Contents
key: KEYCODE or **AnyKey**
modifiers: SETofKEYMASK or **AnyModifier**
grab-window: WINDOW
owner-events: BOOL
pointer-mode, *keyboard-mode*: {**Synchronous, Asynchronous**}

Errors
Window, Value, Access

Description
This request establishes a passive grab on the keyboard. In the future, the keyboard is actively grabbed as described in **GrabKeyboard**, the last-keyboard-grab time is set to the time at which the key was pressed (as transmitted in the **KeyPress** event), and the **KeyPress** event is reported if all of the following conditions are true:

- The keyboard is not grabbed and the specified key (which can itself be a modifier key) is logically pressed when the specified modifier keys are logically down, and no other modifier keys are logically down.

- Either the grab-window is an ancestor of (or is) the focus window or the grab-window is a descendent of the focus window and contains the pointer.

- A passive grab on the same key combination does not exist on any ancestor of grab-window.

The interpretation of the remaining arguments is the same as for **GrabKeyboard**. The active grab is terminated automatically when the logical state of the keyboard has the specified key released, independent of the logical state of modifier keys. Note that the logical state of a device (as seen by means of the protocol) may lag the physical state if device event processing is frozen.

This request overrides all previous passive grabs by the same client on the same key combinations on the same window. A modifier of **AnyModifier** is equivalent to issuing the request for all possible modifier combinations (including the combination of no modifiers). It is not required that all modifiers specified have currently assigned keycodes. A key of **AnyKey** is equivalent to issuing the request for all possible keycodes. Otherwise, the key must be in the range specified by min-keycode and max-keycode in the connection setup (or a **Value** error results).

An **Access** error is generated if some other client has issued a **GrabKey** with the same key combination on the same window. When using **AnyModifier** or **AnyKey**, the request fails completely (no grabs are established), and an **Access** error is generated if there is a conflicting grab for any combination.

Request Encoding

# of Bytes	Value	Description
1	33	opcode
1	BOOL	owner-events
2	4	request length
4	WINDOW	grab-window
2	SETofKEYMASK	modifiers:
	#x8000	**AnyModifier**
1	KEYCODE	key:
	0	**AnyKey**
1		pointer-mode:
	0	**Synchronous**
	1	**Asynchronous**
1		keyboard-mode:
	0	**Synchronous**
	1	**Asynchronous**
3		unused

Name
GrabKeyboard

Request Contents
grab-window: WINDOW
owner-events: BOOL
pointer-mode, *keyboard-mode*: {**Synchronous, Asynchronous**}
time: TIMESTAMP or **CurrentTime**

Reply Contents
status: {**Success, AlreadyGrabbed, Frozen, InvalidTime, NotViewable**}

Errors
Window, Value

Description
This request actively grabs control of the keyboard. Further key events are reported only to the grabbing client. This request overrides any active keyboard grab by this client.

If owner-events is **False**, all generated key events are reported with respect to grab-window. If owner-events is **True** and if a generated key event would normally be reported to this client, it is reported normally. Otherwise, the event is reported with respect to the grab-window. Both **KeyPress** and **KeyRelease** events are always reported, independent of any event selection made by the client.

If keyboard-mode is **Asynchronous**, keyboard event processing continues normally. If the keyboard is currently frozen by this client, then processing of keyboard events is resumed. If keyboard-mode is **Synchronous**, the state of the keyboard (as seen by means of the protocol) appears to freeze. No further keyboard events are generated by the server until the grabbing client issues a releasing **AllowEvents** request or until the keyboard grab is released. Actual keyboard changes are not lost while the keyboard is frozen. They are simply queued for later processing.

If pointer-mode is **Asynchronous**, pointer event processing is unaffected by activation of the grab. If pointer-mode is **Synchronous**, the state of the pointer (as seen by means of the protocol) appears to freeze. No further pointer events are generated by the server until the grabbing client issues a releasing **AllowEvents** request or until the keyboard grab is released. Actual pointer changes are not lost while the pointer is frozen. They are simply queued for later processing.

This request generates **FocusIn** and **FocusOut** events.

The request fails with status **AlreadyGrabbed** if the keyboard is actively grabbed by some other client. The request fails with status **Frozen** if the keyboard is frozen by an active grab of another client. The request fails with status **NotViewable** if grab-window is not viewable. The request fails with status **InvalidTime** if the specified time is earlier than the last-keyboard-grab time or later than the current server time. Otherwise, the last-keyboard-grab time is set to the specified time with **CurrentTime** replaced by the current server time.

Request Encoding

# of Bytes	Value	Description
1	31	opcode
1	BOOL	owner-events
2	4	request length
4	WINDOW	grab-window
4	TIMESTAMP	time:
	0	**CurrentTime**
1		pointer-mode:
	0	**Synchronous**
	1	**Asynchronous**
1		keyboard-mode:
	0	**Synchronous**
	1	**Asynchronous**
2		unused

Reply Encoding

# of Bytes	Value	Description
1	1	reply
1		status:
	0	**Success**
	1	**AlreadyGrabbed**
	2	**InvalidTime**
	3	**NotViewable**
	4	**Frozen**
2	CARD16	sequence number
4	0	reply length
24		unused

Name

GrabPointer

Request Contents

grab-window: WINDOW
owner-events: BOOL
event-mask: SETofPOINTEREVENT
pointer-mode, *keyboard-mode*: {**Synchronous**, **Asynchronous**}
confine-to: WINDOW or **None**
cursor: CURSOR or **None**
time: TIMESTAMP or **CurrentTime**

Reply Contents

status: {**Success**, **AlreadyGrabbed**, **Frozen**, **InvalidTime**, **NotViewable**}

Errors

Cursor, **Window**, **Value**

Description

This request actively grabs control of the pointer. Further pointer events are only reported to the grabbing client. The request overrides any active pointer grab by this client.

If owner-events is **False**, all generated pointer events are reported with respect to grab-window and are only reported if selected by event-mask. If owner-events is **True** and a generated pointer event would normally be reported to this client, it is reported normally. Otherwise, the event is reported with respect to the grab-window and is only reported if selected by event-mask. For either value of owner-events, unreported events are simply discarded.

If pointer-mode is **Asynchronous**, pointer event processing continues normally. If the pointer is currently frozen by this client, then processing of pointer events is resumed. If pointer-mode is **Synchronous**, the state of the pointer (as seen by means of the protocol) appears to freeze, and no further pointer events are generated by the server until the grabbing client issues a releasing **AllowEvents** request or until the pointer grab is released. Actual pointer changes are not lost while the pointer is frozen. They are simply queued for later processing.

If keyboard-mode is **Asynchronous**, keyboard event processing is unaffected by activation of the grab. If keyboard-mode is **Synchronous**, the state of the keyboard (as seen by means of the protocol) appears to freeze, and no further keyboard events are generated by the server until the grabbing client issues a releasing **AllowEvents** request or until the pointer grab is released. Actual keyboard changes are not lost while the keyboard is frozen. They are simply queued for later processing.

If a cursor is specified, then it is displayed regardless of what window the pointer is in. If no cursor is specified, then when the pointer is in grab-window or one of its subwindows, the normal cursor for that window is displayed. Otherwise, the cursor for grab-window is displayed.

If a confine-to window is specified, then the pointer will be restricted to stay contained in that window. The confine-to window need have no relationship to the grab-window. If the pointer is not initially in the confine-to window, then it is warped automatically to the closest edge (and enter/leave events are generated normally) just before the grab activates. If the confine-to window is subsequently reconfigured, the pointer will be warped automatically as necessary to keep it contained in the window.

This request generates **EnterNotify** and **LeaveNotify** events.

The request fails with status **AlreadyGrabbed** if the pointer is actively grabbed by some other client. The request fails with status **Frozen** if the pointer is frozen by an active grab of another client. The request fails with status **NotViewable** if grab-window or confine-to window is not viewable or if the confine-to window lies completely outside the boundaries of the root window. The request fails with status **InvalidTime** if the specified time is earlier than the last-pointer-grab time or later than the current server time. Otherwise, the last-pointer-grab time is set to the specified time, with **CurrentTime** replaced by the current server time.

Request Encoding

# of Bytes	Value	Description
1	26	opcode
1	BOOL	owner-events
2	6	request length
4	WINDOW	grab-window
2	SETofPOINTEREVENT	event-mask
1		pointer-mode:
	0	**Synchronous**
	1	**Asynchronous**
1		keyboard-mode:
	0	**Synchronous**
	1	**Asynchronous**
4	WINDOW	confine-to:
	0	**None**
4	CURSOR	cursor:
	0	**None**
4	TIMESTAMP	time:
	0	**CurrentTime**

Reply Encoding

# of Bytes	Value	Description
1	1	reply
1		status:
	0	**Success**
	1	**AlreadyGrabbed**
	2	**InvalidTime**

# of Bytes	Value	Description
	3	**NotViewable**
	4	**Frozen**
2	CARD16	sequence number
4	0	reply length
24		unused

GrabServer

Name
GrabServer

Request Contents
Opcode and request length only.

Errors
This request generates no errors.

Description
This request disables processing of requests and close-downs on all connections other than the one this request arrived on.

Request Encoding

# of Bytes	Value	Description
1	36	opcode
1		unused
2	1	request length

Name

GraphicsExpose

Event Contents

drawable : DRAWABLE
x, y, width, height : CARD16
count : CARD16
major-opcode : CARD8
minor-opcode : CARD16

Description

This event is reported to clients selecting graphics-exposures in a graphics context and is generated when a destination region could not be computed due to an obscured or out-of-bounds source region. All of the regions exposed by a given graphics request are guaranteed to be reported contiguously. If count is zero, then no more **GraphicsExpose** events for this window follow. If count is nonzero, then at least that many more **GraphicsExpose** events for this window follow (and possibly more).

The x and y coordinates are relative to drawable's origin and specify the upper-left corner of a rectangle. The width and height specify the extent of the rectangle.

The major and minor opcodes identify the graphics request used. For the core protocol, major-opcode is always **CopyArea** or **CopyPlane**, and minor-opcode is always zero.

Request Encoding

# of Bytes	Value	Description
1	13	code
1		unused
2	CARD16	sequence number
4	DRAWABLE	drawable
2	CARD16	x
2	CARD16	y
2	CARD16	width
2	CARD16	height
2	CARD16	minor-opcode
2	CARD16	count
1	CARD8	major-opcode
11		unused

GravityNotify

Name

GravityNotify

Event Contents

event, window: WINDOW
x, y: INT16

Description

This event is reported to clients selecting **SubstructureNotify** on the parent and to clients selecting **StructureNotify** on the window. It is generated when a window is moved because of a change in size of the parent. The event is the window on which the event was generated, and the window is the window that is moved. The x and y coordinates are relative to the new parent's origin and specify the position of the upper-left outer corner of the window.

Request Encoding

# of Bytes	Value	Description
1	24	code
1		unused
2	CARD16	sequence number
4	WINDOW	event
4	WINDOW	window
2	INT16	x
2	INT16	y
16		unused

Name

ImageText8

Request Contents

drawable: DRAWABLE
gc: GCONTEXT
x, y: INT16
string: STRING8

Errors

Drawable, GContext, Match

Description

The x and y coordinates are relative to the drawable's origin and specify the baseline starting position (the initial character origin). The effect is first to fill a destination rectangle with the background pixel defined in gc and then to paint the text with the foreground pixel. The upper-left corner of the filled rectangle is at:

```
[x,y - font-ascent]
```

the width is:

```
overall-width
```

and the height is:

```
font-ascent + font-descent
```

The overall-width, font-ascent, and font-descent are as they would be returned by a **Query-TextExtents** call using gc and string.

The function and fill-style defined in gc are ignored for this request. The effective function is **Copy**, and the effective fill-style **Solid**.

For fonts defined with 2-byte matrix indexing, each STRING8 byte is interpreted as a byte2 value of a CHAR2B with a byte1 value of zero.

GC components: plane-mask, foreground, background, font, subwindow-mode, clip-x-origin, clip-y-origin, clip-mask

Request Encoding

# of Bytes	Value	Description
1	76	opcode
1	n	length of string
2	4+(n+p)/4	request length
4	DRAWABLE	drawable
4	GCONTEXT	gc

# of Bytes	Value	Description
2	INT16	x
2	INT16	y
n	STRING8	string
p		unused, p=pad(n)

Name
ImageText16

Request Contents
drawable: DRAWABLE
gc: GCONTEXT
x, y: INT16
string: STRING16

Errors
Drawable, GContext, Match

Description
This request is similar to **ImageText8**, except 2-byte (or 16-bit) characters are used. For fonts defined with linear indexing rather than 2-byte matrix indexing, the server will interpret each CHAR2B as a 16-bit number that has been transmitted most-significant byte first (that is, byte1 of the CHAR2B is taken as the most-significant byte).

Request Encoding

# of Bytes	Value	Description
1	77	opcode
1	n	number of CHAR2Bs in string
2	4+(2n+p)/4	request length
4	DRAWABLE	drawable
4	GCONTEXT	gc
2	INT16	x
2	INT16	y
2n	STRING16	string
p		unused, p=pad(2n)

InstallColormap

Name
InstallColormap

Request Contents
cmap: COLORMAP

Errors
Colormap

Description
This request makes this colormap an installed map for its screen. All windows associated with this colormap immediately display with true colors. As a side effect, additional colormaps might be implicitly installed or uninstalled by the server. Which other colormaps get installed or uninstalled is server-dependent except that the required list must remain installed.

If cmap is not already an installed map, a **ColormapNotify** event is generated on every window having cmap as an attribute. In addition, for every other colormap that is installed or uninstalled as a result of the request, a **ColormapNotify** event is generated on every window having that colormap as an attribute.

At any time, there is a subset of the installed maps that are viewed as an ordered list and are called the required list. The length of the required list is at most M, where M is the min-installed-maps specified for the screen in the connection setup. The required list is maintained as follows. When a colormap is an explicit argument to **InstallColormap**, it is added to the head of the list; the list is truncated at the tail, if necessary, to keep the length of the list to at most M. When a colormap is an explicit argument to **UninstallColormap** and it is in the required list, it is removed from the list. A colormap is not added to the required list when it is installed implicitly by the server, and the server cannot implicitly uninstall a colormap that is in the required list.

Initially the default colormap for a screen is installed (but is not in the required list).

Request Encoding

# of Bytes	Value	Description
1	81	opcode
1		unused
2	2	request length
4	COLORMAP	cmap

Name
InternAtom

Request Contents
name: STRING8
only-if-exists: BOOL

Reply Contents
atom: ATOM or **None**

Errors
Value, **Alloc**

Description
This request returns the atom for the given name. If only-if-exists is **False**, then the atom is created if it does not exist. The string should use the ISO Latin-1 encoding. Upper case and lower case matter.

The lifetime of an atom is not tied to the interning client. Atoms remained defined until server reset (see Appendix A, *Connection Close*).

Request Encoding

# of Bytes	Value	Description
1	16	opcode
1	BOOL	only-if-exists
2	2+(n+p)/4	request length
2	n	length of name
2		unused
n	STRING8	name
p		unused, p=pad(n)

Reply Encoding

# of Bytes	Value	Description
1	1	reply
1		unused
2	CARD16	sequence number
4	0	reply length

# of Bytes	Value	Description
4	ATOM	atom:
	0	**None**
20		unused

Name
KeymapNotify

Event Contents
keys: LISTofCARD8

Description
The value is a bit vector as described in **QueryKeymap**. This event is reported to clients selecting **KeymapState** on a window and is generated immediately after every **EnterNotify** and **FocusIn**.

Request Encoding

# of Bytes	Value	Description
1	11	code
31	LISTofCARD8	keys
		(byte for keycodes 0-7 is omitted)

KeyPress

Name

KeyPress

Event Contents

root, event: WINDOW
child: WINDOW or **None**
same-screen: BOOL
root-x, root-y, event-x, event-y: INT16
detail: (See Description.)
state: SETofKEYBUTMASK
time: TIMESTAMP

(Same contents as **MotionNotify**.)

Description

KeyPress events are sent by the server to the client when the user presses a keyboard key. Only clients selecting **KeyPress** events will receive them. The window member of this event depends on which window the pointer is in when the button is pressed and on the values of the event-mask and do-not-propagate field for that window and its ancestors.

For more information, see **MotionNotify**.

Request Encoding

# of Bytes	Value	Description
1	2	code
1	KEYCODE	detail
2	CARD16	sequence number
4	TIMESTAMP	time
4	WINDOW	root
4	WINDOW	event
4	WINDOW	child:
	0	**None**
2	INT16	root-x
2	INT16	root-y
2	INT16	event-x
2	INT16	event-y
2	SETofKEYBUTMASK	state
1	BOOL	same-screen
1		unused

Name

KeyRelease

Event Contents

root, *event*: WINDOW
child: WINDOW or **None**
same-screen: BOOL
root-x, *root-y*, *event-x*, *event-y*: INT16
detail: (See Description.)
state: SETofKEYBUTMASK
time: TIMESTAMP

(Same contents as **MotionNotify**.)

Description

KeyRelease events are sent by the server to the client when the user presses a keyboard key. Only clients selecting **KeyRelease** events will receive them. The window member of this event depends on which window the pointer is in when the button is released and on the values of the event-mask and do-not-propagate field for that window and its ancestors.

For more information, see **MotionNotify**.

Request Encoding

# of Bytes	Value	Description
1	3	code
1	KEYCODE	detail
2	CARD16	sequence number
4	TIMESTAMP	time
4	WINDOW	root
4	WINDOW	event
4	WINDOW	child:
	0	**None**
2	INT16	root-x
2	INT16	root-y
2	INT16	event-x
2	INT16	event-y
2	SETofKEYBUTMASK	state
1	BOOL	same-screen
1		unused

KillClient

Name

KillClient

Request Contents

resource: CARD32 or **AllTemporary**

Errors

Value

Description

If a valid resource is specified, **KillClient** forces a close-down of the client that created the resource. If the client has already terminated in either **RetainPermanent** mode or **Retain-Temporary** mode, all of the client's resources are destroyed (see Appendix A, *Connection Close*). If **AllTemporary** is specified, then the resources of all clients that have terminated in **RetainTemporary** are destroyed.

Request Encoding

# of Bytes	Value	Description
1	113	opcode
1		unused
2	2	request length
4	CARD32	resource:
	0	**AllTemporary**

Name

LeaveNotify

Event Contents

root, event : WINDOW
child : WINDOW or **None**
same-screen : BOOL
root-x, root-y, event-x, event-y : INT16
mode : { **Normal, Grab, Ungrab** }
detail : { **Ancestor, Virtual, Inferior, Nonlinear, NonlinearVirtual** }
focus : BOOL
state : SETofKEYBUTMASK
time : TIMESTAMP

Description

If pointer motion or window hierarchy change causes the pointer to be in a different window than before, **EnterNotify** and **LeaveNotify** events are generated instead of a **MotionNotify** event. Only clients selecting **EnterWindow** on a window receive **EnterNotify** events, and only clients selecting **LeaveWindow** receive **LeaveNotify** events. The pointer position reported in the event is always the final position, not the initial position of the pointer. The root is the root window for this position, and root-x and root-y are the pointer coordinates relative to root's origin at the time of the event. Event is the event window. If the event window is on the same screen as root, then event-x and event-y are the pointer coordinates relative to the event window's origin. Otherwise, event-x and event-y are zero. In a **LeaveNotify** event, if a child of the event window contains the initial position of the pointer, then the child component is set to that child. Otherwise, it is **None**. For an **EnterNotify** event, if a child of the event window contains the final pointer position, then the child component is set to that child. Otherwise, it is **None**. If the event window is the focus window or an inferior of the focus window, then focus is **True**. Otherwise, focus is **False**.

Normal pointer motion events have mode **Normal**. Pseudo-motion events when a grab activates have mode **Grab**, and pseudo-motion events when a grab deactivates have mode **Ungrab**.

All **EnterNotify** and **LeaveNotify** events caused by a hierarchy change are generated after any hierarchy event caused by that change (that is, **UnmapNotify, MapNotify, Configure-Notify, GravityNotify, CirculateNotify**), but the ordering of **EnterNotify** and **LeaveNotify** events with respect to **FocusOut, VisibilityNotify**, and **Expose** events is not constrained.

Normal events are generated as follows.

When the pointer moves from window A to window B and A is an inferior of B:

- **LeaveNotify** with detail **Ancestor** is generated on A.

- **LeaveNotify** with detail **Virtual** is generated on each window between A and B exclusive (in that order).

- **EnterNotify** with detail **Inferior** is generated on B.

When the pointer moves from window A to window B and B is an inferior of A:

- **LeaveNotify** with detail **Inferior** is generated on A.

- **EnterNotify** with detail **Virtual** is generated on each window between A and B exclusive (in that order).

- **EnterNotify** with detail **Ancestor** is generated on B.

When the pointer moves from window A to window B and window C is their least common ancestor:

- **LeaveNotify** with detail **Nonlinear** is generated on A.

- **LeaveNotify** with detail **NonlinearVirtual** is generated on each window between A and C exclusive (in that order).

- **EnterNotify** with detail **NonlinearVirtual** is generated on each window between C and B exclusive (in that order).

- **EnterNotify** with detail **Nonlinear** is generated on B.

When the pointer moves from window A to window B on different screens:

- **LeaveNotify** with detail **Nonlinear** is generated on A.

- If A is not a root window, **LeaveNotify** with detail **NonlinearVirtual** is generated on each window above A up to and including its root (in order).

- If B is not a root window, **EnterNotify** with detail **NonlinearVirtual** is generated on each window from B's root down to but not including B (in order).

- **EnterNotify** with detail **Nonlinear** is generated on B.

When a pointer grab activates (but after any initial warp into a confine-to window and before generating any actual **ButtonPress** event that activates the grab), G is the grab-window for the grab, and P is the window the pointer is in:

- **EnterNotify** and **LeaveNotify** events with mode **Grab** are generated (as for **Normal** above) as if the pointer were to suddenly warp from its current position in P to some position in G. However, the pointer does not warp, and the pointer position is used as both the initial and final positions for the events.

When a pointer grab deactivates (but after generating any actual **ButtonRelease** event that deactivates the grab), G is the grab-window for the grab, and P is the window the pointer is in:

- **EnterNotify** and **LeaveNotify** events with mode **Ungrab** are generated (as for **Normal** above) as if the pointer were to suddenly warp from some position in G to its current position in P. However, the pointer does not warp, and the current pointer position is used as both the initial and final positions for the events.

Request Encoding

# of Bytes	Value	Description
1	8	code
1		detail:
	0	**Ancestor**
	1	**Virtual**
	2	**Inferior**
	3	**Nonlinear**
	4	**NonlinearVirtual**
2	CARD16	sequence number
4	TIMESTAMP	time
4	WINDOW	root
4	WINDOW	event
4	WINDOW	child:
	0	**None**
2	INT16	root-x
2	INT16	root-y
2	INT16	event-x
2	INT16	event-y
2	SETofKEYBUTMASK	state
1		mode:
	0	**Normal**
	1	**Grab**
	2	**Ungrab**
1		same-screen, focus:
	#x01	focus (1 is True, 0 is False)
	#x02	same-screen (1 is True, 0 is False)
	#xfc	unused

ListExtensions

Name
ListExtensions

Request Contents
Opcode and request length only.

Reply Contents
names: LISTofSTRING8

Errors
This request generates no errors.

Description
This request returns a list of all extensions supported by the server.

Request Encoding

# of Bytes	Value	Description
1	99	opcode
1		unused
2	1	request length

Reply Encoding

# of Bytes	Value	Description
1	1	reply
1	CARD8	number of STRs in names
2	CARD16	sequence number
4	(n+p)/4	reply length
24		unused
n	LISTofSTR	names
p		unused, p=pad(n)

ListFonts

Name
ListFonts

Request Contents
pattern: STRING8
max-names: CARD16

Reply Contents
names: LISTofSTRING8

Errors
This request generates no errors.

Description
This request returns a list of available font names (as controlled by the font search path; see **SetFontPath** request) that match the pattern. At most, max-names names will be returned. The pattern should use the ISO Latin-1 encoding, and upper case and lower case do not matter. In the pattern, the ''?'' character (octal value 77) will match any single character, and the ''*'' character (octal value 52) will match any number of characters. The returned names are in lower case.

Request Encoding

# of Bytes	Value	Description
1	49	opcode
1		unused
2	2+(n+p)/4	request length
2	CARD16	max-names
2	n	length of pattern
n	STRING8	pattern
p		unused, p=pad(n)

Reply Encoding

# of Bytes	Value	Description
1	1	reply
1		unused
2	CARD16	sequence number
4	(n+p)/4	reply length
2	CARD16	number of STRs in names

# of Bytes	Value	Description
22		unused
n	LISTofSTR	names
p		unused, p=pad(n)

ListFontsWithInfo

Name

ListFontsWithInfo

Request Contents

pattern: STRING8
max-names: CARD16

Reply Contents

name: STRING8
info: FONTINFO
replies-hint: CARD32

where:

FONTINFO:	[draw-direction: { **LeftToRight**, **RightToLeft** }
	min-char-or-byte2, max-char-or-byte2: CARD16
	min-byte1, max-byte1: CARD8
	all-chars-exist: BOOL
	default-char: CARD16
	min-bounds: CHARINFO
	max-bounds: CHARINFO
	font-ascent: INT16
	font-descent: INT16
	properties: LISTofFONTPROP]

Errors

This request generates no errors.

Description

This request is similar to **ListFonts**, but it also returns information about each font. The information returned for each font is identical to what **QueryFont** would return except that the per-character metrics are not returned. Note that this request can generate multiple replies. With each reply, replies-hint may provide an indication of how many more fonts will be returned. This number is a hint only and may be larger or smaller than the number of fonts actually returned. A zero value does not guarantee that no more fonts will be returned. After the font replies, a reply with a zero-length name is sent to indicate the end of the reply sequence.

This request has one reply for each font queried (and it is the only request with multiple replies).

Request Encoding

# of Bytes	Value	Description
1	50	opcode
1		unused
2	2+(n+p)/4	request length

# of Bytes | Value | Description

# of Bytes	Value	Description
2	CARD16	max-names
2	n	length of pattern
n	STRING8	pattern
p		unused, p=pad(n)

Reply Encoding (except for last in series)

# of Bytes	Value	Description
1	1	reply
1	n	length of name in bytes
2	CARD16	sequence number
4	7+2m+(n+p)/4	reply length
12	CHARINFO	min-bounds
4		unused
12	CHARINFO	max-bounds
4		unused
2	CARD16	min-char-or-byte2
2	CARD16	max-char-or-byte2
2	CARD16	default-char
2	m	number of FONTPROPs in properties
1		draw-direction:
	0	**LeftToRight**
	1	**RightToLeft**
1	CARD8	min-byte1
1	CARD8	max-byte1
1	BOOL	all-chars-exist
2	INT16	font-ascent
2	INT16	font-descent
4	CARD32	replies-hint
8m	LISTofFONTPROP	properties
n	STRING8	name
p		unused, p=pad(n)

LISTofFONTPROP is *n* repetitions of the encoding for FONTPROP shown in the table below:

# of Bytes	Value	Description
4	ATOM	name
4		value

The encoding for CHARINFO is shown in the table below:

# of Bytes	Value	Description
2	INT16	left-side-bearing
2	INT16	right-side-bearing
2	INT16	character-width
2	INT16	ascent
2	INT16	descent
2	CARD16	attributes

Reply Encoding (last in series)

# of Bytes	Value	Description
1	1	reply
1	0	last-reply indicator
2	CARD16	sequence number
4	7	reply length
52		unused

ListHosts

Name

ListHosts

Request Contents

Opcode and request length only.

Reply Contents

mode: { **Enabled**, **Disabled** }
hosts: LISTofHOST

Errors

This request generates no errors.

Description

This request returns the hosts on the access control list and states whether use of the list at connection setup is currently enabled or disabled.

Each HOST is padded to a multiple of four bytes.

Request Encoding

# of Bytes	Value	Description
1	110	opcode
1		unused
2	1	request length

Reply Encoding

# of Bytes	Value	Description
1	1	reply
1		mode:
	0	**Disabled**
	1	**Enabled**
2	CARD16	sequence number
4	n/4	reply length
2	CARD16	number of HOSTs in hosts
22		unused
n	LISTofHOST	hosts
		(n always a multiple of 4)

ListInstalledColormaps

Name

ListInstalledColormaps

Request Contents

window: WINDOW

Reply Contents

cmaps: LISTofCOLORMAP

Errors

Window

Description

This request returns a list of the currently installed colormaps for the screen of the specified window. The order of colormaps is not significant, and there is no explicit indication of the required list (see **InstallColormap** request).

Request Encoding

# of Bytes	Value	Description
1	83	opcode
1		unused
2	2	request length
4	WINDOW	window

Reply Encoding

# of Bytes	Value	Description
1	1	reply
1		unused
2	CARD16	sequence number
4	n	reply length
2	n	number of COLORMAPs in cmaps
22		unused
4n	LISTofCOLORMAP	cmaps

ListProperties

Name
ListProperties

Request Contents
window: WINDOW

Reply Contents
atoms: LISTofATOM

Errors
Window

Description
This request returns the atoms of properties currently defined on the window.

Request Encoding

# of Bytes	Value	Description
1	21	opcode
1		unused
2	2	request length
4	WINDOW	window

Reply Encoding

# of Bytes	Value	Description
1	1	reply
1		unused
2	CARD16	sequence number
4	n	reply length
2	n	number of ATOMs in atoms
22		unused
4n	LISTofATOM	atoms

Name
LookupColor

Request Contents
cmap: COLORMAP
name: STRING8

Reply Contents
exact-red, exact-green, exact-blue: CARD16
visual-red, visual-green, visual-blue: CARD16

Errors
Colormap, Name

Description
This request looks up the string name of a color with respect to the screen associated with cmap and returns both the exact color values and the closest values provided by the hardware with respect to the visual type of cmap. The name should use the ISO Latin-1 encoding, and upper case and lower case do not matter.

Request Encoding

# of Bytes	Value	Description
1	92	opcode
1		unused
2	3+(n+p)/4	request length
4	COLORMAP	cmap
2	n	length of name
2		unused
n	STRING8	name
p		unused, p=pad(n)

Reply Encoding

# of Bytes	Value	Description
1	1	reply
1		unused
2	CARD16	sequence number
4	0	reply length
2	CARD16	exact-red
2	CARD16	exact-green
2	CARD16	exact-blue

# of Bytes	Value	Description
2	CARD16	visual-red
2	CARD16	visual-green
2	CARD16	visual-blue
12		unused

Name

MapNotify

Event Contents

event, *window*: WINDOW
override-redirect: BOOL

Description

This event is reported to clients selecting **StructureNotify** on the window and to clients selecting **SubstructureNotify** on the parent. It is generated when the window changes state from
unmapped to mapped. The event is the window on which the event was generated, and the window is the window that is mapped. The override-redirect flag is from the window's attribute.

Request Encoding

# of Bytes	Value	Description
1	19	code
1		unused
2	CARD16	sequence number
4	WINDOW	event
4	WINDOW	window
1	BOOL	override-redirect
19		unused

MappingNotify

Name
MappingNotify

Event Contents
request: { **Modifier**, **Keyboard**, **Pointer** }
first-keycode, *count*: CARD8

Description
This event is sent to all clients. There is no mechanism to express disinterest in this event. The detail indicates the kind of change that occurred: **Modifiers** for a successful **SetModifier-Mapping**, **Keyboard** for a successful **ChangeKeyboardMapping**, and **Pointer** for a successful **SetPointerMapping**. If the detail is **Keyboard**, then first-keycode and count indicate the range of altered keycodes.

Request Encoding

# of Bytes	Value	Description
1	34	code
1		unused
2	CARD16	sequence number
1		request:
	0	**Modifier**
	1	**Keyboard**
	2	**Pointer**
1	KEYCODE	first-keycode
1	CARD8	count
25		unused

Name
MapRequest

Event Contents
parent, window: WINDOW

Description
This event is reported to the client selecting **SubstructureRedirect** on the parent and is generated when a **MapWindow** request is issued on an unmapped window with an override-redirect attribute of **False**.

Request Encoding

# of Bytes	Value	Description
1	20	code
1		unused
2	CARD16	sequence number
4	WINDOW	parent
4	WINDOW	window
20		unused

MapSubwindows

Name
MapSubwindows

Request Contents
window: WINDOW

Errors
Window

Description
This request performs a **MapWindow** request on all unmapped children of the window, in top-to-bottom stacking order.

Request Encoding

# of Bytes	Value	Description
1	9	opcode
1		unused
2	2	request length
4	WINDOW	window

Name

MapWindow

Request Contents

window: WINDOW

Errors

Window

Description

If the window is already mapped, this request has no effect.

If the override-redirect attribute of the window is **False** and some other client has selected **SubstructureRedirect** on the parent, then a **MapRequest** event is generated, but the window remains unmapped. Otherwise, the window is mapped, and a **MapNotify** event is generated.

If the window is now viewable and its contents have been discarded, the window is tiled with its background (if no background is defined, the existing screen contents are not altered), and zero or more exposure events are generated. If a backing-store has been maintained while the window was unmapped, no exposure events are generated. If a backing-store will now be maintained, a full-window exposure is always generated. Otherwise, only visible regions may be reported. Similar tiling and exposure take place for any newly viewable inferiors.

Request Encoding

# of Bytes	Value	Description
1	8	opcode
1		unused
2	2	request length
4	WINDOW	window

MotionNotify

Name
MotionNotify

Event Contents
root, *event*: WINDOW
child: WINDOW or **None**
same-screen: BOOL
root-x, *root-y*, *event-x*, *event-y*: INT16
detail: (See Description.)
state: SETofKEYBUTMASK
time: TIMESTAMP

Description
ButtonPress, **ButtonRelease**, **KeyPress**, **KeyRelease**, and **MotionNotify** are generated either when a key or button logically changes state or when the pointer logically moves. The generation of these logical changes may lag the physical changes if device event processing is frozen. Note that **KeyPress** and **KeyRelease** are generated for all keys, even those mapped to modifier bits. The source of the event is the window the pointer is in. The window the event is reported with respect to is called the event window. The event window is found by starting with the source window and looking up the hierarchy for the first window on which any client has selected interest in the event (provided no intervening window prohibits event generation by including the event type in its do-not-propagate-mask). The actual window used for reporting can be modified by active grabs and, in the case of keyboard events, can be modified by the focus window.

The root is the root window of the source window, and root-x and root-y are the pointer coordinates relative to root's origin at the time of the event. Event is the event window. If the event window is on the same screen as root, then event-x and event-y are the pointer coordinates relative to the event window's origin. Otherwise, event-x and event-y are zero. If the source window is an inferior of the event window, then child is set to the child of the event window that is an ancestor of (or is) the source window. Otherwise, it is set to **None**. The state component gives the logical state of the buttons and modifier keys just before the event. The detail component type varies with the event type:

Event	Component
KeyPress, **KeyRelease**	KEYCODE
ButtonPress, **ButtonRelease**	BUTTON
MotionNotify	{**Normal**, **Hint**}

MotionNotify events are only generated when the motion begins and ends in the window. The granularity of motion events is not guaranteed, but a client selecting for motion events is guaranteed to get at least one event when the pointer moves and comes to rest. Selecting **PointerMotion** receives events independent of the state of the pointer buttons. By selecting some subset of **Button[1-5]Motion** instead, **MotionNotify** events will only be received when one or more of the specified buttons are pressed. By selecting **ButtonMotion**, **MotionNotify** events will be received only when at least one button is pressed. The events are always of type **MotionNotify**, independent of the selection. If **PointerMotionHint** is selected, the server is free to send only one **MotionNotify** event (with detail **Hint**) to the client for the event window until either the key or the button state changes, the pointer leaves the event window, or the client issues a **QueryPointer** or **GetMotionEvents** request.

Request Encoding

# of Bytes	Value	Description
1	6	code
1		detail:
	0	**Normal**
	1	**Hint**
2	CARD16	sequence number
4	TIMESTAMP	time
4	WINDOW	root
4	WINDOW	event
4	WINDOW	child:
	0	**None**
2	INT16	root-x
2	INT16	root-y
2	INT16	event-x
2	INT16	event-y
2	SETofKEYBUTMASK	state
1	BOOL	same-screen
1		unused

Name

NoExpose

Event Contents

drawable: DRAWABLE
major-opcode: CARD8
minor-opcode: CARD16

Description

This event is reported to clients selecting graphics-exposures in a graphics context and is generated when a graphics request that might produce **GraphicsExpose** events does not produce any. The drawable specifies the destination used for the graphics request.

The major and minor opcodes identify the graphics request used. For the core protocol, major-opcode is always **CopyArea** or **CopyPlane**, and the minor-opcode is always zero.

Request Encoding

# of Bytes	Value	Description
1	14	code
1		unused
2	CARD16	sequence number
4	DRAWABLE	drawable
2	CARD16	minor-opcode
1	CARD8	major-opcode
21		unused

Name
NoOperation

Request Contents
Opcode and request length only.

Errors
This request generates no errors.

Description
This request has no arguments and no results, but the request length field can be nonzero, which allows the request to be any multiple of four bytes in length. The bytes contained in the request are uninterpreted by the server.

This request can be used in its minimum four-byte form as padding where necessary by client libraries that find it convenient to force requests to begin on 64-bit boundaries.

Request Encoding

# of Bytes	Value	Description
1	127	opcode
1		unused
2	1	request length

OpenFont

Name
OpenFont

Request Contents
fid: FONT
name: STRING8

Errors
IDChoice, Name, Alloc

Description
This request loads the specified font, if necessary, and associates identifier *fid* with it. The font name should use the ISO Latin-1 encoding, and upper case and lower case do not matter. The interpretation of characters "?" (octal value 77) and "*" (octal value 52) in the name is not defined by the core protocol but is reserved for future definition. A structured lformat for font names is specified in the X Consortium standard *X Logical Font Description Conventions, Release 4*, which is reprinted as Appendix M in this manual.

Fonts are not associated with a particular screen and can be stored as a component of any graphics context.

Request Encoding

# of Bytes	Value	Description
1	45	opcode
1		unused
2	3+(n+p)/4	request length
4	FONT	fid
2	n	length of name
2		unused
n	STRING8	name
p		unused, p=pad(n)

Name
PolyArc

Request Contents
drawable: DRAWABLE
gc: GCONTEXT
arcs: LISTofARC

Errors
Drawable, GContext, Match

Description
This request draws circular or elliptical arcs. Each arc is specified by a rectangle and two angles. The angles are signed integers in degrees scaled by 64, with positive indicating counterclockwise motion and negative indicating clockwise motion. The start of the arc is specified by angle1 relative to the three-o'clock position from the center of the rectangle, and the path and extent of the arc is specified by angle2 relative to the start of the arc. If the magnitude of angle2 is greater than 360 degrees, it is truncated to 360 degrees. The x and y coordinates of the rectangle are relative to the origin of the drawable. For an arc specified as [x,y,w,h,a1,a2], the origin of the major and minor axes is at [x+(w/2),y+(h/2)], and the infinitely thin path describing the entire circle/ellipse intersects the horizontal axis at [x,y+(h/2)] and [x+w,y+(h/2)] and intersects the vertical axis at [x+(w/2),y] and [x+(w/2),y+h]. These coordinates can be fractional; that is, they are not truncated to discrete coordinates. The path should be defined by the ideal mathematical path. For a wide line with line-width lw, the bounding outlines for filling are given by the two infinitely thin paths consisting of all points whose perpendicular distance from the path of the circle/ellipse is equal to lw/2 (which may be a fractional value). The cap-style and join-style are applied the same as for a line corresponding to the tangent of the circle/ellipse at the endpoint.

For an arc specified as [x,y,w,h,a1,a2], the angles must be specified in the effectively skewed coordinate system of the ellipse (for a circle, the angles and coordinate systems are identical). The relationship between these angles and angles expressed in the normal coordinate system of the screen (as measured with a protractor) is as follows:

```
skewed-angle = atan (tan (normal-angle) * w / h) + adjust
```

The skewed-angle and normal-angle are expressed in radians (rather than in degrees scaled by 64) in the range [0,2*PI]. The atan returns a value in the range [–PI/2,PI/2]. The adjust is:

0   for normal-angle in the range [0,PI/2]
PI   for normal-angle in the range [PI/2,(3*PI)/2]
2*PI   for normal-angle in the range [(3*PI)/2,2*PI]

The arcs are drawn in the order listed. If the last point in one arc coincides with the first point in the following arc, the two arcs will join correctly. If the first point in the first arc coincides with the last point in the last arc, the two arcs will join correctly. For any given arc, no pixel is drawn more than once. If two arcs join correctly and the line-width is greater than zero and the arcs intersect, no pixel is drawn more than once. Otherwise, the intersecting pixels of intersecting arcs are drawn multiple times. Specifying an arc with one endpoint and a clockwise extent draws the same pixels as specifying the other endpoint and an equivalent counterclockwise extent, except as it affects joins.

By specifying one axis to be zero, a horizontal or vertical line can be drawn.

Angles are computed based solely on the coordinate system, ignoring the aspect ratio.

GC components: function, plane-mask, line-width, line-style, cap-style, join-style, fill-style, subwindow-mode, clip-x-origin, clip-y-origin, clip-mask

GC mode-dependent components: foreground, background, tile, stipple, tile-stipple-x-origin, tile-stipple-y-origin, dash-offset, dashes

Request Encoding

# of Bytes	Value	Description
1	68	opcode
1		unused
2	3+3n	request length
4	DRAWABLE	drawable
4	GCONTEXT	gc
12n	LISTofARC	arcs

Name

PolyFillArc

Request Contents

drawable: DRAWABLE
gc: GCONTEXT
arcs: LISTofARC

Errors

Drawable, **GContext**, **Match**

Description

For each arc, this request fills the region closed by the infinitely thin path described by the
specified arc and one or two line segments, depending on the arc-mode. For **Chord**, the single
line segment joining the endpoints of the arc is used. For **PieSlice**, the two line segments joining the endpoints of the arc with the center point are used. The arcs are as specified in the
PolyArc request.

The arcs are filled in the order listed. For any given arc, no pixel is drawn more than once. If
regions intersect, the intersecting pixels are drawn multiple times.

GC components: function, plane-mask, fill-style, arc-mode, subwindow-mode, clip-x-origin,
clip-y-origin, clip-mask

GC mode-dependent components: foreground, background, tile, stipple, tile-stipple-x-origin,
tile-stipple-y-origin

Request Encoding

# of Bytes	Value	Description
1	71	opcode
1		unused
2	3+3n	request length
4	DRAWABLE	drawable
4	GCONTEXT	gc
12n	LISTofARC	arcs

PolyFillRectangle

Name

PolyFillRectangle

Request Contents

drawable: DRAWABLE
gc: GCONTEXT
rectangles: LISTofRECTANGLE

Errors

Drawable, **GContext**, **Match**

Description

This request fills the specified rectangles, as if a four-point **FillPoly** were specified for each rectangle:

```
[x,y] [x+width,y] [x+width,y+height] [x,y+height]
```

The x and y coordinates of each rectangle are relative to the drawable's origin and define the upper-left corner of the rectangle.

The rectangles are drawn in the order listed. For any given rectangle, no pixel is drawn more than once. If rectangles intersect, the intersecting pixels are drawn multiple times.

GC components: function, plane-mask, fill-style, subwindow-mode, clip-x-origin, clip-y-origin, clip-mask

GC mode-dependent components: foreground, background, tile, stipple, tile-stipple-x-origin, tile-stipple-y-origin

Request Encoding

# of Bytes	Value	Description
1	70	opcode
1		unused
2	3+2n	request length
4	DRAWABLE	drawable
4	GCONTEXT	gc
8n	LISTofRECTANGLE	rectangles

Name
PolyLine

Request Contents
drawable: DRAWABLE
gc: GCONTEXT
coordinate-mode: { **Origin**, **Previous** }
points: LISTofPOINT

Errors
Drawable, **GContext**, **Value**, **Match**

Description
This request draws lines between each pair of points (point[i],point[i+1]). The lines are drawn in the order listed. The lines join correctly at all intermediate points, and if the first and last points coincide, the first and last lines also join correctly.

For any given line, no pixel is drawn more than once. If thin (zero line-width) lines intersect, the intersecting pixels are drawn multiple times. If wide lines intersect, the intersecting pixels are drawn only once, as though the entire **PolyLine** were a single filled shape.

The first point is always relative to the drawable's origin. The rest are relative either to that origin or to the previous point, depending on the coordinate-mode.

GC components: function, plane-mask, line-width, line-style, cap-style, join-style, fill-style, subwindow-mode, clip-x-origin, clip-y-origin, clip-mask

GC mode-dependent components: foreground, background, tile, stipple, tile-stipple-x-origin, tile-stipple-y-origin, dash-offset, dashes

Request Encoding

# of Bytes	Value	Description
1	65	opcode
1		coordinate-mode:
	0	**Origin**
	1	**Previous**
2	3+n	request length
4	DRAWABLE	drawable
4	GCONTEXT	gc
4n	LISTofPOINT	points

PolyPoint

Name
PolyPoint

Request Contents
drawable: DRAWABLE
gc: GCONTEXT
coordinate-mode: {Origin, Previous}
points: LISTofPOINT

Errors
Drawable, **GContext**, **Value**, **Match**

Description
This request combines the foreground pixel in gc with the pixel at each point in the drawable. The points are drawn in the order listed.

The first point is always relative to the drawable's origin. The rest are relative either to that origin or to the previous point, depending on the coordinate-mode.

GC components: function, plane-mask, foreground, subwindow-mode, clip-x-origin, clip-y-origin, clip-mask

Request Encoding

# of Bytes	Value	Description
1	64	opcode
1		coordinate-mode:
	0	**Origin**
	1	**Previous**
2	3+n	request length
4	DRAWABLE	drawable
4	GCONTEXT	gc
4n	LISTofPOINT	points

PolyRectangle

Name
PolyRectangle

Request Contents
drawable: DRAWABLE
gc: GCONTEXT
rectangles: LISTofRECTANGLE

Errors
Drawable, **GContext**, **Match**

Description
This request draws the outlines of the specified rectangles, as if a five-point **PolyLine** were specified for each rectangle:

```
[x,y] [x+width,y] [x+width,y+height] [x,y+height] [x,y]
```

The x and y coordinates of each rectangle are relative to the drawable's origin and define the upper-left corner of the rectangle.

The rectangles are drawn in the order listed. For any given rectangle, no pixel is drawn more than once. If rectangles intersect, the intersecting pixels are drawn multiple times.

GC components: function, plane-mask, line-width, line-style, join-style, fill-style, subwindow-mode, clip-x-origin, clip-y-origin, clip-mask

GC mode-dependent components: foreground, background, tile, stipple, tile-stipple-x-origin, tile-stipple-y-origin, dash-offset, dashes

Request Encoding

# of Bytes	Value	Description
1	67	opcode
1		unused
2	3+2n	request length
4	DRAWABLE	drawable
4	GCONTEXT	gc
8n	LISTofRECTANGLE	rectangles

PolySegment

Name

PolySegment

Request Contents

drawable: DRAWABLE
gc: GCONTEXT
segments: LISTofSEGMENT

where:

SEGMENT: [x1, y1, x2, y2: INT16]

Errors

Drawable, **GContext**, **Match**

Description

For each segment, this request draws a line between [x1,y1] and [x2,y2]. The lines are drawn in the order listed. No joining is performed at coincident endpoints. For any given line, no pixel is drawn more than once. If lines intersect, the intersecting pixels are drawn multiple times.

GC components: function, plane-mask, line-width, line-style, cap-style, fill-style, subwindow-mode, clip-x-origin, clip-y-origin, clip-mask

GC mode-dependent components: foreground, background, tile, stipple, tile-stipple-x-origin, tile-stipple-y-origin, dash-offset, dashes

Request Encoding

# of Bytes	Value	Description
1	66	opcode
1		unused
2	3+2n	request length
4	DRAWABLE	drawable
4	GCONTEXT	gc
8n	LISTofSEGMENT	segments

LISTofSEGMENT is *n* repetitions of the encoding for SEGMENT shown in the table below:

# of Bytes	Value	Description
2	INT16	x1
2	INT16	y1
2	INT16	x2
2	INT16	y2

Name
PolyText8

Request Contents
drawable : DRAWABLE
gc : GCONTEXT
x, y : INT16
items : LISTofTEXTITEM8

where:

TEXTITEM8:	TEXTELT8 or FONT
TEXTELT8:	[delta: INT8
	string: STRING8]

Errors
Drawable, GContext, Match, Font

Description
The x and y coordinates are relative to the drawable's origin and specify the baseline starting position (the initial character origin). Each text item is processed in turn. A font item causes the font to be stored in gc and to be used for subsequent text. Switching among fonts does not affect the next character origin. A text element delta specifies an additional change in the position along the x axis before the string is drawn; the delta is always added to the character origin. Each character image, as defined by the font in gc, is treated as an additional mask for a fill operation on the drawable.

All contained FONTs are always transmitted most-significant byte first.

If a **Font** error is generated for an item, the previous items may have been drawn.

For fonts defined with 2-byte matrix indexing, each STRING8 byte is interpreted as a byte2 value of a CHAR2B with a byte1 value of zero.

GC components: function, plane-mask, fill-style, font, subwindow-mode, clip-x-origin, clip-y-origin, clip-mask

GC mode-dependent components: foreground, background, tile, stipple, tile-stipple-x-origin, tile-stipple-y-origin

Request Encoding

# of Bytes	Value	Description
1	74	opcode
1		unused
2	4+(n+p)/4	request length
4	DRAWABLE	drawable
4	GCONTEXT	gc

# of Bytes	Value	Description
2	INT16	x
2	INT16	y
n	LISTofTEXTITEM8	items
p		unused, p=pad(n)
		(p must be 0 or 1)

LISTofTEXTITEM8 is *n* repetitions of the encoding for TEXTITEM8 shown in the tables below:

# of Bytes	Value	Description
1	m	length of string (cannot be 255)
1	INT8	delta
m	STRING8	string

or:

# of Bytes	Value	Description
1	255	font-shift indicator
1		font byte 3 (most-significant)
1		font byte 2
1		font byte 1
1		font byte 0 (least-significant)

Name
PolyText16

Request Contents
drawable: DRAWABLE
gc: GCONTEXT
x, y: INT16
items: LISTofTEXTITEM16

where:

TEXTITEM16:	TEXTELT16 or FONT
TEXTELT16:	[delta: INT8
	string: STRING16]

Errors
Drawable, **GContext**, **Match**, **Font**

Description
This request is similar to **PolyText8**, except 2-byte (or 16-bit) characters are used. For fonts defined with linear indexing rather than 2-byte matrix indexing, the server will interpret each CHAR2B as a 16-bit number that has been transmitted most-significant byte first (that is, byte1 of the CHAR2B is taken as the most-significant byte).

Request Encoding

# of Bytes	Value	Description
1	75	opcode
1		unused
2	4+(n+p)/4	request length
4	DRAWABLE	drawable
4	GCONTEXT	gc
2	INT16	x
2	INT16	y
n	LISTofTEXTITEM16	items
p		unused, p=pad(n) (p must be 0 or 1)

LISTofTEXTITEM16 is *n* repetitions of the encoding for TEXTITEM16 shown in the tables below:

# of Bytes	Value	Description
1	m	number of CHAR2Bs in string (cannot be 255)

# of Bytes	Value	Description
1	INT8	delta
n	STRING16	string

or:

# of Bytes	Value	Description
1	255	font-shift indicator
1		font byte 3 (most-significant)
1		font byte 2
1		font byte 1
1		font byte 0 (least-significant)

PropertyNotify

Name

PropertyNotify

Event Contents

window: WINDOW
atom: ATOM
state: {**NewValue**, **Deleted**}
time: TIMESTAMP

Description

This event is reported to clients selecting **PropertyChange** on the window and is generated with state **NewValue** when a property of the window is changed using **ChangeProperty** or **RotateProperties**, even when adding zero-length data using **ChangeProperty** and when replacing all or part of a property with identical data using **ChangeProperty** or **Rotate-Properties**. It is generated with state **Deleted** when a property of the window is deleted using request **DeleteProperty** or **GetProperty**. The timestamp indicates the server time when the property was changed.

Request Encoding

# of Bytes	Value	Description
1	28	code
1		unused
2	CARD16	sequence number
4	WINDOW	window
4	ATOM	atom
4	TIMESTAMP	time
1		state:
	0	**NewValue**
	1	**Deleted**
15		unused

Name

PutImage

Request Contents

drawable: DRAWABLE
gc: GCONTEXT
depth: CARD8
width, *height*: CARD16
dst-x, *dst-y*: INT16
left-pad: CARD8
format: {**Bitmap**, **XYPixmap**, **ZPixmap**}
data: LISTofBYTE

Errors

Drawable, **GContext**, **Match**, **Value**

Description

This request combines an image with a rectangle of the drawable. The dst-x and dst-y coordinates are relative to the drawable's origin.

If **Bitmap** format is used, then depth must be one (or a **Match** error results), and the image must be in XY format. The foreground pixel in gc defines the source for bits set to 1 in the image, and the background pixel defines the source for the bits set to 0.

For **XYPixmap** and **ZPixmap**, the depth must match the depth of the drawable (or a **Match** error results). For **XYPixmap**, the image must be sent in XY format. For **ZPixmap**, the image must be sent in the Z format defined for the given depth.

The left-pad must be zero for **ZPixmap** format (or a **Match** error results). For **Bitmap** and **XYPixmap** format, left-pad must be less than bitmap-scanline-pad as given in the server connection setup information (or a **Match** error results). The first left-pad bits in every scanline are to be ignored by the server. The actual image begins that many bits into the data. The width argument defines the width of the actual image and does not include left-pad.

GC components: function, plane-mask, subwindow-mode, clip-x-origin, clip-y-origin, clip-mask

GC mode-dependent components: foreground, background

Request Encoding

# of Bytes	Value	Description
1	72	opcode
1		format:
	0	**Bitmap**
	1	**XYPixmap**
	2	**ZPixmap**

# of Bytes	Value	Description
2	6+(n+p)/4	request length
4	DRAWABLE	drawable
4	GCONTEXT	gc
2	CARD16	width
2	CARD16	height
2	INT16	dst-x
2	INT16	dst-y
1	CARD8	left-pad
1	CARD8	depth
2		unused
n	LISTofBYTE	data
p		unused, p=pad(n)

QueryBestSize

Name
QueryBestSize

Request Contents
class: { **Cursor**, **Tile**, **Stipple** }
drawable: DRAWABLE
width, *height*: CARD16

Reply Contents
width, height: CARD16

Errors
Drawable, **Value**, **Match**

Description
This request returns the best size that is closest to the argument size. For **Cursor**, this is the largest size that can be fully displayed. For **Tile**, this is the size that can be tiled fastest. For **Stipple**, this is the size that can be stippled fastest.

For **Cursor**, the drawable indicates the desired screen. For **Tile** and **Stipple**, the drawable indicates the screen and also possibly the window class and depth. An **InputOnly** window cannot be used as the drawable for **Tile** or **Stipple** (or a **Match** error results).

Request Encoding

# of Bytes	Value	Description
1	97	opcode
1		class:
	0	**Cursor**
	1	**Tile**
	2	**Stipple**
2	3	request length
4	DRAWABLE	drawable
2	CARD16	width
2	CARD16	height

Reply Encoding

# of Bytes	Value	Description
1	1	reply
1		unused
2	CARD16	sequence number
4	0	reply length

# of Bytes	Value	Description
2	CARD16	width
2	CARD16	height
20		unused

Name
QueryColors

Request Contents
cmap: COLORMAP
pixels: LISTofCARD32

Reply Contents
colors: LISTofRGB

where:

RGB: [red, green, blue: CARD16]

Errors
Colormap, **Value**

Description
This request returns the hardware-specific color values stored in cmap for the specified pixels. The values returned for an unallocated entry are undefined. A **Value** error is generated if a pixel is not a valid index into cmap. If more than one pixel is in error, it is arbitrary as to which pixel is reported.

Request Encoding

# of Bytes	Value	Description
1	91	opcode
1		unused
2	2+n	request length
4	COLORMAP	cmap
4n	LISTofCARD32	pixels

Reply Encoding

# of Bytes	Value	Description
1	1	reply
1		unused
2	CARD16	sequence number
4	2n	reply length
2	n	number of RGBs in colors
22		unused
8n	LISTofRGB	colors

LISTofRGB is *n* repetitions of the encoding for RGB shown in the table below:

# of Bytes	Value	Description
2	CARD16	red
2	CARD16	green
2	CARD16	blue
2		unused

Name
QueryExtension

Request Contents
name: STRING8

Reply Contents
present: BOOL
major-opcode: CARD8
first-event: CARD8
first-error: CARD8

Errors
This request generates no errors.

Description
This request determines if the named extension is present. If so, the major opcode for the extension is returned, if it has one. Otherwise, zero is returned. Any minor opcode and the request formats are specific to the extension. If the extension involves additional event types, the base event type code is returned. Otherwise, zero is returned. The format of the events is specific to the extension. If the extension involves additional error codes, the base error code is returned. Otherwise, zero is returned. The format of additional data in the errors is specific to the extension.

The extension name should use the ISO Latin-1 encoding, and upper case and lower case matter.

Request Encoding

# of Bytes	Value	Description
1	98	opcode
1		unused
2	2+(n+p)/4	request length
2	n	length of name
2		unused
n	STRING8	name
p		unused, p=pad(n)

Reply Encoding

# of Bytes	Value	Description
1	1	reply
1		unused
2	CARD16	sequence number

# of Bytes	Value	Description
4	0	reply length
1	BOOL	present
1	CARD8	major-opcode
1	CARD8	first-event
1	CARD8	first-error
20		unused

Name
QueryFont

Request Contents
font: FONTABLE

Reply Contents
font-info: FONTINFO
char-infos: LISTofCHARINFO

where:

FONTINFO:	[draw-direction: {**LeftToRight**, **RightToLeft**}
	min-char-or-byte2, max-char-or-byte2: CARD16
	min-byte1, max-byte1: CARD8
	all-chars-exist: BOOL
	default-char: CARD16
	min-bounds: CHARINFO
	max-bounds: CHARINFO
	font-ascent: INT16
	font-descent: INT16
	properties: LISTofFONTPROP]
FONTPROP:	[name: ATOM
	value: 32-bit value]
CHARINFO:	[left-side-bearing: INT16
	right-side-bearing: INT16
	character-width: INT16
	ascent: INT16
	descent: INT16
	attributes: CARD16]

Errors
Font

Description
This request returns logical information about a font. If a gcontext is given for font, the currently contained font is used.

The draw-direction is just a hint and indicates whether most char-infos have a positive, **Left-ToRight**, or a negative, **RightToLeft**, character-width metric. The core protocol defines no support for vertical text.

If min-byte1 and max-byte1 are both zero, then min-char-or-byte2 specifies the linear character index corresponding to the first element of char-infos, and max-char-or-byte2 specifies the linear character index of the last element. If either min-byte1 or max-byte1 are nonzero, then both min-char-or-byte2 and max-char-or-byte2 will be less than 256 and the 2-byte character index values corresponding to char-infos element N (counting from 0) are:

```
byte1 = N/D + min-byte1
byte2 = N\D + min-char-or-byte2
```

where:

D   =   max-char-or-byte2 – min-char-or-byte2 + 1
/   =   integer division
\   =   integer modulus

If char-infos has length zero, then min-bounds and max-bounds will be identical, and the effective char-infos is one filled with this char-info, of length:

```
L = D * (max-byte1 - min-byte1 + 1)
```

That is, all glyphs in the specified linear or matrix range have the same information, as given by min-bounds (and max-bounds). If all-chars-exist is **True**, then all characters in char-infos have nonzero bounding boxes.

The default-char specifies the character that will be used when an undefined or nonexistent character is used. Note that default-char is a CARD16, not CHAR2B. For a font using 2-byte matrix format, the default-char has byte1 in the most-significant byte and byte2 in the least-significant byte. If the default-char itself specifies an undefined or nonexistent character, then no printing is performed for an undefined or nonexistent character.

The min-bounds and max-bounds contain the minimum and maximum values of each individual CHARINFO component over all char-infos (ignoring nonexistent characters). The bounding box of the font (that is, the smallest rectangle enclosing the shape obtained by superimposing all characters at the same origin [x,y]) has its upper-left coordinate at:

```
[x+min-bounds.left-side-bearing,y-max-bounds.ascent]
```

with a width of:

```
max-bounds.right-side-bearing - min-bounds.left-side-bearing
```

and a height of:

```
max-bounds.ascent + max-bounds.descent
```

The font-ascent is the logical extent of the font above the baseline and is used for determining line spacing. Specific characters may extend beyond this. The font-descent is the logical extent of the font at or below the baseline and is used for determining line spacing. Specific characters may extend beyond this. If the baseline is at Y-coordinate y, then the logical extent of the font is inclusive between the Y-coordinate values (y-font-ascent) and (y+font-descent-1).

A font is not guaranteed to have any properties. The interpretation of the property value (for example, INT32, CARD32) must be derived from a prior knowledge of the property.

A basic set of font properties is specified in the X Consortium standard *X Logical Font Description Conventions, Release 4*, which is reprinted as Appendix M in this manual.

For a character origin at [x,y], the bounding box of a character (that is, the smallest rectangle enclosing the character's shape), described in terms of CHARINFO components, is a rectangle with its upper-left corner at:

```
[x+left-side-bearing,y-ascent]
```

with a width of:

```
right-side-bearing - left-side-bearing
```

and a height of:

```
ascent + descent
```

and the origin for the next character is defined to be:

```
[x+character-width,y]
```

Note that the baseline is logically viewed as being just below nondescending characters (when descent is zero, only pixels with Y-coordinates less than y are drawn) and that the origin is logically viewed as being coincident with the left edge of a nonkerned character (when left-side-bearing is zero, no pixels with X-coordinate less than x are drawn).

Note that CHARINFO metric values can be negative.

A nonexistent character is represented with all CHARINFO components zero.

The interpretation of the per-character attributes field is server-dependent.

Request Encoding

# of Bytes	Value	Description
1	47	opcode
1		unused
2	2	request length
4	FONTABLE	font

Reply Encoding

# of Bytes	Value	Description
1	1	reply
1		unused
2	CARD16	sequence number
4	7+2n+3m	reply length
12	CHARINFO	min-bounds
4		unused
12	CHARINFO	max-bounds
4		unused

# of Bytes	Value	Description
2	CARD16	min-char-or-byte2
2	CARD16	max-char-or-byte2
2	CARD16	default-char
2	n	number of FONTPROPs in properties
1		draw-direction:
	0	**LeftToRight**
	1	**RightToLeft**
1	CARD8	min-byte1
1	CARD8	max-byte1
1	BOOL	all-chars-exist
2	INT16	font-ascent
2	INT16	font-descent
4	m	number of CHARINFOs in char-infos
8n	LISTofFONTPROP	properties
12m	LISTofCHARINFO	char-infos

LISTofFONTPROP is *n* repetitions of the encoding for FONTPROP shown in the table below:

# of Bytes	Value	Description
4	ATOM	name
4		value

LISTofCHARINFO is *n* repetitions of the encoding for CHARINFO shown in the table below:

# of Bytes	Value	Description
2	INT16	left-side-bearing
2	INT16	right-side-bearing
2	INT16	character-width
2	INT16	ascent
2	INT16	descent
2	CARD16	attributes

QueryKeymap

Name

QueryKeymap

Request Contents

Opcode and request length only.

Reply Contents

keys: LISTofCARD8

Errors

This request generates no errors.

Description

This request returns a bit vector for the logical state of the keyboard. Each bit set to 1 indicates that the corresponding key is currently pressed. The vector is represented as 32 bytes. Byte N (from 0) contains the bits for keys 8N to 8N+7 with the least-significant bit in the byte representing key 8N. Note that the logical state of a device (as seen by means of the protocol) may lag the physical state if device event processing is frozen.

Request Encoding

# of Bytes	Value	Description
1	44	opcode
1		unused
2	1	request length

Reply Encoding

# of Bytes	Value	Description
1	1	reply
1		unused
2	CARD16	sequence number
4	2	reply length
32	LISTofCARD8	keys

Name
QueryPointer

Request Contents
window: WINDOW

Reply Contents
root: WINDOW
child: WINDOW or **None**
same-screen: BOOL
root-x, root-y, win-x, win-y: INT16
mask: SETofKEYBUTMASK

Errors
Window

Description
The root window the pointer is logically on and the pointer coordinates relative to the root's origin are returned. If same-screen is **False**, then the pointer is not on the same screen as the argument window, child is **None**, and win-x and win-y are zero. If same-screen is **True**, then win-x and win-y are the pointer coordinates relative to the argument window's origin, and child is the child containing the pointer, if any. The current logical state of the modifier keys and the buttons are also returned. Note that the logical state of a device (as seen by means of the protocol) may lag the physical state if device event processing is frozen.

Request Encoding

# of Bytes	Value	Description
1	38	opcode
1		unused
2	2	request length
4	WINDOW	window

Reply Encoding

# of Bytes	Value	Description
1	1	reply
1	BOOL	same-screen
2	CARD16	sequence number
4	0	reply length
4	WINDOW	root
4	WINDOW	child:
	0	**None**

# of Bytes	Value	Description
2	INT16	root-x
2	INT16	root-y
2	INT16	win-x
2	INT16	win-y
2	SETofKEYBUTMASK	mask
6		unused

Name
QueryTextExtents

Request Contents
font: FONTABLE
string: STRING16

Reply Contents
draw-direction: {**LeftToRight**, **RightToLeft**}
font-ascent: INT16
font-descent: INT16
overall-ascent: INT16
overall-descent: INT16
overall-width: INT32
overall-left: INT32
overall-right: INT32

Errors
Font

Description
This request returns the logical extents of the specified string of characters in the specified font. If a gcontext is given for font, the currently contained font is used. The draw-direction, font-ascent, and font-descent are the same as described in **QueryFont**. The overall-ascent is the maximum of the ascent metrics of all characters in the string, and the overall-descent is the maximum of the descent metrics. The overall-width is the sum of the character-width metrics of all characters in the string. For each character in the string, let W be the sum of the character-width metrics of all characters preceding it in the string, let L be the left-side-bearing metric of the character plus W, and let R be the right-side-bearing metric of the character plus W. The overall-left is the minimum L of all characters in the string, and the overall-right is the maximum R.

For fonts defined with linear indexing rather than 2-byte matrix indexing, the server will interpret each CHAR2B as a 16-bit number that has been transmitted most-significant byte first (that is, byte1 of the CHAR2B is taken as the most-significant byte).

Characters with all zero metrics are ignored. If the font has no defined default-char, then undefined characters in the string are also ignored.

Request Encoding

# of Bytes	Value	Description
1	48	opcode
1	BOOL	odd length, True if p=2
2	2+(2n+p)/4	request length

# of Bytes	Value	Description
4	FONTABLE	font
2n	STRING16	string
p		unused, p=pad(2n)

Reply Encoding

# of Bytes	Value	Description
1	1	reply
1		draw-direction:
	0	**LeftToRight**
	1	**RightToLeft**
2	CARD16	sequence number
4	0	reply length
2	INT16	font-ascent
2	INT16	font-descent
2	INT16	overall-ascent
2	INT16	overall-descent
4	INT32	overall-width
4	INT32	overall-left
4	INT32	overall-right
4		unused

Name
QueryTree

Request Contents
window: WINDOW

Reply Contents
root: WINDOW
parent: WINDOW or **None**
children: LISTofWINDOW

Errors
Window

Description
This request returns the root, the parent, and the children of the window. The children are listed in bottom-to-top stacking order.

Request Encoding

# of Bytes	Value	Description
1	15	opcode
1		unused
2	2	request length
4	WINDOW	window

Reply Encoding

# of Bytes	Value	Description
1	1	reply
1		unused
2	CARD16	sequence number
4	n	reply length
4	WINDOW	root
4	WINDOW	parent:
	0	**None**
2	n	number of WINDOWs in children
14		unused
4n	LISTofWINDOW	children

RecolorCursor

Name
RecolorCursor

Request Contents
cursor: CURSOR
fore-red, fore-green, fore-blue: CARD16
back-red, back-green, back-blue: CARD16

Errors
Cursor

Description
This request changes the color of a cursor. If the cursor is being displayed on a screen, the change is visible immediately.

Request Encoding

# of Bytes	Value	Description
1	96	opcode
1		unused
2	5	request length
4	CURSOR	cursor
2	CARD16	fore-red
2	CARD16	fore-green
2	CARD16	fore-blue
2	CARD16	back-red
2	CARD16	back-green
2	CARD16	back-blue

ReparentNotify

Name
ReparentNotify

Event Contents
event, *window*, *parent*: WINDOW
x, *y*: INT16
override-redirect: BOOL

Description
This event is reported to clients selecting **SubstructureNotify** on either the old or the new parent and to clients selecting **StructureNotify** on the window. It is generated when the window is reparented. The event is the window on which the event was generated. The window is the window that has been rerooted. The parent specifies the new parent. The x and y coordinates are relative to the new parent's origin and specify the position of the upper-left outer corner of the window. The override-redirect flag is from the window's attribute.

Request Encoding

# of Bytes	Value	Description
1	21	code
1		unused
2	CARD16	sequence number
4	WINDOW	event
4	WINDOW	window
4	WINDOW	parent
2	INT16	x
2	INT16	y
1	BOOL	override-redirect
11		unused

ReparentWindow

Name

ReparentWindow

Request Contents

window, *parent*: WINDOW
x, *y*: INT16

Errors

Window, Match

Description

If the window is mapped, an **UnmapWindow** request is performed automatically first. The window is then removed from its current position in the hierarchy and is inserted as a child of the specified parent. The x and y coordinates are relative to the parent's origin and specify the new position of the upper-left outer corner of the window. The window is placed on top in the stacking order with respect to siblings. A **ReparentNotify** event is then generated. The over-ride-redirect attribute of the window is passed on in this event; a value of **True** indicates that a window manager should not tamper with this window. Finally, if the window was originally mapped, a **MapWindow** request is performed automatically.

Normal exposure processing on formerly obscured windows is performed. The server might not generate exposure events for regions from the initial unmap that are immediately obscured by the final map.

A **Match** error is generated if:

- The new parent is not on the same screen as the old parent.

- The new parent is the window itself or an inferior of the window.

- The window has a **ParentRelative** background, and the new parent is not the same depth as the window.

Request Encoding

# of Bytes	Value	Description
1	7	opcode
1		unused
2	4	request length
4	WINDOW	window
4	WINDOW	parent
2	INT16	x
2	INT16	y

Name

ResizeRequest

Event Contents

window: WINDOW
width, height: CARD16

Description

This event is reported to the client selecting **ResizeRedirect** on the window and is generated when a **ConfigureWindow** request by some other client on the window attempts to change the size of the window. The width and height are the inside size, not including the border.

Request Encoding

# of Bytes	Value	Description
1	25	code
1		unused
2	CARD16	sequence number
4	WINDOW	window
2	CARD16	width
2	CARD16	height
20		unused

RotateProperties

Name
RotateProperties

Request Contents
window: WINDOW
delta: INT16
properties: LISTofATOM

Errors
Window, **Atom**, **Match**

Description

If the property names in the list are viewed as being numbered starting from zero, and there are N property names in the list, then the value associated with property name I becomes the value associated with property name (I+delta)mod N, for all I from zero to N–1. The effect is to rotate the states by delta places around the virtual ring of property names (right for positive delta, left for negative delta).

If delta mod N is nonzero, a **PropertyNotify** event is generated for each property in the order listed.

If an atom occurs more than once in the list or no property with that name is defined for the window, a **Match** error is generated. If an **Atom** or a **Match** error is generated, no properties are changed.

Request Encoding

# of Bytes	Value	Description
1	114	opcode
1		unused
2	3+n	request length
4	WINDOW	window
2	n	number of properties
2	INT16	delta
4n	LISTofATOM	properties

Name

SelectionClear

Event Contents

owner: WINDOW
selection: ATOM
time: TIMESTAMP

Description

This event is reported to the current owner of a selection and is generated when a new owner is being defined by means of **SetSelectionOwner**. The timestamp is the last-change time recorded for the selection. The owner argument is the window that was specified by the current owner in its **SetSelectionOwner** request.

Request Encoding

# of Bytes	Value	Description
1	29	code
1		unused
2	CARD16	sequence number
4	TIMESTAMP	time
4	WINDOW	owner
4	ATOM	selection
16		unused

SelectionNotify

Name

SelectionNotify

Event Contents

requestor: WINDOW
selection, *target*: ATOM
property: ATOM or **None**
time: TIMESTAMP or **CurrentTime**

Description

This event is generated by the server in response to a **ConvertSelection** request when there is no owner for the selection. When there is an owner, it should be generated by the owner using **SendEvent**. The owner of a selection should send this event to a requestor either when a selection has been converted and stored as a property or when a selection conversion could not be performed (indicated with property **None**).

Request Encoding

# of Bytes	Value	Description
1	31	code
1		unused
2	CARD16	sequence number
4	TIMESTAMP	time:
	0	**CurrentTime**
4	WINDOW	requestor
4	ATOM	selection
4	ATOM	target
4	ATOM	property:
	0	**None**
8		unused

SelectionRequest

Name

SelectionRequest

Event Contents

owner: WINDOW
selection: ATOM
target: ATOM
property: ATOM or **None**
requestor: WINDOW
time: TIMESTAMP or **CurrentTime**

Description

This event is reported to the owner of a selection and is generated when a client issues a **ConvertSelection** request. The owner argument is the window that was specified in the **Set-SelectionOwner** request. The remaining arguments are as in the **ConvertSelection** request.

The owner should convert the selection based on the specified target type and send a **Selection-Notify** back to the requestor. A complete specification for using selections is given in the X Consortium standard *Inter-Client Communication Conventions Manual*, which is reprinted as Appendix L in this manual.

Request Encoding

# of Bytes	Value	Description
1	30	code
1		unused
2	CARD16	sequence number
4	TIMESTAMP	time:
	0	**CurrentTime**
4	WINDOW	owner
4	WINDOW	requestor
4	ATOM	selection
4	ATOM	target
4	ATOM	property:
	0	**None**
4		unused

Name

SendEvent

Request Contents

destination: WINDOW or **PointerWindow** or **InputFocus**
propagate: BOOL
event-mask: SETofEVENT
event: any event

Errors

Window, **Value**

Description

If **PointerWindow** is specified, destination is replaced with the window that the pointer is in. If **InputFocus** is specified and the focus window contains the pointer, destination is replaced with the window that the pointer is in. Otherwise, destination is replaced with the focus window.

If the event-mask is the empty set, then the event is sent to the client that created the destination window. If that client no longer exists, no event is sent.

If propagate is **False**, then the event is sent to every client selecting on destination any of the event types in event-mask.

If propagate is **True** and no clients have selected on destination any of the event types in event-mask, then destination is replaced with the closest ancestor of destination for which some client has selected a type in event-mask and no intervening window has that type in its do-not-propagate-mask. If no such window exists or if the window is an ancestor of the focus window and **InputFocus** was originally specified as the destination, then the event is not sent to any clients. Otherwise, the event is reported to every client selecting on the final destination any of the types specified in event-mask.

The event code must be one of the core events or one of the events defined by an extension (or a **Value** error results) so that the server can correctly byte-swap the contents as necessary. The contents of the event are otherwise unaltered and unchecked by the server except to force on the most-significant bit of the event code and to set the sequence number in the event correctly.

Active grabs are ignored for this request.

Request Encoding

# of Bytes	Value	Description
1	25	opcode
1	BOOL	propagate
2	11	request length
4	WINDOW	destination:
	0	**PointerWindow**
	1	**InputFocus**

# of Bytes	Value	Description
4	SETofEVENT	event-mask
32		standard event format

SetAccessControl

Name

SetAccessControl

Request Contents

mode: {**Enable**, **Disable**}

Errors

Value, **Access**

Description

This request enables or disables the use of the access control list at connection setups.

The client must reside on the same host as the server and/or have been granted permission by a server-dependent method to execute this request (or an **Access** error results).

Request Encoding

# of Bytes	Value	Description
1	111	opcode
1		mode:
	0	**Disable**
	1	**Enable**
2	1	request length

SetClipRectangles

Name

SetClipRectangles

Request Contents

gc: GCONTEXT
clip-x-origin, *clip-y-origin*: INT16
rectangles: LISTofRECTANGLE
ordering: { **UnSorted**, **YSorted**, **YXSorted**, **YXBanded** }

Errors

GContext, **Value**, **Alloc**, **Match**

Description

This request changes clip-mask in gc to the specified list of rectangles and sets the clip origin. Output will be clipped to remain contained within the rectangles. The clip origin is interpreted relative to the origin of whatever destination drawable is specified in a graphics request. The rectangle coordinates are interpreted relative to the clip origin. The rectangles should be nonintersecting or graphics results will be undefined. Note that the list of rectangles can be empty, which effectively disables output. This is the opposite of passing **None** as the clip-mask in **CreateGC** and **ChangeGC**.

If known by the client, ordering relations on the rectangles can be specified with the ordering argument. This may provide faster operation by the server. If an incorrect ordering is specified, the server may generate a **Match** error, but it is not required to do so. If no error is generated, the graphics results are undefined. **UnSorted** means that the rectangles are in arbitrary order. **YSorted** means that the rectangles are nondecreasing in their Y origin. **YXSorted** additionally constrains **YSorted** order in that all rectangles with an equal Y origin are nondecreasing in their X origin. **YXBanded** additionally constrains **YXSorted** by requiring that, for every possible Y scanline, all rectangles that include that scanline have identical Y origins and Y extents.

Request Encoding

# of Bytes	Value	Description
1	59	opcode
1		ordering:
	0	**UnSorted**
	1	**YSorted**
	2	**YXSorted**
	3	**YXBanded**
2	3+2n	request length
4	GCONTEXT	gc

# of Bytes	Value	Description
2	INT16	clip-x-origin
2	INT16	clip-y-origin
8n	LISTofRECTANGLE	rectangles

Name

SetCloseDownMode

Request Contents

mode: {**Destroy**, **RetainPermanent**, **RetainTemporary**}

Errors

Value

Description

This request defines what will happen to the client's resources at connection close. A connection starts in **Destroy** mode. The meaning of the close-down mode is described in Appendix A, *Connection Close*.

Request Encoding

# of Bytes	Value	Description
1	112	opcode
1		mode:
	0	**Destroy**
	1	**RetainPermanent**
	2	**RetainTemporary**
2	1	request length

SetDashes

Name

SetDashes

Request Contents

gc: GCONTEXT
dash-offset: CARD16
dashes: LISTofCARD8

Errors

GContext, Value, Alloc

Description

This request sets dash-offset and dashes in gc for dashed line styles. Dashes cannot be empty (or a **Value** error results). Specifying an odd-length list is equivalent to specifying the same list concatenated with itself to produce an even-length list. The initial and alternating elements of dashes are the even dashes; the others are the odd dashes. Each element specifies a dash length in pixels. All of the elements must be nonzero (or a **Value** error results). The dash-offset defines the phase of the pattern, specifying how many pixels into dashes the pattern should actually begin in any single graphics request. Dashing is continuous through path elements combined with a join-style but is reset to the dash-offset between each sequence of joined lines.

The unit of measure for dashes is the same as in the ordinary coordinate system. Ideally, a dash length is measured along the slope of the line, but implementations are only required to match this ideal for horizontal and vertical lines. Failing the ideal semantics, it is suggested that the length be measured along the major axis of the line. The major axis is defined as the x axis for lines drawn at an angle of between -45 and $+45$ degrees or between 315 and 225 degrees from the x axis. For all other lines, the major axis is the y axis.

Request Encoding

# of Bytes	Value	Description
1	58	opcode
1		unused
2	3+(n+p)/4	request length
4	GCONTEXT	gc
2	CARD16	dash-offset
2	n	length of dashes
n	LISTofCARD8	dashes
p		unused, p=pad(n)

Name

SetFontPath

Request Contents

path: LISTofSTRING8

Errors

Value

Description

This request defines the search path for font lookup. There is only one search path per server, not one per client. The interpretation of the strings is operating-system-dependent, but the strings are intended to specify directories to be searched in the order listed.

Setting the path to the empty list restores the default path defined for the server.

As a side effect of executing this request, the server is guaranteed to flush all cached information about fonts for which there currently are no explicit resource IDs allocated.

The meaning of an error from this request is system specific.

Request Encoding

# of Bytes	Value	Description
1	51	opcode
1		unused
2	2+(n+p)/4	request length
2	CARD16	number of STRs in path
2		unused
n	LISTofSTR	path
p		unused, p=pad(n)

SetInputFocus

Name

SetInputFocus

Request Contents

focus: WINDOW or **PointerRoot** or **None**
revert-to: {**Parent**, **PointerRoot**, **None**}
time: TIMESTAMP or **CurrentTime**

Errors

Window, **Value**, **Match**

Description

This request changes the input focus and the last-focus-change time. The request has no effect if the specified time is earlier than the current last-focus-change time or is later than the current server time. Otherwise, the last-focus-change time is set to the specified time with **Current-Time** replaced by the current server time.

If **None** is specified as the focus, all keyboard events are discarded until a new focus window is set. In this case, the revert-to argument is ignored.

If a window is specified as the focus, it becomes the keyboard's focus window. If a generated keyboard event would normally be reported to this window or one of its inferiors, the event is reported normally. Otherwise, the event is reported with respect to the focus window.

If **PointerRoot** is specified as the focus, the focus window is dynamically taken to be the root window of whatever screen the pointer is on at each keyboard event. In this case, the revert-to argument is ignored.

This request generates **FocusIn** and **FocusOut** events.

The specified focus window must be viewable at the time of the request (or a **Match** error results). If the focus window later becomes not viewable, the new focus window depends on the revert-to argument. If revert-to is **Parent**, the focus reverts to the parent (or the closest viewable ancestor) and the new revert-to value is taken to be **None**. If revert-to is **Pointer-Root** or **None**, the focus reverts to that value. When the focus reverts, **FocusIn** and **Focus-Out** events are generated, but the last-focus-change time is not affected.

Request Encoding

# of Bytes	Value	Description
1	42	opcode
1		revert-to:
	0	**None**
	1	**PointerRoot**
	2	**Parent**
2	3	request length

# of Bytes	Value	Description
4	WINDOW	focus:
	0	**None**
	1	**PointerRoot**
4	TIMESTAMP	time:
	0	**CurrentTime**

SetModifierMapping

Name
SetModifierMapping

Request Contents
keycodes-per-modifier : CARD8
keycodes : LISTofKEYCODE

Reply Contents
status: {**Success**, **Busy**, **Failed**}

Errors
Value, **Alloc**

Description
This request specifies the keycodes (if any) of the keys to be used as modifiers. The number of keycodes in the list must be 8*keycodes-per-modifier (or a **Length** error results). The keycodes are divided into eight sets, with each set containing keycodes-per-modifier elements. The sets are assigned to the modifiers **Shift**, **Lock**, **Control**, **Mod1**, **Mod2**, **Mod3**, **Mod4**, and **Mod5**, in order. Only nonzero keycode values are used within each set; zero values are ignored. All of the nonzero keycodes must be in the range specified by min-keycode and max-keycode in the connection setup (or a **Value** error results). The order of keycodes within a set does not matter. If no nonzero values are specified in a set, the use of the corresponding modifier is disabled, and the modifier bit will always be zero. Otherwise, the modifier bit will be one whenever at least one of the keys in the corresponding set is in the down position.

A server can impose restrictions on how modifiers can be changed (for example, if certain keys do not generate up transitions in hardware, if auto-repeat cannot be disabled on certain keys, or if multiple keys per modifier are not supported). The status reply is **Failed** if some such restriction is violated, and none of the modifiers are changed.

If the new nonzero keycodes specified for a modifier differ from those currently defined and any (current or new) keys for that modifier are logically in the down state, then the status reply is **Busy**, and none of the modifiers are changed.

This request generates a **MappingNotify** event on a **Success** status.

Request Encoding

# of Bytes	Value	Description
1	118	opcode
1	n	keycodes-per-modifier
2	1+2n	request length
8n	LISTofKEYCODE	keycodes

Reply Encoding

# of Bytes	Value	Description
1	1	reply
1		status:
	0	**Success**
	1	**Busy**
	2	**Failed**
2	CARD16	sequence number
4	0	reply length
24		unused

SetPointerMapping

Name
SetPointerMapping

Request Contents
map: LISTofCARD8

Reply Contents
status: {**Success**, **Busy**}

Errors
Value

Description
This request sets the mapping of the pointer. Elements of the list are indexed starting from one. The length of the list must be the same as **GetPointerMapping** would return (or a **Value** error results). The index is a core button number, and the element of the list defines the effective number.

A zero element disables a button. Elements are not restricted in value by the number of physical buttons, but no two elements can have the same nonzero value (or a **Value** error results).

If any of the buttons to be altered are logically in the down state, the status reply is **Busy**, and the mapping is not changed.

This request generates a **MappingNotify** event on a **Success** status.

Request Encoding

# of Bytes	Value	Description
1	116	opcode
1	n	length of map
2	1+(n+p)/4	request length
n	LISTofCARD8	map
p		unused, p=pad(n)

Reply Encoding

# of Bytes	Value	Description
1	1	reply
1		status:
	0	**Success**
	1	**Busy**

# of Bytes	Value	Description
2	CARD16	sequence number
4	0	reply length
24		unused

SetScreenSaver

Name

SetScreenSaver

Request Contents

timeout, *interval*: INT16
prefer-blanking: {**Yes**, **No**, **Default**}
allow-exposures: {**Yes**, **No**, **Default**}

Errors

Value

Description

The timeout and interval are specified in seconds; setting a value to –1 restores the default. Other negative values generate a **Value** error. If the timeout value is zero, screen-saver is disabled (but an activated screen-saver is not deactivated). If the timeout value is nonzero, screen-saver is enabled. Once screen-saver is enabled, if no input from the keyboard or pointer is generated for timeout seconds, screen-saver is activated. For each screen, if blanking is preferred and the hardware supports video blanking, the screen will simply go blank. Otherwise, if either exposures are allowed or the screen can be regenerated without sending exposure events to clients, the screen is changed in a server-dependent fashion to avoid phosphor burn. Otherwise, the state of the screens does not change, and screen-saver is not activated. At the next keyboard or pointer input or at the next **ForceScreenSaver** with mode **Reset**, screen-saver is deactivated, and all screen states are restored.

If the server-dependent screen-saver method is amenable to periodic change, interval serves as a hint about how long the change period should be, with zero hinting that no periodic change should be made. Examples of ways to change the screen include scrambling the color map periodically, moving an icon image about the screen periodically, or tiling the screen with the root window background tile, randomly reoriginated periodically.

Request Encoding

# of Bytes	Value	Description
1	107	opcode
1		unused
2	3	request length
2	INT16	timeout
2	INT16	interval
1		prefer-blanking:
	0	**No**
	1	**Yes**
	2	**Default**

# of Bytes	Value	Description
1		allow-exposures:
	0	**No**
	1	**Yes**
	2	**Default**
2		unused

SetSelectionOwner

Name

SetSelectionOwner

Request Contents

selection: ATOM
owner: WINDOW or **None**
time: TIMESTAMP or **CurrentTime**

Errors

Atom, **Window**

Description

This request changes the owner, owner window, and last-change time of the specified selection. This request has no effect if the specified time is earlier than the current last-change time of the specified selection or is later than the current server time. Otherwise, the last-change time is set to the specified time with **CurrentTime** replaced by the current server time. If the owner window is specified as **None**, then the owner of the selection becomes **None** (that is, no owner). Otherwise, the owner of the selection becomes the client executing the request. If the new owner (whether a client or **None**) is not the same as the current owner and the current owner is not **None**, then the current owner is sent a **SelectionClear** event.

If the client that is the owner of a selection is later terminated (that is, its connection is closed) or if the owner window it has specified in the request is later destroyed, then the owner of the selection automatically reverts to **None**, but the last-change time is not affected.

The selection atom is uninterpreted by the server. The owner window is returned by the **Get-SelectionOwner** request and is reported in **SelectionRequest** and **SelectionClear** events.

Selections are global to the server.

Request Encoding

# of Bytes	Value	Description
1	22	opcode
1		unused
2	4	request length
4	WINDOW	owner:
	0	**None**
4	ATOM	selection
4	TIMESTAMP	time:
	0	**CurrentTime**

Name

StoreColors

Request Contents

cmap: COLORMAP
items: LISTofCOLORITEM

where:

      COLORITEM: [pixel: CARD32
                      do-red, do-green, do-blue: BOOL
                      red, green, blue: CARD16]

Errors

Colormap, **Access**, **Value**

Description

This request changes the colormap entries of the specified pixels. The do-red, do-green, and do-blue fields indicate which components should actually be changed. If the colormap is an installed map for its screen, the changes are visible immediately.

All specified pixels that are allocated writable in cmap (by any client) are changed, even if one or more pixels produce an error. A **Value** error is generated if a specified pixel is not a valid index into cmap, and an **Access** error is generated if a specified pixel is unallocated or is allocated read-only. If more than one pixel is in error, it is arbitrary as to which pixel is reported.

Request Encoding

# of Bytes	Value	Description
1	89	opcode
1		unused
2	2+3n	request length
4	COLORMAP	cmap
12n	LISTofCOLORITEM	items

LISTofCOLORITEM is *n* repetitions of the encoding for COLORITEM shown in the table below:

# of Bytes	Value	Description
4	CARD32	pixel
2	CARD16	red
2	CARD16	green
2	CARD16	blue

# of Bytes	Value	Description
1		do-red, do-green, do-blue:
	#x01	do-red (1 is True, 0 is False)
	#x02	do-green (1 is True, 0 is False)
	#x04	do-blue (1 is True, 0 is False)
	#xf8	unused
1		unused

StoreNamedColor

Name

StoreNamedColor

Request Contents

cmap: COLORMAP
pixel: CARD32
name: STRING8
do-red, do-green, do-blue: BOOL

Errors

Colormap, **Name**, **Access**, **Value**

Description

This request looks up the named color with respect to the screen associated with cmap and then does a **StoreColors** in cmap. The name should use the ISO Latin-1 encoding, and upper case and lower case do not matter. The **Access** and **Value** errors are the same as in **StoreColors**.

Request Encoding

# of Bytes	Value	Description
1	90	opcode
1		do-red, do-green, do-blue:
	#x01	do-red (1 is True, 0 is False)
	#x02	do-green (1 is True, 0 is False)
	#x04	do-blue (1 is True, 0 is False)
	#xf8	unused
2	4+(n+p)/4	request length
4	COLORMAP	cmap
4	CARD32	pixel
2	n	length of name
2		unused
n	STRING8	name
p		unused, p=pad(n)

TranslateCoordinates

Name

TranslateCoordinates

Request Contents

src-window, *dst-window*: WINDOW
src-x, *src-y*: INT16

Reply Contents

same-screen: BOOL
child: WINDOW or **None**
dst-x, dst-y: INT16

Errors

Window

Description

The src-x and src-y coordinates are taken relative to src-window's origin and are returned as dst-x and dst-y coordinates relative to dst-window's origin. If same-screen is **False**, then src-window and dst-window are on different screens, and dst-x and dst-y are zero. If the coordinates are contained in a mapped child of dst-window, then that child is returned.

Request Encoding

# of Bytes	Value	Description
1	40	opcode
1		unused
2	4	request length
4	WINDOW	src-window
4	WINDOW	dst-window
2	INT16	src-x
2	INT16	src-y

Reply Encoding

# of Bytes	Value	Description
1	1	reply
1	BOOL	same-screen
2	CARD16	sequence number
4	0	reply length
4	WINDOW	child:
	0	**None**

# of Bytes	Value	Description
2	INT16	dst-x
2	INT16	dst-y
16		unused

UngrabButton

Name

UngrabButton

Request Contents

modifiers: SETofKEYMASK or **AnyModifier**
button: BUTTON or **AnyButton**
grab-window: WINDOW

Errors

Window, **Value**

Description

This request releases the passive button/key combination on the specified window if it was grabbed by this client. A modifiers argument of **AnyModifier** is equivalent to issuing the request for all possible modifier combinations (including the combination of no modifiers). A button of **AnyButton** is equivalent to issuing the request for all possible buttons. The request has no effect on an active grab.

Request Encoding

# of Bytes	Value	Description
1	29	opcode
1	BUTTON	button:
	0	**AnyButton**
2	3	request length
4	WINDOW	grab-window
2	SETofKEYMASK	modifiers:
	#x8000	**AnyModifier**
2		unused

Name

UngrabKey

Request Contents

key: KEYCODE or **AnyKey**
modifiers: SETofKEYMASK or **AnyModifier**
grab-window: WINDOW

Errors

Window, **Value**

Description

This request releases the key combination on the specified window if it was grabbed by this client. A modifiers argument of **AnyModifier** is equivalent to issuing the request for all possible modifier combinations (including the combination of no modifiers). A key of **AnyKey** is equivalent to issuing the request for all possible keycodes. This request has no effect on an active grab.

Request Encoding

# of Bytes	Value	Description
1	34	opcode
1	KEYCODE	key:
	0	**AnyKey**
2	3	request length
4	WINDOW	grab-window
2	SETofKEYMASK	modifiers:
	#x8000	**AnyModifier**
2		unused

UngrabKeyboard

Name

UngrabKeyboard

Request Contents

time: TIMESTAMP or **CurrentTime**

Errors

This request generates no errors.

Description

This request releases the keyboard if this client has it actively grabbed (as a result of either **GrabKeyboard** or **GrabKey**) and releases any queued events. The request has no effect if the specified time is earlier than the last-keyboard-grab time or is later than the current server time.

This request generates **FocusIn** and **FocusOut** events.

An **UngrabKeyboard** is performed automatically if the event window for an active keyboard grab becomes not viewable.

Request Encoding

# of Bytes	Value	Description
1	32	opcode
1		unused
2	2	request length
4	TIMESTAMP	time:
	0	**CurrentTime**

Name

UngrabPointer

Request Contents

time: TIMESTAMP or **CurrentTime**

Errors

This request generates no errors.

Description

This request releases the pointer if this client has it actively grabbed (from either **GrabPointer** or **GrabButton** or from a normal button press) and releases any queued events. The request has no effect if the specified time is earlier than the last-pointer-grab time or is later than the current server time.

This request generates **EnterNotify** and **LeaveNotify** events.

An **UngrabPointer** request is performed automatically if the event window or confine-to window for an active pointer grab becomes not viewable or if window reconfiguration causes the confine-to window to lie completely outside the boundaries of the root window.

Request Encoding

# of Bytes	Value	Description
1	27	opcode
1		unused
2	2	request length
4	TIMESTAMP	time:
	0	**CurrentTime**

UngrabServer

Name
UngrabServer

Request Contents
Opcode and request length only.

Errors
This request generates no errors.

Description
This request restarts processing of requests and close-downs on other connections.

Request Encoding

# of Bytes	Value	Description
1	37	opcode
1		unused
2	1	request length

UninstallColormap

Name

UninstallColormap

Request Contents

cmap: COLORMAP

Errors

Colormap

Description

If cmap is on the required list for its screen (see **InstallColormap** request), it is removed from the list. As a side effect, cmap might be uninstalled, and additional colormaps might be implicitly installed or uninstalled. Which colormaps get installed or uninstalled is server-dependent except that the required list must remain installed.

If cmap becomes uninstalled, a **ColormapNotify** event is generated on every window having cmap as an attribute. In addition, for every other colormap that is installed or uninstalled as a result of the request, a **ColormapNotify** event is generated on every window having that colormap as an attribute.

Request Encoding

# of Bytes	Value	Description
1	82	opcode
1		unused
2	2	request length
4	COLORMAP	cmap

UnmapNotify

Name

UnmapNotify

Event Contents

event, window: WINDOW
from-configure: BOOL

Errors

This request generates no errors.

Description

This event is reported to clients selecting **StructureNotify** on the window and to clients selecting **SubstructureNotify** on the parent. It is generated when the window changes state from mapped to unmapped. The event is the window on which the event was generated, and the window is the window that is unmapped. The from-configure flag is **True** if the event was generated as a result of the window's parent being resized when the window itself had a win-gravity of **Unmap**.

Request Encoding

# of Bytes	Value	Description
1	18	code
1		unused
2	CARD16	sequence number
4	WINDOW	event
4	WINDOW	window
1	BOOL	from-configure
19		unused

Name
UnmapSubwindows

Request Contents
window: WINDOW

Errors
Window

Description
This request performs an **UnmapWindow** request on all mapped children of the window, in bottom-to-top stacking order.

Request Encoding

# of Bytes	Value	Description
1	11	opcode
1		unused
2	2	request length
4	WINDOW	window

UnmapWindow

Name

UnmapWindow

Request Contents

window: WINDOW

Errors

Window

Description

If the window is already unmapped, this request has no effect. Otherwise, the window is unmapped, and an **UnmapNotify** event is generated. Normal exposure processing on formerly obscured windows is performed.

Request Encoding

# of Bytes	Value	Description
1	10	opcode
1		unused
2	2	request length
4	WINDOW	window

VisibilityNotify

Name

VisibilityNotify

Event Contents

window: WINDOW
state: {**Unobscured**, **PartiallyObscured**, **FullyObscured**}

Description

This event is reported to clients selecting **VisibilityChange** on the window. In the following, the state of the window is calculated ignoring all of the window's subwindows. When a window changes state from partially or fully obscured or not viewable to viewable and completely unobscured, an event with **Unobscured** is generated. When a window changes state from viewable and completely unobscured or not viewable to viewable and partially obscured, an event with **PartiallyObscured** is generated. When a window changes state from viewable and completely unobscured, from viewable and partially obscured, or from not viewable to viewable and fully obscured, an event with **FullyObscured** is generated.

VisibilityNotify events are never generated on **InputOnly** windows.

All **VisibilityNotify** events caused by a hierarchy change are generated after any hierarchy event caused by that change (for example, **UnmapNotify**, **MapNotify**, **ConfigureNotify**, **GravityNotify**, **CirculateNotify**). Any **VisibilityNotify** event on a given window is generated before any **Expose** events on that window, but it is not required that all **Visibility-Notify** events on all windows be generated before all **Expose** events on all windows. The ordering of **VisibilityNotify** events with respect to **FocusOut**, **EnterNotify**, and **LeaveNotify** events is not constrained.

Request Encoding

# of Bytes	Value	Description
1	15	code
1		unused
2	CARD16	sequence number
4	WINDOW	window
1		state:
	0	**Unobscured**
	1	**PartiallyObscured**
	2	**FullyObscured**
23		unused

WarpPointer

Name

WarpPointer

Request Contents

src-window: WINDOW or **None**
dst-window: WINDOW or **None**
src-x, src-y: INT16
src-width, src-height: CARD16
dst-x, dst-y: INT16

Errors

Window

Description

If dst-window is **None**, this request moves the pointer by offsets [dst-x,dst-y] relative to the current position of the pointer. If dst-window is a window, this request moves the pointer to [dst-x,dst-y] relative to dst-window's origin. However, if src-window is not **None**, the move only takes place if src-window contains the pointer and the pointer is contained in the specified rectangle of src-window.

The src-x and src-y coordinates are relative to src-window's origin. If src-height is zero, it is replaced with the current height of src-window minus src-y. If src-width is zero, it is replaced with the current width of src-window minus src-x.

This request cannot be used to move the pointer outside the confine-to window of an active pointer grab. An attempt will only move the pointer as far as the closest edge of the confine-to window.

This request will generate events just as if the user had instantaneously moved the pointer.

Request Encoding

# of Bytes	Value	Description
1	41	opcode
1		unused
2	6	request length
4	WINDOW	src-window:
	0	**None**
4	WINDOW	dst-window:
	0	**None**
2	INT16	src-x
2	INT16	src-y

# of Bytes	Value	Description
2	CARD16	src-width
2	CARD16	src-height
2	INT16	dst-x
2	INT16	dst-y

Part Three:

Appendices

Part Three consists of background material from the X protocol specification (Appendices A through F), reference aids (Appendices G through K), and convention manuals (Appendices L and M).

Connection Close
Keysyms
Errors
Predefined Atoms
Flow Control and Concurrency

Request Group Summary
Alphabetical Listing of Requests
Xlib Functions to Protocol Requests
Protocol Requests to Xlib Functions
Events Briefly Described

Interclient Communications Conventions
Logical Font Description Conventions, Release 4

A
Connection Close

At connection close, all event selections made by the client are discarded. If the client has the pointer actively grabbed, an **UngrabPointer** is performed. If the client has the keyboard actively grabbed, an **UngrabKeyboard** is performed. All passive grabs by the client are released. If the client has the server grabbed, an **UngrabServer** is performed. All selections (see **SetSelectionOwner** request) owned by the client are disowned. If close-down mode (see **SetCloseDownMode** request) is **RetainPermanent** or **RetainTemporary**, then all resources (including colormap entries) allocated by the client are marked as permanent or temporary, respectively (but this does not prevent other clients from explicitly destroying them). If the mode is **Destroy**, all of the client's resources are destroyed.

When a client's resources are destroyed, for each window in the client's save-set, if the window is an inferior of a window created by the client, the save-set window is reparented to the closest ancestor such that the save-set window is not an inferior of a window created by the client. If the save-set window is unmapped, a **MapWindow** request is performed on it (even if it was not an inferior of a window created by the client). The reparenting leaves unchanged the absolute coordinates (with respect to the root window) of the upper-left outer corner of the save-set window. After save-set processing, all windows created by the client are destroyed. For each nonwindow resource created by the client, the appropriate **Free** request is performed. All colors and colormap entries allocated by the client are freed.

A server goes through a cycle of having no connections and having some connections. At every transition to the state of having no connections as a result of a connection closing with a **Destroy** close-down mode, the server resets its state as if it had just been started. This starts by destroying all lingering resources from clients that have terminated in **Retain-Permanent** or **RetainTemporary** mode. It additionally includes deleting all but the predefined atom identifiers, deleting all properties on all root windows, resetting all device maps and attributes (key click, bell volume, acceleration), resetting the access control list, restoring the standard root tiles and cursors, restoring the default font path, and restoring the input focus to state **PointerRoot**.

Note that closing a connection with a close-down mode of **RetainPermanent** or **Retain-Temporary** will not cause the server to reset.

B
Keysyms

X Protocol X11, Release 3

For convenience, keysym values are viewed as split into four bytes:

- Byte 1 (for the purposes of this encoding) is the most-significant 5 bits (because of the 29-bit effective values).

- Byte 2 is the next most-significant 8 bits.

- Byte 3 is the next most-significant 8 bits.

- Byte 4 is the least-significant 8 bits.

There are two special KEYSYM values: NoSymbol and VoidSymbol.

Byte 1	Byte 2	Byte 3	Byte 4	Name
0	0	0	0	NoSymbol
0	255	255	255	VoidSymbol

All other standard KEYSYM values have zero values for bytes 1 and 2. Byte 3 indicates a character code set, and byte 4 indicates a particular character within that set.

Byte 3	Byte 4
0	Latin-1
1	Latin-2
2	Latin-3
3	Latin-4
4	Kana
5	Arabic
6	Cyrillic
7	Greek
8	Technical
9	Special
10	Publishing
11	Apl

Byte 3	Byte 4
12	Hebrew
255	Keyboard

Each character set contains gaps where codes have been removed that were duplicates with codes in previous character sets (that is, character sets with lesser byte 3 value).

The 94 and 96 character code sets have been moved to occupy the right-hand quadrant (decimal 129 through 256), so the ASCII subset has a unique encoding across byte 4, which corresponds to the ASCII character code. However, this cannot be guaranteed with future registrations and does not apply to all of the Keyboard set.

To the best of our knowledge, the Latin, Kana, Arabic, Cyrillic, Greek, Apl, and Hebrew sets are from the appropriate ISO and/or ECMA international standards. There are no Technical, Special, or Publishing international standards, so these sets are based on Digital Equipment Corporation standards.

The ordering between the sets (byte 3) is essentially arbitrary. National and international standards bodies were commencing deliberations regarding international 2-byte and 4-byte character sets at the time these keysyms were developed, but we did not know of any proposed layouts.

The order may be arbitrary, but it is important in dealing with duplicate coding. As far as possible, keysym values (byte 4) follow the character set encoding standards, except for the Greek and Cyrillic keysyms, which are based on early draft standards. In the Latin-1 to Latin-4 sets, all duplicate glyphs occupy the same code position. However, duplicates between Greek and Technical do not occupy the same code position. Applications that wish to use the Latin-2, Latin-3, Latin-4, Greek, Cyrillic, or Technical sets may find it convenient to use arrays to transform the keysyms.

There is a difference between European and U.S. usage of the names Pilcrow, Paragraph, and Section, as follows:

U.S. Name	European Name	Code Position in Latin-1
Section sign	Paragraph sign	10/07
Paragraph sign	Pilcrow sign	11/06

We have adopted the U.S. names (by accident rather than by design).

The Keyboard set is a miscellaneous collection of commonly occurring keys on keyboards. Within this set, the keypad symbols are generally duplicates of symbols found on keys on the main part of the keyboard, but they are distinguished here because they often have a distinguishable semantics associated with them.

Keyboards tend to be comparatively standard with respect to the alphanumeric keys, but they differ radically on the miscellaneous function keys. Many function keys are left over from early timesharing days or are designed for a specific application. Keyboard layouts from large manufacturers tend to have lots of keys for every conceivable purpose, whereas small workstation manufacturers often add keys that are solely for support of some of their unique functionality. There are two ways of thinking about how to define keysyms for such a world:

- The Engraving approach

- The Common approach

The Engraving approach is to create a keysym for every unique key engraving. This is effectively taking the union of all key engravings on all keyboards. For example, some keyboards label function keys across the top as F1 through Fn, and others label them as PF1 through PFn. These would be different keys under the Engraving approach. Likewise, Lock would differ from Shift Lock, which is different from the up-arrow symbol that has the effect of changing lower case to upper case. There are lots of other aliases such as Del, DEL, Delete, Remove, and so forth. The Engraving approach makes it easy to decide if a new entry should be added to the keysym set: if it does not exactly match an existing one, then a new one is created. One estimate is that there would be on the order of 300 to 500 Keyboard keysyms using this approach, without counting foreign translations and variations.

The Common approach tries to capture all of the keys present on an interesting number of keyboards, folding likely aliases into the same keysym. For example, Del, DEL, and Delete are all merged into a single keysym. Vendors would be expected to augment the keysym set (using the vendor-specific encoding space) to include all of their unique keys that were not included in the standard set. Each vendor decides which of its keys map into the standard keysyms, which presumably can be overridden by a user. It is more difficult to implement this approach, because judgment is required about when a sufficient set of keyboards implements an engraving to justify making it a keysym in the standard set and about which engravings should be merged into a single keysym. Under this scheme, there are an estimated 100 to 150 keysyms.

Although neither scheme is perfect or elegant, the Common approach has been selected because it makes it easier to write a portable application. Having the Delete functionality merged into a single keysym allows an application to implement a deletion function and expect reasonable bindings on a wide set of workstations. Under the Common approach, application writers are still free to look for and interpret vendor-specific keysyms, but because they are in the extended set, the application developer is more conscious that they are writing the application in a nonportable fashion.

In the listings below, Code Pos is a representation of byte 4 of the keysym value, expressed as most-significant/least-significant 4-bit values. The Code Pos numbers are for reference only and do not affect the keysym value. In all cases, the keysym value is:

```
byte3 * 256 + byte4
```

Byte	Byte	Code	Name	Set
000	032	02/00	Space	Latin-1
000	033	02/01	Exclamation Point	Latin-1
000	034	02/02	Quotation Mark	Latin-1
000	035	02/03	Number Sign	Latin-1
000	036	02/04	Dollar Sign	Latin-1
000	037	02/05	Percent Sign	Latin-1
000	038	02/06	Ampersand	Latin-1
000	039	02/07	Apostrophe	Latin-1
000	040	02/08	Left Parenthesis	Latin-1
000	041	02/09	Right Parenthesis	Latin-1
000	042	02/10	Asterisk	Latin-1
000	043	02/11	Plus Sign	Latin-1
000	044	02/12	Comma	Latin-1
000	045	02/13	Minus Sign	Latin-1
000	046	02/14	Full Stop	Latin-1
000	047	02/15	Solidus	Latin-1
000	048	03/00	Digit Zero	Latin-1
000	049	03/01	Digit One	Latin-1
000	050	03/02	Digit Two	Latin-1
000	051	03/03	Digit Three	Latin-1
000	052	03/04	Digit Four	Latin-1
000	053	03/05	Digit Five	Latin-1
000	054	03/06	Digit Six	Latin-1
000	055	03/07	Digit Seven	Latin-1
000	056	03/08	Digit Eight	Latin-1
000	057	03/09	Digit Nine	Latin-1
000	058	03/10	Colon	Latin-1
000	059	03/11	SemiColon	Latin-1
000	060	03/12	Less Than Sign	Latin-1
000	061	03/13	Equals Sign	Latin-1
000	062	03/14	Greater Than Sign	Latin-1
000	063	03/15	Question Mark	Latin-1
000	064	04/00	Commercial At	Latin-1
000	065	04/01	Latin Capital Letter A	Latin-1
000	066	04/02	Latin Capital Letter B	Latin-1
000	067	04/03	Latin Capital Letter C	Latin-1
000	068	04/04	Latin Capital Letter D	Latin-1
000	069	04/05	Latin Capital Letter E	Latin-1
000	070	04/06	Latin Capital Letter F	Latin-1
000	071	04/07	Latin Capital Letter G	Latin-1
000	072	04/08	Latin Capital Letter H	Latin-1
000	073	04/09	Latin Capital Letter I	Latin-1
000	074	04/10	Latin Capital Letter J	Latin-1
000	075	04/11	Latin Capital Letter K	Latin-1
000	076	04/12	Latin Capital Letter L	Latin-1
000	077	04/13	Latin Capital Letter M	Latin-1

Byte	Byte	Code	Name	Set
000	078	04/14	Latin Capital Letter N	Latin-1
000	079	04/15	Latin Capital Letter O	Latin-1
000	080	05/00	Latin Capital Letter P	Latin-1
000	081	05/01	Latin Capital Letter Q	Latin-1
000	082	05/02	Latin Capital Letter R	Latin-1
000	083	05/03	Latin Capital Letter S	Latin-1
000	084	05/04	Latin Capital Letter T	Latin-1
000	085	05/05	Latin Capital Letter U	Latin-1
000	086	05/06	Latin Capital Letter V	Latin-1
000	087	05/07	Latin Capital Letter W	Latin-1
000	088	05/08	Latin Capital Letter X	Latin-1
000	089	05/09	Latin Capital Letter Y	Latin-1
000	090	05/10	Latin Capital Letter Z	Latin-1
000	091	05/11	Left Square Bracket	Latin-1
000	092	05/12	Reverse Solidus	Latin-1
000	093	05/13	Right Square Bracket	Latin-1
000	094	05/14	Circumflex Accent	Latin-1
000	095	05/15	Low Line	Latin-1
000	096	06/00	Grave Accent	Latin-1
000	097	06/01	Latin Small Letter a	Latin-1
000	098	06/02	Latin Small Letter b	Latin-1
000	099	06/03	Latin Small Letter c	Latin-1
000	100	06/04	Latin Small Letter d	Latin-1
000	101	06/05	Latin Small Letter e	Latin-1
000	102	06/06	Latin Small Letter f	Latin-1
000	103	06/07	Latin Small Letter g	Latin-1
000	104	06/08	Latin Small Letter h	Latin-1
000	105	06/09	Latin Small Letter i	Latin-1
000	106	06/10	Latin Small Letter j	Latin-1
000	107	06/11	Latin Small Letter k	Latin-1
000	108	06/12	Latin Small Letter l	Latin-1
000	109	06/13	Latin Small Letter m	Latin-1
000	110	06/14	Latin Small Letter n	Latin-1
000	111	06/15	Latin Small Letter o	Latin-1
000	112	07/00	Latin Small Letter p	Latin-1
000	113	07/01	Latin Small Letter q	Latin-1
000	114	07/02	Latin Small Letter r	Latin-1
000	115	07/03	Latin Small Letter s	Latin-1
000	116	07/04	Latin Small Letter t	Latin-1
000	117	07/05	Latin Small Letter u	Latin-1
000	118	07/06	Latin Small Letter v	Latin-1
000	119	07/07	Latin Small Letter w	Latin-1
000	120	07/08	Latin Small Letter x	Latin-1
000	121	07/09	Latin Small Letter y	Latin-1
000	122	07/10	Latin Small Letter z	Latin-1
000	123	07/11	Left Curly Bracket	Latin-1

Byte	Byte	Code	Name	Set
000	124	07/12	Vertical Line	Latin-1
000	125	07/13	Right Curly Bracket	Latin-1
000	126	07/14	Tilde	Latin-1
000	160	10/00	No-Break Space	Latin-1
000	161	10/01	Inverted Exclamation Mark	Latin-1
000	162	10/02	Cent Sign	Latin-1
000	163	10/03	Pound Sign	Latin-1
000	164	10/04	Currency Sign	Latin-1
000	165	10/05	Yen Sign	Latin-1
000	166	10/06	Broken Vertical Bar	Latin-1
000	167	10/07	Section Sign	Latin-1
000	173	10/13	Hyphen	Latin-1
000	168	10/08	DiaeresiS	Latin-1
000	169	10/09	Copyright Sign	Latin-1
000	170	10/10	Feminine Ordinal Indicator	Latin-1
000	171	10/11	Left Angle Quotation Mark	Latin-1
000	172	10/12	Not Sign	Latin-1
000	174	10/14	Registered Trademark Sign	Latin-1
000	175	10/15	Macron	Latin-1
000	176	11/00	Degree Sign, Ring Above	Latin-1
000	177	11/01	Plus-Minus Sign	Latin-1
000	178	11/02	SuperScript Two	Latin-1
000	179	11/03	SuperScript Three	Latin-1
000	180	11/04	Acute Accent	Latin-1
000	181	11/05	Micro Sign	Latin-1
000	182	11/06	Paragraph Sign	Latin-1
000	183	11/07	Middle Dot	Latin-1
000	184	11/08	Cedilla	Latin-1
000	185	11/09	SuperScript One	Latin-1
000	186	11/10	Masculine Ordinal Indicator	Latin-1
000	187	11/11	Right Angle Quotation Mark	Latin-1
000	188	11/12	Vulgar Fraction One Quarter	Latin-1
000	189	11/13	Vulgar Fraction One Half	Latin-1
000	190	11/14	Vulgar Fraction Three Quarters	Latin-1
000	191	11/15	Inverted Question Mark	Latin-1
000	192	12/00	Latin Capital Letter A with Grave Accent	Latin-1
000	193	12/01	Latin Capital Letter A with Acute Accent	Latin-1
000	194	12/02	Latin Capital Letter A with Circumflex Accent	Latin-1
000	195	12/03	Latin Capital Letter A with Tilde	Latin-1
000	196	12/04	Latin Capital Letter A with Diaeresis	Latin-1
000	197	12/05	Latin Capital Letter A with Ring above	Latin-1
000	198	12/06	Latin Capital Diphthong Ae	Latin-1
000	199	12/07	Latin Capital Letter C witH Cedilla	Latin-1
000	200	12/08	Latin Capital Letter E with Grave Accent	Latin-1
000	201	12/09	Latin Capital Letter E with Acute Accent	Latin-1
000	202	12/10	Latin Capital Letter E with Circumflex Accent	Latin-1

Byte	Byte	Code	Name	Set
000	203	12/11	Latin Capital Letter E with Diaeresis	Latin-1
000	204	12/12	Latin Capital Letter I with Grave Accent	Latin-1
000	205	12/13	Latin Capital Letter I with Acute Accent	Latin-1
000	206	12/14	Latin Capital Letter I with Circumflex Accent	Latin-1
000	207	12/15	Latin Capital Letter I with Diaeresis	Latin-1
000	208	13/00	Icelandic Capital Letter Eth	Latin-1
000	209	13/01	Latin Capital Letter N with Tilde	Latin-1
000	210	13/02	Latin Capital Letter O with Grave Accent	Latin-1
000	211	13/03	Latin Capital Letter O with Acute Accent	Latin-1
000	212	13/04	Latin Capital Letter O with Circumflex Accent	Latin-1
000	213	13/05	Latin Capital Letter O with Tilde	Latin-1
000	214	13/06	Latin Capital Letter O with Diaeresis	Latin-1
000	215	13/07	Multiplication Sign	Latin-1
000	216	13/08	Latin Capital Letter O with Obilque Stroke	Latin-1
000	217	13/09	Latin Capital Letter U with Grave Accent	Latin-1
000	218	13/10	Latin Capital Letter U with Acute Accent	Latin-1
000	219	13/11	Latin Capital Letter U with Circumflex Accent	Latin-1
000	220	13/12	Latin Capital Letter U with Diaeresis	Latin-1
000	221	13/13	Latin Capital Letter Y with Acute Accent	Latin-1
000	222	13/14	Icelandic Capital Letter Thorn	Latin-1
000	223	13/15	German Small Letter Sharp s	Latin-1
000	224	14/00	Latin Small Letter a with Grave Accent	Latin-1
000	225	14/01	Latin Small Letter a with Acute Accent	Latin-1
000	226	14/02	Latin Small Letter a with Circumflex Accent	Latin-1
000	227	14/03	Latin Small Letter a with Tilde	Latin-1
000	228	14/04	Latin Small Letter a with Diaeresis	Latin-1
000	229	14/05	Latin Small Letter a with Ring Above	Latin-1
000	230	14/06	Latin Small Diphthong ae	Latin-1
000	231	14/07	Latin Small Letter c with Cedilla	Latin-1
000	232	14/08	Latin Small Letter e with Grave Accent	Latin-1
000	233	14/09	Latin Small Letter e with Acute Accent	Latin-1
000	234	14/10	Latin Small Letter e with Circumflex Accent	Latin-1
000	235	14/11	Latin Small Letter e with Diaeresis	Latin-1
000	236	14/12	Latin Small Letter i with Grave Accent	Latin-1
000	237	14/13	Latin Small Letter i with Acute Accent	Latin-1
000	238	14/14	Latin Small Letter i with Circumflex Accent	Latin-1
000	239	14/15	Latin Small Letter i with Diaeresis	Latin-1
000	240	15/00	Icelandic Small Letter Eth	Latin-1
000	241	15/01	Latin Small Letter n with Tilde	Latin-1
000	242	15/02	Latin Small Letter o with Grave Accent	Latin-1
000	243	15/03	Latin Small Letter o with Acute Accent	Latin-1
000	244	15/04	Latin Small Letter o with Circumflex Accent	Latin-1
000	245	15/05	Latin Small Letter o with Tilde	Latin-1
000	246	15/06	Latin Small Letter o with Diaeresis	Latin-1
000	247	15/07	Division Sign	Latin-1
000	248	15/08	Latin Small Letter o with Obilque Stroke	Latin-1

Keysyms

Byte	Byte	Code	Name		Set
000	249	15/09	Latin Small Letter u with Grave Accent		Latin-1
000	250	15/10	Latin Small Letter u with Acute Accent		Latin-1
000	251	15/11	Latin Small Letter u with Circumflex Accent		Latin-1
000	252	15/12	Latin Small Letter u with Diaeresis		Latin-1
000	253	15/13	Latin Small Letter y with Acute Accent		Latin-1
000	254	15/14	Icelandic Small Letter Thorn		Latin-1
000	255	15/15	Latin Small Letter y with Diaeresis		Latin-1
001	161	10/01	Latin Capital Letter A with Ogonek		Latin-2
001	162	10/02	Breve		Latin-2
001	163	10/03	Latin Capital Letter L with Stroke		Latin-2
001	165	10/05	Latin Capital Letter L with Caron		Latin-2
001	166	10/06	Latin Capital Letter S with Acute Accent		Latin-2
001	169	10/09	Latin Capital Letter S with Caron		Latin-2
001	170	10/10	Latin Capital Letter S with Cedilla		Latin-2
001	171	10/11	Latin Capital Letter T with Caron		Latin-2
001	172	10/12	Latin Capital Letter Z with Acute Accent		Latin-2
001	174	10/14	Latin Capital Letter Z with Caron		Latin-2
001	175	10/15	Latin Capital Letter Z with Dot Above		Latin-2
001	177	11/01	Latin Small Letter a with Ogonek		Latin-2
001	178	11/02	Ogonek		Latin-2
001	179	11/03	Latin Small Letter l with Stroke		Latin-2
001	181	11/05	Latin Small Letter l with Caron		Latin-2
001	182	11/06	Latin Small Letter s with Acute Accent		Latin-2
001	183	11/07	Caron		Latin-2
001	185	11/09	Latin Small Letter s with Caron		Latin-2
001	186	11/10	Latin Small Letter s with Cedilla		Latin-2
001	187	11/11	Latin Small Letter t with Caron		Latin-2
001	188	11/12	Latin Small Letter z with Acute Accent		Latin-2
001	189	11/13	Double Acute Accent		Latin-2
001	190	11/14	Latin Small Letter z with Caron		Latin-2
001	191	11/15	Latin Small Letter z with Dot Above		Latin-2
001	192	12/00	Latin Capital Letter R with Acute Accent		Latin-2
001	195	12/03	Latin Capital Letter A with Breve		Latin-2
001	197	12/05	Latin Capital Letter L with Acute Accent		Latin-2
001	198	12/06	Latin Capital Letter C with Acute Accent		Latin-2
001	200	12/08	Latin Capital Letter C with Caron		Latin-2
001	202	12/10	Latin Capital Letter E with Ogonek		Latin-2
001	204	12/12	Latin Capital Letter E with Caron		Latin-2
001	207	12/15	Latin Capital Letter D with Caron		Latin-2
001	208	13/00	Latin Capital Letter D with Stroke		Latin-2
001	209	13/01	Latin Capital Letter N with Acute Accent		Latin-2
001	210	13/02	Latin Capital Letter N with Caron		Latin-2
001	213	13/05	Latin Capital Letter O with Double Acute Accent		Latin-2
001	216	13/08	Latin Capital Letter R with Caron		Latin-2

Byte	Byte	Code	Name	Set
001	217	13/09	Latin Capital Letter U with Ring Above	Latin-2
001	219	13/11	Latin Capital Letter U with Double Acute Accent	Latin-2
001	222	13/14	Latin Capital Letter T with Cedilla	Latin-2
001	224	14/00	Latin Small Letter r with Acute Accent	Latin-2
001	227	14/03	Latin Small Letter a with Breve	Latin-2
001	229	14/05	Latin Small Letter l with Acute Accent	Latin-2
001	230	14/06	Latin Small Letter c with Acute Accent	Latin-2
001	232	14/08	Latin Small Letter c with Caron	Latin-2
001	234	14/10	Latin Small Letter e with Ogonek	Latin-2
001	236	14/12	Latin Small Letter e with Caron	Latin-2
001	239	14/15	Latin Small Letter d with Caron	Latin-2
001	240	15/00	Latin Small Letter d with Stroke	Latin-2
001	241	15/01	Latin Small Letter n with Acute Accent	Latin-2
001	242	15/02	Latin Small Letter n with Caron	Latin-2
001	245	15/05	Latin Small Letter o with Double Acute Accent	Latin-2
001	248	15/08	Latin Small Letter r with Caron	Latin-2
001	249	15/09	Latin Small Letter u with RING Above	Latin-2
001	251	15/11	Latin Small Letter u with Double Acute Accent	Latin-2
001	254	15/14	Latin Small Letter t with Cedilla	Latin-2
001	255	15/15	Dot Above	Latin-2
002	161	10/01	Latin Capital Letter H with Stroke	Latin-3
002	166	10/06	Latin Capital Letter H with Circumflex Accent	Latin-3
002	169	10/09	Latin Capital Letter I with Dot Above	Latin-3
002	171	10/11	Latin Capital Letter G with Breve	Latin-3
002	172	10/12	Latin Capital Letter J with Circumflex Accent	Latin-3
002	177	11/01	Latin Small Letter h with Stroke	Latin-3
002	182	11/06	Latin Small Letter h with Circumflex Accent	Latin-3
002	185	11/09	Small Dotless Letter i	Latin-3
002	187	11/11	Latin Small Letter g with Breve	Latin-3
002	188	11/12	Latin Small Letter j with Circumflex Accent	Latin-3
002	197	12/05	Latin Capital Letter C with Dot Above	Latin-3
002	198	12/06	Latin Capital Letter C with Circumflex Accent	Latin-3
002	213	13/05	Latin Capital Letter G with Dot Above	Latin-3
002	216	13/08	Latin Capital Letter G with Circumflex Accent	Latin-3
002	221	13/13	Latin Capital Letter U with Breve	Latin-3
002	222	13/14	Latin Capital Letter S with Circumflex Accent	Latin-3
002	229	14/05	Latin Small Letter c with Dot Above	Latin-3
002	230	14/06	Latin Small Letter c with Circumflex Accent	Latin-3
002	245	15/05	Latin Small Letter g with Dot Above	Latin-3
002	248	15/08	Latin Small Letter g with Circumflex Accent	Latin-3
002	253	15/13	Latin Small Letter u with Breve	Latin-3
002	254	15/14	Latin Small Letter s with Circumflex Accent	Latin-3

Keysyms

Byte	Byte	Code	Name	Set
003	162	10/02	Small Greenlandic Letter Kra	Latin-4
003	163	10/03	Latin Capital Letter R with Cedilla	Latin-4
003	165	10/05	Latin Capital Letter I with Tilde	Latin-4
003	166	10/06	Latin Capital Letter L with Cedilla	Latin-4
003	170	10/10	Latin Capital Letter E with Macron	Latin-4
003	171	10/11	Latin Capital Letter G with Cedilla	Latin-4
003	172	10/12	Latin Capital Letter T with Oblique Stroke	Latin-4
003	179	11/03	Latin Small Letter r with Cedilla	Latin-4
003	181	11/05	Latin Small Letter i with Tilde	Latin-4
003	182	11/06	Latin Small Letter l with Cedilla	Latin-4
003	186	11/10	Latin Small Letter e with Macron	Latin-4
003	187	11/11	Latin Small Letter g with Cedilla Above	Latin-4
003	188	11/12	Latin Small Letter t with Oblique Stroke	Latin-4
003	189	11/13	Lappish Capital Letter Eng	Latin-4
003	191	11/15	Lappish Small Letter Eng	Latin-4
003	192	12/00	Latin Capital Letter A with Macron	Latin-4
003	199	12/07	Latin Capital Letter I with Ogonek	Latin-4
003	204	12/12	Latin Capital Letter E with Dot Above	Latin-4
003	207	12/15	Latin Capital Letter I with Macron	Latin-4
003	209	13/01	Latin Capital Letter N with Cedilla	Latin-4
003	210	13/02	Latin Capital Letter O with Macron	Latin-4
003	211	13/03	Latin Capital Letter K with Cedilla	Latin-4
003	217	13/09	Latin Capital Letter U with Ogonek	Latin-4
003	221	13/13	Latin Capital Letter U with Tilde	Latin-4
003	222	13/14	Latin Capital Letter U with Macron	Latin-4
003	224	14/00	Latin Small Letter a with Macron	Latin-4
003	231	14/07	Latin Small Letter i with Ogonek	Latin-4
003	236	14/12	Latin Small Letter e with Dot Above	Latin-4
003	239	14/15	Latin Small Letter i with Macron	Latin-4
003	241	15/01	Latin Small Letter n with Cedilla	Latin-4
003	242	15/02	Latin Small Letter o with Macron	Latin-4
003	243	15/03	Latin Small Letter k with Cedilla	Latin-4
003	249	15/09	Latin Small Letter u with Ogonek	Latin-4
003	253	15/13	Latin Small Letter u with Tilde	Latin-4
003	254	15/14	Latin Small Letter u with Macron	Latin-4
004	126	07/14	Overline	Kana
004	161	10/01	Kana Full STop	Kana
004	162	10/02	Kana Opening Bracket	Kana
004	163	10/03	Kana Closing Bracket	Kana
004	164	10/04	Kana Comma	Kana
004	165	10/05	Kana Conjunctive	Kana
004	166	10/06	Kana Letter Wo	Kana
004	167	10/07	Kana Letter Small A	Kana
004	168	10/08	Kana Letter Small I	Kana

Byte	Byte	Code	Name		Set
004	169	10/09	Kana Letter Small U		Kana
004	170	10/10	Kana Letter Small E		Kana
004	171	10/11	Kana Letter Small O		Kana
004	172	10/12	Kana Letter Small Ya		Kana
004	173	10/13	Kana Letter Small Yu		Kana
004	174	10/14	Kana Letter Small Yo		Kana
004	175	10/15	Kana Letter Small Tsu		Kana
004	176	11/00	Prolonged Sound Symbol		Kana
004	177	11/01	Kana Letter A		Kana
004	178	11/02	Kana Letter I		Kana
004	179	11/03	Kana Letter U		Kana
004	180	11/04	Kana Letter E		Kana
004	181	11/05	Kana Letter O		Kana
004	182	11/06	Kana Letter Ka		Kana
004	183	11/07	Kana Letter Ki		Kana
004	184	11/08	Kana Letter Ku		Kana
004	185	11/09	Kana Letter Ke		Kana
004	186	11/10	Kana Letter Ko		Kana
004	187	11/11	Kana Letter Sa		Kana
004	188	11/12	Kana Letter Shi		Kana
004	189	11/13	Kana Letter Su		Kana
004	190	11/14	Kana Letter Se		Kana
004	191	11/15	Kana Letter So		Kana
004	192	12/00	Kana Letter Ta		Kana
004	193	12/01	Kana Letter Chi		Kana
004	194	12/02	Kana Letter Tsu		Kana
004	195	12/03	Kana Letter Te		Kana
004	196	12/04	Kana Letter To		Kana
004	197	12/05	Kana Letter Na		Kana
004	198	12/06	Kana Letter Ni		Kana
004	199	12/07	Kana Letter Nu		Kana
004	200	12/08	Kana Letter Ne		Kana
004	201	12/09	Kana Letter No		Kana
004	202	12/10	Kana Letter Ha		Kana
004	203	12/11	Kana Letter Hi		Kana
004	204	12/12	Kana Letter Fu		Kana
004	205	12/13	Kana Letter He		Kana
004	206	12/14	Kana Letter Ho		Kana
004	207	12/15	Kana Letter Ma		Kana
004	208	13/00	Kana Letter Mi		Kana
004	209	13/01	Kana Letter Mu		Kana
004	210	13/02	Kana Letter Me		Kana
004	211	13/03	Kana Letter Mo		Kana
004	212	13/04	Kana Letter Ya		Kana
004	213	13/05	Kana Letter Yu		Kana
004	214	13/06	Kana Letter Yo		Kana

Byte	Byte	Code	Name	Set
004	215	13/07	Kana Letter Ra	Kana
004	216	13/08	Kana Letter Ri	Kana
004	217	13/09	Kana Letter Ru	Kana
004	218	13/10	Kana Letter Re	Kana
004	219	13/11	Kana Letter Ro	Kana
004	220	13/12	Kana Letter Wa	Kana
004	221	13/13	Kana Letter N	Kana
004	222	13/14	Voiced Sound Symbol	Kana
004	223	13/15	Semivoiced Sound Symbol	Kana
005	172	10/12	Arabic Comma	Arabic
005	187	11/11	Arabic Semicolon	Arabic
005	191	11/15	Arabic Question Mark	Arabic
005	193	12/01	Arabic Letter Hamza	Arabic
005	194	12/02	Arabic Letter Madda On Alef	Arabic
005	195	12/03	Arabic Letter Hamza On Alef	Arabic
005	196	12/04	Arabic Letter Hamza On Waw	Arabic
005	197	12/05	Arabic Letter Hamza Under Alef	Arabic
005	198	12/06	Arabic Letter Hamza On Yeh	Arabic
005	199	12/07	Arabic Letter Alef	Arabic
005	200	12/08	Arabic Letter Beh	Arabic
005	201	12/09	Arabic Letter Teh Marbuta	Arabic
005	202	12/10	Arabic Letter Teh	Arabic
005	203	12/11	Arabic Letter Theh	Arabic
005	204	12/12	Arabic Letter Jeem	Arabic
005	205	12/13	Arabic Letter Hah	Arabic
005	206	12/14	Arabic Letter Khah	Arabic
005	207	12/15	Arabic Letter Dal	Arabic
005	208	13/00	Arabic Letter Thal	Arabic
005	209	13/01	Arabic Letter Ra	Arabic
005	210	13/02	Arabic Letter Zain	Arabic
005	211	13/03	Arabic Letter Seen	Arabic
005	212	13/04	Arabic Letter Sheen	Arabic
005	213	13/05	Arabic Letter Sad	Arabic
005	214	13/06	Arabic Letter Dad	Arabic
005	215	13/07	Arabic Letter Tah	Arabic
005	216	13/08	Arabic Letter Zah	Arabic
005	217	13/09	Arabic Letter Ain	Arabic
005	218	13/10	Arabic Letter Ghain	Arabic
005	224	14/00	Arabic Letter Tatweel	Arabic
005	225	14/01	Arabic Letter Feh	Arabic
005	226	14/02	Arabic Letter Qaf	Arabic
005	227	14/03	Arabic Letter Kaf	Arabic
005	228	14/04	Arabic Letter Lam	Arabic
005	229	14/05	Arabic Letter Meem	Arabic

Byte	Byte	Code	Name	Set
005	230	14/06	Arabic Letter Noon	Arabic
005	231	14/07	Arabic Letter Ha	Arabic
005	232	14/08	Arabic Letter Waw	Arabic
005	233	14/09	Arabic Letter Alef Maksura	Arabic
005	234	14/10	Arabic Letter Yeh	Arabic
005	235	14/11	Arabic Letter Fathatan	Arabic
005	236	14/12	Arabic Letter Dammatan	Arabic
005	237	14/13	Arabic Letter Kasratan	Arabic
005	238	14/14	Arabic Letter Fatha	Arabic
005	239	14/15	Arabic Letter Damma	Arabic
005	240	15/00	Arabic Letter Kasra	Arabic
005	241	15/01	Arabic Letter Shadda	Arabic
005	242	15/02	Arabic Letter Sukun	Arabic
006	161	10/01	Serbocroation Cyrillic Small Letter Dje	Cyrillic
006	162	10/02	Macedonian Cyrillic Small Letter Gje	Cyrillic
006	163	10/03	Cyrillic Small Letter Io	Cyrillic
006	164	10/04	Ukrainian Cyrillic Small Letter Ie	Cyrillic
006	165	10/05	Macedonian Small Letter DSE	Cyrillic
006	166	10/06	Byelorussian/Ukrainian Cyrillic Small Letter I	Cyrillic
006	167	10/07	Ukrainian Small Letter Yi	Cyrillic
006	168	10/08	Cyrillic Small Letter Je	Cyrillic
006	169	10/09	Cyrillic Small Letter Lje	Cyrillic
006	170	10/10	Cyrillic Small Letter Nje	Cyrillic
006	171	10/11	Serbian Small Letter Tshe	Cyrillic
006	172	10/12	Macedonian Cyrillic Small Letter Kje	Cyrillic
006	174	10/14	Byelorussian Small Letter Short U	Cyrillic
006	175	10/15	Cyrillic Small Letter Dzhe	Cyrillic
006	176	11/00	Numero Sign	Cyrillic
006	177	11/01	Serbocroatian Cyrillic Capital Letter Dje	Cyrillic
006	178	11/02	Macedonian Cyrillic Capital Letter Gje	Cyrillic
006	179	11/03	Cyrillic Capital Letter Io	Cyrillic
006	180	11/04	Ukrainian Cyrillic Capital Letter Ie	Cyrillic
006	181	11/05	Macedonian Capital Letter Dse	Cyrillic
006	182	11/06	Byelorussian/Ukrainian Cyrillic Capital Letter I	Cyrillic
006	183	11/07	Ukrainian Capital Letter Yi	Cyrillic
006	184	11/08	Cyrillic Capital Letter Je	Cyrillic
006	185	11/09	Cyrillic Capital Letter Lje	Cyrillic
006	186	11/10	Cyrillic Capital Letter Nje	Cyrillic
006	187	11/11	Serbian Capital Letter Tshe	Cyrillic
006	188	11/12	Macedonian Cyrillic Capital Letter Kje	Cyrillic
006	190	11/14	Byelorussian Capital Letter Short U	Cyrillic
006	191	11/15	Cyrillic Capital Letter Dzhe	Cyrillic
006	192	12/00	Cyrillic Small Letter Yu	Cyrillic
006	193	12/01	Cyrillic Small Letter A	Cyrillic

Keysyms

Byte	Byte	Code	Name	Set
006	194	12/02	Cyrillic Small Letter Be	Cyrillic
006	195	12/03	Cyrillic Small Letter Tse	Cyrillic
006	196	12/04	Cyrillic Small Letter De	Cyrillic
006	197	12/05	Cyrillic Small Letter Ie	Cyrillic
006	198	12/06	Cyrillic Small Letter Ef	Cyrillic
006	199	12/07	Cyrillic Small Letter Ghe	Cyrillic
006	200	12/08	Cyrillic Small Letter Ha	Cyrillic
006	201	12/09	Cyrillic Small Letter I	Cyrillic
006	202	12/10	Cyrillic Small Letter Short I	Cyrillic
006	203	12/11	Cyrillic Small Letter Ka	Cyrillic
006	204	12/12	Cyrillic Small Letter El	Cyrillic
006	205	12/13	Cyrillic Small Letter Em	Cyrillic
006	206	12/14	Cyrillic Small Letter En	Cyrillic
006	207	12/15	Cyrillic Small Letter O	Cyrillic
006	208	13/00	Cyrillic Small Letter Pe	Cyrillic
006	209	13/01	Cyrillic Small Letter Ya	Cyrillic
006	210	13/02	Cyrillic Small Letter Er	Cyrillic
006	211	13/03	Cyrillic Small Letter Es	Cyrillic
006	212	13/04	Cyrillic Small Letter Te	Cyrillic
006	213	13/05	Cyrillic Small Letter U	Cyrillic
006	214	13/06	Cyrillic Small Letter Zhe	Cyrillic
006	215	13/07	Cyrillic Small Letter Ve	Cyrillic
006	216	13/08	Cyrillic Small Soft Sign	Cyrillic
006	217	13/09	Cyrillic Small Letter Yeru	Cyrillic
006	218	13/10	Cyrillic Small Letter Ze	Cyrillic
006	219	13/11	Cyrillic Small Letter Sha	Cyrillic
006	220	13/12	Cyrillic Small Letter E	Cyrillic
006	221	13/13	Cyrillic Small Letter Shcha	Cyrillic
006	222	13/14	Cyrillic Small Letter Che	Cyrillic
006	223	13/15	Cyrillic Small Hard Sign	Cyrillic
006	224	14/00	Cyrillic Capital Letter Yu	Cyrillic
006	225	14/01	Cyrillic Capital Letter A	Cyrillic
006	226	14/02	Cyrillic Capital Letter Be	Cyrillic
006	227	14/03	Cyrillic Capital Letter Tse	Cyrillic
006	228	14/04	Cyrillic Capital Letter De	Cyrillic
006	229	14/05	Cyrillic Capital Letter Ie	Cyrillic
006	230	14/06	Cyrillic Capital Letter Ef	Cyrillic
006	231	14/07	Cyrillic Capital Letter Ghe	Cyrillic
006	232	14/08	Cyrillic Capital Letter Ha	Cyrillic
006	233	14/09	Cyrillic Capital Letter I	Cyrillic
006	234	14/10	Cyrillic Capital Letter Short I	Cyrillic
006	235	14/11	Cyrillic Capital Letter Ka	Cyrillic
006	236	14/12	Cyrillic Capital Letter El	Cyrillic
006	237	14/13	Cyrillic Capital Letter Em	Cyrillic
006	238	14/14	Cyrillic Capital Letter En	Cyrillic
006	239	14/15	Cyrillic Capital Letter O	Cyrillic

Byte	Byte	Code	Name	Set
006	240	15/00	Cyrillic Capital Letter Pe	Cyrillic
006	241	15/01	Cyrillic Capital Letter Ya	Cyrillic
006	242	15/02	Cyrillic Capital Letter Er	Cyrillic
006	243	15/03	Cyrillic Capital Letter Es	Cyrillic
006	244	15/04	Cyrillic Capital Letter Te	Cyrillic
006	245	15/05	Cyrillic Capital Letter U	Cyrillic
006	246	15/06	Cyrillic Capital Letter Zhe	Cyrillic
006	247	15/07	Cyrillic Capital Letter Ve	Cyrillic
006	248	15/08	Cyrillic Capital Soft Sign	Cyrillic
006	249	15/09	Cyrillic Capital Letter Yeru	Cyrillic
006	250	15/10	Cyrillic Capital Letter Ze	Cyrillic
006	251	15/11	Cyrillic Capital Letter Sha	Cyrillic
006	252	15/12	Cyrillic Capital Letter E	Cyrillic
006	253	15/13	Cyrillic Capital Letter Shcha	Cyrillic
006	254	15/14	Cyrillic Capital Letter Che	Cyrillic
006	255	15/15	Cyrillic Capital Hard Sign	Cyrillic
007	161	10/01	Greek Capital Letter Alpha with Accent	Greek
007	162	10/02	Greek Capital Letter Epsilon with Accent	Greek
007	163	10/03	Greek Capital Letter Eta with Accent	Greek
007	164	10/04	Greek Capital Letter Iota with Accent	Greek
007	165	10/05	Greek Capital Letter Iota with Diaeresis	Greek
007	166	10/06	Greek Capital Letter Iota with Accent+Diaeresis	Greek
007	167	10/07	Greek Capital Letter Omicron with Accent	Greek
007	168	10/08	Greek Capital Letter Upsilon with Accent	Greek
007	174	10/14	Diaeresis And Accent	Greek
007	175	10/15	Horizontal Bar	Greek
007	169	10/09	Greek Capital Letter Upsilon with Diaeresis	Greek
007	170	10/10	Greek Capital Letter Upsilon with Accent+Diaeresis	Greek
007	171	10/11	Greek Capital Letter Omega with Accent	Greek
007	177	11/01	Greek Small Letter Alpha with Accent	Greek
007	178	11/02	Greek Small Letter Epsilon with Accent	Greek
007	179	11/03	Greek Small Letter ETA with Accent	Greek
007	180	11/04	Greek Small Letter Iota with Accent	Greek
007	181	11/05	Greek Small Letter Iota with Diaeresis	Greek
007	182	11/06	Greek Small Letter Iota with Accent+Diaeresis	Greek
007	183	11/07	Greek Small Letter Omicron with Accent	Greek
007	184	11/08	Greek Small Letter Upsilon with Accent	Greek
007	185	11/09	Greek Small Letter Upsilon with Diaeresis	Greek
007	186	11/10	Greek Small Letter Upsilon with Accent+Diaeresis	Greek
007	187	11/11	Greek Small Letter Omega with Accent	Greek
007	193	12/01	Greek Capital Letter Alpha	Greek
007	194	12/02	Greek Capital Letter Beta	Greek
007	195	12/03	Greek Capital Letter Gamma	Greek
007	196	12/04	Greek Capital Letter Delta	Greek

Byte	Byte	Code	Name	Set
007	197	12/05	Greek Capital Letter Epsilon	Greek
007	198	12/06	Greek Capital Letter Zeta	Greek
007	199	12/07	Greek Capital Letter Eta	Greek
007	200	12/08	Greek Capital Letter Theta	Greek
007	201	12/09	Greek Capital Letter Iota	Greek
007	202	12/10	Greek Capital Letter Kappa	Greek
007	203	12/11	Greek Capital Letter LAMDA	Greek
007	204	12/12	Greek Capital Letter Mu	Greek
007	205	12/13	Greek Capital Letter Nu	Greek
007	206	12/14	Greek Capital Letter Xi	Greek
007	207	12/15	Greek Capital Letter Omicron	Greek
007	208	13/00	Greek Capital Letter Pi	Greek
007	209	13/01	Greek Capital Letter Rho	Greek
007	210	13/02	Greek Capital Letter Sigma	Greek
007	212	13/04	Greek Capital Letter Tau	Greek
007	213	13/05	Greek Capital Letter Upsilon	Greek
007	214	13/06	Greek Capital Letter Phi	Greek
007	215	13/07	Greek Capital Letter Chi	Greek
007	216	13/08	Greek Capital Letter Psi	Greek
007	217	13/09	Greek Capital Letter Omega	Greek
007	225	14/01	Greek Small Letter Alpha	Greek
007	226	14/02	Greek Small Letter Beta	Greek
007	227	14/03	Greek Small Letter Gamma	Greek
007	228	14/04	Greek Small Letter Delta	Greek
007	229	14/05	Greek Small Letter Epsilon	Greek
007	230	14/06	Greek Small Letter Zeta	Greek
007	231	14/07	Greek Small Letter Eta	Greek
007	232	14/08	Greek Small Letter Theta	Greek
007	233	14/09	Greek Small Letter Iota	Greek
007	234	14/10	Greek Small Letter Kappa	Greek
007	235	14/11	Greek Small Letter Lambda	Greek
007	236	14/12	Greek Small Letter Mu	Greek
007	237	14/13	Greek Small Letter Nu	Greek
007	238	14/14	Greek Small Letter Xi	Greek
007	239	14/15	Greek Small Letter Omicron	Greek
007	240	15/00	Greek Small Letter Pi	Greek
007	241	15/01	Greek Small Letter Rho	Greek
007	242	15/02	Greek Small Letter Sigma	Greek
007	243	15/03	Greek Small Letter Final Small Sigma	Greek
007	244	15/04	Greek Small Letter Tau	Greek
007	245	15/05	Greek Small Letter Upsilon	Greek
007	246	15/06	Greek Small Letter Phi	Greek
007	247	15/07	Greek Small Letter Chi	Greek
007	248	15/08	Greek Small Letter Psi	Greek
007	249	15/09	Greek Small Letter Omega	Greek

Byte	Byte	Code	Name	Set
008	161	10/01	Left Radical	Technical
008	162	10/02	Top Left Radical	Technical
008	163	10/03	Horizontal Connector	Technical
008	164	10/04	Top Integral	Technical
008	165	10/05	Bottom Integral	Technical
008	166	10/06	Vertical Connector	Technical
008	167	10/07	Top Left Square Bracket	Technical
008	168	10/08	Bottom Left Square Bracket	Technical
008	169	10/09	Top Right Square Bracket	Technical
008	170	10/10	Bottom Right Square Bracket	Technical
008	171	10/11	Top Left Parenthesis	Technical
008	172	10/12	Bottom Left Parenthesis	Technical
008	173	10/13	Top Right Parenthesis	Technical
008	174	10/14	Bottom Right Parenthesis	Technical
008	175	10/15	Left Middle Curly Brace	Technical
008	176	11/00	Right Middle Curly Brace	Technical
008	177	11/01	Top Left Summation	Technical
008	178	11/02	Bottom Left Summation	Technical
008	179	11/03	Top Vertical Summation Connector	Technical
008	180	11/04	Bottom Vertical Summation Connector	Technical
008	181	11/05	Top Right Summation	Technical
008	182	11/06	Bottom Right Summation	Technical
008	183	11/07	Right Middle Summation	Technical
008	188	11/12	Less Than Or Equal Sign	Technical
008	189	11/13	Not Equal Sign	Technical
008	190	11/14	Greater Than Or Equal Sign	Technical
008	191	11/15	Integral	Technical
008	192	12/00	Therefore	Technical
008	193	12/01	Variation, Proportional To	Technical
008	194	12/02	Infinity	Technical
008	197	12/05	Nabla, Del	Technical
008	200	12/08	Is Approximate To	Technical
008	201	12/09	Similar Or Equal To	Technical
008	205	12/13	If And Only If	Technical
008	206	12/14	Implies	Technical
008	207	12/15	Identical To	Technical
008	214	13/06	Radical	Technical
008	218	13/10	IS Included In	Technical
008	219	13/11	Includes	Technical
008	220	13/12	Intersection	Technical
008	221	13/13	Union	Technical
008	222	13/14	Logical And	Technical
008	223	13/15	Logical Or	Technical
008	239	14/15	Partial Derivative	Technical
008	246	15/06	Function	Technical
008	251	15/11	Left Arrow	Technical

Byte	Byte	Code	Name	Set
008	252	15/12	Upward Arrow	Technical
008	253	15/13	Right Arrow	Technical
008	254	15/14	Downward Arrow	Technical
009	223	13/15	Blank	Special
009	224	14/00	Solid Diamond	Special
009	225	14/01	Checkerboard	Special
009	226	14/02	"Ht"	Special
009	227	14/03	"Ff"	Special
009	228	14/04	"Cr"	Special
009	229	14/05	"Lf"	Special
009	232	14/08	"Nl"	Special
009	233	14/09	"Vt"	Special
009	234	14/10	Lower-Right Corner	Special
009	235	14/11	Upper-Right Corner	Special
009	236	14/12	Upper-Left Corner	Special
009	237	14/13	Lower-Left Corner	Special
009	238	14/14	Crossing-Lines	Special
009	239	14/15	Horizontal Line, Scan 1	Special
009	240	15/00	Horizontal Line, Scan 3	Special
009	241	15/01	Horizontal Line, Scan 5	Special
009	242	15/02	Horizontal Line, Scan 7	Special
009	243	15/03	Horizontal Line, Scan 9	Special
009	244	15/04	Left "T"	Special
009	245	15/05	Right "T"	Special
009	246	15/06	Bottom "T"	Special
009	247	15/07	Top "T"	Special
009	248	15/08	Vertical Bar	Special
010	161	10/01	Em Space	Publish
010	162	10/02	En Space	Publish
010	163	10/03	3/Em Space	Publish
010	164	10/04	4/Em Space	Publish
010	165	10/05	Digit Space	Publish
010	166	10/06	Punctuation Space	Publish
010	167	10/07	Thin Space	Publish
010	168	10/08	Hair Space	Publish
010	169	10/09	Em Dash	Publish
010	170	10/10	En Dash	Publish
010	172	10/12	Significant Blank Symbol	Publish
010	174	10/14	Ellipsis	Publish
010	175	10/15	Double Baseline Dot	Publish
010	176	11/00	Vulgar Fraction One Third	Publish
010	177	11/01	Vulgar Fraction Two Thirds	Publish

Byte	Byte	Code	Name	Set
010	178	11/02	Vulgar Fraction One Fifth	Publish
010	179	11/03	Vulgar Fraction Two Fifths	Publish
010	180	11/04	Vulgar Fraction Three Fifths	Publish
010	181	11/05	Vulgar Fraction Four Fifths	Publish
010	182	11/06	Vulgar Fraction One Sixth	Publish
010	183	11/07	Vulgar Fraction Five Sixths	Publish
010	184	11/08	Care Of	Publish
010	187	11/11	Figure Dash	Publish
010	188	11/12	Left Angle Bracket	Publish
010	189	11/13	Decimal Point	Publish
010	190	11/14	Right Angle Bracket	Publish
010	191	11/15	Marker	Publish
010	195	12/03	Vulgar Fraction One Eighth	Publish
010	196	12/04	Vulgar Fraction Three Eighths	Publish
010	197	12/05	Vulgar Fraction Five Eighths	Publish
010	198	12/06	Vulgar Fraction Seven Eighths	Publish
010	201	12/09	Trademark Sign	Publish
010	202	12/10	Signature Mark	Publish
010	203	12/11	Trademark Sign In Circle	Publish
010	204	12/12	Left Open Triangle	Publish
010	205	12/13	Right Open Triangle	Publish
010	206	12/14	Em Open Circle	Publish
010	207	12/15	Em Open Rectangle	Publish
010	208	13/00	Left Single Quotation Mark	Publish
010	209	13/01	Right Single Quotation Mark	Publish
010	210	13/02	Left Double Quotation Mark	Publish
010	211	13/03	Right Double Quotation Mark	Publish
010	212	13/04	Prescription, Take, Recipe	Publish
010	214	13/06	Minutes	Publish
010	215	13/07	Seconds	Publish
010	217	13/09	Latin Cross	Publish
010	218	13/10	Hexagram	Publish
010	219	13/11	Filled Rectangle Bullet	Publish
010	220	13/12	Filled Left Triangle Bullet	Publish
010	221	13/13	Filled Right Triangle Bullet	Publish
010	222	13/14	Em Filled Circle	Publish
010	223	13/15	Em Filled Rectangle	Publish
010	224	14/00	En Open Circle Bullet	Publish
010	225	14/01	En Open Square Bullet	Publish
010	226	14/02	Open Rectangular Bullet	Publish
010	227	14/03	Open Triangular Bullet Up	Publish
010	228	14/04	Open Triangular Bullet Down	Publish
010	229	14/05	Open Star	Publish
010	230	14/06	En Filled Circle Bullet	Publish
010	231	14/07	En Filled Square Bullet	Publish
010	232	14/08	Filled Triangular Bullet Up	Publish

Keysyms

Byte	Byte	Code	Name		Set
010	233	14/09	Filled Triangular Bullet Down		Publish
010	234	14/10	Left Pointer		Publish
010	235	14/11	Right Pointer		Publish
010	236	14/12	Club		Publish
010	237	14/13	Diamond		Publish
010	238	14/14	Heart		Publish
010	240	15/00	Maltese Cross		Publish
010	241	15/01	Dagger		Publish
010	242	15/02	Double Dagger		Publish
010	243	15/03	Check Mark, Tick		Publish
010	244	15/04	Ballot Cross		Publish
010	245	15/05	Musical Sharp		Publish
010	246	15/06	Musical Flat		Publish
010	247	15/07	Male Symbol		Publish
010	248	15/08	Female Symbol		Publish
010	249	15/09	Telephone Symbol		Publish
010	250	15/10	Telephone Recorder Symbol		Publish
010	251	15/11	Phonograph CopyRight Sign		Publish
010	252	15/12	Caret		Publish
010	253	15/13	Single Low Quotation Mark		Publish
010	254	15/14	Double Low Quotation Mark		Publish
010	255	15/15	Cursor		Publish
011	163	10/03	Left Caret		Apl
011	166	10/06	Right Caret		Apl
011	168	10/08	Down Caret		Apl
011	169	10/09	Up Caret		Apl
011	192	12/00	Overbar		Apl
011	194	12/02	Down Tack		Apl
011	195	12/03	Up Shoe (Cap)		Apl
011	196	12/04	Down Stile		Apl
011	198	12/06	Underbar		Apl
011	202	12/10	Jot		Apl
011	204	12/12	Quad		Apl
011	206	12/14	Up Tack		Apl
011	207	12/15	Circle		Apl
011	211	13/03	Up Stile		Apl
011	214	13/06	Down Shoe (Cup)		Apl
011	216	13/08	Right Shoe		Apl
011	218	13/10	Left Shoe		Apl
011	220	13/12	Left Tack		Apl
011	252	15/12	Right Tack		Apl

Byte	Byte	Code	Name	Set
012	223	13/15	Double Low Line	Hebrew
012	224	14/00	Hebrew Letter Aleph	Hebrew
012	225	14/01	Hebrew Letter Bet	Hebrew
012	226	14/02	Hebrew Letter Gimel	Hebrew
012	227	14/03	Hebrew Letter Dalet	Hebrew
012	228	14/04	Hebrew Letter He	Hebrew
012	229	14/05	Hebrew Letter Waw	Hebrew
012	230	14/06	Hebrew Letter Zain	Hebrew
012	231	14/07	Hebrew Letter Chet	Hebrew
012	232	14/08	Hebrew Letter Tet	Hebrew
012	233	14/09	Hebrew Letter Yod	Hebrew
012	234	14/10	Hebrew Letter Final Kaph	Hebrew
012	235	14/11	Hebrew Letter Kaph	Hebrew
012	236	14/12	Hebrew Letter Lamed	Hebrew
012	237	14/13	Hebrew Letter Final Mem	Hebrew
012	238	14/14	Hebrew Letter Mem	Hebrew
012	239	14/15	Hebrew Letter Final Nun	Hebrew
012	240	15/00	Hebrew Letter Nun	Hebrew
012	241	15/01	Hebrew Letter Samech	Hebrew
012	242	15/02	Hebrew Letter A'yin	Hebrew
012	243	15/03	Hebrew Letter Final Pe	Hebrew
012	244	15/04	Hebrew Letter PE	Hebrew
012	245	15/05	Hebrew Letter Final Zade	Hebrew
012	246	15/06	Hebrew Letter Zade	Hebrew
012	247	15/07	Hebrew Qoph	Hebrew
012	248	15/08	Hebrew Resh	Hebrew
012	249	15/09	Hebrew Shin	Hebrew
012	250	15/10	Hebrew Taw	Hebrew
255	008	00/08	BackSpace, Back Space, Back Char	Keyboard
255	009	00/09	Tab	Keyboard
255	010	00/10	Linefeed, Lf	Keyboard
255	011	00/11	Clear	Keyboard
255	013	00/13	Return, Enter	Keyboard
255	019	01/03	Pause, Hold	Keyboard
255	020	01/04	Scroll Lock	Keyboard
255	027	01/11	Escape	Keyboard
255	032	02/00	Multi-Key Character Preface	Keyboard
255	033	02/01	Kanji, Kanji Convert	Keyboard
255	034	02/02	Muhenkan	Keyboard
255	035	02/03	Henkan Mode	Keyboard
255	036	02/04	Romaji	Keyboard
255	037	02/05	Hiragana	Keyboard
255	038	02/06	Katakana	Keyboard
255	039	02/07	Hiragana/Katakana Toggle	Keyboard

Byte	Byte	Code	Name		Set
255	040	02/08	Zenkaku		Keyboard
255	041	02/09	Hankaku		Keyboard
255	042	02/10	Zenkaku/Hankaku Toggle		Keyboard
255	043	02/11	Touroku		Keyboard
255	044	02/12	Massyo		Keyboard
255	045	02/13	Kana Lock		Keyboard
255	046	02/14	Kana Shift		Keyboard
255	047	02/15	Eisu Shift		Keyboard
255	048	03/00	Eisu Toggle		Keyboard
255	080	05/00	Home		Keyboard
255	081	05/01	Left, Move Left, Left Arrow		Keyboard
255	082	05/02	Up, Move Up, Up Arrow		Keyboard
255	083	05/03	Right, Move Right, Right Arrow		Keyboard
255	084	05/04	Down, Move Down, Down Arrow		Keyboard
255	085	05/05	Prior, Previous		Keyboard
255	086	05/06	Next		Keyboard
255	087	05/07	End, Eol		Keyboard
255	088	05/08	Begin, Bol		Keyboard
255	096	06/00	Select, Mark		Keyboard
255	097	06/01	Print		Keyboard
255	098	06/02	Execute, Rdn, Do		Keyboard
255	099	06/03	Insert, Insert Here		Keyboard
255	101	06/05	Undo, Oops		Keyboard
255	102	06/06	Redo, Again		Keyboard
255	103	06/07	Menu		Keyboard
255	104	06/08	Find, Search		Keyboard
255	105	06/09	Cancel, Stop, Abort, Exit		Keyboard
255	106	06/10	Help, Question Mark		Keyboard
255	107	06/11	Break		Keyboard
255	126	07/14	Mode Switch, Script Switch, Character Set Switch		Keyboard
255	127	07/15	Num Lock		Keyboard
255	128	08/00	Keypad Space		Keyboard
255	137	08/09	Keypad Tab		Keyboard
255	141	08/13	Keypad Enter		Keyboard
255	145	09/01	Keypad F1, PF1, A		Keyboard
255	146	09/02	Keypad F2, PF2, B		Keyboard
255	147	09/03	Keypad F3, PF3, C		Keyboard
255	148	09/04	Keypad F4, PF4, D		Keyboard
255	170	10/10	Keypad Multiplication Sign, Asterisk		Keyboard
255	171	10/11	Keypad Plus Sign		Keyboard
255	172	10/12	Keypad Separator, Comma		Keyboard
255	173	10/13	Keypad Minus Sign, Hyphen		Keyboard
255	174	10/14	Keypad Decimal Point, Full Stop		Keyboard
255	175	10/15	Keypad Division Sign, Solidus		Keyboard
255	176	11/00	Keypad Digit Zero		Keyboard
255	177	11/01	Keypad Digit One		Keyboard

Byte	Byte	Code	Name		Set
255	178	11/02	Keypad Digit Two		Keyboard
255	179	11/03	Keypad Digit Three		Keyboard
255	180	11/04	Keypad Digit Four		Keyboard
255	181	11/05	Keypad Digit Five		Keyboard
255	182	11/06	Keypad Digit Six		Keyboard
255	183	11/07	Keypad Digit Seven		Keyboard
255	184	11/08	Keypad Digit Eight		Keyboard
255	185	11/09	Keypad Digit Nine		Keyboard
255	189	11/13	Keypad Equals Sign		Keyboard
255	190	11/14	F1		Keyboard
255	191	11/15	F2		Keyboard
255	192	12/00	F3		Keyboard
255	193	12/01	F4		Keyboard
255	194	12/02	F5		Keyboard
255	195	12/03	F6		Keyboard
255	196	12/04	F7		Keyboard
255	197	12/05	F8		Keyboard
255	198	12/06	F9		Keyboard
255	199	12/07	F10		Keyboard
255	200	12/08	F11, L1		Keyboard
255	201	12/09	F12, L2		Keyboard
255	202	12/10	F13, L3		Keyboard
255	203	12/11	F14, L4		Keyboard
255	204	12/12	F15, L5		Keyboard
255	205	12/13	F16, L6		Keyboard
255	206	12/14	F17, L7		Keyboard
255	207	12/15	F18, L8		Keyboard
255	208	13/00	F19, L9		Keyboard
255	209	13/01	F20, L10		Keyboard
255	210	13/02	F21, R1		Keyboard
255	211	13/03	F22, R2		Keyboard
255	212	13/04	F23, R3		Keyboard
255	213	13/05	F24, R4		Keyboard
255	214	13/06	F25, R5		Keyboard
255	215	13/07	F26, R6		Keyboard
255	216	13/08	F27, R7		Keyboard
255	217	13/09	F28, R8		Keyboard
255	218	13/10	F29, R9		Keyboard
255	219	13/11	F30, R10		Keyboard
255	220	13/12	F31, R11		Keyboard
255	221	13/13	F32, R12		Keyboard
255	222	13/14	F33, R13		Keyboard
255	223	13/15	F34, R14		Keyboard
255	224	14/00	F35, R15		Keyboard
255	225	14/01	Left Shift		Keyboard
255	226	14/02	Right Shift		Keyboard

Keysyms

Byte	Byte	Code	Name		Set
255	227	14/03	Left Control		Keyboard
255	228	14/04	Right Control		Keyboard
255	229	14/05	Caps Lock		Keyboard
255	230	14/06	Shift Lock		Keyboard
255	231	14/07	Left Meta		Keyboard
255	232	14/08	Right Meta		Keyboard
255	233	14/09	Left ALT		Keyboard
255	234	14/10	Right ALT		Keyboard
255	235	14/11	Left Super		Keyboard
255	236	14/12	Right Super		Keyboard
255	237	14/13	Left Hyper		Keyboard
255	238	14/14	Right Hyper		Keyboard
255	255	15/15	Delete, Rubout		Keyboard

C
Errors

This section lists and describes the various types of errors. In general, when a request terminates with an error, the request has no side effects (that is, there is no partial execution). The only requests for which this is not true are **ChangeWindowAttributes**, **ChangeGC**, **Poly-Text8**, **PolyText16**, **FreeColors**, **StoreColors**, and **ChangeKeyboardControl**. All these requests perform an operation multiple times or set multiple values, and all the operations or values up to the one containing the error will be performed.

The following error codes can be returned by the various requests.

Access
An attempt is made to grab a key/button combination already grabbed by another client.

An attempt is made to free a colormap entry not allocated by the client.

An attempt is made to store into a read-only or an unallocated colormap entry.

An attempt is made to modify the access control list from other than the local host (or otherwise authorized client).

An attempt is made to select an event type that only one client can select at a time when another client has already selected it.

Alloc
The server failed to allocate the requested resource. Note that the explicit listing of **Alloc** errors in request only covers allocation errors at a very coarse level and is not intended to cover all cases of a server running out of allocation space in the middle of service. The semantics when a server runs out of allocation space are left unspecified, but a server may generate an **Alloc** error on any request for this reason, and clients should be prepared to receive such errors and handle or discard them.

Atom
A value for an ATOM argument does not name a defined ATOM.

Colormap
A value for a COLORMAP argument does not name a defined COLORMAP.

Cursor	A value for a CURSOR argument does not name a defined CURSOR.
Drawable	A value for a DRAWABLE argument does not name a defined WINDOW or PIXMAP.
Font	A value for a FONT argument does not name a defined FONT.
	A value for a FONTABLE argument does not name a defined FONT or a defined GCONTEXT.
GContext	A value for a GCONTEXT argument does not name a defined GCONTEXT.
IDChoice	The value chosen for a resource identifier either is not included in the range assigned to the client or is already in use.
Implementation	The server does not implement some aspect of the request. A server that generates this error for a core request is deficient. As such, this error is not listed for any of the requests, but clients should be prepared to receive such errors and handle or discard them.
Length	The length of a request is shorter or longer than that required to minimally contain the arguments.
	The length of a request exceeds the maximum length accepted by the server.
Match	An **InputOnly** window is used as a DRAWABLE.
	In a graphics request, the GCONTEXT argument does not have the same root and depth as the destination DRAWABLE argument.
	Some argument (or pair of arguments) has the correct type and range, but it fails to match in some other way required by the request.
Name	A font or color of the specified name does not exist.
Pixmap	A value for a PIXMAP argument does not name a defined PIXMAP.
Request	The major or minor opcode does not specify a valid request.
Value	Some numeric value falls outside the range of values accepted by the request. Unless a specific range is specified for an argument, the full range defined by the argument's type is accepted. Any argument defined as a set of alternatives typically can generate this error (due to the encoding).

Window   A value for a WINDOW argument does not name a defined
                           WINDOW.

NOTE

The **BadAtom**, **BadColormap**, **BadCursor**, **Bad-
Drawable**, **BadFont**, **BadGContext**, **BadPixmap**,
and **BadWindow** errors are also used when the argument type is extended by union with a set of fixed
alternatives; for example, <WINDOW or **Pointer-
Root** or None>.

Encoding

The encoding of each error follows:

Access

# Bytes	Value	Description
1	0	Error
1	10	code
2	CARD16	sequence number
4		unused
2	CARD16	minor opcode
1	CARD8	major opcode
21		unused

Alloc

# Bytes	Value	Description
1	0	Error
1	11	code
2	CARD16	sequence number
4		unused
2	CARD16	minor opcode
1	CARD8	major opcode
21		unused

Atom

# Bytes	Value	Description
1	0	Error
1	5	code
2	CARD16	sequence number
4	CARD32	bad atom id
2	CARD16	minor opcode
1	CARD8	major opcode
21		unused

Colormap

# Bytes	Value	Description
1	0	Error
1	12	code
2	CARD16	sequence number
4	CARD32	bad resource id
2	CARD16	minor opcode
1	CARD8	major opcode
21		unused

Cursor

# Bytes	Value	Description
1	0	Error
1	6	code
2	CARD16	sequence number
4	CARD32	bad resource id
2	CARD16	minor opcode
1	CARD8	major opcode
21		unused

Drawable

# Bytes	Value	Description
1	0	Error
1	9	code
2	CARD16	sequence number
4	CARD32	bad resource id
2	CARD16	minor opcode
1	CARD8	major opcode
21		unused

Font

# Bytes	Value	Description
1	0	Error
1	7	code
2	CARD16	sequence number
4	CARD32	bad resource id
2	CARD16	minor opcode
1	CARD8	major opcode
21		unused

GContext

# Bytes	Value	Description
1	0	Error
1	13	code
2	CARD16	sequence number
4	CARD32	bad resource id
2	CARD16	minor opcode
1	CARD8	major opcode
21		unused

IDChoice

# Bytes	Value	Description
1	0	Error
1	14	code
2	CARD16	sequence number
4	CARD32	bad resource id
2	CARD16	minor opcode
1	CARD8	major opcode
21		unused

Implementation

# Bytes	Value	Description
1	0	Error
1	17	code
2	CARD16	sequence number
4		unused
2	CARD16	minor opcode
1	CARD8	major opcode
21		unused

Length

# Bytes	Value	Description
1	0	Error
1	16	code
2	CARD16	sequence number
4		unused
2	CARD16	minor opcode
1	CARD8	major opcode
21		unused

Match

# Bytes	Value	Description
1	0	Error
1	8	code
2	CARD16	sequence number
4		unused
2	CARD16	minor opcode
1	CARD8	major opcode
21		unused

Name

# Bytes	Value	Description
1	0	Error
1	15	code
2	CARD16	sequence number
4		unused
2	CARD16	minor opcode
1	CARD8	major opcode
21		unused

Pixmap

# Bytes	Value	Description
1	0	Error
1	4	code
2	CARD16	sequence number
4	CARD32	bad resource id
2	CARD16	minor opcode
1	CARD8	major opcode
21		unused

Request

# Bytes	Value	Description
1	0	Error
1	1	code
2	CARD16	sequence number
4		unused
2	CARD16	minor opcode
1	CARD8	major opcode
21		unused

Value

# Bytes	Value	Description
1	0	Error
1	2	code
2	CARD16	sequence number
4	<32-bits>	bad value
2	CARD16	minor opcode
1	CARD8	major opcode
21		unused

Window

# Bytes	Value	Description
1	0	Error
1	3	code
2	CARD16	sequence number
4	CARD32	bad resource id
2	CARD16	minor opcode
1	CARD8	major opcode
21		unused

D
Predefined Atoms

*A property is a named piece of data attached to a window, stored by the server. Clients use them primarily to pass information between clients through the server. For this to work, both clients need to know the name of the property where the data will be stored. Property names are strings, so instead of passing arbitrary-length strings over the network, the server chooses an ID to represent each property name. This ID is called an Atom. When a client wants to use a particular property, it knows the name but not the Atom, so it calls **Intern-Atom** to get the Atom for the property name. This is a round-trip because the server maintains the mapping between strings and atoms. Since there are a number of standard properties that are used by many clients, the X protocol defines the Atoms of these properties ahead of time, so that clients need not call **InternAtom**. These are called predefined atoms. This speeds the startup of applications. Client libraries such as Xlib provide symbolic constants that contain the predefined values for these atoms, which clients can use in their code. -Ed.*

Predefined atoms are not strictly necessary and may not be useful in all environments, but they will eliminate many **InternAtom** requests in most applications. Note that they are predefined only in the sense of having numeric values, not in the sense of having required semantics. The core protocol imposes no semantics on these names, but semantics are specified in other X Consortium standards, such as Appendix L, *Interclient Communications Conventions*, and Appendix M, *Logical Font Description Conventions, Release 4*.

To avoid conflicts with possible future names for which semantics might be imposed (either at the protocol level or in terms of higher level user interface models), names beginning with an underscore should be used for atoms that are private to a particular vendor or organization. To guarantee no conflicts between vendors and organizations, additional prefixes need to be used. However, the protocol does not define the mechanism for choosing such prefixes. For names private to a single application or end user but stored in globally accessible locations, it is suggested that two leading underscores be used to avoid conflicts with other names.

The following names have predefined atom values. Note that upper case and lower case matter.

Arc	End_Space	Resolution	Underline_Position
Atom	Family_Name	Resource_Manager	Underline_Thickness
Bitmap	Font	Rgb_Best_Map	Visualid
Cap_Height	Font_Name	Rgb_Blue_Map	Weight
Cardinal	Full_Name	Rgb_Color_Map	Window
Colormap	Integer	Rgb_Default_Map	Wm_Class
Copyright	Italic_Angle	Rgb_Gray_Map	Wm_Client_Machine
Cursor	Max_Space	Rgb_Green_Map	Wm_Command
Cut_Buffer0	Min_Space	Rgb_Red_Map	Wm_Hints
Cut_Buffer1	Norm_Space	Secondary	Wm_Icon_Name
Cut_Buffer2	Notice	Strikeout_Ascent	Wm_Icon_Size
Cut_Buffer3	Pixmap	Strikeout_Descent	Wm_Name
Cut_Buffer4	Point	String	Wm_Normal_Hints
Cut_Buffer5	Point_Size	Subsc.Lpt_X	Wm_Size_Hints
Cut_Buffer6	Primary	Subsc.Lpt_Y	Wm_Transient_For
Cut_Buffer7	Quad_Width	Supersc.Lpt_X	Wm_Zoom_Hints
Drawable	Rectangle	Supersc.Lpt_Y	X_Height

Encoding

Primary	1	Rgb_Color_Map	24	Supersc.Lpt_X	47
Secondary	2	Rgb_Best_Map	25	Supersc.Lpt_Y	48
Arc	3	Rgb_Blue_Map	26	Subsc.Lpt_X	49
Atom	4	Rgb_Default_Map	27	Subsc.Lpt_Y	50
Bitmap	5	Rgb_Gray_Map	28	Underline_Position	51
Cardinal	6	Rgb_Green_Map	29	Underline_Thickness	52
Colormap	7	Rgb_Red_Map	30	Strikeout_Ascent	53
Cursor	8	String	31	Strikeout_Descent	54
Cut_Buffer0	9	VisualId	32	Italic_Angle	55
Cut_Buffer1	10	Window	33	X_Height	56
Cut_Buffer2	11	Wm_Command	34	Quad_Width	57
Cut_Buffer3	12	Wm_Hints	35	Weight	58
Cut_Buffer4	13	Wm_Client_Machine	36	Point_Size	59
Cut_Buffer5	14	Wm_Icon_Name	37	Resolution	60
Cut_Buffer6	15	Wm_Icon_Size	38	Copyright	61
Cut_Buffer7	16	Wm_Name	39	Notice	62
Drawable	17	Wm_Normal_Hints	40	Font_Name	63
Font	18	Wm_Size_Hints	41	Family_Name	64
Integer	19	Wm_Zoom_Hints	42	Full_Name	65
Pixmap	20	Min_Space	43	Cap_Height	66
Point	21	Norm_Space	44	Wm_Class	67
Rectangle	22	Max_Space	45	Wm_Transient_For	68
Resource_Manager	23	End_Space	46		

E
Keyboards and Pointers

Keyboards

A keycode represents a physical (or logical) key. Keycodes lie in the inclusive range [8,255]. A keycode value carries no intrinsic information, although server implementors may attempt to encode geometry information (for example, matrix) to be interpreted in a server-dependent fashion. The mapping between keys and keycodes cannot be changed using the protocol.

A keysym is an encoding of a symbol on the cap of a key. The set of defined keysyms include the character sets Latin-1, Latin-2, Latin-3, Latin-4, Kana, Arabic, Cryllic, Greek, Technical, Special, Publish, Apl, and Hebrew as well as a set of symbols common on keyboards (Return, Help, Tab, and so on). Keysyms with the most-significant bit (of the 29 bits) set are reserved as vendor-specific.

A list of KEYSYMs is associated with each KEYCODE. The list is intended to convey the set of symbols on the corresponding key. If the list (ignoring trailing NoSymbol entries) is a single KEYSYM, "*K*," then the list is treated as if it were the list "*K* NoSymbol *K* NoSymbol." If the list (ignoring trailing NoSymbol entries) is a pair of KEYSYMs, "*K1 K2*," then the list is treated as if it were the list "*K1 K2 K1 K2*." If the list (ignoring trailing NoSymbol entries) is a triple of KEYSYMs, "*K1 K2 K3*," then the list is treated as if it were the list "*K1 K2 K3* No-Symbol." When an explicit "void" element is desired in the list, the value VoidSymbol can be used.

The first four elements of the list are split into two groups of KEYSYMs. Group 1 contains the first and second KEYSYMs; Group 2 contains the third and fourth KEYSYMs. Within each group, if the second element of the group is NoSymbol, then the group should be treated as if the second element were the same as the first element, except when the first element is an alphabetic KEYSYM "*K*" for which both lower-case and upper-case forms are defined. In that case, the group should be treated as if the first element were the upper-case form of "*K*."

The standard rules for obtaining a KEYSYM from a **KeyPress** event make use of only the Group 1 and Group 2 KEYSYMs; no interpretation of other KEYSYMs in the list is given here. Which group to use is determined by modifier state. Switching between groups is controlled by the KEYSYM named MODE SWITCH, by attaching that KEYSYM to some KEYCODE and attaching that KEYCODE to any one of the modifiers Mod1 through Mod5. This modifier is called the "group modifier." For any KEYCODE, Group 1 is used when the group modifier is off, and Group 2 is used when the group modifier is on.

Within a group, which KEYSYM to use is also determined by the modifier state. The first KEYSYM is used when the Shift and Lock modifiers are off. The second KEYSYM is used when the Shift modifier is on, or when the Lock modifier is on and the second KEYSYM is upper-case alphabetic, or when the Lock modifier is on and is interpreted as Shift Lock. Otherwise, when the Lock modifier is on and is interpreted as Caps Lock, the state of the Shift modifier is applied first to select a KEYSYM, but if that KEYSYM is lower-case alphabetic, then the corresponding upper-case KEYSYM is used instead.

The mapping between KEYCODEs and KEYSYMs is not used directly by the server; it is merely stored for reading and writing by clients.

The keymask modifier named **Lock** is intended to be mapped to either a Caps Lock or a Shift Lock key, but which one is left as application-specific and/or user-specific. However, it is suggested that the determination be made according to the associated KEYSYMs of the corresponding KEYCODE.

Pointers

When a button press is processed with the pointer in some window W and no active pointer grab is in progress, the ancestors of W are searched from the root down, looking for a passive grab to activate. If no matching passive grab on the button exists, then an active grab is started automatically for the client receiving the event, and the last-pointer-grab time is set to the current server time. The effect is essentially equivalent to a **GrabButton** with arguments:

Argument	Value
event-mask	Client's selected pointer events on the event window
pointer-mode and keyboard-mode	**Asynchronous**
owner-events	**True**, if the client has **OwnerGrabButton** selected on the event window; otherwise, **False**
confine-to	**None**
cursor	**None**

The grab is terminated automatically when the logical state of the pointer has all buttons released. **UngrabPointer** and **ChangeActivePointerGrab** can both be used to modify the active grab.

Buttons are always numbered starting with one.

Encoding

Keyboards

Keycode values are always greater than 7 (and less than 256).

Keysym values with the bit #x10000000 set are reserved as vendor-specific.

The names and encodings of the standard keysym values are contained in Appendix B, *Keysyms*.

Pointers

Button values are numbered starting with one.

F
Flow Control and Concurrency

Whenever the server is writing to a given connection, it is permissible for the server to stop reading from that connection (but if the writing would block, it must continue to service other connections). The server is not required to buffer more than a single request per connection at one time. For a given connection to the server, a client can block while reading from the connection but should undertake to read (events and errors) when writing would block. Failure on the part of a client to obey this rule could result in a deadlocked connection, although deadlock is probably unlikely unless either the transport layer has very little buffering or the client attempts to send large numbers of requests without ever reading replies or checking for errors and events.

Whether or not a server is implemented with internal concurrency, the overall effect must be as if individual requests are executed to completion in some serial order, and requests from a given connection must be executed in delivery order (that is, the total execution order is a shuffle of the individual streams). The execution of a request includes validating all arguments, collecting all data for any reply, and generating and queueing all required events. However, it does not include the actual transmission of the reply and the events. In addition, the effect of any other cause that can generate multiple events (for example, activation of a grab or pointer motion) must effectively generate and queue all required events indivisibly with respect to all other causes and requests. For a request from a given client, any events destined for that client that are caused by executing the request must be sent to the client before any reply or error is sent.

G
Request Group Summary

Group Listing with Brief Description

This quick reference will help you find and use the correct protocol request for a particular application. It supplies two lists:

• Group Listing with Brief Descriptions

• Alphabetical Listing of Requests

Request Group Summary

Colors and Colormaps

AllocColor	Allocate a read-only colorcell specifying the color with RGB values.
AllocColorCells	Allocate read/write colorcells. This request does not set the colors of the allocated cells.
AllocColorPlanes	Allocate read/write colorcells for overlays. This request does not set the colors of the allocated cells.
AllocNamedColor	Allocate a read-only colorcell specifying the color with a color name.
CopyColormapAndFree	Copy into a new virtual colormap the colorcells that one client has allocated, and free these colorcells in the old colormap.
CreateColormap	Create a virtual colormap.
FreeColormap	Free a virtual colormap.
FreeColors	Deallocate colorcells.
InstallColormap	Copy a virtual colormap into the display hardware, so that it will actually be used to translate pixel values.

ListInstalledColormaps	List the IDs of the colormaps installed in the hardware.
LookupColor	Return the RGB values associated with a color name, and return the closest RGB values available on the display hardware.
QueryColors	Return the colors in the specified cells of a colormap.
StoreColors	Store colors into cells allocated by **AllocColorCells** or **AllocColorPlanes.**
StoreNamedColor	Store colors into cells allocated by **AllocColorCells** or **AllocColorPlanes.**
UninstallColormap	Remove a virtual colormap from the display hardware, so it will not be used to translate pixel values.

Cursors

CreateCursor	Create a cursor resource from characters in a special cursor font.
CreateGlyphCursor	Create a cursor resource from characters in any font.
FreeCursor	Destroy a cursor resource.
RecolorCursor	Change the foreground and background colors of a cursor.

Drawing Graphics

ClearArea	Clear an area of a window.
CopyArea	Copy an area of a window to another area in the same or a different window. If the source area is obscured, this request will generate a **GraphicsExpose** event to identify the area of the destination for which the source is not available.
CopyPlane	Copy a single plane of one drawable into any number of planes of another, applying two pixel values to translate the depth of the single plane.
FillPoly	Fill a polygon, without drawing the complete outline.
PolyArc	Draw one or more arcs, each of which is a partial ellipse aligned with the x and y axis.
PolyFillArc	Fill one or more arcs, without drawing the arc itself.
PolyFillRectangle	Fill one or more rectangles, without drawing the entire outline.
PolyLine	Draw one or more connected lines.

PolyPoint	Draw one or more points.
PolyRectangle	Draw one or more rectangles.
PolySegment	Draw one or more disconnected lines.

Events

GetInputFocus	Return the current keyboard focus window.
GetMotionEvents	Some servers are equipped with a buffer that records the position history of the pointer. This request will return segments of this history for selected time periods.
SetInputFocus	Set a window and its descendants to receive all keyboard input.

Fonts and Text

CloseFont	Disclaim interest in a particular font. If this is the last client to be using the specified font, then the font is unloaded.
GetFontPath	Get the path that the server uses to search for fonts.
ImageText8	Draw text string in 8-bit font. The bounding rectangle of the string is drawn in the background color from the GC before the text is drawn.
ImageText16	Draw text string in 16-bit font. The bounding rectangle of the string is drawn in the background color from the GC before the text is drawn.
ListFonts	List the fonts available on a server.
ListFontsWithInfo	List the fonts available on a server, with information about each font.
OpenFont	Load a font for drawing. If the font has already been loaded, this request simply returns the ID.
PolyText8	Draw text items using 8-bit fonts. Each item can specify a string, a font, and a horizontal offset.
PolyText16	Draw text items using 16-bit fonts. Each item can specify a string, a font, and a horizontal offset.
QueryFont	Get the table of information describing a font and each character in it.
QueryTextExtents	Calculate the width of a string in a certain font.
SetFontPath	Set the path that the server uses to search for fonts.

The Graphics Context

ChangeGC	Change any or all characteristics of an existing GC.
CopyGC	Copy any or all characteristics of one GC into another.
CreateGC	Create a graphics context, and optionally set any or all of its characteristics. If not set, each characteristic has a reasonable default.
FreeGC	Free the memory in the server associated with a GC.
SetClipRectangles	Set the clip region of a GC to the union of a set of rectangles.
SetDashes	Set the dash pattern for lines, in a more powerful way than is possible using **CreateGC** or **ChangeGC**.

Images

GetImage	Place an image from a drawable into a representation in memory.
PutImage	Dump an image into a drawable.

Interclient Communication

ChangeProperty	Set the value of a property.
ConvertSelection	Request that the owner of a particular selection convert it to a particular format, then send an event informing the requestor of the conversion's success and the name of the property containing the result.
DeleteProperty	Delete the data associated with a particular property on a particular window.
GetAtomName	Get the string name of a property given it ID.
GetProperty	Get the value of a property.
GetSelectionOwner	Get the current owner of a particular selection property.
InternAtom	Get the ID of a property given its string name, and optionally create the ID if no property with the specified name exists.
ListHosts	Obtain a list of hosts having access to a display.
ListProperties	List the IDs of the current list of properties.
RotateProperties	Rotate the values of a list of properties.

SetSelectionOwner	Set a window as the current owner of a particular selection property.

Keyboard and Pointer

AllowEvents	Release events queued in the server due to grabs with certain parameters.
Bell	Ring the keyboard bell.
ChangeActivePointerGrab	Change the events that are sent to a window that has grabbed the pointer or keyboard.
ChangeKeyboardControl	Change personal preference features of the keyboard such as click and auto-repeat.
ChangeKeyboardMapping	Change the keyboard mapping seen by all clients.
ChangePointerControl	Change personal preference features of the pointer, such as acceleration (the ratio of the amount the physical mouse is moved to the amount the cursor moves on the screen).
GetKeyboardControl	Get personal preference features of the keyboard such as click and auto-repeat.
GetKeyboardMapping	Return the keyboard mapping seen by all clients.
GetModifierMapping	Get the mapping of physical keys to logical modifiers.
GetPointerControl	Return personal preference features of the pointer.
GetPointerMapping	Get the mapping of physical buttons to logical buttons.
GrabButton	For all pointer events (button presses and motion) occurring while the specified combination of buttons and modifier keys are pressed, declare that these pointer events will be delivered to a particular window regardless of the pointer's location on the screen.
GrabKey	For all keyboard events occurring while the specified combination of buttons and modifier keys are pressed, declare that these keyboard events will be delivered to a particular window regardless of the pointer's location on the screen.
GrabKeyboard	Declare that all keyboard events will be delivered to a particular window regardless of the pointer's location on the screen.
GrabPointer	Declare that all pointer events (button presses and motion) will be delivered to a particular window regardless of the pointer's location on the screen.
QueryKeymap	Get the current state of the entire keyboard.

Request Group Summary

QueryPointer	Get the current pointer position.
SetModifierMapping	Set the mapping of physical keys to logical modifiers such as Shift and Control.
SetPointerMapping	Set the mapping of physical buttons to logical buttons.
UngrabButton	Release a grab on a button.
UngrabKey	Release a grab on a button.
UngrabKeyboard	Release a grab on the keyboard.
UngrabPointer	Release a grab on the pointer.
WarpPointer	Move the pointer.

Security

ChangeHosts	Modify the list of hosts that are allowed access to a server.
SetAccessControl	Turn on or off the mechanism that checks the host access list before allowing a connection.

Window Characteristics

ChangeWindowAttributes	Set any or all window attributes. For a brief description of the window attributes, see Section 1.3.2.
GetGeometry	Return the position, dimensions, border width, and depth of a window; return the ID of the root window at the top of the window's hierarchy.
GetWindowAttributes	Get the current values of some of the window attributes described for **ChangeWindowAttributes**; also find out the characteristics of the window that were set when it was created (**InputOnly** or **InputOutput**, and visual), whether its colormap is installed and whether it is mapped or viewable.

Window Manipulation by the Client

CreateWindow	Create a window.
DestroySubwindows	Destroy an entire hierarchy of windows.
DestroyWindow	Destroy a window.
MapSubwindows	Map all subwindows of a window.

MapWindow	Mark a window as eligible for display.
UnmapSubwindows	Remove all subwindows of a window, but not the window itself, from the screen.
UnmapWindow	Remove a window and all its subwindows from the screen.

Window Manipulation by the Window Manager

ChangeSaveSet	Add or remove windows from a save-set.
CirculateWindow	Lower the highest window on the screen or raise the lowest one, depending on the parameters of this request.
ConfigureWindow	Allow the window manager to move, resize, change the border width, or change the stacking order of a window.
QueryTree	Allow the window manager to get the window IDs of windows it did not create.
ReparentWindow	Allow the window manager to change the window hierarchy to insert a frame window between each top-level window on the screen and the root window. The window manager can then decorate this frame window with a title for the application, buttons for moving and resizing the window, etc.

Miscellaneous

CreatePixmap	Create an off-screen drawable.
ForceScreenSaver	Activate or reset the screen saver.
FreePixmap	Free the memory associated with an off-screen drawable.
GetScreenSaver	Get the characteristics of the mechanism that blanks the screen after an idle period.
GrabServer	Initiate a state where requests only from a single client will be acted upon. The server will queue events for other clients and requests made by other clients until the grab is released.
KillClient	After a client exits because of the **SetCloseDownMode** request, kill the resources that remain alive.
ListExtensions	List the extensions available on the server.
NoOperation	The minimum request, it contains only the opcode and request length.

QueryBestSize	Query the server for the fastest size for creating tiles or stipples or the largest support size for cursors.
QueryExtension	Determine whether a certain extension is available in the server.
SendEvent	Send any type of event to a particular window.
SetCloseDownMode	Determine whether resources created by a client are preserved after the client exits. Normally, they are not, but if the client can reclaim its resources in a later incarnation, the client can use this request.
SetScreenSaver	Set characteristics that blank the screen after an idle period.
TranslateCoordinates	Translate coordinates from a window frame of reference to a screen frame of reference.
UngrabServer	Release the grab on the server, process all outstanding requests, and send all queued events.

H
Alphabetical Listing of Requests

This appendix provides a table that lists all protocol requests in alphabetical order with brief descriptions.

Table H-1. Alphabetical Listing of Requests

Request	Description
AllocColor	Allocate a read-only colorcell specifying the color with RGB values.
AllocColorCells	Allocate read/write colorcells. This request does not set the colors of the allocated cells.
AllocColorPlanes	Allocate read/write colorcells for overlays. This request does not set the colors of the allocated cells.
AllocNamedColor	Allocate a read-only colorcell specifying the color with a color name.
AllowEvents	Release events queued in the server due to grabs with certain parameters.
Bell	Ring the keyboard bell.
ChangeActivePointerGrab	Change the events that are sent to a window that has grabbed the pointer or keyboard.
ChangeGC	Change any or all characteristics of an existing GC.
ChangeHosts	Modify the list of hosts that are allowed access to a server.
ChangeKeyboardControl	Change personal preference features of the keyboard such as click and auto-repeat.
ChangeKeyboardMapping	Change the keyboard mapping seen by all clients.
ChangePointerControl	Change personal preference features of the pointer, such as acceleration (the ratio of the amount the physical mouse is moved to the amount the cursor moves on the screen).
ChangeProperty	Set the value of a property.
ChangeSaveSet	Add or remove windows from a save-set.
ChangeWindowAttributes	Set any or all window attributes. For a brief description of the window attributes, see Section 1.3.2.
CirculateWindow	Lower the highest window on the screen or raise the lowest one, depending on the parameters of this request.
ClearArea	Clear an area of a window.
CloseFont	Disclaim interest in a particular font. If this is the last client to be using the specified font, then the font is unloaded.

Listing of
Requests

Request	Description
ConfigureWindow	Allow the window manager to move, resize, change the border width, or change the stacking order of a window.
ConvertSelection	Request that the owner of a particular selection convert it to a particular format, then send an event informing the requestor of the conversion's success and the name of the property containing the result.
CopyArea	Copy an area of a window to another area in the same or a different window. If the source area is obscured, this request will generate a **GraphicsExpose** event to identify the area of the destination for which the source is not available.
CopyColormapAndFree	Copy into a new virtual colormap the colorcells that one client has allocated, and free these colorcells in the old colormap.
CopyGC	Copy any or all characteristics of one GC into another.
CopyPlane	Copy a single plane of one drawable into any number of planes of another, applying two pixel values to translate the depth of the single plane.
CreateColormap	Create a virtual colormap.
CreateCursor	Create a cursor resource from characters in a special cursor font.
CreateGC	Create a graphics context, and optionally set any or all of its characteristics. If not set, each characteristic has a reasonable default.
CreateGlyphCursor	Create a cursor resource from characters in any font.
CreatePixmap	Create an off-screen drawable.
CreateWindow	Create a window.
DeleteProperty	Delete the data associated with a particular property on a particular window.
DestroySubwindows	Destroy an entire hierarchy of windows.
DestroyWindow	Destroy a window.
FillPoly	Fill a polygon, without drawing the complete outline.
ForceScreenSaver	Activate or reset the screen saver.
FreeColormap	Free a virtual colormap.
FreeColors	Deallocate colorcells.
FreeCursor	Destroy a cursor resource.
FreeGC	Free the memory in the server associated with a GC.
FreePixmap	Free the memory associated with an off-screen drawable.
GetAtomName	Get the string name of a property given it ID.
GetFontPath	Get the path that the server uses to search for fonts.
GetGeometry	Return the position, dimensions, border width, and depth of a window; return the ID of the root window at the top of the window's hierarchy.
GetImage	Place an image from a drawable into a representation in memory.
GetInputFocus	Return the current keyboard focus window.
GetKeyboardControl	Get personal preference features of the keyboard such as click and auto-repeat.
GetKeyboardMapping	Return the keyboard mapping seen by all clients.
GetModifierMapping	Get the mapping of physical keys to logical modifiers.

Request	Description
GetMotionEvents	Some servers are equipped with a buffer that records the position history of the pointer. This request will return segments of this history for selected time periods.
GetPointerControl	Return personal preference features of the pointer.
GetPointerMapping	Get the mapping of physical buttons to logical buttons.
GetProperty	Get the value of a property.
GetScreenSaver	Get the characteristics of the mechanism that blanks the screen after an idle period.
GetSelectionOwner	Get the current owner of a particular selection property.
GetWindowAttributes	Get the current values of some of the window attributes described for **ChangeWindowAttributes**; also find out the characteristics of the window that were set when it was created (**InputOnly** or **InputOutput**, and visual), whether its colormap is installed and whether it is mapped or viewable.
GrabButton	For all pointer events (button presses and motion) occurring while the specified combination of buttons and modifier keys are pressed, declare that these pointer events will be delivered to a particular window regardless of the pointer's location on the screen.
GrabKey	For all keyboard events occurring while the specified combination of buttons and modifier keys are pressed, declare that these keyboard events will be delivered to a particular window regardless of the pointer's location on the screen.
GrabKeyboard	Declare that all keyboard events will be delivered to a particular window regardless of the pointer's location on the screen.
GrabPointer	Declare that all pointer events (button presses and motion) will be delivered to a particular window regardless of the pointer's location on the screen.
GrabServer	Initiate a state where requests only from a single client will be acted upon. The server will queue events for other clients and requests made by other clients until the grab is released.
ImageText8	Draw text string in 8-bit font. The bounding rectangle of the string is drawn in the background color from the GC before the text is drawn.
ImageText16	Draw text string in 16-bit font. The bounding rectangle of the string is drawn in the background color from the GC before the text is drawn.
InstallColormap	Copy a virtual colormap into the display hardware, so that it will actually be used to translate pixel values.
InternAtom	Get the ID of a property given its string name, and optionally create the ID if no property with the specified name exists.
KillClient	After a client exits because of the **SetCloseDownMode** request, kill the resources that remain alive.
ListExtensions	List the extensions available on the server.
ListFonts	List the fonts available on a server.
ListFontsWithInfo	List the fonts available on a server, with information about each font.
ListHosts	Obtain a list of hosts having access to a display.
ListInstalledColormaps	List the IDs of the colormaps installed in the hardware.
ListProperties	List the IDs of the current list of properties.

Listing of
Requests

Request	Description
LookupColor	Return the RGB values associated with a color name, and return the closest RGB values available on the display hardware.
MapSubwindows	Map all subwindows of a window.
MapWindow	Mark a window as eligible for display.
NoOperation	The minimum request, it contains only the opcode and request length.
OpenFont	Load a font for drawing. If the font has already been loaded, this request simply returns the ID.
PolyArc	Draw one or more arcs, each of which is a partial ellipse aligned with the x and y axis.
PolyFillArc	Fill one or more arcs, without drawing the arc itself.
PolyFillRectangle	Fill one or more rectangles, without drawing the entire outline.
PolyLine	Draw one or more connected lines.
PolyPoint	Draw one or more points.
PolyRectangle	Draw one or more rectangles.
PolySegment	Draw one or more disconnected lines.
PolyText8	Draw text items using 8-bit fonts. Each item can specify a string, a font, and a horizontal offset.
PolyText16	Draw text items using 16-bit fonts. Each item can specify a string, a font, and a horizontal offset.
PutImage	Dump an image into a drawable.
QueryBestSize	Query the server for the fastest size for creating tiles or stipples or the largest support size for cursors.
QueryColors	Return the colors in the specified cells of a colormap.
QueryExtension	Determine whether a certain extension is available in the server.
QueryFont	Get the table of information describing a font and each character in it.
QueryKeymap	Get the current state of the entire keyboard.
QueryPointer	Get the current pointer position.
QueryTextExtents	Calculate the width of a string in a certain font.
QueryTree	Allow the window manager to get the window IDs of windows it did not create.
RecolorCursor	Change the foreground and background colors of a cursor.
ReparentWindow	Allow the window manager to change the window hierarchy to insert a frame window between each top-level window on the screen and the root window. The window manager can then decorate this frame window with a title for the application, buttons for moving and resizing the window, etc.
RotateProperties	Rotate the values of a list of properties.
SendEvent	Send any type of event to a particular window.
SetAccessControl	Turn on or off the mechanism that checks the host access list before allowing a connection.
SetClipRectangles	Set the clip region of a GC to the union of a set of rectangles.
SetCloseDownMode	Determine whether resources created by a client are preserved after the client exits. Normally, they are not, but if the client can reclaim its resources in a later incarnation, the client can use this request.

Request	Description
SetDashes	Set the dash pattern for lines, in a more powerful way than is possible using **CreateGC** or **ChangeGC**.
SetFontPath	Set the path that the server uses to search for fonts.
SetInputFocus	Set a window and its descendants to receive all keyboard input.
SetModifierMapping	Set the mapping of physical keys to logical modifiers such as Shift and Control.
SetPointerMapping	Set the mapping of physical buttons to logical buttons.
SetScreenSaver	Set characteristics that blank the screen after an idle period.
SetSelectionOwner	Set a window as the current owner of a particular selection property.
StoreColors	Store colors into cells allocated by **AllocColorCells** or **AllocColorPlanes**.
StoreNamedColor	Store colors into cells allocated by **AllocColorCells** or **AllocColorPlanes**.
TranslateCoordinates	Translate coordinates from a window frame of reference to a screen frame of reference.
UngrabButton	Release a grab on a button.
UngrabKey	Release a grab on a button.
UngrabKeyboard	Release a grab on the keyboard.
UngrabPointer	Release a grab on the pointer.
UngrabServer	Release the grab on the server, process all outstanding requests, and send all queued events.
UninstallColormap	Remove a virtual colormap from the display hardware, so it will not be used to translate pixel values.
UnmapSubwindows	Remove all subwindows of a window, but not the window itself, from the screen.
UnmapWindow	Remove a window and all its subwindows from the screen.
WarpPointer	Move the pointer.

Listing of
Requests

I

Xlib Functions to Protocol Requests

This appendix provides a table that lists each Xlib function (in alphabetical order) and the corresponding protocol request that it generates.

Xlib Function	Protocol Request
XActivateScreenSaver	ForceScreenSaver
XAddHost	ChangeHosts
XAddHosts	ChangeHosts
XAddToSaveSet	ChangeSaveSet
XAllocColor	AllocColor
XAllocColorCells	AllocColorCells
XAllocColorPlanes	AllocColorPlanes
XAllocNamedColor	AllocNamedColor
XAllowEvents	AllowEvents
XAutoRepeatOff	ChangeKeyboardControl
XAutoRepeatOn	ChangeKeyboardControl
XBell	Bell
XChangeActivePointerGrab	ChangeActivePointerGrab
XChangeGC	ChangeGC
XChangeKeyboardControl	ChangeKeyboardControl
XChangeKeyboardMapping	ChangeKeyboardMapping
XChangePointerControl	ChangePointerControl
XChangeProperty	ChangeProperty
XChangeSaveSet	ChangeSaveSet
XChangeWindowAttributes	ChangeWindowAttributes
XCirculateSubwindows	CirculateWindow
XCirculateSubwindowsDown	CirculateWindow
XCirculateSubwindowsUp	CirculateWindow
XClearArea	ClearArea
XClearWindow	ClearArea
XConfigureWindow	ConfigureWindow
XConvertSelection	ConvertSelection
XCopyArea	CopyArea
XCopyColormapAndFree	CopyColormapAndFree
XCopyGC	CopyGC

Xlib Function	Protocol Request
XCopyPlane	CopyPlane
XCreateBitmapFromData	CreateGC
	CreatePixmap
	FreeGC
	PutImage
XCreateColormap	CreateColormap
XCreateFontCursor	CreateGlyphCursor
XCreateGC	CreateGC
XCreateGlyphCursor	CreateGlyphCursor
XCreatePixmap	CreatePixmap
XCreatePixmapCursor	CreateCursor
XCreatePixmapFromBitmapData	CreateGC
	CreatePixmap
	FreeGC
	PutImage
XCreateSimpleWindow	CreateWindow
XCreateWindow	CreateWindow
XDefineCursor	ChangeWindowAttributes
XDeleteProperty	DeleteProperty
XDestroySubwindows	DestroySubwindows
XDestroyWindow	DestroyWindow
XDisableAccessControl	SetAccessControl
XDrawArc	PolyArc
XDrawArcs	PolyArc
XDrawImageString	ImageText8
XDrawImageString16	ImageText16
XDrawLine	PolySegment
XDrawLines	PolyLine
XDrawPoint	PolyPoint
XDrawPoints	PolyPoint
XDrawRectangle	PolyRectangle
XDrawRectangles	PolyRectangle
XDrawSegments	PolySegment
XDrawString	PolyText8
XDrawString16	PolyText16
XDrawText	PolyText8
XDrawText16	PolyText16
XEnableAccessControl	SetAccessControl
XFetchBuffer	GetProperty
XFetchBytes	GetProperty
XFetchName	GetProperty
XFillArc	PolyFillArc
XFillArcs	PolyFillArc
XFillPolygon	FillPoly
XFillRectangle	PolyFillRectangle
XFillRectangles	PolyFillRectangle

Xlib Function	Protocol Request
XForceScreenSaver	ForceScreenSaver
XFreeColormap	FreeColormap
XFreeColors	FreeColors
XFreeCursor	FreeCursor
XFreeFont	CloseFont
XFreeGC	FreeGC
XFreePixmap	FreePixmap
XGetAtomName	GetAtomName
XGetFontPath	GetFontPath
XGetGeometry	GetGeometry
XGetIconName	GetProperty
XGetIconSizes	GetProperty
XGetImage	GetImage
XGetInputFocus	GetInputFocus
XGetKeyboardControl	GetKeyboardControl
XGetKeyboardMapping	GetKeyboardMapping
XGetModifierMapping	GetModifierMapping
XGetMotionEvents	GetMotionEvents
XGetModifierMapping	GetModifierMapping
XGetNormalHints	GetProperty
XGetPointerControl	GetPointerControl
XGetPointerMapping	GetPointerMapping
XGetRGBColormap	GetProperty
XGetScreenSaver	GetScreenSaver
XGetSelectionOwner	GetSelectionOwner
XGetSizeHints	GetProperty
XGetSubImage	GetImage
XGetTextProperty	GetProperty
XGetWMClientMachine	GetProperty
XGetWMHints	GetProperty
XGetWMCommand	GetProperty
XGetWMIconName	GetProperty
XGetWMProtocols	GetProperty
XGetWMNormalHints	GetProperty
XGetWMSizeHints	GetProperty
XGetWindowAttributes	GetWindowAttributes
	GetGeometry
XGetWindowProperty	GetProperty
XGetZoomHints	GetProperty
XGrabButton	GrabButton
XGrabKey	GrabKey
XGrabKeyboard	GrabKeyboard
XGrabPointer	GrabPointer
XGrabServer	GrabServer
XIconifyWindow	SendEvent
XInitExtension	QueryExtension

Xlib Function	Protocol Request
XInstallColormap	InstallColormap
XInternAtom	InternAtom
XKillClient	KillClient
XListExtensions	ListExtensions
XListFonts	ListFonts
XListFontsWithInfo	ListFontsWithInfo
XListHosts	ListHosts
XListInstalledColormaps	ListInstalledColormaps
XListProperties	ListProperties
XLoadFont	OpenFont
XLoadQueryFont	OpenFont
	QueryFont
XLookupColor	LookupColor
XLowerWindow	ConfigureWindow
XMapRaised	ConfigureWindow
	MapWindow
XMapSubwindows	MapSubwindows
XMapWindow	MapWindow
XMoveResizeWindow	ConfigureWindow
XMoveWindow	ConfigureWindow
XNoOp	NoOperation
XOpenDisplay	see Connection Setup
XParseColor	LookupColor
XPutImage	PutImage
XQueryBestCursor	QueryBestSize
XQueryBestSize	QueryBestSize
XQueryBestStipple	QueryBestSize
XQueryBestTile	QueryBestSize
XQueryColor	QueryColors
XQueryColors	QueryColors
XQueryExtension	QueryExtension
XQueryFont	QueryFont
XQueryKeymap	QueryKeymap
XQueryPointer	QueryPointer
XQueryTextExtents	QueryTextExtents
XQueryTextExtents16	QueryTextExtents
XQueryTree	QueryTree
XRaiseWindow	ConfigureWindow
XReadBitmapFile	CreateGC
	CreatePixmap
	FreeGC
	PutImage
XRecolorCursor	RecolorCursor
XReconfigureWMWindow	ConfigureWindow
XRemoveFromSaveSet	ChangeSaveSet
XRemoveHost	ChangeHosts

Xlib Function	Protocol Request
XRemoveHosts	ChangeHosts
XReparentWindow	ReparentWindow
XResetScreenSaver	ForceScreenSaver
XResizeWindow	ConfigureWindow
XRestackWindows	ConfigureWindow
XRotateBuffers	RotateProperties
XRotateWindowProperties	RotateProperties
XSelectInput	ChangeWindowAttributes
XSendEvent	SendEvent
XSetAccessControl	SetAccessControl
XSetArcMode	ChangeGC
XSetBackground	ChangeGC
XSetClipMask	ChangeGC
XSetClipOrigin	ChangeGC
XSetClipRectangles	SetClipRectangles
XSetCloseDownMode	SetCloseDownMode
XSetCommand	ChangeProperty
XSetDashes	SetDashes
XSetFillRule	ChangeGC
XSetFillStyle	ChangeGC
XSetFont	ChangeGC
XSetFontPath	SetFontPath
XSetForeground	ChangeGC
XSetFunction	ChangeGC
XSetGraphicsExposures	ChangeGC
XSetIconName	ChangeProperty
XSetIconSizes	ChangeProperty
XSetInputFocus	SetInputFocus
XSetLineAttributes	ChangeGC
XSetModifierMapping	SetModifierMapping
XSetNormalHints	ChangeProperty
XSetPlaneMask	ChangeGC
XSetPointerMapping	SetPointerMapping
XSetRGBColormap	ChangeProperty
XSetScreenSaver	SetScreenSaver
XSetSelectionOwner	SetSelectionOwner
XSetSizeHints	ChangeProperty
XSetStandardProperties	ChangeProperty
XSetState	ChangeGC
XSetStipple	ChangeGC
XSetSubwindowMode	ChangeGC
XSetTextProperty	ChangeProperty
XSetTile	ChangeGC
XSetTSOrigin	ChangeGC
XSetWMClientMachine	ChangeProperty
XSetWMColormapWindows	ChangeProperty

Xlib Function	Protocol Request
XSetWMCommand	ChangeProperty
XSetWMHints	ChangeProperty
XSetWMIconName	ChangeProperty
XSetWMNormalHints	ChangeProperty
XSetWMProtocols	ChangeProperty
XSetWMProperties	ChangeProperty
XSetWMSizeHints	ChangeProperty
XSetWindowBackground	ChangeWindowAttributes
XSetWindowBackgroundPixmap	ChangeWindowAttributes
XSetWindowBorder	ChangeWindowAttributes
XSetWindowBorderPixmap	ChangeWindowAttributes
XSetWindowBorderWidth	ConfigureWindow
XSetWindowColormap	ChangeWindowAttributes
XSetZoomHints	ChangeProperty
XStoreBuffer	ChangeProperty
XStoreBytes	ChangeProperty
XStoreColor	StoreColors
XStoreColors	StoreColors
XStoreName	ChangeProperty
XStoreNamedColor	StoreNamedColor
XTranslateCoordinates	TranslateCoordinates
XUndefineCursor	ChangeWindowAttributes
XUngrabButton	UngrabButton
XUngrabKey	UngrabKey
XUngrabKeyboard	UngrabKeyboard
XUngrabPointer	UngrabPointer
XUngrabServer	UngrabServer
XUninstallColormap	UninstallColormap
XUnloadFont	CloseFont
XUnmapSubwindows	UnmapSubwindows
XUnmapWindow	UnmapWindow
XWarpPointer	WarpPointer
XWithdrawWindow	SendEvent

J

Protocol Requests to Xlib Functions

The following table lists each X protocol request (in alphabetical order) and the Xlib functions that reference it.

Protocol Request	Xlib Function
AllocColor	XAllocColor
AllocColorCells	XAllocColorCells
AllocColorPlanes	XAllocColorPlanes
AllocNamedColor	XAllocNamedColor
AllowEvents	XAllowEvents
Bell	XBell
SetAccessControl	XDisableAccessControl
	XEnableAccessControl
	XSetAccessControl
ChangeActivePointerGrab	XChangeActivePointerGrab
SetCloseDownMode	XSetCloseDownMode
ChangeGC	XChangeGC
	XSetArcMode
	XSetBackground
	XSetClipMask
	XSetClipOrigin
	XSetFillRule
	XSetFillStyle
	XSetFont
	XSetForeground
	XSetFunction
	XSetGraphicsExposures
	XSetLineAttributes
	XSetPlaneMask
	XSetState
	XSetStipple
	XSetSubwindowMode
	XSetTile
	XSetTSOrigin
ChangeHosts	XAddHost

Protocol Request	Xlib Function
	XAddHosts
	XRemoveHost
	XRemoveHosts
ChangeKeyboardControl	XAutoRepeatOff
	XAutoRepeatOn
	XChangeKeyboardControl
ChangeKeyboardMapping	XChangeKeyboardMapping
ChangePointerControl	XChangePointerControl
ChangeProperty	XChangeProperty
	XSetCommand
	XSetIconName
	XSetIconSizes
	XSetNormalHints
	XSetSizeHints
	XSetStandardProperties
	XSetWMHints
	XSetZoomHints
	XStoreBuffer
	XStoreBytes
	XStoreName
ChangeSaveSet	XAddToSaveSet
	XChangeSaveSet
	XRemoveFromSaveSet
ChangeWindowAttributes	XChangeWindowAttributes
	XDefineCursor
	XSelectInput
	XSetWindowBackground
	XSetWindowBackgroundPixmap
	XSetWindowBorder
	XSetWindowBorderPixmap
	XSetWindowColormap
	XUndefineCursor
CirculateWindow	XCirculateSubwindowsDown
	XCirculateSubwindowsUp
	XCirculateSubwindows
ClearArea	XClearArea
	XClearWindow
CloseFont	XFreeFont
	XUnloadFont
ConfigureWindow	XConfigureWindow
	XLowerWindow
	XMapRaised
	XMoveResizeWindow
	XMoveWindow
	XRaiseWindow
	XResizeWindow

Protocol Request	Xlib Function
	XRestackWindows
	XSetWindowBorderWidth
ConvertSelection	XConvertSelection
CopyArea	XCopyArea
CopyColormapAndFree	XCopyColormapAndFree
CopyGC	XCopyGC
CopyPlane	XCopyPlane
CreateColormap	XCreateColormap
CreateCursor	XCreatePixmapCursor
CreateGC	XCreateGC
	XCreateBitmapFromData
	XCreatePixmapFromData
	XOpenDisplay
	XReadBitmapFile
CreateGlyphCursor	XCreateFontCursor
	XCreateGlyphCursor
CreatePixmap	XCreatePixmap
	XCreateBitmapFromData
	XCreatePixmapFromData
	XReadBitmapFile
CreateWindow	XCreateSimpleWindow
	XCreateWindow
DeleteProperty	XDeleteProperty
DestroySubwindows	XDestroySubwindows
DestroyWindow	XDestroyWindow
FillPoly	XFillPolygon
ForceScreenSaver	XActivateScreenSaver
	XForceScreenSaver
	XResetScreenSaver
FreeColormap	XFreeColormap
FreeColors	XFreeColors
FreeCursor	XFreeCursor
FreeGC	XFreeGC
	XCreateBitmapFromData
	XCreatePixmapFromData
	XReadBitmapFile
FreePixmap	XFreePixmap
GetAtomName	XGetAtomName
GetFontPath	XGetFontPath
GetGeometry	XGetGeometry
	XGetWindowAttributes
GetImage	XGetImage
GetInputFocus	XGetInputFocus
	XSync
GetKeyboardControl	XGetKeyboardControl
GetKeyboardMapping	XGetKeyboardMapping

Protocol Request	Xlib Function
GetModifierMapping	XGetModifierMapping
GetMotionEvents	XGetMotionEvents
GetPointerControl	XGetPointerControl
GetPointerMapping	XGetPointerMapping
GetProperty	XFetchBytes
	XFetchName
	XGetIconSizes
	XGetNormalHints
	XGetSizeHints
	XGetWMHints
	XGetWindowProperty
	XGetZoomHints
GetSelectionOwner	XGetSelectionOwner
GetWindowAttributes	XGetWindowAttributes
GrabButton	XGrabButton
GrabKey	XGrabKey
GrabKeyboard	XGrabKeyboard
GrabPointer	XGrabPointer
GrabServer	XGrabServer
ImageText8	XDrawImageString
ImageText16	XDrawImageString16
InstallColormap	XInstallColormap
InternAtom	XInternAtom
KillClient	XKillClient
ListExtensions	XListExtensions
ListFonts	XListFonts
ListFontsWithInfo	XListFontsWithInfo
ListHosts	XListHosts
ListInstalledColormaps	XListInstalledColormaps
ListProperties	XListProperties
LookupColor	XLookupColor
	XParseColor
MapSubwindows	XMapSubwindows
MapWindow	XMapRaised
	XMapWindow
NoOperation	XNoOp
OpenFont	XLoadFont
	XLoadQueryFont
PolyArc	XDrawArc
	XDrawArcs
PolyFillArc	XFillArc
	XFillArcs
PolyFillRectangle	XFillRectangle
	XFillRectangles
PolyLine	XDrawLines
PolyPoint	XDrawPoint

Protocol Request	Xlib Function
	XDrawPoints
PolyRectangle	XDrawRectangle
	XDrawRectangles
PolySegment	XDrawLine
	XDrawSegments
PolyText8	XDrawString
	XDrawText
PolyText16	XDrawString16
	XDrawText16
PutImage	XPutImage
	XCreateBitmapFromData
	XCreatePixmapFromData
	XReadBitmapFile
QueryBestSize	XQueryBestCursor
	XQueryBestSize
	XQueryBestStipple
	XQueryBestTile
QueryColors	XQueryColor
	XQueryColors
QueryExtension	XInitExtension
	XQueryExtension
QueryFont	XLoadQueryFont
	XQueryFont
QueryKeymap	XQueryKeymap
QueryPointer	XQueryPointer
QueryTextExtents	XQueryTextExtents
	XQueryTextExtents16
QueryTree	XQueryTree
RecolorCursor	XRecolorCursor
ReparentWindow	XReparentWindow
RotateProperties	XRotateBuffers
	XRotateWindowProperties
SendEvent	XSendEvent
SetClipRectangles	XSetClipRectangles
SetCloseDownMode	XSetCloseDownMode
SetDashes	XSetDashes
SetFontPath	XSetFontPath
SetInputFocus	XSetInputFocus
SetModifierMapping	XSetModifierMapping
SetPointerMapping	XSetPointerMapping
SetScreenSaver	XGetScreenSaver
	XSetScreenSaver
SetSelectionOwner	XSetSelectionOwner
StoreColors	XStoreColor
	XStoreColors
StoreNamedColor	XStoreNamedColor

Protocol Request	Xlib Function
TranslateCoordinates	XTranslateCoordinates
UngrabButton	XUngrabButton
UngrabKey	XUngrabKey
UngrabKeyboard	XUngrabKeyboard
UngrabPointer	XUngrabPointer
UngrabServer	XUngrabServer
UninstallColormap	XUninstallColormap
UnmapSubwindows	XUnmapSubWindows
UnmapWindow	XUnmapWindow
WarpPointer	XWarpPointer

K
Events Briefly Described

The X server is capable of sending many types of events to the client, only some of which most clients need. Therefore, X provides a mechanism whereby the client can express an interest in certain events but not others. Not only does this prevent wasting of network time on unneeded events, but it also speeds and simplifies clients by avoiding the testing and throwing away of these unnecessary events. Events are selected on a per-window basis.

As mentioned in the sample session in Section 1.3, all events begin with an 8-bit type code. The following is a list of all the event types, what they signify, and any special notes about how they are selected.

ButtonPress, ButtonRelease
> A pointer button was pressed or released. These events include the pointer position and the state of the modifier keys on the keyboard (such as Shift).

CirculateNotify, ConfigureNotify, CreateNotify, DestroyNotify, MapNotify, UnmapNotify
> This event is generated when one of these requests is actually made on a window. These are used to tell a client when some other client has manipulated a window. Usually this other client is the window manager. All these events and **GravityNotify** and **ReparentNotify** can only be selected together.

CirculateRequest, ConfigureRequest, MapRequest, ResizeRequest
> These events are selected by the window manager to enforce its window management policy. Once selected by the window manager, any request to resize, map, reconfigure, or circulate a window by any client other than the window manager will not be acted on by the server but instead will result in one of these events being sent to the window manager. The window manager then can decide whether to allow, modify, or deny the parameters of the request given in the event and then reissue the request to the server.

ClientMessage
> These events, or any other type, can be sent from one client to another using the **SendEvent** request. This event type is for client-specific information.

ColormapNotify
> This event tells a client when a colormap has been modified or when it is installed or uninstalled from the hardware colormap.

EnterNotify, LeaveNotify

The pointer entered or left a window. These events are generated even for each window not visible on the screen that is an ancestor of the origin or destination window.

Expose

As explained in Section 1.2.2, **Expose** events signify that a section of a window has become visible and should be redrawn by the client.

FocusIn, FocusOut

The keyboard focus window has been changed. Like **EnterNotify** and **Leave-Notify**, these events can be generated even for invisible windows.

GraphicsExpose, NoExpose

GraphicsExpose and **NoExpose** are generated only as the result of **CopyArea** and **CopyPlane** requests. If the source area specified in either request is unavailable, one or more **GraphicsExpose** events are generated, and they specify the areas of the destination that could not be drawn. If the source area was available, a single **NoExpose** event is generated. **GraphicsExpose** and **No-Expose** events are not selected normally but instead are turned on or off by a member of the graphics context.

GravityNotify

This event notifies a client when a window has been moved in relation to its parent because of its window gravity attribute. This window attribute is designed to allow automatic positioning of subwindows in certain simple cases when the parent is resized.

KeymapNotify

Always following **EnterNotify** or **FocusIn**, **KeymapNotify** gives the complete status of all the keys on the keyboard.

KeyPress, KeyRelease

A keyboard key was pressed or released. Even the Shift and Control keys generate these events. There is no way to select just the events on particular keys.

MappingNotify

This event tells the client that a client has changed the keyboard symbol table in the server. This event cannot be selected; it is always sent to the client when any client calls **ChangeKeyboardMapping**.

MotionNotify

The pointer moved. **MotionNotify** events can be selected such that they are delivered only when certain pointer buttons are pressed or regardless of the pointer buttons. Also, they can be selected such that only one **MotionNotify** event is sent between each query of the pointer position or button press. This reduces the number of **MotionNotify** events sent for clients that do not need complete pointer position history.

PropertyNotify

This event is issued whenever a client changes or deletes a property, even if the change is to replace data with identical data.

ReparentNotify

This event tells the client that a window has been given a new parent. Reparenting is used by the window manager to decorate and provide space around each window for a user interface for window management. One meaning of this event is that the coordinates of this window are no longer in relation to the old parent, which is normally the screen.

SelectionClear, SelectionNotify, SelectionRequest

These three events are used in the selection method of communicating between clients. See Section 1.3.2.1 for a description of selecting events. These events are not selected, but are always generated by the requests involved in the selection procedure.

VisibilityNotify

This event is generated when a window changes from fully obscured, partially obscured, or unobscured to any other of these states and also when this window becomes viewable (all its ancestors are mapped).

As mentioned in the list, a few of these event types cannot be selected because they are automatically delivered to all clients whenever they occur. This is either because virtually all clients need them or because they only get generated by clients that have an interest in them.

Unused bytes within an event are not guaranteed to be zero. Event codes 64 through 127 are reserved for extensions, although the core protocol does not define a mechanism for selecting interest in such events. Every core event (with the exception of **KeymapNotify**) also contains the least significant 16 bits of the sequence number of the last request issued by the client that was (or is currently being) processed by the server.

The server may retain the recent history of pointer motion and to a finer granularity than is reported by **MotionNotify** events. Such history is available by means of the **GetMotion-Events** request. The approximate size of the history buffer is given by motion-buffer-size.

L
Interclient Communication Conventions*

It was an explicit design goal of X11 to specify mechanism, not policy. As a result, a client that converses with the server using the protocol defined by the X Window System Protocol, Version 11, may operate "correctly" in isolation but may not coexist properly with others sharing the same server.

Being a good citizen in the X11 world involves adhering to conventions governing interclient communication in a number of areas:

- The selection mechanism.

- The cut buffers.

- The window manager.

- The session manager.

- The manipulation of shared resources.

- The resource database.

In the following sections, we propose suitable conventions for each area, insofar as it is possible to do so *without* enforcing a particular user interface. In order to permit clients written in different languages to communicate, the conventions are expressed solely in terms of the protocol operations, not in the (probably more familiar) Xlib interface. The binding of these operations to the Xlib interface for C, and to the equivalent interfaces for other languages, is the subject of other documents.

*This appendix reprints *Inter-Client Communication Conventions Manual, Version 1.0, MIT X Consortium Standard*, by David S. H. Rosenthal, Sun Microsystems, Inc.

L.1 Evolution of the Conventions

In the interests of timely acceptance, this first edition of the manual covers only a minimal set of required conventions. It is expected that as experience is gained, these conventions will be added to and conventions governing other optional areas will be agreed on. The X Consortium is expected to develop mechanisms for doing this.

As far as possible, these conventions are upward-compatible with those in the February 25, 1988, draft of this manual distributed with the X11R2 release. In some areas, semantic problems were discovered with those conventions and thus complete upward-compatibility could not be assured. Areas of incompatibility are noted in the text and summarized in Section L.8.

In the course of developing these conventions, a number of minor changes to the protocol have been identified as desirable. They are identified in the text and summarized in Section L.9, as input to a future protocol revision process. If and when a protocol revision incorporating them is undertaken, this document will need some revision. Since it is difficult to ensure that clients and servers are upgraded simultaneously, clients using the revised conventions should examine the minor protocol revision number and be prepared to use the older conventions when communicating with an older server.

It is expected that the conventions will be revised in such a way as to ensure that clients using the conventions appropriate to protocol minor revision n will interoperate correctly with those using conventions appropriate to protocol minor revision $n+1$ if the server supports both.

L.1.1 Atoms

Many of the conventions described below use Atoms. The following sections amplify the description of Atoms in the protocol specification, to assist the reader.

L.1.2 What are Atoms?

At the conceptual level, Atoms are unique names. Clients can use them to communicate information to each other. They can be thought of as a bundle of octets, like a string, but without an encoding being specified. The elements are not necessarily ASCII characters, and no case folding happens.*

The protocol designers felt that passing these sequences of bytes back and forth across the wire would be too costly. Further, it is important that events as they appear "on the wire" have a fixed size (in fact, 32 bytes), and since some events contain Atoms, a fixed-size representation for them was needed.

---

*The comment in the protocol specification for `InternAtom` that ISO Latin-1 encoding should be used is in the nature of a convention; the server treats the string as a byte sequence.

To provide a fixed-size representation, a protocol request (`InternAtom`) was provided to register a byte sequence with the server, which returns a 32-bit value (with the top three bits zero) that maps to the byte sequence. The inverse operator is also available (`GetAtom-Name`).

L.1.3 Predefined Atoms

The protocol specifies a number of Atoms as being predefined:

> "Predefined atoms are not strictly necessary and may not be useful in all environments but will eliminate many `InternAtom` requests in most applications. Note that "predefined" is only in the sense of having numeric values, not in the sense of having required semantics."

They are an implementation trick to avoid the cost of Interning many atoms that are expected to be used during the startup phase of all applications. The results of the `InternAtom` requests (which require a handshake) can be assumed *a priori*.

Language interfaces should probably cache the Atom-name mappings, and get them only when required. The CLX interface, for instance, makes no distinction between predefined atoms and other atoms; all atoms are viewed as symbols at the interface. However, a CLX implementation will typically keep a symbol/atom cache and will typically prefill this cache with the predefined atoms.

L.1.4 Naming Conventions

The built-in atoms are composed of upper-case ASCII characters with the logical words separated by an underscore ("_") (for example, `WM_ICON_NAME`). The protocol specification recommends that Atoms used for private vendor specific reasons should begin with an underscore. To prevent conflicts among organizations, additional prefixes should be chosen (for example, `_DEC_WM_DECORATION_GEOMETRY`).

The names were chosen in this fashion to make it easy to use them in a "natural" way within LISP. Keyword constructors allow the programmer to specify the atoms as LISP atoms. If the atoms were not all upper case, then special quoting conventions would have to be used.

L.1.5 Semantics

The core protocol imposes no semantics on atoms except as they are used in FONTPROP structures. See the definition of `QueryFont` in the protocol specification for more information on FONTPROP semantics.

L.1.6 Name Spaces

The protocol defines six distinct spaces in which Atoms are interpreted, as shown in Table L-1. Any particular Atom may or may not have some valid interpretation with respect to each of these name spaces.

Table L-1. Atom Name Spaces

Space	a.k.a	Examples
Property name	name	WM_HINTS, WM_NAME, RGB_BEST_MAP, etc.
Property type	type	WM_HINTS, CURSOR, RGB_COLOR_MAP, etc.
Selection name	selection	PRIMARY, SECONDARY, CLIPBOARD
Selection target	target	FILE_NAME, POSTSCRIPT, PIXMAP, etc.
Font property		QUAD_WIDTH, POINT_SIZE, etc.
ClientMessage type		WM_SAVE_YOURSELF, _DEC_SAVE_EDITS, etc.

L.2 Peer-to-Peer Communication via Selections

The primary mechanism X11 defines for clients that want to exchange information, for example, by cutting and pasting between windows, is *selections*. There can be an arbitrary number of selections, each named by an atom, and they are global to the server. The choice of an atom to be used is discussed in Section L.2.6. Each selection is owned by a client and is attached to a window.

Selections communicate between an *owner* and a *requestor*. The owner has the data representing the value of its selection, and the requestor receives it. A requestor wishing to obtain the value of a selection provides:

- The name of the selection.

- The name of a property.

- A window.

- An atom representing the data type required.

If the selection is currently owned, the owner receives an event and is expected to:

- Convert the contents of the selection to the requested data type.

- Place this data in the named property on the named window.

- Send the requestor an event to let it know the property is available.

Clients are strongly encouraged to use this mechanism. In particular, displaying text in a permanent window without providing the ability to select it and convert it into a string is definitely antisocial.

Note that in the X11 environment, *all* data transferred between an owner and a requestor must normally go via the server. An X11 client cannot assume that another client can open the same files or even communicate directly. The other client may be talking to the server via a completely different networking mechanism (for example, one client might be DECnet and the other TCP/IP). Thus, passing indirect references to data such as file names, hostnames and port numbers, and so on is permitted only if both clients specifically agree.

L.2.1 Acquiring Selection Ownership

A client wishing to acquire ownership of a particular selection should call Set-SelectionOwner:

```
SetSelectionOwner
     selection:    ATOM
     owner:        WINDOW or None
     time:         TIMESTAMP or CurrentTime
```

The client should set *selection* to the Atom representing the selection, set *owner* to some window that it created, and set *time* to some time between the current last-change time of the selection concerned and the current server time. This time value will normally be obtained from the timestamp of the event triggering the acquisition of the selection. Clients should *not* set the time value to CurrentTime, since if they do so they have no way of finding when they gained ownership of the selection. Clients must use a window they created in order for requestors to be able to route events to the owner of the selection.*

> Convention: *Clients attempting to acquire a selection must set the time value of the* SetSelectionOwner *request to the timestamp of the event triggering the acquisition attempt, not to* CurrentTime. *A zero-length append to a property is a way to obtain a timestamp for this purpose; the timestamp is in the corresponding* PropertyNotify *event.*

Note that if the time in the SetSelectionOwner request is in the future relative to the server's current time or if it is in the past relative to the last time the selection concerned changed hands, the SetSelectionOwner request appears to the client to succeed, but ownership is *not* actually transferred.

Since clients cannot name other clients directly, the "owner" window is used to refer to the owning client in the replies to GetSelectionOwner, in SelectionRequest and SelectionClear events, and possibly as a place to put properties describing the selection in question. To discover the owner of a particular selection, a client should invoke:

```
GetSelectionOwner
     selection:    ATOM
   =>
     owner:        WINDOW or None
```

---

*There is at present no part of the protocol which requires requestors to send events to the owner of a selection. This restriction is imposed in order to prepare for possible future extensions.

Convention: *Clients are normally expected to provide some visible confirmation of selection ownership. To make this feedback reliable, a client must perform a sequence like:*

```
SetSelectionOwner(selection=PRIMARY, owner=Window,
        time=timestamp)
owner = GetSelectionOwner(selection=PRIMARY)
if (owner != Window) Failure
```

If the `SetSelectionOwner` request succeeds (not merely appears to succeed), the client issuing it is recorded by the server as being the owner of the selection for the time period starting at "time."

Problem: *There is no way for anyone to find out the last-change time of a selection. At the next protocol revision, `GetSelectionOwner` should be changed to return the last-change time as well as the owner.*

L.2.2 Responsibilities of the Selection Owner

When a requestor wants the value of a selection, the owner receives a `Selection-Request` event:

```
SelectionRequest
    owner:       WINDOW
    selection:   ATOM
    target:      ATOM
    property:    ATOM or None
    requestor:   WINDOW
    time:        TIMESTAMP or CurrentTime
```

The *owner* and the *selection* fields will be the values specified in the `Set-SelectionOwner` request. The owner should compare the timestamp with the period it has owned the selection and, if the time is outside, refuse the `SelectionRequest` by sending the requestor window a `SelectionNotify` event with the "property" set to `None`, using `SendEvent` with an empty event mask.

More advanced selection owners are free to maintain a history of the value of the selection and to respond to requests for the value of the selection during periods they owned it even though they do not own it now.

If the *property* field is `None`, the requestor is an obsolete client. Owners are encouraged to support these clients by using the *target* atom as the property name to be used for the reply.

Otherwise, the owner should use the *target* field to decide the form to convert the selection into and, if the selection cannot be converted into that form, refuse the `Selection-Request` similarly.

If the *property* field is not `None`, the owner should place the data resulting from converting the selection into the specified property on the requestor window, setting the property's type to some appropriate value (which need not be the same as *target*).

Convention: *All properties used to reply to* `SelectionRequest` *events must be placed on the requestor window.*

In either case, if the data comprising the selection cannot be stored on the requestor window (for example, because the server cannot provide sufficient memory), the owner must refuse the `SelectionRequest` as above. See Section L.2.5.

If the property is successfully stored, the owner should acknowledge the successful conversion by sending the requestor window a `SelectionNotify` event, using `SendEvent` with an empty mask:

```
SelectionNotify
     requestor:      WINDOW
     selection:      ATOM
     target:         ATOM
     property:       ATOM or None
     time:           TIMESTAMP or CurrentTime
```

The `selection`, `target`, `property`, and `time` fields of the `SelectionNotify` event should be set to the values received in the `SelectionRequest` event (setting the `property` field to None indicates that the conversion requested could not be made).

Convention: *The* `selection`, `target`, `property`, *and* `time` *fields in the* `SelectionNotify` *event should be set to the values received in the* `SelectionRequest` *event.*

The data stored in the property must eventually be deleted. A convention is needed to assign the responsibility for doing so.

Convention: *Selection requestors are responsible for deleting properties whose names they receive in* `SelectionNotify` *events (see Section L.2.4) or in properties with type MULTIPLE.*

A selection owner will often need confirmation that the data comprising the selection has actually been transferred (for example, if the operation has side effects on the owner's internal data structures, these should not take place until the requestor has indicated that it has successfully received the data). They should express interest in `PropertyNotify` events for the `requestor` window and wait until the property in the `SelectionNotify` event has been deleted before assuming that the selection data has been transferred.

When some other client acquires a selection, the previous owner receives a `Selection-Clear` event:

```
SelectionClear
     owner:          WINDOW
     selection:      ATOM
     time:           TIMESTAMP
```

The `timestamp` field is the time at which the ownership changed hands, and the `owner` field is the window the new owner specified in its `SetSelectionOwner` request.

If an owner loses ownership while it has a transfer in progress, that is to say, before it receives notification that the requestor has received all the data, it must continue to service the ongoing transfer until it is complete.

L.2.3 Giving Up Selection Ownership

Clients may give up selection ownership voluntarily, or they may lose it forcibly as the result of some other client's actions.

L.2.3.1 Voluntarily

To relinquish ownership of a selection voluntarily, a client should execute a Set-SelectionOwner request for that selection atom, with *owner* specified as None and *time* the timestamp that was used to acquire the selection.

Alternatively, the client may destroy the window used as the *owner* value of the Set-SelectionOwner request, or it may terminate. In both cases, the ownership of the selection involved will revert to None.

L.2.3.2 Forcibly

If a client gives up ownership of a selection, or if some other client executes a Set-SelectionOwner for it and thus reassigns it forcibly, the previous owner will receive a SelectionClear event:

```
SelectionClear
    owner:          WINDOW
    selection:      ATOM
    time:           TIMESTAMP
```

The timestamp is the time the selection changed hands. The owner argument is the window that was specified by the current owner in its SetSelectionOwner request.

L.2.4 Requesting a Selection

A client wishing to obtain the value of a selection in a particular form issues a Convert-Selection request:

```
ConvertSelection
    selection:      ATOM
    target:         ATOM
    property:       ATOM or None
    requestor:      WINDOW
    time:           TIMESTAMP or CurrentTime
```

The *selection* field specifies the particular selection involved, and the *target* specifies the required form of the information. The choice of suitable atoms to use is discussed in Section L.2.6. The *requestor* field should be set to a window the requestor created; the *owner* will place the reply property on it. The *time* field should be set to the timestamp on the event triggering the request for the selection value; clients should *not* use Current-Time for this field.

Convention: *Clients should not use* CurrentTime *for the time field of* ConvertSelection *requests. They should use the timestamp of the event that caused the request to be made.*

The *property* field should be set to the name of a property that the owner can use to report the value of the selection. Note that the requestor of a selection needs to know neither the client owning the selection nor the window to which it is attached.

Although the protocol allows the property field to be set to None (in which case the owner is supposed chose a property name), it is difficult for the owner to do so safely.

Convention: *Requestors should not use* None *for the property field of* ConvertSelection *requests.*

Convention: *Owners receiving* ConvertSelection *requests with property field* None *are talking to an obsolete client. They should choose the target atom as the property name to be used for the reply.*

The result of the ConvertSelection request is that a SelectionNotify event will be received:

```
SelectionNotify
     requestor:    WINDOW
     selection:    ATOM
     target:       ATOM
     property:     ATOM or None
     time:         TIMESTAMP or CurrentTime
```

The *requestor*, *selection*, *target*, and *time* fields will be the same as those on the ConvertSelection request.

If the *property* field is None, the conversion has been refused. This can mean that there is no owner for the selection, that the owner does not support the conversion implied by *target*, or that the server did not have sufficient space to accommodate the data.

If the *property* field is not None, then that property will exist on the *requestor* window. The value of the selection can be retrieved from this *property* by using the GetProperty request:

```
GetProperty
     window:       WINDOW
     property:     ATOM
     type:         ATOM or AnyPropertyType
     long-offset:  CARD32
     long-length:  CARD32
     delete:       BOOL
=>
     type:         ATOM or None
     format:       {0, 8, 16, 32}
     bytes-after:  CARD32
     value:        LISTofINT8 or LISTofINT16 or LISTofINT32
```

When using GetProperty to retrieve the value of a selection, the *property* field should be set to the corresponding value in the SelectionNotify event. The *type* field should be set to AnyPropertyType, because the *requestor* has no way of knowing beforehand what type the selection owner will use. Several GetProperty requests may be needed to retrieve all the data in the selection; each should set the *long-offset* field to the amount of data received so far and the *size* field to some reasonable buffer size (see Section L.2.5). If the returned value of *bytes-after* is zero, the whole property has been transferred.

Once all the data in the selection has been retrieved, which may require getting the values of several properties (see Section L.2.7), the property in the `SelectionNotify` should be deleted by invoking `GetProperty` with the *delete* field set to `True`.

As discussed above, the owner has no way of knowing when the data has been transferred to the *requestor* unless the property is removed.

> Convention: *The requestor must delete the property named in the* `SelectionNotify` *once all the data has been retrieved. They should invoke either* `DeleteProperty` *or* `GetWindowProperty(delete==TRUE)` *after they have successfully retrieved all data comprising the selection. See the next section.*

L.2.5 Large Data Transfers

Selections can get large, and this poses two problems:

- Transferring large amounts of data to the server is expensive.

- All servers will have limits on the amount of data that can be stored in properties. Exceeding this limit will result in an `Alloc` error on the `ChangeProperty` request that the selection owner uses to store the data.

The problem of limited server resources is addressed by the following conventions:

> Convention: *Selection owners should transfer the data describing a selection large compared with maximum-request-size in the connection handshake using the INCR property mechanism (see below).*

> Convention: *Any client using* `SetSelectionOwner` *to acquire selection ownership should arrange to process* `Alloc` *errors in property change requests. For clients using Xlib, this involves using* `XSetErrorHandler()` *to override the default handler.*

> Convention: *A selection owner must confirm that no* `Alloc` *error occurred while storing the properties for a selection before replying with a confirming* `SelectionNotify` *event.*

> Convention: *When storing large amounts (relative to max-request-size) of data, clients should use a sequence of* `ChangeProperty(mode==Append)` *requests for reasonable quantities of data. This is to avoid locking up servers and to limit the waste of data transfer caused by an* `Alloc` *error.*

Convention: *If an* Alloc *error occurs during storing the selection data, all properties stored for this selection should be deleted, and the* Convert-Selection *request refused by replying with a* SelectionNotify *event with* property *set to* None.

Convention: *In order to avoid locking up servers for inordinate lengths of time, requestors retrieving large quantities of data from a property should perform a series of* GetProperty *requests, each asking for a reasonable amount of data.*

Problem: *Single-threaded servers should be changed to avoid locking up during large data transfers.*

L.2.6 Usage of Selection Atoms

It is important to observe that defining a new atom consumes resources in the server, and they are not released until the server reinitializes. Thus, it must be a goal to reduce the need for newly minted atoms.

L.2.6.1 Selection Atoms

There can be an arbitrary number of selections, each named by an atom. To conform with the interclient conventions, however, clients need deal with only these three selections:

*   PRIMARY
*   SECONDARY
*   CLIPBOARD

Other selections may be used freely for private communication among related groups of clients.

Problem: *How does a client find out which selection atoms are valid?*

L.2.6.2 The PRIMARY Selection

The selection named by the atom PRIMARY is used for all commands which take only a single argument. It is the principal means of communication between clients which use the selection mechanism.

L.2.6.3 The SECONDARY Selection

The selection named by the atom SECONDARY is used:

- As the second argument to commands taking two arguments, for example, "exchange primary and secondary selections."

- As a means of obtaining data when there is a primary selection and the user does not wish to disturb it.

L.2.6.4 The CLIPBOARD Selection

The selection named by the atom CLIPBOARD is used to hold data being transferred between clients, normally being "cut" or "copied" and then "pasted." Whenever a client wants to transfer data to the clipboard, it should:

- Assert ownership of the CLIPBOARD.

- If it succeeds in acquiring ownership, it should be prepared to respond to a request for the contents of the CLIPBOARD in the normal way, retaining the data in order to be able to return it. The request may be generated by the clipboard client described below.

- If it fails to acquire ownership, a cutting client should not actually perform the cut nor provide feedback suggesting that it has actually transferred data to the clipboard.

This process should be repeated whenever the data to be transferred would change.

Clients wishing to "paste" data from the clipboard should request the contents of the CLIPBOARD selection in the usual way.

Except while a client is actually deleting data, the owner of the CLIPBOARD selection may be a single, special client implemented for the purpose. It should:

- Assert ownership of the CLIPBOARD selection, and reassert it any time the clipboard data changes.

- If it loses the selection (which will be because someone has some new data for the clipboard):

  - Obtain the contents of the selection from the new owner, using the timestamp in the `SelectionClear` event.

  - Attempt to reassert ownership of the CLIPBOARD selection, using the same timestamp.

  - If the attempt fails, restart the process using a newly acquired timestamp. This timestamp should be obtained by asking the current owner of the CLIPBOARD selection to convert it to a TIMESTAMP. If this conversion is refused, or if the same timestamp is received twice, the clipboard client should acquire a fresh timestamp in the normal way, for example, by a zero-length append to a property.

- Respond to requests for the CLIPBOARD contents in the normal way.

A special CLIPBOARD client is not necessary. The protocol used by the "cutting" client and the "pasting" client is the same whether the CLIPBOARD client is running or not. The reasons for running the special client include:

- Stability – If the "cutting" client were to crash or terminate, the clipboard value would still be available.

- Feedback – The clipboard client can display the contents of the clipboard.

- Simplicity – A client deleting data does not have to retain it for so long, reducing the chance of race conditions causing problems.

The reasons not to run the clipboard client include:

- Performance – Data is only transferred if it is actually required (when some client actually wants the data).

- Flexibility – The clipboard data may be available as more than one target.

L.2.6.5 Target Atoms

The atom that a requestor supplies as the `target` of a `ConvertSelection` request determines the form of the data supplied. The set of such atoms is extensible, but a generally accepted base set of target atoms is needed. As a starting point for this, Table L-2 contains those that have been suggested so far.

Table L-2. Initial Set of Target Atoms and Their Meanings

Atom	Type (See Table L-3)	Meaning
TARGETS	ATOM	List of valid target atoms
MULTIPLE	ATOM_PAIR	Look in the `ConvertSelection` property
TIMESTAMP	INTEGER	Timestamp used to acquire selection
STRING	STRING	ISO Latin-1 (+TAB+NEWLINE) text
TEXT	TEXT	Text in owner's encoding
LIST_LENGTH	INTEGER	Number of disjoint parts of selection
PIXMAP	DRAWABLE	Pixmap ID
DRAWABLE	DRAWABLE	Drawable ID
BITMAP	BITMAP	Bitmap ID
FOREGROUND	PIXEL	Pixel value
BACKGROUND	PIXEL	Pixel value
COLORMAP	COLORMAP	Colormap ID
ODIF	TEXT	ISO Office Document Interchange Format
OWNER_OS	TEXT	Operating system of owner
FILE_NAME	TEXT	Full path name of a file
HOST_NAME	TEXT	See `WM_CLIENT_MACHINE`
CHARACTER_POSITION	SPAN	Start and end of selection in bytes
LINE_NUMBER	SPAN	Start and end line numbers

Table L-2. Initial Set of Target Atoms and Their Meanings (continued)

Atom	Type (See Table L-3)	Meaning
COLUMN_NUMBER	SPAN	
LENGTH	INTEGER	Number of bytes in selection
USER	TEXT	Name of user running owner
PROCEDURE	TEXT	Name of selected procedure
MODULE	TEXT	Name of selected module
PROCESS	INTEGER, TEXT	Process ID of owner
TASK	INTEGER, TEXT	Task ID of owner
CLASS	TEXT	Class of owner; see WM_CLASS
NAME	TEXT	Name of owner; see WM_NAME
CLIENT_WINDOW	WINDOW	Top-level window of owner
DELETE	NULL	True if owner deleted selection
INSERT_SELECTION	NULL	Insert specified selection
INSERT_PROPERTY	NULL	Insert specified property

This table will grow.

Selection owners are required to support the following targets:

- **TARGETS.** The owner should return a list of Atoms representing the targets for which an attempt to convert the current selection will succeed (barring unforeseeable problems such as `Alloc` errors). This list should include all the required Atoms.

- **MULTIPLE.** The MULTIPLE target atom is valid only when a property is specified on the `ConvertSelection` request. If the *property* field in the `Selection-Request` event is `None` and the target is MULTIPLE, it should be refused.

  When a selection owner receives a `SelectionRequest(target=MULTIPLE)` request, the contents of the property named in the request will be a list of atom pairs, the first atom naming a target and the second naming a property (`None` is not valid here). The effect should be as if the owner had received a sequence of `SelectionRequest` events, one for each atom pair, except that:

  - The owner should reply with a `SelectionNotify` only when all the requested conversions have been performed.

  - The owner should replace in the MULTIPLE property any property atoms for targets it failed to convert with `None`.

    Convention: *The entries in a MULTIPLE property must be processed in the order they appear in the property. See Section L.2.6.3.*

- **TIMESTAMP.** To avoid some race conditions, it is important that requestors be able to discover the timestamp the owner used to acquire ownership. Until and unless the protocol is changed so that `GetSelectionOwner` returns the timestamp used to acquire ownership, selection owners must support conversion to TIMESTAMP, returning the timestamp they used to obtain the selection.

> Problem: *The protocol should be changed to return in response to a* Get-SelectionOwner *the timestamp used to acquire the selection.*

All other targets are optional.

L.2.6.6 Selection with Side Effects

Some targets, DELETE is an example, have side effects. To render them unambiguous, the entries in a MULTIPLE property must be processed in the order they appear in the property.

In general, targets with side effects will return no information (i.e., a zero-length property of type NULL). In all cases, the requested side effect must be performed before the conversion is accepted. If the requested side effect cannot be performed, the corresponding conversion request must be refused.

> Convention: *Targets with side effects should return no information (i.e., a zero-length property of type* NULL*).*

> Convention: *The side effect of a target must be performed before the conversion is accepted.*

> Convention: *If the side effect of a target cannot be performed, the corresponding conversion request must be refused.*

> Problem: *The need to delay responding to the* ConvertSelection *request until a further conversion has succeeded poses problems for the Intrinsics interface that need to be addressed.*

These side-effect targets are used to implement operations such as "exchange primary and secondary selections."

L.2.6.7 DELETE

When the owner of a selection receives a request to convert it to DELETE, it should delete the corresponding selection (whatever doing so means for its internal data structures) and return a zero-length property of type NULL if the deletion was successful.

L.2.6.8 INSERT_SELECTION

When the owner of a selection receives a request to convert it to INSERT_SELECTION, the property named will be of type ATOM_PAIR. The first atom will name a selection, and the second will name a target. The owner should use the selection mechanism to convert the named selection into the named target and insert it at the location of the selection for which it got the INSERT_SELECTION request (whatever doing so means for its internal data structures).

L.2.6.9 INSERT_PROPERTY

When the owner of a selection receives a request to convert it to INSERT_PROPERTY, it should insert the property named in the request at the location of the selection for which it got the INSERT_SELECTION request (whatever doing so means for its internal data structures).

L.2.7 Usage of Selection Properties

The names of the properties used in selection data transfer are chosen by the requestor. The use of None property fields in ConvertSelection requests, which request the selection owner to choose a name, is not permitted by these conventions.

The type of the property involved is always chosen by the selection owner and can involve some types with special semantics assigned by convention. These special types are reviewed in the following sections.

In all cases, a request for conversion to a target should return a property of one of the types listed in Table L-2 for that property, or a property of type INCR and then a property of one of the listed types.

The selection owner will return a list of zero or more items of the type indicated by the property type. In general, the number of items in the list will correspond to the number of disjoint parts of the selection. Some targets, such as side-effect targets, will be of length 0 irrespective of the number of disjoint selection parts. In the case of fixed-size items, the requestor may determine the number of items by the property size; for variable-length items such as text, the separators are listed in Table L-3.

Table L-3. Property Types, Formats, and Separators

Type Atom	Format	Separator
STRING	8	Null
ATOM	32	Fixed-size
ATOM_PAIR	32	Fixed-size
BITMAP	32	Fixed-size
PIXMAP	32	Fixed-size
DRAWABLE	32	Fixed-size
SPAN	32	Fixed-size
INTEGER	32	Fixed-size
WINDOW	32	Fixed-size
INCR	32	Fixed-size

This table will grow.

L.2.7.1 TEXT Properties

In general, the encoding for the characters in a text string property is specified by its type. It is highly desirable for there to be a simple, invertible mapping between string property types and any character set names embedded within font names in any font-naming standard adopted by the Consortium.

The atom TEXT is a polymorphic target. Requesting conversion into TEXT will convert into whatever encoding is convenient for the owner. The encoding chosen will be indicated by the type of the property returned. TEXT is not defined as a type; it will never be the returned type from a selection conversion request.

If the requestor wants the owner to return the contents of the selection in a specific encoding, it should request conversion into the name of that encoding.

In Table L-2, the word TEXT is used to indicate one of the registered encoding names. The type would not actually be TEXT; it would be STRING or some other ATOM naming the encoding chosen by the owner.

STRING as a type or a target specifies the ISO Latin-1 character set plus the "control" characters TAB (octal 11) and NEWLINE (octal 12). The spacing interpretation of TAB is context-dependent. Other ASCII control characters are explicitly not included in STRING at the present time.

Type STRING properties will consist of a list of elements separated by NULL characters; other encodings will need to specify an appropriate list format.

L.2.7.2 INCR Properties

Requestors may receive a property of type INCR* in response to any target that results in selection data. This indicates that the owner will send the actual data incrementally. The contents of the INCR property will be an integer, representing a lower bound on the number of bytes of data in the selection. The requestor and the selection owner transfer the data comprising the selection in the following manner.

The selection requestor starts the transfer process by deleting the (*type*==INCR) property forming the reply to the selection.

The selection owner then:

- Appends the data in suitable-size chunks to the same property on the same window as the selection reply, with a type corresponding to the actual type of the converted selection. The size should be less than the maximum-request-size in the connection handshake.

- Between each append, waits for a PropertyNotify (*state*==Deleted) event showing that the requestor has read the data. The reason for doing this is to limit the consumption of space in the server.

---

*These properties were called INCREMENTAL in an earlier draft. The protocol for using them has changed, and so the name has changed to avoid confusion.

- When the entire data has been transferred to the server, waits until a `Property-Notify` (*state*==`Deleted`), showing that the data has been read by the requestor, and then writes zero-length data to the property.

The selection requestor:

- Waits for the `SelectionNotify` event.
- Loops—
  - Retrieving data using `GetProperty` with *delete* `True`.
  - Waiting for a `PropertyNotify` with *state*==`NewValue`.

  —until a zero-length property is obtained.
- Deletes the zero-length property.

The type of the converted selection is the type of the first partial property. The remaining partial properties must have the same type.

L.2.7.3 DRAWABLE Properties

Requestors may receive properties of type PIXMAP, BITMAP, DRAWABLE, or WINDOW, containing an appropriate ID. Some information about these drawables is available from the server via the `GetGeometry` request, but the following items are not:

- Foreground pixel
- Background pixel
- Colormap ID

In general, requestors converting into targets whose returned type in Table L-2 is one of the DRAWABLE types should expect to convert also into the following targets (using the MULTIPLE mechanism):

- FOREGROUND returns a PIXEL value.
- BACKGROUND returns a PIXEL value.
- COLORMAP returns a colormap ID.

L.2.7.4 SPAN Properties

Properties with type SPAN contain a list of cardinal-pairs, with the length of the cardinals determined by the format. The first specifies the starting position, and the second the ending position plus one. The base is zero. If they are the same, the span is zero-length and before the specified position. The units are implied by the target atom, such as LINE_NUMBER or CHARACTER_POSITION.

L.3 Peer-to-Peer Communication via Cut Buffers

Communication via cut buffers is much simpler but much less powerful than via the selection mechanism. The selection mechanism is active, in that it provides a link between the owner and requestor clients. The cut buffer mechanism is passive; an owner places data in a cut buffer, from where a requestor retrieves it at some later time.

The cut buffers consist of eight properties on the root of screen 0, named by the predefined atoms CUT_BUFFER0 to CUT_BUFFER7. These properties must (at present) have type STRING and format 8. A client using the cut buffer mechanism must initially ensure that all eight exist, using ChangeProperty to append zero-length data to each.

A client storing data in the cut buffers (an owner) must first rotate the ring of buffers by +1, using RotateProperties to rename CUT_BUFFER0 to CUT_BUFFER1 to ..... to CUT_BUFFER7 to CUT_BUFFER0. It must then store the data into CUT_BUFFER0, using ChangeProperty in mode Replace.

A client obtaining data from the cut buffers should use GetProperty to retrieve the contents of CUT_BUFFER0.

A client may, in response to a specific user request, rotate the cut buffers by -1, using RotateProperties to rename CUT_BUFFER7 to CUT_BUFFER6 to ..... to CUT_BUFFER0 to CUT_BUFFER7.

Data should be stored to the cut buffers and the ring rotated only when requested by explicit user action. Users depend on their mental model of cut buffer operation and need to be able to identify operations that transfer data to and fro.

L.4 Client-to-Window-Manager Communication

To permit window managers to perform their role of mediating the competing demands for resources such as screen space, the clients being managed must adhere to certain conventions and must expect the window managers to do likewise. These conventions are covered here from the client's point of view and again from the window manager's point of view in the *Window and Session Manager Conventions Manual.**

---

*The *Window and Session Manager Conventions Manual* has not yet been written.

In general, these conventions are somewhat complex and will undoubtedly change as new window management paradigms are developed. There is thus a strong bias towards defining only those conventions that are essential and which apply generally to all window management paradigms. Clients designed to run with a particular window manager can easily define private protocols to add to these conventions but must be aware that their users may decide to run some other window manager no matter how much the designers of the private protocol are convinced that they have seen the "one true light" of user interfaces.

It is a principle of these conventions that a general client should neither know nor care which window manager is running or, indeed, if one is running at all. The conventions do not support all client functions without a window manager running—for example, the concept of Iconic is not directly supported by clients. If no window manager is running, the concept of Iconic does not apply. A goal of the conventions is to make it possible to kill and restart window managers without loss of functionality.

Each window manager will implement a particular window management policy; the choice of an appropriate window management policy for the user's circumstances is not one for an individual client to make but will be made by the user or the user's system administrator. This does not exclude the possibility of writing clients that use a private protocol to restrict themselves to operating only under a specific window manager; it merely ensures that no claim of general utility is made for such programs.

For example, the claim is often made that "the client I'm writing is important, and it needs to be on top." Perhaps it is important when it is being run in earnest, and it should then be run under the control of a window manager that recognizes "important" windows through some private protocol and ensures that they are on top. However, imagine, for example, that the "important" client is being debugged. Then, ensuring that it is always on top is no longer the appropriate window management policy, and it should be run under a window manager that allows other windows (e.g., the debugger) to appear on top.

L.4.1 Client's Actions

In general, the object of the X11 design is that clients should as far as possible do exactly what they would do in the absence of a window manager, except for:

- Hinting to the window manager about the resources they would like to obtain.

- Cooperating with the window manager by accepting the resources they are allocated, even if they are not those requested.

- Being prepared for resource allocations to change at any time.

L.4.1.1 Creating a Top-level Window

A client would normally expect to create its top-level windows as children of one or more of the root windows, using some boiler plate like:

```
win = XCreateSimpleWindow(dpy, DefaultRootWindow(dpy),
            xsh.x, xsh.y, xsh.width, xsh.height,
            bw, bd, bg);
```

or, if a particular one of the roots was required, like:

```
win = XCreateSimpleWindow(dpy, RootWindow(dpy, screen),
            xsh.x, xsh.y, xsh.width, xsh.height,
            bw, bd, bg);
```

Ideally, it should be possible to override the choice of a root window and allow clients (including window managers) to treat a nonroot window as a pseudo-root. This would allow, for example, testing of window managers and the use of application-specific window managers to control the subwindows owned by the members of a related suite of clients. Doing so properly requires an extension, the design of which is under study.*

From the client's point of view, the window manager will regard its top-level window as being in one of three states:

- Normal
- Iconic
- Withdrawn

Newly created windows start in the Withdrawn state. Transitions between states happen when the top-level window is mapped and unmapped and when the window manager receives certain messages. For details, see Sections L.4.1.2 and L.4.1.14.

L.4.1.2 Client Properties

Once the client has one or more top-level windows, it should place properties on those windows to inform the window manager of its desired behavior. Window managers will assume values they find convenient for any of these properties that are not supplied; clients that depend on particular values must explicitly supply them. Properties written by the client will not be changed by the window manager.

The window manager will examine the contents of these properties when the window makes the transition from Withdrawn state and will monitor some for changes while the window is in Iconic or Normal state. When the client changes one of these properties, it must use Replace mode to overwrite the entire property with new data; the window manager will retain no memory of the old value of the property. All fields of the property must be set to suitable values in a single Replace-mode ChangeProperty request. This is to ensure that the full contents of the property will be available to a new window manager if the existing

---

*The mechanism proposed in the earlier drafts turned out to be inadequate to support all the proposed uses of the pseudo-root facility.

one crashes or is shut down and restarted, or if the session needs to be shut down and restarted by the session manager.

> Convention: *Clients writing or rewriting window manager properties must ensure that the entire content of the property remains valid at all times.*

If these properties are longer than expected, clients should ignore the remainder of the property. Extending these properties is reserved to the X Consortium; private extensions to them are forbidden. Private additional communication between clients and window managers should take place using separate properties. The next sections describe each of the properties the clients needs to set in turn. They are summarized in Table L-13.

L.4.1.3 WM_NAME

The WM_NAME property is an uninterpreted string that the client wishes the window manager to display in association with the window (for example, in a window headline bar).

The encoding used for this string (and all other uninterpreted string properties) is implied by the type of the property. The ATOMS to be used for this purpose are described in Section L.2.7.1.

Window managers are expected to make an effort to display this information; simply ignoring WM_NAME is not acceptable behavior. Clients can assume that at least the first part of this string is visible to the user and that, if the information is not visible to the user, it is because the user has taken an explicit decision to make it invisible.

On the other hand, there is no guarantee that the user can see the WM_NAME string even if the window manager supports window headlines. The user may have placed the headline off-screen or covered it by other windows. WM_NAME should not be used for application-critical information nor to announce asynchronous changes of application state that require timely user response. The expected uses are:

- To permit the user to identify one of a number of instances of the same client.

- To provide the user with noncritical state information.

Note that even window managers that support headline bars will place some limit on the length of string that can be visible; brevity here will pay dividends.

> Problem: *A change is needed to* XFetchName *and similar Xlib routines to allow for multiple encodings.*

L.4.1.4 WM_ICON_NAME

The WM_ICON_NAME property is an uninterpreted string that the client wishes displayed in association with the window when it is iconified (for example, in an icon label). In other respects, including the type, it is similar to WM_NAME. Fewer characters will normally be visible in WM_ICON_NAME than WM_NAME, for obvious geometric reasons.

Clients should not attempt to display this string in their icon pixmaps or windows; they should rely on the window manager to do so.

L.4.1.5 WM_NORMAL_HINTS

The type of the WM_NORMAL_HINTS property is WM_SIZE_HINTS. Its contents are shown in Table L-4.

Table L-4. WM_SIZE_HINTS Type Property Contents

Field	Type	Comments
flags	CARD32	See Table L-5 below
pad	4*CARD32	For backward-compatibility
min_width	INT32	If missing, assume base_width
min_height	INT32	If missing, assume base_height
max_width	INT32	
max_height	INT32	
width_inc	INT32	
height_inc	INT32	
min_aspect	(INT32,INT32)	
max_aspect	(INT32,INT32)	
base_width	INT32	If missing, assume min_width
base_height	INT32	If missing, assume min_height
win_gravity	INT32	If missing, assume NorthWest

Table L-5. WM_SIZE_HINTS.flags Bit Definitions

Name	Value	Field
USPosition	1	User-specified x, y
USSize	2	User-specified width, height
PPosition	4	Program-specified position
PSize	8	Program-specified size
PMinSize	16	Program-specified minimum size
PMaxSize	32	Program-specified maximum size
PResizeInc	64	Program-specified resize increments
PAspect	128	Program-specified min and max aspect ratios
PBaseSize	256	Program-specified base size

Table L-5. WM_SIZE_HINTS.flags Bit Definitions (continued)

Name	Value	Field
PWinGravity	512	Program-specified window gravity

To indicate that the size and position of the window (when mapped from Withdrawn state) was specified by the user, the client should set the USPosition and USSize flags. To indicate that it was specified by the client without any user involvement, the client should set PPosition and PSize. USPosition and USSize allow a window manager to know that the user specifically asked where the window should be placed or how the window should be sized and that further interaction is superfluous.

The size specifiers refer to the width and height of the client's window, excluding borders. The window manager will interpret the position of the window, and its border width, to position the point of the outer rectangle of the overall window specified by the win_gravity in the size hints. The outer rectangle of the window includes any borders or decorations supplied by the window manager. In other words, if the window manager decides to place the window where the client asked, the position on the parent window's border named by the win_gravity will be placed where the client window would have been placed in the absence of a window manager.

The defined values for win_gravity are those specified for WINGRAVITY in the core X protocol, with the exception of Unmap and Static: NorthWest (1), North (2), NorthEast (3), West (4), Center (5), East (6), SouthWest (7), South (8), and SouthEast (9).

The min_width and min_height elements specify the minimum size that the window can be for the client to be useful. The max_width and max_height elements specify the maximum size. The base_width and base_height elements in conjunction with width_inc and height_inc define an arithmetic progression of preferred window widths and heights:

```
width = base_width + ( i * width_inc )
height = base_height + ( j * height_inc )
```

for nonnegative integers i and j. Window managers are encouraged to use i and j instead of width and height in reporting window sizes to users. If a base size is not provided, the minimum size is to be used in its place and vice versa.

The min_aspect and max_aspect fields are fractions, with the numerator first and the denominator second, and they allow a client to specify the range of aspect ratios it prefers.

Problem: *The* base *and* win_gravity *fields need a change to Xlib.*

L.4.1.6 WM_HINTS

The WM_HINTS property, whose type is WM_HINTS, is used to communicate to the window manager the information it needs other than the window geometry, which is available from the window itself; the constraints on that geometry, which is available from the WM_NORMAL_HINTS structure; and various strings, which need separate properties such as WM_NAME. The contents of these properties are shown in Table L-6.

Table L-6. WM_HINTS Type Property Contents

Field	Type	Comments
flags	CARD32	See Table L-7 below
input	CARD32	Client's input model
initial_state	CARD32	State when first mapped
icon_pixmap	PIXMAP	Pixmap for icon image
icon_window	WINDOW	Window for icon image
icon_x	INT32	Icon location
icon_y	INT32	
icon_mask	PIXMAP	Mask for icon shape
window_group	WINDOW	ID of group leader window

Table L-7. WM_HINTS.flags Bit Definitions

Name	Value	Field
InputHint	1	input
StateHint	2	initial_state
IconPixmapHint	4	icon_pixmap
IconWindowHint	8	icon_window
IconPositionHint	16	icon_x and icon_y
IconMaskHint	32	icon_mask
WindowGroupHint	64	window_group
MessageHint	128	This bit is obsolete

Window managers are free to assume convenient values for all fields of the WM_HINTS property if a window is mapped without one.

The input field is used to communicate to the window manager the input focus model used by the client (see Section 4.1.7).

Clients with the Globally Active and No Input models should set the *input* flag to False. Clients with the Passive and Locally Active models should set the *input* flag to True.

From the client's point of view, the window manager will regard the client's top-level window as being in one of three states:

- Normal

- Iconic

- Withdrawn

The semantics of these states are described in Section L.4.1.14. Newly created windows start in the Withdrawn state. Transitions between states happen when a non-override-redirect top-level window is mapped and unmapped and when the window manager receives certain messages.

The value of the *initial_state* field determines the state the client wishes to be in at the time the top-level window is mapped from Withdrawn state, as shown in Table L-8.

Table L-8. WM_HINTS.initial_state Values

State	Value	Comments
NormalState	1	Window is visible
IconicState	3	Icon is visible

The *icon_pixmap* field may specify a pixmap to be used as an icon. This pixmap should be:

- One of the sizes specified in the WM_ICON_SIZE property on the root, if it exists (see Section L.4.1.11).

- 1-bit deep. The window manager will select, through the defaults database, suitable background (for the 0 bits) and foreground (for the 1 bits) colors. These defaults can, of course, specify different colors for the icons of different clients.

The *icon_mask* specifies which pixels of the icon_pixmap should be used as the icon, allowing for icons to appear nonrectangular.

The *icon_window* field is the ID of a window the client wants used as its icon. Most, but not all, window managers will support icon windows; those that do not are likely to have a user interface in which small windows that behave like icons are completely inappropriate, so that clients should not attempt to remedy the omission by working around it.

Clients needing more capabilities from the icons than a simple two-color bitmap should use icon windows. Rules for clients that do are set out in Section L.4.1.9.

The (*icon_x,icon_y*) coordinate is a hint to the window manager as to where it should position the icon. The policies of the window manager control the positioning of icons, so clients should not depend on attention being paid to this hint.

The *window_group* field lets the client specify that this window belongs to a group of windows. An example is a single client manipulating multiple children of the root window.

Convention: *The* `window_group` *field should be set to the ID of the group leader. The window group leader may be a window which exists only for that purpose. A place-holder group leader of this kind would never be mapped, either by the client or by the window manager.*

Convention: *The properties of the window group leader are those for the group as a whole (for example, the icon to be shown when the entire group is iconified).*

Window managers may provide facilities for manipulating the group as a whole. Clients, at present, have no way to operate on the group as a whole.

The `messages` bit, if set in the flags field, indicates that the client is using an obsolete window manager communication protocol,* rather than the `WM_PROTOCOLS` mechanism of Section L.4.1.9.

L.4.1.7 WM_CLASS

The `WM_CLASS` property, of type STRING (without control characters), contains two consecutive null-terminated strings specifying the Instance and Class names to be used by both the client and the window manager for looking up resources for the application or as identifying information. This property must be present when the window leaves Withdrawn state and may be changed only while the window is in Withdrawn state. Window managers may examine the property only when they start up and when the Window leaves Withdrawn state, but there should be no need for a client to change its state dynamically.

The two strings are, respectively:

- A string naming the particular instance of the application to which the client owning this window belongs. Resources that are specified by instance name override any resources that are specified by class name. Instance names may be specified by the user in an operating-system-specific manner. Under UNIX, the following conventions are used:

  - If *-name name* is given on the command line, *name* is used as the instance name.

  - Otherwise, if the environment variable `RESOURCE_NAME` is set, its value will be used as the instance name.

  - Otherwise, the trailing part of the name used to invoke the program (argv[0] stripped of any directory names) is used as the instance name.

- A string naming the general class of applications to which the client owning this window belongs. Resources that are specified by class apply to all applications that have the same class name. Class names are specified by the application writer. Examples of commonly used class names include "Emacs", "XTerm", "XClock", "XLoad", etc.

---

*This obsolete protocol was described in the July 27, 1988, draft of this manual. Windows using it can also be detected because their `WM_HINTS` properties are four bytes longer than expected. Window managers are free to support clients using the obsolete protocol in a "backward-compatibility" mode.

Note that `WM_CLASS` strings, being null-terminated, differ from the general conventions that STRING properties are null-separated. This inconsistency is necessary for backward-compatibility.

L.4.1.8 WM_TRANSIENT_FOR

The `WM_TRANSIENT_FOR` property, of type WINDOW, contains the ID of another top-level window. The implication is that this window is a pop up on behalf of the named window, and window managers may decide not to decorate transient windows or treat them differently in other ways. In particular, window managers should present newly mapped `WM_TRANSIENT_FOR` windows without requiring any user interaction, even if mapping top-level windows normally does require interaction. Dialogue boxes, for example, are an example of windows that should have `WM_TRANSIENT_FOR` set.

It is important not to confuse `WM_TRANSIENT_FOR` with override-redirect. `WM_TRANSIENT_FOR` should be used in those cases where the pointer is not grabbed while the window is mapped; in other words, if other windows are allowed to be active while the transient is up. If other windows must be prevented from processing input (for example, when implementing pop-up menus), use override-redirect and grab the pointer while the window is mapped.

L.4.1.9 WM_PROTOCOLS

The `WM_PROTOCOLS` property, of type ATOM, is a list of atoms. Each atom identifies a communication protocol between the client and the window manager in which the client is willing to participate. Atoms can identify both standard protocols and private protocols specific to individual window managers.

All the protocols in which a client can volunteer to take part involve the window manager sending the client a `ClientMessage` event and the client taking appropriate action. For details of the contents of the event, see Section L.4.2.8. In each case, the protocol transactions are initiated by the window manager.

The `WM_PROTOCOLS` property is not required. If it is not present, the client does not wish to participate in any window manager protocols.

The X Consortium will maintain a registry of protocols to avoid collisions in the name space. Table L-9 contains the protocols that have been defined to date.

Table L-9. Current WM_PROTOCOLS

Protocol	Section	Purpose
WM_TAKE_FOCUS	L.4.1.17	Assignment of input focus
WM_SAVE_YOURSELF	L.5.2.1	Save client state warning
WM_DELETE_WINDOW	L.5.2.2	Request to delete top-level window
This table will grow.		

L.4.1.10 WM_COLORMAP_WINDOWS

The WM_COLORMAP_WINDOWS property, of type WINDOW, on a top-level window is a list of the the IDs of windows that may need colormaps installed that differ from the colormap of the top-level window. The window manager will watch this list of windows for changes in their colormap attributes. The top-level window is always (implicitly or explicitly) on the watch list.

See Section L.4.1.18 for the details of this mechanism.

L.4.1.11 Window Manager Properties

The properties described above are those which the client is responsible for maintaining on its top-level windows. This section describes the properties that the window manager places on client's top-level windows and on the root.

L.4.1.12 WM_STATE

The window manager will place a WM_STATE property, of type WM_STATE, on each top-level client window. In general, clients should not need to examine the contents of this property; it is intended for communication between window and session managers. See Section L.5.1.4 for more details.

L.4.1.13 WM_ICON_SIZE

A window manager that wishes to place constraints on the sizes of icon pixmaps and/or windows should place a property called WM_ICON_SIZE on the root. The contents of this property are shown in Table L-10.

Table L-10. WM_ICON_SIZE Type Property Contents

Field	Type	Comments
min_width	CARD32	Data for icon size series
min_height	CARD32	
max_width	CARD32	
max_height	CARD32	
width_inc	CARD32	
height_inc	CARD32	

For more details, see Chapter 10, *Interclient Communication*, Section 10.2.4.2, of Volume One, *Xlib Programming Manual*.

L.4.1.14 Changing Window State

From the client's point of view, the window manager will regard each of the client's top-level non-override-redirect windows as being in one of three states. The semantics of the states are:

- `NormalState`. The client's top-level window is visible.

- `IconicState`. The client's top-level window is iconic, whatever that means for this window manager. The client can assume that its `icon_window` (if any) will be visible, and failing that, its `icon_pixmap` (if any) or its `WM_ICON_NAME` will be visible.

- `WithdrawnState`. Neither the client's top-level window nor its icon are visible.

In fact, the window manager may implement states with semantics other than those described above. For example, a window manager might implement a concept of `InactiveState` in which an infrequently used client's window would be represented as a string in a menu. But this state is invisible to the client, which would see itself merely as being in `IconicState`.

Newly created top-level windows are in Withdrawn state. Once the window has been provided with suitable properties, the client is free to change its state as follows:*

- **Withdrawn → Normal.** The client should map the window with `WM_HINTS.initial_state` being `NormalState`.

- **Withdrawn → Iconic.** The client should map the window with `WM_HINTS.initial_state` being `IconicState`.

- **Normal → Iconic.** The client should send a client message event as described below.

- **Normal → Withdrawn.** The client should unmap the window and follow it with a synthetic UnmapNotify event as described below.†

- **Iconic → Normal.** The client should map the window. The contents of `WM_HINTS.initial_state` are irrelevant in this case.

- **Iconic → Withdrawn.** The client should unmap the window and follow it with a synthetic `UnmapNotify` event as described below.

Once a client's non-override-redirect top-level window has left Withdrawn state, the client will know that the window is in Normal state if it is mapped and that the window is in Iconic state if it is not mapped. It may select for `StructureNotify` on the top-level window, and it will receive an `UnmapNotify` event when it moves to Iconic state and a `MapNotify` when it moves to Normal state. This implies that a reparenting window manager will unmap the top-level window as well as the parent window when going Iconic.

---

*The conventions described in earlier drafts of this manual had some serious semantic problems. These new conventions are designed to be compatible with clients using earlier conventions, except in areas where the earlier conventions would not actually have worked.

†For compatibility with obsolete clients, window managers should trigger the transition on the real UnmapNotify rather than wait for the synthetic one. They should also trigger the transition if they receive a synthetic UnmapNotify on a window for which they have not yet received a real UnmapNotify.

Convention: *Reparenting window managers must unmap the client's top-level window whenever they unmap the window to which they have reparented it.*

If the transition is to Withdrawn state, in addition to unmapping the window itself, a synthetic `UnmapNotify` event must be sent using `SendEvent` with the following parameters:

destination:	the root
propagate:	False
event-mask:	(SubstructureRedirect|SubstructureNotify)
event: an UnmapNotify with:	
event:	the root
window:	the window itself
from-configure:	False

The reason for doing this is to ensure that the window manager gets some notification of the desire to change state, even though the window may already be unmapped when the desire is expressed.

If the transition is from Normal to Iconic state, the client should send a `ClientMessage` event to the root with:

- *window* == the window to be iconified

- *type* == the atom `WM_CHANGE_STATE`*

- *format* == 32

- *data*[0] == `IconicState`

Other values of data[0] are reserved for future extensions to these conventions.† The parameters of the `SendEvent` should be as above.

Clients can also select for `VisibilityChange` on their (top-level or icon) windows. They will then receive a `VisibilityNotify` (*state*=FullyObscured) event when the window concerned becomes completely obscured even though mapped (and thus perhaps a waste of time to update) and a `VisibilityNotify` (*state!*=FullyObscured) when it becomes even partly viewable.

L.4.1.15 Configuring the Window

Clients can resize and reposition their top-level windows using the `ConfigureWindow` request. The attributes of the window that can be altered with this request are:

- The [*x,y*] location of the window's upper-left outer corner.

- The [*width,height*] of the inner region of the window (excluding borders).

---

*The *type* field of the `ClientMessage` event (called the *message_type* field by Xlib) should not be confused with the *code* field of the event itself, which will have the value 33 (`ClientMessage`).

†The format of this `ClientMessage` event does not match the format of `ClientMessages` in Section L.4.2.8. This is because they are sent by the window manager to clients, and this is sent by clients to the window manager.

- The border width of the window.

- The window's position in the stack.

The coordinate system in which the location is expressed is that of the root, irrespective of any reparenting that may have occurred, and the border width to be used and `win_gravity` position hint to be used are those most recently requested by the client. Client configure requests are interpreted by the window manager in the same manner as the initial window geometry mapped from Withdrawn state, as described in Section L.4.1.5. Clients must be aware that there is no guarantee that the window manager will allocate them the requested size or location and must be prepared to deal with *any* size and location. If the window manager decides to respond to a `ConfigureRequest` by:

- Not changing the size or location of the window at all, a client will receive a synthetic `ConfigureNotify` event describing the (unchanged) state of the window. The [*x,y*] coordinates will be in the root coordinate system, adjusted for the border width the client requested, irrespective of any reparenting that has taken place. The `border_width` will be the border width the client requested. The client will not receive a real `ConfigureNotify`, since no change has actually taken place.

- Moving the window without resizing it, a client will receive a synthetic `Configure-Notify` event following the move describing the new state of the window, whose [*x,y*] coordinates will be in the root coordinate system adjusted for the border width the client requested. The `border_width` will be the border width the client requested. The client may not receive a real `ConfigureNotify` event describing this change, since the window manager may have reparented the top-level window. If it does receive a real event, the synthetic event will follow the real one.

- Resizing the window (whether or not it is moved), a client which has selected for `StructureNotify` will receive a `ConfigureNotify` event. Note that the coordinates in this event are relative to the parent, which may not be the root if the window has been reparented and will reflect the actual border width of the window, which the window manager may have changed. The `TranslateCoordinates` request can be used to convert the coordinates if required.

The general rule is that coordinates in real `ConfigureNotify` events are in the parent's space, whereas in synthetic events they are in the root space.

Clients should be aware that their borders may not be visible. Window managers are free to use reparenting techniques to decorate client's top-level windows with "borders" containing titles, controls, and other details to maintain a consistent look and feel. If they do, they are likely to override the client's attempts to set the border width and set it to zero. Clients, therefore, should not depend on the top-level window's border being visible nor use it to display any critical information. Other window managers will allow the top-level window's border to be visible.

> Convention: *Clients should set their desired border width on all* `Configure-Window` *requests, to avoid a race condition.*

Clients changing their position in the stack must be aware that they may have been reparented, which means that windows that used to be siblings no longer are. Using a non-sibling as the sibling parameter on a `ConfigureWindow` request will cause an error.

> Convention: *Clients using* `ConfigureWindow` *to request a change in their position in the stack should do so using None in the sibling field.*

Clients that must position themselves in the stack relative to some window that was origi-nally a sibling must do the `ConfigureWindow` request (in case they are running under a nonreparenting window manager), be prepared to deal with a resulting error, and then follow with a synthetic `ConfigureRequest` event by invoking `SendEvent` with:

```
destination:                    the root
propagate:                      False
event-mask:                     (SubstructureRedirect|SubstructureNotify)
event: a ConfigureRequest with:
    event:                      the root
    window:                     the window itself
    ....                        other parameters from the ConfigureWindow
```

Doing this is deprecated, and window managers are, in any case, free to position windows in the stack as they see fit. Clients should ignore the *above* field of both real and synthetic `ConfigureNotify` events that they receive on their non-override-redirect top-level win-dows, since they cannot be guaranteed to contain useful information.

L.4.1.16 Changing Window Attributes

The attributes that may be supplied when a window is created may be changed using the `ChangeWindowAttributes` request. They are shown in Table L-11.

Table L-11. Window Attributes

Attribute	Private to Client
Background pixmap	Yes
Background pixel	Yes
Border pixmap	Yes
Border pixel	Yes
Bit gravity	Yes
Window gravity	No
Backing-store hint	Yes
Save-under hint	No
Event mask	No
Do-not-propagate mask	Yes
Override-redirect flag	No
Colormap	Yes
Cursor	Yes

Most are private to the client and will never be interfered with by the window manager. As regards the attributes that are not private to the client:

- The window manager is free to override the window gravity; a reparenting window manager may want to set the top-level window's window gravity for its own purposes.

- Clients are free to set the save-under hint on their top-level windows, but they must be aware that the hint may be overridden by the window manager.

- Windows, in effect, have per-client event masks, and so clients may select for whatever events are convenient, irrespective of any events the window manager is selecting for. There are some events for which only one client at a time may select, but the window manager should not select for them on any of the client's windows.

- Clients can set override-redirect on top-level windows but are encouraged not to do so except as described in Sections L.4.1.20 and L.4.2.9.

L.4.1.17 Input Focus

There are four models of input handling:

- **No Input.** The client never expects keyboard input.

  An example would be *xload*, or another output-only client.

- **Passive Input.** The client expects keyboard input but never explicitly sets the input focus.

  An example would be a simple client with no subwindows, which will accept input in `PointerRoot` mode or when the window manager sets the input focus to its top-level window (in click-to-type mode).

- **Locally Active Input.** The client expects keyboard input and explicitly sets the input focus, but only does so when one of its windows already has the focus.

  An example would be a client with subwindows defining various data entry fields that uses Next and Prev keys to move the input focus between the fields, once its top-level window has acquired the focus in `PointerRoot` mode or when the window manager sets the input focus to its top-level window (in click-to-type mode).

- **Globally Active Input.** The client expects keyboard input and explicitly sets the input focus even when it is in windows the client does not own.

  An example would be a client with a scrollbar that wants to allow users to scroll the window without disturbing the input focus even if it is in some other window. It wants to acquire the input focus when the user clicks in the scrolled region but not when the user clicks in the scroll bar itself. Thus, it wants to prevent the window manager setting the input focus to any of its windows.

The four input models and the corresponding values of the `input` field and the presence or absence of the `WM_TAKE_FOCUS` atom in the `WM_PROTOCOLS` property are shown in Table L-12.

Table L-12. Input Models

Input Model	Input Field	WM_TAKE_FOCUS
No Input	False	Absent
Passive	True	Absent
Locally Active	True	Present
Globally Active	False	Present

Passive and Locally Active clients set the *input* field of WM_HINTS True to indicate that they require window manager assistance in acquiring the input focus. No Input and Globally Active clients set the *input* field False to request that the window manager not set the input focus to their top-level window.

Clients using SetInputFocus must set the *time* field to the timestamp of the event that caused them to make the attempt. Note that this cannot be a FocusIn event, since they do not have timestamps, and that clients may acquire the focus without a corresponding EnterNotify. Clients must not use CurrentTime in the *time* field.

Clients using the Globally Active model can only use SetInputFocus to acquire the input focus when they do not already have it on receipt of one of the following events:

- ButtonPress

- ButtonRelease

- Passive-grabbed KeyPress

- Passive-grabbed KeyRelease

In general, clients should avoid using passive-grabbed Key events for this purpose except when they are unavoidable (as, for example, a selection tool that establishes a passive grab on the keys that cut, copy, or paste).

The method by which the user commands the window manager to set the focus to a window is up to the window manager. For example, clients cannot determine whether they will see the click that transfers the focus.

Windows with the atom WM_TAKE_FOCUS in their WM_PROTOCOLS property may receive a ClientMessage from the window manager as described in Section L.4.2.8 with WM_TAKE_FOCUS in their data[0] field. If they want the focus, they should respond with a SetInputFocus request with its *window* field set to the window of theirs that last had the input focus, or to their *default input window*, and the *time* field set to the time-stamp in the message. See Section L.4.2.7.

A client could receive WM_TAKE_FOCUS when opening from an icon or when the user has clicked outside the top-level window in an area that indicates to the window manager that it should assign the focus (for example, clicking in the headline bar can be used to assign the focus).

The goal is to support window managers that want to assign the input focus to a top-level window in such a way that the top-level window can either assign it to one of its subwindows or decline the offer of the focus. A clock, for example, or a text editor with no currently open frames might not want to take focus even though the window manager generally believes that clients should take the input focus after being deiconified or raised.

> Problem: *There would be no need for* WM_TAKE_FOCUS *if the* FocusIn *event contained a timestamp and a previous-focus field. This could avoid the potential race condition. There is space in the event for this information; it should be added at the next protocol revision.*

Clients that set the input focus need to decide a value for the *revert-to* field of the Set-InputFocus request. This determines the behavior of the input focus if the window the focus has been set to becomes not viewable. It can be any of:

- Parent. In general, clients should use this value when assigning focus to one of their subwindows. Unmapping the subwindow will cause focus to revert to the parent, which is probably what you want.

- PointerRoot. Using this value with a click-to-type focus management policy leads to race conditions, since the window becoming unviewable may coincide with the window manager deciding to move the focus elsewhere.

- None. Using this value causes problems if the window manager reparents the window (most window managers will) and then crashes. The input focus will be None, and there will probably be no way to change it.

The convention is:

> Convention: *Clients invoking* SetInputFocus *should set* revert-to *to* Parent.

A convention is also required for clients that want to give up the input focus:

> Convention: *Clients should not give up the input focus of their own volition. They should ignore input that they receive instead.*

L.4.1.18 Colormaps

The window manager is responsible for installing and uninstalling colormaps.* Clients provide the window manager with hints on which colormaps to install and uninstall but must not install or uninstall colormaps themselves. When a client's top-level window gets the colormap focus (as a result of whatever colormap focus policy is implemented by the window manager), the window manager will insure that one or more of the client's colormaps are installed. The reason for this convention is that there is no safe way for multiple clients to install and uninstall Colormaps.

---

*The conventions described in earlier drafts by which clients and window managers shared responsibility for installing colormaps suffered from semantic problems.

Convention: *Clients must not use* `InstallColormap` *or* `Uninstall-Colormap`.

There are two possible ways in which clients could hint to the window manager about the colormaps they want installed. Using a property, they could tell the window manager:

- A priority-ordered list of the colormaps they want installed or

- A priority-ordered list of the windows whose colormaps they want installed.

The second of these alternatives has been selected because:

- It allows window managers to know the visuals for the colormaps, permitting visual-dependent colormap installation policies.

- It allows window managers to select for `VisibilityChange` on the windows concerned and ensure that maps are only installed if the windows that need them are visible.

Clients whose top-level windows and subwindows all use the same colormap should set its ID in the colormap field of the window's attributes. They should not set a `WM_COLORMAP_WINDOWS` property on the top-level window. If they want to change the colormap, they should change the window attribute, and the window manager will install the colormap for them.

Clients creating windows may use the value `CopyFromParent` to inherit their parent's colormap. Window managers will ensure that the root window's colormap field contains a colormap that is suitable for clients to inherit; in particular, the colormap will provide distinguishable colors for `BlackPixel` and `WhitePixel`.

Top-level windows that have subwindows, or override-redirect pop-up windows, whose colormap requirements differ from the top-level window should have a `WM_COLORMAP_-WINDOWS` property. This property contains a list of window IDs of windows whose colormaps the window manager should attempt to have installed when, in the course of its individual colormap focus policy, it assigns the colormap focus to the top-level window (see Section L.4.1.10). The list is ordered by the importance to the client of having the colormaps installed. If this order changes, the property should be updated. The window manager will track changes to this property and will track changes to the colormap attribute of the windows in the property.

`WM_TRANSIENT_FOR` windows either can have their own `WM_COLORMAP_WINDOWS` property or appear in the property of the window they are transient for, as appropriate.

Clients should be aware of the min-installed-maps and max-installed-maps fields of the connection startup information and the effect that the minimum value has on the "required list":

> "At any time, there is a subset of the installed maps, viewed as an ordered list, called the "required list." The length of the required list is at most M, where M is the min-installed-maps specified for the screen in the connection setup. The required list is maintained as follows. When a colormap is an explicit argument to `InstallColormap`, it is added to the head of the list, and the list is truncated at the tail if necessary to keep the length of the list to at most M. When a colormap is an explicit argument to `UninstallColormap` and it is in the required list, it is removed from the list. A colormap is not added to the required

list when it is installed implicitly by the server, and the server cannot implicitly uninstall a colormap that is in the required list."

In less precise words, the min-installed-maps most recently installed maps are guaranteed to be installed. This number will often be one; clients needing multiple colormaps should beware.

The window manager will identify and track changes to the colormap attribute of the windows identified by the `WM_COLORMAP_WINDOWS` property and the top-level window if it does not appear in the list. If the top-level window does not appear in the list, it will be assumed to be higher priority than any window in the list. It will also track changes in the contents of the `WM_COLORMAP_WINDOWS` property, in case the set of windows or their relative priority changes. The window manager will define some colormap focus policy, and whenever the top-level window has the colormap focus will attempt to maximize the number of colormaps from the head of the `WM_COLORMAP_WINDOWS` list that are installed.

L.4.1.19 Icons

A client can hint to the window manager about the desired appearance of its icon in several ways:

- Set a string in `WM_ICON_NAME`. All clients should do this, as it provides a fall-back for window managers whose ideas about icons differ widely from those of the client.

- Set a pixmap into the *icon_pixmap* field of the `WM_HINTS` property and possibly another into the *icon_mask* field. The window manager is expected to display the pixmap masked by the mask. The pixmap should be one of the sizes found in the `WM_ICON_SIZE` property on the root. If this property is not found, the window manager is unlikely to display icon pixmaps. Window managers will normally clip or tile pixmaps which do not match `WM_ICON_SIZE`.

- Set a window into the *icon_window* field of the `WM_HINTS` property. The window manager is expected to map that window whenever the client is in Iconic state. In general, the size of the icon window should be one of those specified in `WM_ICON_SIZE` on the root, if it exists. Window managers are free to resize icon windows.

In Iconic state, the window manager will normally ensure that:

- If the window's *WM_HINTS.icon_window* is set, the window it names is visible.

- If not, if the window's *WM_HINTS.icon_pixmap* is set, the pixmap it names is visible.

- Otherwise, the window's `WM_ICON_NAME` string is visible.

Clients should observe the following conventions about their icon windows:

Convention: *The icon window should be an* InputOutput *child of the root.*

Convention: *The icon window should be one of the sizes specified in the* `WM_ICON_SIZE` *property on the root.*

Convention: *The icon window should use the root visual and default colormap for the screen in question.*

Convention: *Clients should not map their icon windows.*

Convention: *Clients should not unmap their icon windows.*

Convention: *Clients should not configure their icon windows.*

Convention: *Clients should not set override-redirect on their icon windows nor select for* ResizeRedirect *on them.*

Convention: *Clients must not depend on being able to receive input events via their icon windows.*

Convention: *Clients must not manipulate the borders of their icon windows.*

Convention: *Clients must select for Exposure on their icon window and repaint it when requested.*

Window managers will differ as to whether they support input events to client's icon windows; most will allow some subset of the keys and buttons through.

Window managers will ignore any WM_NAME, WM_ICON_NAME, WM_NORMAL_HINTS, WM_HINTS, WM_CLASS, WM_TRANSIENT_FOR, WM_PROTOCOLS, or WM_COLORMAP_WINDOWS properties they find on icon windows. Session managers will ignore any WM_COMMAND or WM_CLIENT_MACHINE properties they find on icon windows.

L.4.1.20 Pop-up Windows

Clients wishing to pop up a window can do one of three things:

- They can create and map another normal top-level window, which will get decorated and managed as normal by the window manager. See the discussion of window groups below.

- If the window will be visible for a relatively short time and deserves a somewhat lighter treatment, they can set the WM_TRANSIENT_FOR property. They can expect less decoration but can set all the normal window manager properties on the window. An example would be a dialogue box.

- If the window will be visible for a very short time and should not be decorated at all, the client can set override-redirect on the window. In general, this should be done only if the pointer is grabbed while the window is mapped. The window manager will never interfere with these windows, which should be used with caution. An example of an appropriate use is a pop-up menu.

Window managers are free to decide if WM_TRANSIENT_FOR windows should be iconified when the window they are transient for is. Clients displaying WM_TRANSIENT_FOR windows which have (or request to have) the window they are transient for iconified do not need to request that the same operation be performed on the WM_TRANSIENT_FOR window; the window manager will change its state if that is the policy it wishes to enforce.

L.4.1.21 Window Groups

A set of top-level windows that should be treated from the user's point of view as related (even though they may belong to a number of clients) should be linked together using the `window_group` field of the `WM_HINTS` structure.

One of the windows (the one the others point to) will be the group leader and will carry the group, as opposed to the individual properties. Window managers may treat the group leader differently from other windows in the group. For example, group leaders may have the full set of decorations, and other group members a restricted set.

It is not necessary that the client ever map the group leader; it may be a window that exists solely as a place-holder.

It is up to the window manager to determine the policy for treating the windows in a group. There is, at present, no way for a client to request a group, as opposed to an individual, operation.

L.4.2 Client Responses to Window Manager Actions

The window manager performs a number of operations on client resources, primarily on their top-level windows. Clients must not try to fight this but may elect to receive notification of the window manager's operations.

L.4.2.1 Reparenting

Clients must be aware that some window managers will reparent their non-override-redirect top-level windows, so that a window that was created as a child of the root will be displayed as a child of some window belonging to the window manager. The effects that this reparenting will have on the client are:

- The parent value returned by a `QueryTree` request will no longer be the value supplied to the `CreateWindow` request that created the reparented window. There should normally be no need for the client to be aware of the identity of the window to which the top-level window has been reparented. In particular, a client wishing to create further top-level windows should continue to use the root as the parent for these new windows.

- The server will interpret the (x,y) coordinates in a `ConfigureWindow` request in the new parent's coordinate space. They will, in fact, normally not be interpreted by the server, because a reparenting window manager will normally have intercepted these operations (see below). Clients should use the root coordinate space for these requests (see Section L.4.1.15).

- `ConfigureWindow` requests that name a specific sibling window may fail because the window named, which used to be a sibling, no longer is after the reparenting operation (see Section L.4.1.15).

- The (x,y) coordinates returned by a `GetGeometry` request are in the parent's coordinate space and are thus not directly useful after a reparent operation.

- A background of `ParentRelative` will have unpredictable results.

- A cursor of `None` will have unpredictable results.

Clients wishing to be notified when they are reparented can select for `StructureNotify` on their top-level window. They will receive a `ReparentNotify` event if and when reparenting takes place.

If the window manager reparents a client's window, the reparented window will be placed in the "save-set" of the parent window. This means that if the window manager terminates, the reparented window will not be destroyed and will be remapped if it was unmapped. Note that this applies to *all* client windows the window manager reparents, including transient windows and client icon windows.

When the window manager gives up control over a client's top-level window, it will reparent it (and any associated windows, such as `WM_TRANSIENT_FOR` windows) back to the root.

There is a potential race condition here. A client might wish to reuse the top-level window, reparenting it somewhere else.

> Convention: *Clients wishing to reparent their top-level windows should do so only when they have their original parents. They may select for* Structure-Notify *on their top-level windows and will receive* ReparentNotify *events informing them when this is true.*

L.4.2.2 Redirection of Operations

Clients must be aware that some window managers will arrange for some client requests to be intercepted and redirected. Redirected requests are not executed; they result instead in events being sent to the window manager, which may decide to do nothing, to alter the arguments, or to perform the request on behalf of the client.

The possibility that a request may be redirected means that a client may not assume that any redirectable request is actually performed when the request is issued or at all. For example, the sequence:

```
MapWindow A
PolyLine A GC <point> <point> ....
```

is incorrect, since the `MapWindow` request may be intercepted and the `PolyLine` output made to an unmapped window. The client must wait for an `Expose` event before drawing in the window.* Another example is:

```
ConfigureWindow width=N height=M
<output assuming window is N by M>
```

which incorrectly assumes that the `ConfigureWindow` request is actually executed with the arguments supplied.

---

*This is true even if the client set backing store to `Always`. The backing store value is a only a hint, and the server may stop maintaining backing store contents at any time.

The requests which may be redirected are:

- `MapWindow`

- `ConfigureWindow`

- `CirculateWindow`

A window with the override-redirect bit set is immune from redirection, but the bit should be set on top-level windows only in cases where other windows should be prevented from processing input while the override-redirect window is mapped (see Section L.4.1.20) and while responding to `ResizeRequest` events (see Section L.4.2.9).

Clients which have no non-Withdrawn top-level windows and which map an override-redirect top-level window are taking over total responsibility for the state of the system. It is their responsibility to:

- Prevent any pre-existing window manager from interfering with their activities.

- Restore the status quo exactly after they unmap the window, so that any pre-existing window manager does not get confused.

In effect, clients of this kind are acting as temporary window managers. Doing so is strongly discouraged, since these clients will be unaware of the user interface policies the window manager is trying to maintain and their user interface behavior is likely to conflict with that of less demanding clients.

L.4.2.3 Window Move

If the window manager moves a top-level window without changing its size, the client will receive a synthetic `ConfigureNotify` event following the move describing the new location, in terms of the root coordinate space. Clients must not respond to being moved by attempting to move themselves to a better location.

Any real `ConfigureNotify` event on a top-level window implies that the window's position on the root may have changed, even though the event reports that the window's position in its parent is unchanged, because the window may have been reparented. And note that the coordinates in the event will not, in this case, be directly useful.

The window manager will send these events using `SendEvent` with:

```
destination:        the client's window
propagate:          False
event-mask:         StructureNotify
```

L.4.2.4 Window Resize

The client can elect to receive notification of being resized by selecting for Structure-Notify on its top-level window(s). It will receive a ConfigureNotify event. The size information in the event will be correct, but the location will be in the parent window (which may not be the root).

The response of the client to being resized should be to accept the size it has been given and to do its best with it. Clients must not respond to being resized by attempting to resize themselves to a better size. If the size is impossible to work with, clients are free to request to change to Iconic state.

L.4.2.5 (De)Iconify

A non-override-redirect window that is not Withdrawn will be in Normal state if it is mapped and in Iconic state if it is unmapped. This will be true even if the window has been reparented; the window manager will unmap the window as well as its parent when switching to Iconic state.

The client can elect to be notified of these state changes by selecting for Structure-Notify on the top-level window. It will receive UnmapNotify when it goes Iconic and MapNotify when it goes Normal.

L.4.2.6 Colormap Change

Clients that wish to be notified of their colormaps being installed or uninstalled should select for ColormapNotify on their top-level windows and on any windows they have named in WM_COLORMAP_WINDOWS properties on their top-level windows. They will receive ColormapNotify events with the *new* field False when the colormap for that window is installed or uninstalled.

> Problem: *There is an inadequacy in the protocol. At the next revision, the* InstallColormap *request should be changed to include a timestamp to avoid the possibility of race conditions if more than one client attempts to install and uninstall colormaps. These conventions attempt to avoid the problem by restricting use of these requests to the window manager.*

L.4.2.7 Input Focus

Clients can request notification that they have the input focus by selecting for Focus-Change on their top-level windows; they will receive FocusIn and FocusOut events. Clients that need to set the input focus to one of their subwindows should not do so unless they have set WM_TAKE_FOCUS in their WM_PROTOCOLS property and have:

*   Set the *input* field of WM_HINTS to True and actually have the input focus in (one of) their top-level windows or

- Set the *input* field of `WM_HINTS` to `False` and have received a suitable event as described in Section L.4.1.17 or

- Received a `WM_TAKE_FOCUS` message as described in Section L.4.1.17.

Clients should not warp the pointer in an attempt to transfer the focus; they should set the focus and leave the pointer alone. See Section L.6.2.

Once a client satisfies these conditions, it may transfer the focus to another of its windows using the `SetInputFocus` request:

```
SetInputFocus
    focus:          WINDOW or PointerRoot or None
    revert-to:      {Parent, PointerRoot, None}
    time:           TIMESTAMP or CurrentTime
```

Convention: *Clients using* `SetInputFocus` *must set the* `time` *field to the timestamp of the event that caused them to make the attempt. Note that this cannot be a* `FocusIn` *event, since they do not have timestamps and that clients may acquire the focus without a corresponding* `EnterNotify`. *Clients must not use* `CurrentTime` *in the* `time` *field.*

Convention: *Clients using* `SetInputFocus` *to set the focus to one of their windows must set the* `revert-to` *field to Parent.*

L.4.2.8 ClientMessage Events

There is no way for clients to prevent themselves being sent `ClientMessage` events.

Top-level windows with a `WM_PROTOCOLS` property may be sent `ClientMessage` events specific to the protocols named by the atoms in the property (see Section L.4.1.9). For all protocols, the `ClientMessage` events have:

- `WM_PROTOCOLS` as the type field.*

- Format 32.

- The atom naming their protocol in the data[0] field.†

- A timestamp in their data[1] field.

The remaining fields, including the *window* field, of the event are determined by the protocol.

These events will be sent using `SendEvent` with:

```
    destination:        the client's window
    propagate:          False
```

---

*The *type* field of the `ClientMessage` event (called the *message_type* field by Xlib) should not be confused with the *code* field of the event itself, which will have the value 33 (`ClientMessage`).

†We use the notation data[*n*] to indicate the *n*[th] element of the LISTofINT8, LISTofINT16, or LISTofINT32 in the data field of the `ClientMessage`, according to the format field. The list is indexed from zero.

```
event-mask:          () empty
event:               as specified by the protocol
```

L.4.2.9   Redirecting Requests

Normal clients can use the redirection mechanism just as window managers do, by selecting for `SubstructureRedirect` on a parent window or `ResizeRedirect` on a window itself. However, at most one client per window can select for these events, and a convention is needed to avoid clashes:

> Convention: *Clients (including window managers) should select for* `SubstructureRedirect` *and* `ResizeRedirect` *only on windows that they own.*

In particular, clients that need to take some special action if they are resized can select for `ResizeRedirect` on their top-level windows. They will receive a `ResizeRequest` event if the window manager resizes their window, and the resize will not actually take place. Clients are free to make what use they like of the information that the window manager wants to change their size, but they must configure the window to the width and height specified in the event in a timely fashion. To ensure that the resize will actually happen at this stage, instead of being intercepted and executed by the window manager (and thus restarting the process) the client needs temporarily to set override-redirect on the window.

> Convention: *Clients receiving* `ResizeRequest` *events must respond by: (a) setting override-redirect on the window specified in the event, (b) configuring the window specified in the event to the width and height specified in the event as soon as possible and before making any other geometry requests, and then (c) clearing override-redirect on the window specified in the event.*

If a window manager detects that a client is not obeying this convention, it is free to take whatever measures it deems appropriate to deal with the client.

L.4.3   Summary of Window Manager Property Types

The window manager properties are summarized in Table L-13.

Table L-13. Window Manager Properties

Name	Type	Format	Section
WM_CLASS	STRING	8	L.4.1.7
WM_COLORMAP_WINDOWS	WINDOW	32	L.4.1.10
WM_HINTS	WM_HINTS	32	L.4.1.6
WM_ICON_NAME	TEXT		L.4.1.4
WM_ICON_SIZE	WM_ICON_SIZE	32	L.4.1.13
WM_NAME	TEXT		L.4.1.3
WM_NORMAL_HINTS	WM_SIZE_HINTS	32	L.4.1.5
WM_PROTOCOLS	ATOM	32	L.4.1.9

Table L-13. Window Manager Properties (continued)

Name	Type	Format	Section
WM_STATE	WM_STATE	32	L.4.1.12
WM_TRANSIENT_FOR	WINDOW	32	L.4.1.8

L.5 Client-to-Session-Manager Communication

The role of the session manager is to manage a collection of clients. It should be capable of:

- Starting a collection of clients as a group.
- Remembering the state of a collection of clients so that they can be restarted in the same state.
- Stopping a collection of clients in a controlled way.

It may also provide a user interface to these capabilities.

L.5.1 Client Actions

There are two ways in which clients should cooperate with the session manager:

- Stateful clients should cooperate with the session manager by providing it with information it can use to restart them if it should become necessary.
- Clients, typically those with more than one top-level window, whose server connection needs to survive the deletion of their top-level window should take part in the WM_DELETE_WINDOW protocol (see Section L.5.2.2).

L.5.1.1 Properties

The client communicates with the session manager by placing two properties (WM_COM-MAND and WM_CLIENT_MACHINE) on its top-level window. If the client has a group of top-level windows, these properties should be placed on the group leader window.

The window manager is responsible for placing a WM_STATE property on each top-level client window for use by session managers and other clients that need to be able to identify top-level client windows and their state.

L.5.1.2 WM_COMMAND

The WM_COMMAND property represents the command used to (re)start the client. Clients should ensure, by resetting this property, that it always reflects a command that will restart them in their current state. The content and type of the property depends on the operating system of the machine running the client. In UNIX systems using ISO Latin-1 characters for their command lines, the property should:

- Be of type STRING,

- Contain a list of NULL-terminated strings, and

- Be initialized from *argv*. Other systems will need to set appropriate conventions for the type and contents and type of WM_COMMAND properties. Window and session managers should not assume that STRING is the type of WM_COMMAND nor that they will be able to understand or display its contents.

Note that WM_COMMAND strings, being null-terminated, differ from the general conventions that STRING properties are null-separated. This inconsistency is necessary for backward-compatibility.

A client with multiple top-level windows should ensure that exactly one of them should have a WM_COMMAND with nonzero length. Zero-length WM_COMMAND properties can be used to reply to WM_SAVE_YOURSELF messages on other top-level windows but will otherwise be ignored (see Section L.5.2.1).

L.5.1.3 WM_CLIENT_MACHINE

The client should set the WM_CLIENT_MACHINE property, of one of the TEXT types, to a string forming the name of the machine running the client, as seen from the machine running the server.

L.5.1.4 WM_STATE

The window manager will place a WM_STATE property, of type WM_STATE, on each top-level client window.

Programs like *xprop* that want to operate on client's top-level windows can use this property to identify them. A client's top-level window is one that:

- Has override-redirect False and

- Has a WM_STATE property or

- Is a mapped child of the root that has no descendant with a WM_STATE property.

Recursion is necessary to cover all window manager reparenting possibilities. Note that clients other than window and session managers should not need to examine the contents of WM_STATE properties; which are not formally defined by this document. The presence or absence of the property is all they need to know.

Suggested contents of the WM_STATE property are shown in Table L-14.

Table L-14. WM_STATE Type Property Contents

Field	Type	Comments
state	CARD32	See Table L-15 below
icon	WINDOW	ID of icon window

Table L-15. WM_STATE.state Values

State	Value	Comments
WithdrawnState	0	
NormalState	1	
IconicState	3	

Adding other fields to this property is reserved to the X Consortium.

The icon field should contain the window ID of the window which the window manager uses as the icon window for the window on which this property is set, if any; otherwise, None. Note that this window may not be the same as the icon window which the client may have specified. It may be:

- The client's icon window.

- A window that the window manager supplied which contains the client's icon pixmap.

- The least ancestor of the client's icon window (or of the window which contains the client's icon pixmap) which contains no other icons.

The state field describes the window manager's idea of the state the window is in, which may not match the client's idea as expressed in the *initial_state* field of the WM_HINTS property (for example, if the user has asked the window manager to iconify the window). If it is NormalState, the window manager believes the client should be animating its window; if it is IconicState, it should animate its icon window. Note that in either state, clients should be prepared to handle exposure events from either window.

The contents of WM_STATE properties and other aspects of the communication between window and session managers will be specified in the *Window and Session Manager Conventions Manual*.

L.5.1.5 Termination

Since they communicate via unreliable network connections, X11 clients must be prepared for their connection to the server to be terminated at any time without warning. They cannot depend on getting notification that termination is imminent nor on being able to use the server to negotiate with the user (for example, using dialogue boxes for confirmation) about their fate.

Equally, clients may terminate at any time without notice to the session manager. When a client terminates itself, rather than being terminated by the session manager, it is viewed as having resigned from the session in question, and it will not be revived if the session is revived.

L.5.2 Client Responses to Session Manager Actions

Clients may need to respond to session manager actions in two ways:

- Saving their internal state.

- Deleting a window.

L.5.2.1 Saving Client State

Clients that wish to be warned when the session manager feels that they should save their internal state (for example, when termination impends) should include the atom WM_SAVE_YOURSELF in the WM_PROTOCOLS property on their top-level windows to participate in the WM_SAVE_YOURSELF protocol. They will receive a ClientMessage as described in Section L.4.2.8 with the atom WM_SAVE_YOURSELF in its data[0] field.

Clients receiving WM_SAVE_YOURSELF should place themselves in a state from which they can be restarted and should update WM_COMMAND to be a command that will restart them in this state. The session manager will be waiting for a PropertyNotify on WM_COMMAND as a confirmation that the client has saved its state, so that WM_COMMAND should be updated (perhaps with a zero-length append) even if its contents are correct. No interactions with the user are permitted during this process.

Once it has received this confirmation, the session manager will feel free to terminate the client if that is what the user asked for. Otherwise, if the user asked for the session to be put to sleep, the session manager will ensure that the client does not receive any mouse or key-board events.

After receiving a WM_SAVE_YOURSELF, saving its state, and updating WM_COMMAND, the client should not change its state (in the sense of doing anything that would require a change to WM_COMMAND) until it receives a mouse or keyboard event. Once it does so, it can assume that the danger is over. The session manager will ensure that these events do not reach clients until the danger is over or until the clients have been killed.

Clients with multiple top-level windows should ensure that, irrespective of how they are arranged in window groups:

- Only one of their top-level windows has a non-zero-length WM_COMMAND property.

- They respond to a WM_SAVE_YOURSELF message by (in this order):

  1. Updating the non-zero-length WM_COMMAND property, if necessary.

  2. Updating the WM_COMMAND property on the window for which they received the WM_SAVE_YOURSELF message if it was not updated in step 1.

Receiving WM_SAVE_YOURSELF on a window is (conceptually) a command to save the entire client state.*

L.5.2.2 Window Deletion

Clients, normally those with multiple top-level windows, whose server connection must survive the deletion of some of their top-level windows should include the atom WM_DELETE_WINDOW in the WM_PROTOCOLS property on each such window. They will receive a ClientMessage, as described in Section L.4.2.8, whose data[0] field is WM_DELETE_WINDOW.

Clients receiving a WM_DELETE_WINDOW message should behave as if the user selected "delete window" from a (hypothetical) menu. They should perform any confirmation dialogue with the user, and if they decide to complete the deletion:

- Either change the window's state to Withdrawn (as described in Section L.4.1.14) or destroy the window.

- Destroy any internal state associated with the window.

If the user aborts the deletion during the confirmation dialogue, the client should ignore the message.

Clients are permitted to interact with the user and ask (for example) whether a file associated with the window to be deleted should be saved or the window deletion should be cancelled. Clients are not required to destroy the window itself; the resource may be reused, but all associated state (backing store, for example) should be released.

If the client aborts a destroy and the user then selects "delete window" again, the WM should start the WM_DELETE_WINDOW protocol again. WMs should not use DestroyWindow on a window that has WM_DELETE_WINDOW in its WM_PROTOCOLS property.

Clients which choose not to include WM_DELETE_WINDOW in the WM_PROTOCOLS property may be disconnected from the server if the user asks for one of the client's top-level windows to be deleted.

---

*This convention has changed since earlier drafts because of the introduction of the protocol in the next section. In the public review draft, there was ambiguity as to whether WM_SAVE_YOURSELF was a checkpoint or a shutdown facility. It is now unambiguously a checkpoint facility; if a shutdown facility is judged to be necessary, a separate WM_PROTOCOLS protocol will be developed and registered with the X Consortium.

Note that the `WM_SAVE_YOURSELF` and `WM_DELETE_WINDOW` protocols are orthogonal to each other and may be selected independently.

L.5.3 Summary of Session Manager Property Types

The session manager properties are summarized in Table L-16.

Table L-16. Window Manager Properties

Name	Type	Format	Section
WM_CLIENT_MACHINE	TEXT		L.5.1.3
WM_COMMAND	TEXT		L.5.1.2
WM_STATE	WM_STATE	32	L.5.1.4

L.6 Manipulation of Shared Resources

X11 permits clients to manipulate a number of shared resources, among them the input focus, the pointer, and colormaps. Conventions are required so that clients do so in an orderly fashion.

L.6.1 The Input Focus

Clients that explicitly set the input focus can do so in one of two modes, as described in the following conventions:

> Convention: *Locally Active clients should set the input focus to one of their windows only when it is already in one of their windows or when they receive a* `WM_TAKE_FOCUS` *message. They should set the* `input` *field of the* `WM_HINTS` *structure* `True`.

> Convention: *Globally Active clients should set the input focus to one of their windows only when they receive a button event or a passive-grabbed key event or when they receive a* `WM_TAKE_FOCUS` *message. They should set the* `input` *field of the* `WM_HINTS` *structure* `False`.

> Convention: *Clients should use the timestamp of the event that caused them to attempt to set the input focus as the* `time` *field on the* `SetInputFocus` *request, not* `CurrentTime`.

L.6.2 The Pointer

In general, clients should not warp the pointer. Window managers may do so, for example, to maintain the invariant that the pointer is always in the window with the input focus. Other window managers may wish to preserve the illusion that the user is in sole control of the pointer.

> Convention: *Clients should not warp the pointer.*

> Convention: *Clients which insist on warping the pointer should do so only with the `src-window` field of the `WarpPointer` request set to one of their windows.*

L.6.3 Grabs

A client's attempt to establish a button or a key grab on a window will fail if some other client has already established a conflicting grab on the same window. The grabs are, therefore, shared resources, and their use requires conventions.

In conformance with the principle that clients should behave as far as possible when a window manager is running as they would when it is not, a client that has the input focus may assume that it can receive all the available keys and buttons.

> Convention: *Window managers should ensure that they provide some mechanism for their clients to receive events from all keys and all buttons, except events involving keys whose keysyms are registered as being for window management functions (e.g., a hypothetical WINDOW keysym).*

In other words, window managers must provide some mechanism by which a client can receive events from *every* key and button (regardless of modifiers) unless and until the X Consortium registers some keysyms as being reserved for window management functions. No keysyms are currently registered for window management functions.

Even so, clients are well advised to allow the key and button combinations used to elicit program actions to be modified, since some window managers may choose not to observe this convention or may not provide a convenient method for the user to transmit events from some keys.

> Convention: *Clients should establish button and key grabs only on windows that they own.*

In particular, this means that a window manager wishing to establish a grab over the client's top-level window should either establish the grab on the root or reparent the window and establish the grab on a proper ancestor. In some cases, a window manager may want to consume the event received, placing the window in a state where a subsequent such event will go to the client. Examples are clicking in a window to set focus, with the click not being offered to the client, or clicking in a buried window to raise it, again with the click not offered to the client. More typically, a window manager should add to rather than replace the client's semantics for key-plus-button combinations by allowing the event to be used by the client after the window manager is done with it. To ensure this, the window manager should establish the grab on the parent using:

```
pointer/keyboard-mode = Synchronous
```

and release the grab using `AllowEvents` with:

```
mode = ReplayPointer/Keyboard
```

In this way, the client will receive the events as if they had not been intercepted.

Obviously, these conventions place some constraints on possible user interface policies. There is a tradeoff here between freedom for window managers to implement their user interface policies and freedom for clients to implement theirs. We resolve this dilemma by:

- Allowing window managers to decide if and when a client will receive an event from any given key or button.

- Placing a requirement on the window manager to provide some mechanism, perhaps a "Quote" key, by which the user can send an event from *any* key or button to the client.

L.6.4 Colormaps

Convention: *If a client has a top-level window that has subwindows or override-redirect pop-up windows whose colormap requirements differ from the top-level window, it should set a* WM_COLORMAP_WINDOWS *property on the top-level window. The* WM_COLORMAP_WINDOWS *property contains a list of the window IDs of windows that the window manager should track for colormap changes.*

Convention: *When a client's colormap requirements change, the client should change the colormap window attribute of a top-level window or one of the windows indicated by a* WM_COLORMAP_WINDOWS *property.*

Convention: *Clients must not use* InstallColormap *or* Uninstall-Colormap.

Clients with `DirectColor` type applications should consult Chapter 7, *Color*, Section 7.8, of Volume One, *Xlib Programming Manual*, for conventions connected with sharing standard colormaps. They should look for and create the properties described there on the root window of the appropriate screen.

Note, however, that the conventions described there are not adequate if the server supports multiple visuals and if standard colormaps need to be deleted. To address this, two additional fields (*visual_id* and *kill_id*) are required in RGB_COLOR_MAP type properties, as shown in Table L-17. The colormap described by the property is one appropriate for the screen on whose root the property is found.

Table L-17. RGB_COLOR_MAP Type Property Contents

Field	Type	Comments
colormap	COLORMAP	ID of the colormap described
red_max	CARD32	Values for pixel calculations
red_mult	CARD32	
green_max	CARD32	
green_mult	CARD32	
blue_max	CARD32	
blue_mult	CARD32	
base_pixel	CARD32	
visual_id	VISUALID	Visual to which colormap belongs
kill_id	CARD32	ID for destroying the resources

When deleting or replacing an RGB_COLOR_MAP, it is not sufficient to delete the property; it is important to free the associated colormap resources as well. If *kill_id* is greater than one, then the resources should be freed by issuing a KillClient protocol request with *kill_id* as the argument. If *kill_id* is one, then the resources should be freed by issuing a FreeColormap protocol request with *colormap* as the colormap argument. If *kill_id* is zero, then no attempt should be made to free the resources. A client creating an RGB_COLOR_MAP for which the *colormap* resource is created specifically for this purpose should set *kill_id* to one (and can create more than one such standard colormap using a single connection). A client creating an RGB_COLOR_MAP for which the *colormap* resource is shared in some way (e.g., is the default colormap for the root window) should create an arbitrary resource and use its resource id for *kill_id* (and should create no other standard colormaps on the connection).

> Convention: *If an* RGB_COLOR_MAP *property is too short to contain the* visual_id *field, it can be assumed that the* visual_id *is the root visual of the appropriate screen. If an* RGB_COLOR_MAP *property is too short to contain the* kill_id *field, a value of zero can be assumed.*

During the connection handshake, the server informs the client of the default colormap for each screen. This is a colormap for the root visual, and clients can use it to improve the extent of colormap sharing if they use the root visual.

A similar capability is desirable for other visuals and can be supported by changing the definition of the RGB_DEFAULT_MAP property to read:

> "This atom names a property. The value of the property is an array of XStandardColormap structures (as extended to include *visual_id* and *kill_id* fields)."

> "Each entry in the array describes an RGB subset of the default color map for the visual specified by *visual_id*."

L.6.5 The Keyboard Mapping

The X server contains a table (read by `GetKeyboardMapping`) that describes, for each keycode generated by the server, the set of symbols appearing on the corresponding key. This table does not affect the server's operations in any way; it is simply a database used by clients attempting to understand the keycodes they receive. Nevertheless, it is a shared resource and requires conventions.

It is possible for clients to modify this table, using `ChangeKeyboardMapping`. In general, clients should not do this. In particular, this is *not* the way in which clients should implement key bindings or key remapping. The conversion between a sequence of keycodes received from the server and a string in a particular encoding is a private matter for each client, as it must be in a world where applications may be using different encodings to support different languages and fonts. This conversion for ISO Latin-1 is implemented by the Xlib *XLookupString()* function; there will presumably be equivalent functions for other encodings.

The only valid reason for using `ChangeKeyboardMapping` is when the symbols written on the keys have changed; as, for example, when a Dvorak key conversion kit or a set of Apl keycaps has been installed. Of course, a client may have to take the change to the keycap on trust.

It is permissible for a client to interact with a user thus:

* "You just started me on a server without a Pause key. Please choose a key to be the Pause key and press it now."

* \<User presses the Scroll Lock key>

* "Adding Pause to the symbols on the Scroll Lock key: Confirm or Abort."

* \<User confirms>

* Client uses `ChangeKeyboardMapping` to add Pause to the keycode that already contains Scroll Lock.

* "Please paint Pause on the Scroll Lock key."

  Convention: *Clients should not use* `ChangeKeyboardMapping`.

If a client succeeds in changing the keyboard mapping table, all clients will receive `MappingNotify(`*request*`=Keyboard)` events. There is no mechanism to avoid receiving these events.

  Convention: *Clients receiving* `MappingNotify(`*request*`=Keyboard)` *events should update any internal keycode translation tables they are using.*

L.6.6 The Modifier Mapping

X11 supports eight modifier bits, of which three are preassigned to Shift, Lock, and Control. Each modifier bit is controlled by the state of a set of keys, and these sets are specified in a table accessed by `GetModifierMapping` and `SetModifierMapping`. This table is a shared resource and requires conventions.

A client needing to use one of the preassigned modifiers should assume that the modifier table has been set up correctly to control these modifiers. The Lock modifier should be interpreted as Caps Lock or Shift Lock according as the keycodes in its controlling set include `XK_Caps_Lock` or `XK_Shift_Lock`.

> Convention: *Clients should determine the meaning of a modifier bit from the keysyms being used to control it.*

A client needing to use an extra modifier, for example, META, should:

- Scan the existing modifier mappings. If it finds a modifier that contains a keycode whose set of keysyms includes `XK_Meta_L` or `XK_Meta_R`, it should use that modifier bit.

- If there is no existing modifier controlled by `XK_Meta_L` or `XK_Meta_R`, it should select an unused modifier bit (one with an empty controlling set), and:

  - If there is a keycode with `XL_Meta_L` in its set of keysyms, add that keycode to the set for the chosen modifier, then

  - If there is a keycode with `XL_Meta_R` in its set of keysyms, add that keycode to the set for the chosen modifier, then

  - If the controlling set is still empty, interact with the user to select one or more keys to be META.

- If there are no unused modifier bits, ask the user to take corrective action.

> Convention: *Clients needing a modifier not currently in use should assign keycodes carrying suitable keysyms to an unused modifier bit.*

> Convention: *Clients assigning their own modifier bits should ask the user politely to remove his or her hands from the key in question if their `SetModifierMapping` request returns a Busy status.*

There is no good solution to the problem of reclaiming assignments to the five non-preassigned modifiers when they are no longer being used.

> Convention: *The user has to use xmodmap or some other utility to deassign obsolete modifier mappings by hand.*

> Problem: *This is kind of low-tech.*

When a client succeeds in performing a `SetModifierMapping`, all clients will receive `MappingNotify(request=Modifier)` events. There is no mechanism for preventing these events being received. A client using one of the non-preassigned modifiers which receives one of these events should do a `GetModifierMapping` to discover the new mapping, and if the modifier it is using has been cleared, it should reinstall the modifier.

Note that `GrabServer` must be used to make the `GetModifierMapping, Set-ModifierMapping` pair in these transactions atomic.

L.7 Resource Manager Conventions

This section has yet to be generated.

L.8 Conclusion

This document provides the protocol-level specification of the minimal conventions needed to ensure that X11 clients can interoperate properly. Further documents are required:

- A *Window and Session Manager Conventions Manual* to cover these convention from the opposite point of view and to add extra conventions of interest to window and session manager implementors.

- An addendum to the *Xlib–C Language X Interface* covering the additional routines, `XIconify()` would be an example, needed to ensure that adhering to these conventions is convenient for the C programmer.

Acknowledgements

David Rosenthal had overall architectural responsibility for the conventions defined in this document, wrote most of the text, and edited the document, but the development has been a communal effort. The details were thrashed out in meetings at the January 1988 MIT X Conference and at the summer 1988 Usenix conference and through months (and megabytes) of argument on the *wmtalk* mail alias. Thanks are due to everyone who contributed, and especially to the following:

- For Section L.2, Jerry Farrell, Phil Karlton, Loretta Guarino Reid, Mark Manasse, and Bob Scheifler.

- For Section L.3, Andrew Palay.

- For Sections L.4 and L.5, Todd Brunhoff, Ellis Cohen, Jim Fulton, Hania Gajewska, Jordan Hubbard, Kerry Kimbrough, Audrey Ishizaki, Matt Landau, Mark Manasse, Bob Scheifler, Ralph Swick, Mike Wexler, and Glenn Widener.

Thanks are also due to those who contributed to the public review, including Gary Combs, Errol Crary, Nancy Cyprych, John Diamant, Clive Feather, Burns Fisher, Richard Greco, Tim Greenwood, Kee Hinckley, Brian Holt, John Interrante, John Irwin, Vania Joloboff, John Laporta, Ken Lee, Stuart Marks, Allan Mimms, Colas Nahaboo, Mark Patrick, Steve Pitschke, Brad Reed, and John Thomas.

Interclient Communications

L.9 Compatibility with Earlier Drafts

This appendix summarizes the incompatibilities between this and earlier drafts.

L.9.1 The R2 Draft

The February 25, 1988, draft that was distributed as part of X11R2 was clearly labeled as such, and many areas were explicitly labeled as liable to change. Nevertheless, in the revision work since then, we have been very careful not to introduce gratuitous incompatibility. A far as possible, we have tried to ensure that clients obeying the conventions in the earlier draft would still work.

The areas in which incompatibilities have become necessary are:

- The use of property `None` in `ConvertSelection` requests is no longer allowed. Owners receiving them are free to use the target atom as the property to respond with, which will work in most cases.

- The protocol for INCREMENTAL type properties as selection replies has changed, and the name has been changed to INCR. Selection requestors are free to implement the earlier protocol if they receive properties of type INCREMENTAL.

- The protocol for INDIRECT type properties as selection replies has changed, and the name has been changed to MULTIPLE. Selection requestors are free to implement the earlier protocol if they receive properties of type INDIRECT.

- The protocol for the special CLIPBOARD client has changed. The earlier protocol is subject to race conditions and should not be used.

- The set of state values in *WM_HINTS.initial_state* has been reduced, but the values that are still valid are unchanged. Window managers should treat the other values sensibly.

- The methods an application uses to change the state of its top-level window have changed but in such a way that cases that used to work will still work.

- The *x*, *y*, *width*, and *height* fields have been removed from the WM_NORMAL_HINTS property and replaced by pad fields. Values set into these fields will be ignored. The position and size of the window should be set by setting the appropriate window attributes.

- A pair of *base* fields and a *win_gravity* field have been added to the WM_NORMAL_HINTS property. Window managers will assume values for these fields if the client sets a short property.

L.9.2 The July 27, 1988, Draft

The Consortium review was based on a draft dated July 27, 1988. Incompatibilities have been introduced in the following areas:

- The *messages* field of the WM_HINTS property was found to be unwieldy and difficult to evolve. It has been replaced by the WM_PROTOCOLS property, but clients using the earlier mechanism can be detected because they set the *messages* bit in the flags field of the WM_HINTS property, and window managers can provide a backward-compatibility mode.

- The mechanism described in the earlier draft by which clients installed their own subwindow colormaps could not be made to work reliably and mandated some features of the look and feel. It has been replaced by the WM_COLORMAP_WINDOWS property. Clients using the earlier mechanism can be detected by the WM_COLORMAPS property they set on their top-level window, but providing a reliable backward-compatibility mode is not possible.

- The recommendations for window manager treatment of top-level window borders have been changed, as those in the earlier draft produced problems with visibility events. For non-window-manager clients, there is no incompatibility.

- The pseudo-root facility in the earlier draft has been removed. Although it has been successfully implemented, it turns out to be inadequate to support the uses envisaged. An extension will be required to support these uses fully, and it was felt that the maximum freedom should be left to the designers of the extension. In general, the previous mechanism was invisible to clients, and no incompatibility should result.

- The addition of the WM_DELETE_WINDOW protocol (which prevents the danger that multi-window clients may be terminated unexpectedly) has meant some changes in the WM_SAVE_YOURSELF protocol to ensure that the two protocols are orthogonal. Clients using the earlier protocol can be detected (see WM_PROTOCOLS above) and supported in a backward-compatibility mode.

- The conventions regarding properties of type RGB_COLOR_MAP have been changed, but clients using the earlier conventions can be detected because their properties are four bytes shorter. These clients will work correctly if the server supports only a single visual or if they use only the visual of the root. These are the only cases in which they would have worked anyway.

L.9.3 The Public Review Drafts

The public review resulted in a set of mostly editorial changes. The changes that introduced some degree of incompatibility are:

- A new section (Section L.6.3) was added covering the window manager's use of grabs. The restrictions it imposes should affect only window managers.

- The TARGETS selection target has been clarified, and it may be necessary for clients to add some entries to their replies.

- A selection owner using INCR transfer should no longer replace targets in a MULTIPLE property with the atom INCR.

- The contents of the `ClientMessage` sent by a client to iconify itself has been clarified, but there should be no incompatibility, since the earlier contents would not, in fact, have worked.

- The border width in synthetic `ConfigureNotify` events is now specified, but this should not cause any incompatibility.

- Clients are now asked to set a border width on all `ConfigureWindow` requests.

- Window manager properties on icon windows will now be ignored, but there should be no incompatibility, since there was no specification that they be obeyed previously.

- The ordering of real and synthetic `ConfigureNotify` events is now specified, but any incompatibility should affect only window managers.

- The semantics of `WM_SAVE_YOURSELF` have been clarified and restricted to be a checkpoint operation only. Clients which were using it as part of a shutdown sequence may need to be modified, especially if they were interacting with the user during the shutdown.

- A `kill_id` field has been added to `RGB_COLOR_MAP` properties. Clients using earlier conventions can be detected by the size of their `RGB_COLOR_MAP` properties, and the cases that would have worked will still work.

L.10 Suggested Protocol Revisions

During the development of these conventions, a number of inadequacies have been discovered in the protocol. They are summarized here as input to an eventual protocol revision design process.

- There is no way for anyone to find out the last-change time of a selection. At the next protocol revision, `GetSelectionOwner` should be changed to return the last-change time as well as the owner.

- How does a client find out which selection atoms are valid?

- The protocol should be changed to return in response to a `GetSelectionOwner` the timestamp used to acquire the selection.

- There would be no need for `WM_TAKE_FOCUS` if the `FocusIn` event contained a timestamp and a previous-focus field. This could avoid the potential race condition. There is space in the event for this information; it should be added at the next protocol revision.

- There is a race condition in `InstallColormap`; the request does not take a timestamp, and it may be executed after the top-level colormap has been uninstalled. The next protocol revision should provide the timestamp in `InstallColormap`, `UninstallColormap`, `ListInstalledColormaps`, and the `Colormap-Notify` event. The timestamp should be used in a similar way to the last-focus-change time for the input focus.

- The protocol needs to be changed to provide some way of identifying the visual and the screen of a colormap.

- There should be some way to reclaim assignments to the five non-preassigned modifiers when they are no longer needed.

Interclient
Communications

M
Logical Font Description
Conventions, Release 4[*]

It is a requirement that X client applications must be portable across server implementations with very different file systems, naming conventions, and font libraries. However, font access requests, as defined by the X Window System Protocol, Version 11, do not specify server-independent conventions for font names, nor do they provide adequate font properties for logically describing typographic fonts.

X clients must be able to dynamically determine fonts available on any given server, in what sizes and styles, etc., so that understandable information can be presented to the user or intelligent font fallbacks can be chosen. It is desirable that the most common queries could be accomplished without the overhead of opening each font and inspection of font properties, i.e., through simple ListFonts requests (e.g., if a user selected a Helvetica typeface family, a client application should be able to query the server for all Helvetica fonts and present only those setwidths, weights, slants, point sizes, character sets available for that family).

This document gives a standard logical font description (XLFD) and conventions to be used in the X protocol so that clients can query and access screen type libraries in a consistent manner across all X servers. In addition to completely specifying a given font via its Font-Name, the XLFD also provides for a standard set of key FontProperties that describe the font in more detail.

The XLFD provides an adequate set of typographic font properties, such as CAP_HEIGHT, RELATIVE_SETWIDTH, X_HEIGHT, for publishing and other applications to do intelligent font matching or substitution when handling documents created on some foreign server using potentially unknown fonts. In addition, this information is required by certain clients to automatically place subscripts and to determine small capital heights, recommended leading, wordspace values, etc.

---

[*]This appendix reprints *Logical Font Description Conventions, Version 1.3, MIT X Consortium Standard.*

Examples are for illustrative purposes only.

M.1 Requirements and Goals

This specification meets the short- and long-term goals to have a standard logical font description which:

- Provides unique, descriptive font names that support simple pattern matching.
- Supports multiple font vendors, arbitrary character sets and encodings.
- Is X server- and operating/file-system-independent.
- Provides adequate descriptive font information for arbitrarily complex font matching/substitution.
- Is extensible.

M.1.1 Unique, Descriptive Font Names

It should be possible to have font names that are long enough and descriptive enough to have a reasonable probability of being unique without inventing a new registration organization. Resolution/size-dependent font masters, multi-vendor font libraries, etc. must be anticipated and handled by the font name alone.

The name itself should be structured to be amenable to simple pattern matching and parsing, allowing X clients to restrict font queries to some subset of all possible fonts in the server.

M.1.2 Supports Multiple Font Vendors and Character Sets

The font name and properties should distinguish between fonts that were supplied by different font vendors but that possibly share the same name. We anticipate a highly competitive font market where users will be able to buy fonts from a number of sources according to their particular requirements.

A number of font vendors deliver each font with all glyphs designed for that font, where charset mappings are defined by encoding vectors. Some server implementations may force these mappings to proprietary or standard charsets statically in the font data, while others may desire to perform the mapping dynamically in the server. Provision must be made in the font name which allows a font request to specify/identify specific charset mappings in server environments where multiple charsets are supported.

M.1.3 Server, Operating, and File System Independent

X client applications that require a particular font should be able to use the descriptive name without knowledge of the file system or other repository in use by the server. However, it should be possible for servers to translate a given font name into a file name syntax that it knows how to deal with, without compromising the uniqueness of the font name. This algorithm should be reversible (exactly how this translation is done is implementation-dependent).

M.1.4 Supports Arbitrarily Complex Font Matching/Substitution

In addition to the font name, the XLFD should define a standard list of descriptive font properties with agreed-upon fallbacks for all fonts, so that client applications can derive font-specific formatting/display data and perform font matching/substitution when asked to handle potentially unknown fonts, as required.

M.1.5 Extensible

The XLFD must be extensible so that new and/or private descriptive font properties can be added to conforming fonts without obsoleting existing X client or server implementations.

M.2 X Logical Font Description

XLFD is divided into two basic components: the `FontName`, which gives all font information needed to uniquely identify a font in X protocol requests (e.g., `ListFonts`, `OpenFont`, etc.), and a variable list of optional `FontProperties`, which describes a font in more detail.

The `FontName` is used in font queries and returned as data in certain X protocol requests. The `FontName` is also specified as the data value for the `FONT` item in the X Consortium Character Bitmap Distribution Format specification (BDF V2.1).

The `FontProperties` are supplied on a font-by-font basis and are returned as data in certain X protocol requests as part of the `XFontStruct` data structure. The `FontProperties` names and associated data values may also appear as items of the **STARTPROPERTIES ... ENDPROPERTIES** list in the BDF V2.1 specification.

M.2.1 FontName

The `FontName` is logically composed of two strings: a `FontNameRegistry` prefix, followed by a `FontNameSuffix`. The `FontNameRegistry` is an x-registered-name that identifies the registration authority that owns the specified `FontNameSuffix` syntax and semantics.

All font names that conform to this specification are to use a `FontNameRegistry` prefix defined to be the string "–", i.e., ISO 8859-1 HYPHEN (Column/Row 02/13). All `Font-NameRegistry` prefixes of the form "+*version*–", where *version* is the version of some future XLFD specification, are reserved by the X Consortium for future extensions to XLFD font names. If required, extensions to the current XLFD font name shall be constructed by appending new fields to the current structure, each delimited by the existing field delimiter. The availability of other `FontNameRegistry` prefixes or fonts that support other registries is server-implementation-dependent.

In the X protocol specification, the `FontName` is required to be a string; hence, numeric field values are represented in the name as string equivalents. All `FontNameSuffix` fields are also defined as `FontProperties`, in which case numeric property values are represented as signed or unsigned integers as appropriate.

M.2.1.1 FontName Syntax

The `FontName` is a structured, parsable string (X data type STRING8) whose Backus-Naur Form syntax description is as follows:

Table M-1. FontName Syntax

FontName ::=	XFontNameRegistry XFontNameSuffix | PrivFontNameRegistry PrivFontNameSuffix	
XFontNameRegistry ::=	XFNDelim | XFNExtPrefix Version XFNDelim	
XFontNameSuffix ::=	FOUNDRY XFNDelim FAMILY_NAME XFNDelim WEIGHT_NAME XFNDelim SLANT XFNDelim SETWIDTH_NAME XFNDelim ADD_STYLE_NAME XFNDelim PIXEL_SIZE XFNDelim POINT_SIZE XFNDelim RESOLUTION_X XFNDelim RESOLUTION_Y XFNDelim SPACING XFNDelim AVERAGE_WIDTH XFNDelim CHARSET_REGISTRY XFNDelim CHARSET_ENCODING	
Version ::=	STRING8 — the XLFD version that defines an extension to the font name syntax (e.g., "2.0")	
XFNExtPrefix ::=	OCTET — the value of ISO8859-1 PLUS (Column/Row 02/13)	
XFNDelim ::=	OCTET — the value of ISO8859-1 HYPHEN (Column/Row 02/13)	

```
    PrivFontNameRegistry ::=    STRING8 — other than those strings
                                reserved by XLFD
      PrivFontNameSuffix ::=    STRING8
```

Field values are constructed as strings of ISO8859-1 graphic characters, excluding the following:

*   HYPHEN (02/13), the XLFD font name delimiter character.

*   QUESTION MARK (03/15) and ASTERISK (02/10), the X protocol font name wildcard characters.

Alphabetic case distinctions are allowed but are for human readability concerns only. Conforming X servers will perform matching on font name query/open requests independent of case. The entire font name string must have no more than 255 characters. It is recommended that clients construct font name query patterns by explicitly including all field delimiters to avoid unexpected results. Note that SPACE is a valid character of a FontName field, e.g., a FAMILY_NAME might be ITC Avant Garde Gothic.

M.2.1.2   FontName Field Definitions

FOUNDRY : x-registered-name

FOUNDRY is an x-registered-name, the name or identifier of the digital type foundry that digitized and supplied the font data or, if different, the identifier of the organization that last modified the font shape or metric information.

The reason this distinction is necessary is that a given font design may be licensed from one source (e.g., ITC) but digitized and sold by any number of different type suppliers. Each digital version of the original design will in general be somewhat different in metrics and shape from the idealized original font data, as each font foundry, for better or for worse, has its own standards and practices for tweaking a typeface for a particular generation of output technologies or has its own perception of market needs.

It is up to the type supplier to register with the X Consortium a suitable name for this FontName field, according to the registration procedures defined by the Consortium.

The X Consortium shall define procedures for registering foundry names and shall maintain and publish in a timely manner a registry of such registered names for use in XLFD font names and properties.

FAMILY_NAME : string

FAMILY_NAME is a string that identifies the range or "family" of typeface designs that are all variations of one basic typographic style. This must be spelled out in full, with words separated by spaces as required. This name must be human-understandable and suitable for presentation to a font user to identify the typeface family.

It is up to the type supplier to supply and maintain a suitable string for this field and font property, to secure the proper legal title to a given name, and to guard against the infringement of other's copyrights or trademarks. By convention, FAMILY_NAME is not translated.

`FAMILY_NAME` may include an indication of design ownership if considered a valid part of the typeface family name (see examples below).

Examples of `FAMILY_NAME`s:

```
Helvetica
ITC Avant Garde Gothic
Times
Times Roman
Bitstream Amerigo
Stone
```

WEIGHT_NAME : string

`WEIGHT_NAME` is a string that identifies the font's typographic weight, i.e., the nominal blackness of the font, according to the FOUNDRY's judgment. This name must be human-understandable and suitable for presentation to a font user.

The interpretation of this field is somewhat problematic, as the typographic judgment of weight has traditionally depended on the overall design of the typeface family in question (i.e., it is possible that the DemiBold weight of one font could be almost equivalent in typographic feel to a Bold font from another family).

`WEIGHT_NAME` is captured as an arbitrary string, since it is an important part of a font's complete human-understandable name, but it should not be used for font matching/substitution. X client applications should use the weight-related font properties (RELA-TIVE_WEIGHT and WEIGHT) that give the coded relative weight and the calculated weight, respectively, for this purpose.

SLANT : code-string

SLANT is a code-string that indicates the overall posture of the typeface design used in the font. The encoding is as follows:

Code	English Translation	Description
"R"	Roman	Upright design
"I"	Italic	Italic design, slanted clockwise from vertical
"O"	Oblique	Obliqued upright design, slanted clockwise from vertical
"RI"	Reverse Italic	Italic design, slanted counter clockwise from vertical
"RO"	Reverse Oblique	Obliqued upright design, slanted counter clockwise from vertical
"OT"	Other	Other

The SLANT codes are for programming convenience only and usually are converted into their equivalent human-understandable form before being presented to a user.

SETWIDTH_NAME : string

`SETWIDTH_NAME` is a string that gives the font's typographic proportionate width, i.e., the nominal width per horizontal unit of the font, according to the FOUNDRY's judgment.

As with WEIGHT_NAME, the interpretation of this field or font property is somewhat problematic, as the designer's judgment of setwidth has traditionally depended on the overall design of the typeface family in question. X client applications should use the RELATIVE_SETWIDTH font property that gives the relative coded proportionate width or calculate the proportionate width for purposes of font matching or substitution.

Examples of SETWIDTH_NAMEs:

```
Normal
Condensed
Narrow
Double Wide
```

ADD_STYLE_NAME : string

ADD_STYLE_NAME is a string that identifies additional typographic style information not captured by other fields but needed to uniquely identify the font.

ADD_STYLE_NAME is not a typeface classification field and is only used for uniqueness. Its usage, as such, is not limited to typographic style distinctions.

Examples of ADD_STYLE_NAMEs:

```
Serif
Sans Serif
Informal
Decorated
```

PIXEL_SIZE : integer-string

PIXEL_SIZE is an unsigned integer-string typographic metric in device pixels which gives the body size of the font at a particular POINT_SIZE and RESOLUTION_Y. PIXEL_SIZE normally incorporates additional vertical spacing considered part of the font design. (Note, however, that this value is not necessarily equivalent to the height of the font bounding box). PIXEL_SIZE is in the range zero to a "very-large-number."

PIXEL_SIZE would normally be used by X client applications that need to query fonts according to device-dependent size, regardless of the point size or vertical resolution for which the font was designed.

POINT_SIZE : integer-string

POINT_SIZE is an unsigned integer-string typographic metric in device-independent units which gives the body size for which the font was designed. This field normally incorporates additional vertical spacing considered part of the font design. (Note, however, that POINT_SIZE is not necessarily equivalent to the height of the font bounding box). POINT_SIZE is expressed in decipoints (where points are as defined in the X protocol or 72.27 points = 1 inch) in the range zero to a "very-large-number."

POINT_SIZE and RESOLUTION_Y would be used by X clients to query fonts according to device-independent size in order to maintain constant text size on the display regardless of the PIXEL_SIZE used for the font.

RESOLUTION_X : integer-string
RESOLUTION_Y : integer-string

RESOLUTION_X and RESOLUTION_Y are unsigned integer-strings, the horizontal and vertical resolution for which the font was designed, measured in pixels/dots per inch (dpi). Horizontal and vertical values are required, since a separate bitmap font must be designed for displays with very different aspect ratios (e.g., 1:1, 4:3, 2:1, etc.).

The separation of pixel/point size and resolution is necessary because X allows for servers with very different video characteristics (e.g., horizontal and vertical resolution, screen and pixel size, pixel shape, etc.) to potentially access the same font library. The font name, then, must differentiate between a 14-point font designed for 75 dpi (body size of about 14 pixels) or a 14-point font designed for 150 dpi (about 28 pixels), etc. Further, in servers that implement some or all fonts as continuously scaled outlines, POINT_SIZE and RESOLUTION_Y will help the server to differentiate between potentially separate font masters for text, title, and display sizes or for other typographic considerations.

SPACING : code-string

SPACING is a code-string that indicates the escapement class of the font, i.e., monospace (fixed pitch), proportional (variable pitch), or charcell (a special monospaced font that conforms to the traditional data processing character cell font model).

Code	English Translation	Description
"P"	Proportional	A font whose logical character widths vary for each glyph. Note that no other restrictions are placed on the metrics of a proportional font.
"M"	Monospaced	A font whose logical character widths are constant (i.e., all char widths of the font are = max_bounds.width). No other restrictions are placed on the metrics of a monospaced font.
"C"	CharCell	A monospaced font which follows the standard typewriter character cell model (i.e., the glyphs of the font can be modeled by X clients as "boxes" of the same width and height which are imaged side by side to form text strings or top to bottom to form text lines). By definition, all glyphs have the same logical character width and no glyphs have "ink" outside of the character cell— there is no kerning (i.e., on a per-char basis with positive metrics:

$$0 <= \text{left-bearing} <= \text{right-bearing} <= \text{width}$$

and with negative metrics:

$$\text{width} <= \text{left-bearing} <= \text{right-bearing} <= 0)$$

and the vertical extents of the font do not exceed the vertical spacing (i.e., on a per-char basis:

$$\text{ascent} <= \text{font-ascent and descent} <= \text{font-descent}).$$

Code	English Translation	Description
		The cell height = font-descent + font-ascent and width = AVERAGE_WIDTH.

AVERAGE_WIDTH : integer-string

AVERAGE_WIDTH is an unsigned integer-string typographic metric value giving the unweighted arithmetic mean width of all glyphs in the font, measured in 1/10th pixels. Note that for monospaced and character cell fonts, this is the width of all glyphs in the font.

CHARSET_REGISTRY : x-registered-name
CHARSET_ENCODING : registered-name

The character set used to encode the glyphs of the font (and implicitly the font's glyph repertoire), as maintained by the X Consortium character set registry. CHARSET_REGISTRY is an x-registered-name that identifies the registration authority that owns the specified encoding. CHARSET_ENCODING is a registered-name that identifies the coded character set as defined by that registration authority.

Although the X protocol does not explicitly have any knowledge about character set encodings, it is expected that server implementers will prefer to embed knowledge of certain proprietary or industry standard charsets into their font library for reasons of performance and convenience. The CHARSET_REGISTRY and CHARSET_ENCODING fields/properties allow an X client font request to specify a specific charset mapping in server environments where multiple charsets are supported. The availability of any particular character set is font- and server-implementation-dependent.

To prevent collisions when defining character set names, it is recommended that CHARSET_REGISTRY/CHARSET_ENCODING name pairs be constructed according to the following conventions:

Table M-2. CHARSET Syntax

```
        CharsetRegistry ::=    StdCharsetRegistryName | PrivCharsetRe-
                               gistryName
        CharsetEncoding ::=    StdCharsetEncodingName | PrivCharsetEn-
                               codingName
   StdCharsetRegistryName ::=  StdOrganizationId StdNumber | StdOrgan-
                               izationId StdNumber Dot Year
  PrivCharsetRegistryName ::=  OrganizationId STRING8
   StdCharsetEncodingName ::=  STRING8 — numeric part # of referenced
                               standard
  PrivCharsetEncodingName ::=  STRING8
        StdOrganizationId ::=  STRING8 — the registered name or acro-
                               nym of the referenced standard organi-
                               zation
               StdNumber ::=   STRING8 — referenced standard number
```

```
OrganizationId ::=   STRING8 — the registered name or acro-
                     nym of the organization
         Dot ::=     "." — ISO 8859-1 FULL STOP (Column/Row
                     2/14)
        Year ::=     STRING8 — numeric year (for example,
                     1989)
```

The X Consortium shall maintain and publish in a timely manner a registry of such character set names for use in X protocol font names and properties as specified in XLFD.

The ISO Latin-1 character set shall be registered by the X Consortium as the CHARSET_REGISTRY-CHARSET_ENCODING value pair: "ISO8859-1."

M.2.1.3 Examples

The following examples of font names are derived from the screen fonts shipped with the R3 server.

Font	X FontName
75dpi Fonts	
Charter 12pt	-Bitstream-Charter-Medium-R-Normal—12-120-75-75-P-68-ISO8859-1
Charter Bold 12pt	-Bitstream-Charter-Bold-R-Normal--12-120-75-75-P-76-ISO8859-1
Charter BoldItalic 12pt	-Bitstream-Charter-Bold-I-Normal--12-120-75-75-P-75-ISO8859-1C
Charter Italic 12pt	-Bitstream-Charter-Medium-I-Normal--12-120-75-75-P-66-ISO8859-1
Courier 8pt	-Adobe-Courier-Medium-R-Normal--8-80-75-75-M-50-ISO8859-1
Courier 10pt	-Adobe-Courier-Medium-R-Normal--10-100-75-75-M-60-ISO8859-1
Courier 12pt	-Adobe-Courier-Medium-R-Normal--12-120-75-75-M-70-ISO8859-1
Courier 14pt	-Adobe-Courier-Medium-R-Normal--14-140-75-75-M-90-ISO8859-1
Courier 18pt	-Adobe-Courier-Medium-R-Normal--18-180-75-75-M-110-ISO8859-1
Courier 24pt	-Adobe-Courier-Medium-R-Normal--24-240-75-75-M-150-ISO8859-1
Courier Bold 10pt	-Adobe-Courier-Bold-R-Normal--10-100-75-75-M-60-ISO8859-1
Courier BoldOblique 10pt	-Adobe-Courier-Bold-O-Normal--10-100-75-75-M-60-ISO8859-1
Courier Oblique 10pt	-Adobe-Courier-Medium-O-Normal--10-100-75-75-M-60-ISO8859-1

Font	X FontName
100dpi Fonts	
Symbol 8pt	`-Adobe-Symbol-Medium-R-Normal--11-80-100-100-P-61-Adobe-FONTSPECIFIC`
Symbol 10pt	`-Adobe-Symbol-Medium-R-Normal--14-100-100-100-P-85-Adobe-FONTSPECIFIC`
Symbol 12pt	`-Adobe-Symbol-Medium-R-Normal--17-120-100-100-P-95-Adobe-FONTSPECIFIC`
Symbol 14pt	`-Adobe-Symbol-Medium-R-Normal--20-140-100-100-P-107-Adobe-FONTSPECIFIC`
Symbol 18pt	`-Adobe-Symbol-Medium-R-Normal--25-180-100-100-P-142-Adobe-FONTSPECIFIC`
Symbol 24pt	`-Adobe-Symbol-Medium-R-Normal--34-240-100-100-P-191-Adobe-FONTSPECIFIC`
Times Bold 10pt	`-Adobe-Times-Bold-R-Normal--14-100-100-100-P-76-ISO8859-1`
Times BoldItalic 10pt	`-Adobe-Times-Bold-I-Normal--14-100-100-100-P-77-ISO8859-1`
Times Italic 10pt	`-Adobe-Times-Medium-I-Normal--14-100-100-100-P-73-ISO8859-1`
Times Roman 10pt	`-Adobe-Times-Medium-R-Normal--14-100-100-100-P-74-ISO8859-1`

M.2.2 FontProperties

All font properties are optional but will generally include the font name fields and, on a font-by-font basis, any other useful font descriptive/usage information that may be required to use the font intelligently. The XLFD specifies an extensive set of standard X font properties, their interpretation, and fallback rules when the property is not defined for a given font. The goal is to provide client applications with enough font information to be able to make automatic formatting/display decisions with good typographic results.

Additional standard X font property definitions may be defined in the future, and private properties may exist in X fonts at any time. Private font properties should be defined to conform to the general mechanism defined in the X protocol to prevent overlap of name space and ambiguous property names, i.e., private font property names are of the form: ISO8859-1 UNDERSCORE (Column/Row 05/15), followed by the organizational identifier, followed by UNDERSCORE, and terminated with the property name.

The Backus-Naur Form syntax description of X Font Properties is:

```
         Properties ::=    OptFontPropList
    OptFontPropList ::=    NULL | OptFontProp OptFontPropList
        OptFontProp ::=    PrivateFontProp | XFontProp
    PrivateFontProp ::=    STRING8  |  Underscore  OrganizationId
                           Underscore STRING8
          XFontProp ::=    FOUNDRY | FAMILY_NAME | WEIGHT_NAME |
                           SLANT | SETWIDTH_NAME | ADD_STYLE_NAME
                           |   PIXEL_SIZE    |   POINT_SIZE    |
                           RESOLUTION_X | RESOLUTION_Y | SPACING |
                           AVERAGE_  WIDTH  |  CHARSET_REGISTRY  |
                           CHARSET_  ENCODING  |  QUAD_WIDTH    |
                           RESOLUTION | MIN_SPACE | NORM_SPACE  |
                           MAX_SPACE | END_SPACE | SUPERSCRIPT_X |
                           SUPERSCRIPT_Y    |    SUBSCRIPT_X    |
                           SUBSCRIPT_Y   |   UNDERLINE_POSITION  |
                           UNDERLINE_THICKNESS | STRIKEOUT_ASCENT
                           |  STRIKEOUT_DESCENT  |  ITALIC_ANGLE  |
                           X_HEIGHT  |   WEIGHT   |  FACE_NAME    |
                           COPYRIGHT | AVG_CAPITAL_WIDTH | AVG_
                           LOWERCASE_WIDTH | RELATIVE_SETWIDTH |
                           RELATIVE_  WEIGHT   |   CAP_HEIGHT    |
                           SUPERSCRIPT_SIZE   |   FIGURE_WIDTH   |
                           SUBSCRIPT_ SIZE  |  SMALL_CAP_SIZE   |
                           NOTICE | DESTINATION
         Underscore ::=    OCTET  —  the  value  of  ISO8859-1
                           UNDERSCORE character (Column/Row 05/15)
     OrganizationId ::=    STRING8 — the registered name of the
                           organization
```

FOUNDRY : ATOM

As defined in the `FontName`, except the property type is ATOM.

FOUNDRY cannot be calculated or defaulted if not supplied as a font property.

FAMILY_NAME : ATOM

As defined in the `FontName`, except the property type is ATOM.

`FAMILY_NAME` cannot be calculated or defaulted if not supplied as a font property.

WEIGHT_NAME : ATOM

As defined in the `FontName`, except the property type is ATOM.

`WEIGHT_NAME` can be defaulted if not supplied as a font property, as follows:

```
if (WEIGHT_NAME undefined) then
    WEIGHT_NAME = ATOM(``Medium'')
```

SLANT : ATOM

As defined in the `FontName`, except the property type is ATOM.

SLANT can be defaulted if not supplied as a font property, as follows:

```
if (SLANT undefined) then
    SLANT = ATOM(''R'')
```

SETWIDTH_NAME : ATOM

As defined in the `FontName`, except the property type is ATOM.

`SETWIDTH_NAME` can be defaulted if not supplied as a font property, as follows:

```
if (SETWIDTH_NAME undefined) then
    SETWIDTH_NAME = ATOM(''Normal'')
```

ADD_STYLE_NAME : ATOM

As defined in the `FontName`, except the property type is ATOM.

`ADD_STYLE_NAME` can be defaulted if not supplied as a font property, as follows:

```
if (ADD_STYLE_NAME undefined) then
    ADD_STYLE_NAME = ATOM('''')
```

PIXEL_SIZE : CARD32

As defined in the `FontName`, except the property type is CARD32.

X clients requiring pixel values for the various typographic fixed spaces (EMspace, ENspace, and THINspace) can use the following algorithm for computing these values from other properties specified for a font:

```
DeciPointsPerInch = 722.7
EMspace = ROUND ((RESOLUTION_X * POINT_SIZE) / DeciPointsPerInch)
ENspace = ROUND (EMspace / 2)
THINspace = ROUND (EMspace / 3)
```

Note that a "/" denotes real division, "*" denotes real multiplication, and "ROUND" denotes a function that rounds its real argument "a" up/down to the next integer, according to $x = \text{FLOOR}(a + 0.5)$, where FLOOR is a function that rounds its argument down to an integer.

`PIXEL_SIZE` can be approximated if not supplied as a font property, according to the algorithm:

```
DeciPointsPerInch = 722.7
if (PIXEL_SIZE undefined) then
    PIXEL_SIZE = ROUND ((RESOLUTION_Y * POINT_SIZE) / DeciPointsPerInch)
```

POINT_SIZE : CARD32

As defined in the `FontName`, except the property type is CARD32.

X clients requiring device-independent values for EMspace, ENspace, and THINspace can use the following algorithm:

```
EMspace = ROUND (POINT_SIZE / 10)
ENspace = ROUND (POINT_SIZE / 20)
THINspace = ROUND (POINT_SIZE / 30)
```

Design `POINT_SIZE` cannot be calculated or approximated.

RESOLUTION_X : CARD32

As defined in the `FontName`, except the property type is CARD32.

`RESOLUTION_X` cannot be calculated or approximated.

RESOLUTION_Y : CARD32

As defined in the `FontName`, except the property type is CARD32.

`RESOLUTION_Y` cannot be calculated or approximated.

SPACING : ATOM

As defined in the `FontName`, except the property type is ATOM.

SPACING can be calculated if not supplied as a font property, according to the definitions given above for the `FontName`.

AVERAGE_WIDTH : CARD32

As defined in the `FontName`, except the property type is CARD32.

`AVERAGE_WIDTH` can be calculated if not provided as a font property, according to the following algorithm:

```
if (AVERAGE_WIDTH undefined) then
    AVERAGE_WIDTH = ROUND (MEAN (all glyph widths in font) * 10)
```

where `MEAN` is a function that returns the arithmetic mean of its arguments.

X clients requiring values for the number of characters per inch (pitch) of a monospaced font can use the following algorithm using the `AVERAGE_WIDTH` and `RESOLUTION_X` font properties:

```
if (SPACING not proportional) then
    CharPitch = (RESOLUTION_X * 10) / AVERAGE_WIDTH
```

CHARSET_REGISTRY : ATOM

As defined in the `FontName`, except the property type is ATOM.

`CHARSET_REGISTRY` cannot be defaulted if not supplied as a font property.

CHARSET_ENCODING : ATOM

As defined in the `FontName`, except the property type is ATOM.

`CHARSET_ENCODING` cannot be defaulted if not supplied as a font property.

MIN_SPACE : CARD32

`MIN_SPACE` is an unsigned integer value that gives the recommended minimum wordspace value to be used with this font.

`MIN_SPACE` can be approximated if not provided as a font property, according to the algorithm:

```
if (MIN_SPACE undefined) then
    MIN_SPACE = ROUND(0.75 * NORM_SPACE)
```

NORM_SPACE : CARD32

`NORM_SPACE` is an unsigned integer value that gives the recommended normal wordspace value to be used with this font.

`NORM_SPACE` can be approximated if not provided as a font property, according to the following algorithm:

```
DeciPointsPerInch = 722.7
if (NORM_SPACE undefined) then
    if (SPACE glyph exists) then
        NORM_SPACE = width of SPACE
    else NORM_SPACE = ROUND((0.33 * RESOLUTION_X * POINT_SIZE) /
                    DeciPointsPerInch)
```

MAX_SPACE : CARD32

`MAX_SPACE` is an unsigned integer value that gives the recommended maximum wordspace value to be used with this font.

`MAX_SPACE` can be approximated if not provided as a font property, according to the following algorithm:

```
if (MAX_SPACE undefined) then
    MAX_SPACE = ROUND(1.5 * NORM_SPACE)
```

END_SPACE : CARD32

`END_SPACE` is an unsigned integer value that gives the recommended spacing at the end of sentences.

`END_SPACE` can be approximated if not provided as a font property, according to the following algorithm:

```
if (END_SPACE undefined) then
    END_SPACE = NORM_SPACE
```

AVG_CAPITAL_WIDTH : INT32

AVG_CAPITAL_WIDTH is an integer value that gives the unweighted arithmetic mean width of all the capital glyphs in the font, in 1/10th pixels (applies to Latin and non-Latin fonts). For Latin fonts, capitals are the glyphs A to Z. Normally used for font matching/substitution.

AVG_CAPITAL_WIDTH can be calculated if not provided as a font property, according to the following algorithm:

```
if (AVG_CAPITAL_WIDTH undefined) then
    AVG_CAPITAL_WIDTH = ROUND (MEAN (capital glyph widths) * 10)
```

Note that MEAN is a function that returns the arithmetic mean of its arguments.

AVG_LOWERCASE_WIDTH : INT32

AVG_LOWERCASE_WIDTH is an integer value that gives the unweighted arithmetic mean width of all the lower-case glyphs in the font in 1/10th pixels. For Latin fonts, lower case are the glyphs a to z. Normally used for font matching or substitution.

Where appropriate, AVG_LOWERCASE_WIDTH can be approximated if not provided as a font property, according to the following algorithm:

```
if (AVG_LOWERCASE_WIDTH undefined) then
    if (lower case exists) then
        AVG_LOWERCASE_WIDTH = ROUND (MEAN (lower case glyph widths) * 10)
    else AVG_LOWERCASE_WIDTH undefined
```

QUAD_WIDTH : INT32 (DEPRECATED)

QUAD_WIDTH was incorrectly defined in the X protocol and is redundant since all typographic fixed spaces (EM, EN, and THIN) are constant for a given font size (i.e., they do not vary according to setwidth). X clients requiring these properties are encouraged to discontinue usage of QUAD_WIDTH and compute these values from other font properties. X clients requiring a font-dependent width value should use either the FIGURE_WIDTH or one of the average character width font properties (AVERAGE_WIDTH, AVG_CAPITAL_WIDTH, or AVG_LOWERCASE_WIDTH) for this purpose.

See also AVERAGE_WIDTH, AVG_CAPITAL_WIDTH, AVG_LOWERCASE_WIDTH, FIGURE_WIDTH, and PIXEL_SIZE font property definitions.

FIGURE_WIDTH : INT32

FIGURE_WIDTH is an integer typographic metric that gives the width of the tabular figures and the dollar sign, if suitable for tabular setting (all widths equal). For Latin fonts, these tabular figures are the arabic numerals 0 to 9.

FIGURE_WIDTH can be approximated if not supplied as a font property, according to the following algorithm:

```
if (numerals and DOLLAR sign are defined & widths are equal) then
    FIGURE_WIDTH = width of DOLLAR
else FIGURE_WIDTH property undefined
```

SUPERSCRIPT_X : INT32

SUPERSCRIPT_X is an integer value that gives the recommended horizontal offset in pixels from the position point to the X origin of synthetic superscript text. If the current position point is at [X,Y], then superscripts should begin at [X+SUPERSCRIPT_X, Y-SUPERSCRIPT_Y].

according to the following algorithm:

```
if (SUPERSCRIPT_X undefined) then
    if (TANGENT(ITALIC_ANGLE) defined) then
        SUPERSCRIPT_X = ROUND((0.40 * CAP_HEIGHT) / TANGENT(ITALIC_ANGLE))
    else SUPERSCRIPT_X = ROUND(0.40 * CAP_HEIGHT)
```

Note that TANGENT is a trigonometric function that returns the tangent of its argument (in degrees scaled by 64).

SUPERSCRIPT_Y : INT32

SUPERSCRIPT_Y is an integer value that gives the recommended vertical offset in pixels from the position point to the Y origin of synthetic superscript text. If the current position point is at [X,Y], then superscripts should begin at [X+SUPERSCRIPT_X, Y-SUPERSCRIPT_Y].

SUPERSCRIPT_Y can be approximated if not provided as a font property, according to the following algorithm:

```
if (SUPERSCRIPT_Y undefined) then
    SUPERSCRIPT_Y = ROUND(0.40 * CAP_HEIGHT)
```

SUBSCRIPT_X : INT32

SUBSCRIPT_X is an integer value that gives the recommended horizontal offset in pixels from the position point to the X origin of synthetic subscript text. If the current position point is at [X,Y], then subscripts should begin at [X+SUBSCRIPT_X, Y+SUBSCRIPT_Y].

SUBSCRIPT_X can be approximated if not provided as a font property, according to the following algorithm:

```
if (SUBSCRIPT_X undefined) then
    if (TANGENT(ITALIC_ANGLE) defined) then
        SUBSCRIPT_X = ROUND((0.40 * CAP_HEIGHT) / TANGENT(ITALIC_ANGLE))
    else SUBSCRIPT_X = ROUND(0.40 * CAP_HEIGHT)
```

SUBSCRIPT_Y : INT32

SUBSCRIPT_Y is an integer value that gives the recommended vertical offset in pixels from the position point to the Y origin of synthetic subscript text. If the current position point is at [X,Y], then subscripts should begin at [X+SUBSCRIPT_X, Y+SUBSCRIPT_Y].

SUBSCRIPT_Y can be approximated if not provided as a font property, according to the following algorithm:

```
if (SUBSCRIPT_Y undefined) then
    SUBSCRIPT_Y = ROUND(0.40 * CAP_HEIGHT)
```

Logical Font Description

SUPERSCRIPT_SIZE : CARD32

SUPERSCRIPT_SIZE is an unsigned integer value that gives the recommended body size of synthetic superscripts to be used with this font, in pixels. Note that this will generally be smaller than the size of the current font, i.e., superscripts are imaged from a smaller font, offset according to SUPERSCRIPT_X and SUPERSCRIPT_Y.

SUPERSCRIPT_SIZE can be approximated if not provided as a font property, according to the following algorithm:

```
if (SUPERSCRIPT_SIZE undefined) then
    SUPERSCRIPT_SIZE = ROUND(0.60 * PIXEL_SIZE)
```

SUBSCRIPT_SIZE : CARD32

SUBSCRIPT_SIZE is an unsigned integer value that gives the recommended body size of synthetic subscripts to be used with this font, in pixels. As with SUPERSCRIPT_SIZE, this will generally be smaller than the size of the current font, i.e., subscripts are imaged from a smaller font, offset according to SUBSCRIPT_X and SUBSCRIPT_Y.

SUBSCRIPT_SIZE can be approximated if not provided as a font property, according to the algorithm:

```
if (SUBSCRIPT_SIZE undefined) then
    SUBSCRIPT_SIZE = ROUND(0.60 * PIXEL_SIZE)
```

SMALL_CAP_SIZE : CARD32

SMALL_CAP_SIZE is an integer value that gives the recommended body size of synthetic small capitals to be used with this font, in pixels. Small capitals are generally imaged from a smaller font of slightly more weight. No offset [X,Y] is necessary.

SMALL_CAP_SIZE can be approximated if not provided as a font property, according to the following algorithm:

```
if (SMALL_CAP_SIZE undefined) then
    SMALL_CAP_SIZE = ROUND(PIXEL_SIZE * ((X_HEIGHT
        + ((CAP_HEIGHT - X_HEIGHT) / 3)) / CAP_HEIGHT))
```

UNDERLINE_POSITION : INT32

UNDERLINE_POSITION is an integer value that gives the recommended vertical offset in pixels from the baseline to the top of the underline. If the current position point is at [X,Y], the top of the baseline is given by [X, Y+UNDERLINE_POSITION].

UNDERLINE_POSITION can be approximated if not provided as a font property, according to the following algorithm:

```
if (UNDERLINE_POSITION undefined) then
    UNDERLINE_POSITION = ROUND(max_bounds.descent / 2)
```

UNDERLINE_THICKNESS : CARD32

UNDERLINE_POSITION is an unsigned integer value that gives the recommended underline thickness, in pixels.

UNDERLINE_THICKNESS can be approximated if not provided as a font property, according to the following algorithm:

```
CapStemWidth = average width of the stems of capitals
if (UNDERLINE_THICKNESS undefined) then
    UNDERLINE_THICKNESS = CapStemWidth
```

STRIKEOUT_ASCENT : INT32

STRIKEOUT_ASCENT is an integer value that gives the vertical ascent for boxing or voiding glyphs in this font. If the current position is at [X,Y] and the string extent is EXTENT, the upper-left corner of the strikeout box is at [X, Y-STRIKEOUT_ASCENT] and the lower right corner of the box is at [X+EXTENT, Y+STRIKEOUT_DESCENT].

STRIKEOUT_ASCENT can be approximated if not provided as a font property, according to the following algorithm:

```
if (STRIKEOUT_ASCENT undefined)
    STRIKEOUT_ASCENT =  max_bounds.ascent
```

STRIKEOUT_DESCENT : INT32

STRIKEOUT_DESCENT is an integer value that gives the vertical descent for boxing or voiding glyphs in this font. If the current position is at [X,Y] and the string extent is EXTENT, the upper-left corner of the strikeout box is at [X, Y-STRIKEOUT_ASCENT] and the lower right corner of the box is at [X+EXTENT, Y+STRIKEOUT_DESCENT].

STRIKEOUT_DESCENT can be approximated if not provided as a font property, according to the following algorithm:

```
if (STRIKEOUT_DESCENT undefined)
    STRIKEOUT_DESCENT =  max_bounds.descent
```

ITALIC_ANGLE : INT32

ITALIC_ANGLE is an integer value that gives the nominal posture angle of the typeface design, in 1/64th degrees, measured from the glyph origin counterclockwise from the three o'clock position.

ITALIC_ANGLE can be defaulted if not provided as a font property, according to the following algorithm:

```
if (ITALIC_ANGLE undefined) then
    ITALIC_ANGLE = (90 * 64)
```

CAP_HEIGHT : CARD32

CAP_HEIGHT is an unsigned integer, the nominal height of the capital letters contained in the font, as specified by the FOUNDRY or typeface designer. Where applicable, it is defined to be the height of the Latin upper case X.

CAP_HEIGHT is required by certain clients to compute scale factors and positioning offsets for algorithmically generated glyphs where this information or designed glyphs are not explicitly provided by the font (e.g., small capitals, superiors, inferiors, etc.). Capital height is also a critical factor in font matching and substitution.

CAP_HEIGHT can be approximated if not provided as a font property, according to the following algorithm:

```
if (CAP_HEIGHT undefined) then
    if (Latin font) then
        CAP_HEIGHT = XCharStruct.ascent[glyph X]
    else if (capitals exist) then
        CAP_HEIGHT = XCharStruct.ascent[some capital glyph]
    else CAP_HEIGHT undefined
```

X_HEIGHT : CARD32

X_HEIGHT is a unsigned integer, the nominal height above the baseline of the lower-case glyphs contained in the font, as specified by the FOUNDRY or typeface designer. Where applicable, it is defined to be the height of the Latin lower case x.

As with CAPHEIGHT, X_HEIGHT is required by certain clients to compute scale factors for algorithmically generated small capitals, where not explicitly provided by the font resource, and is a critical factor in font matching and substitution. X_HEIGHT can be approximated if not provided as a font property, according to the following algorithm:

```
if (X_HEIGHT undefined) then
    if (Latin font) then
        X_HEIGHT = XCharStruct.ascent[glyph x]
    else if (lower case exists) then
        X_HEIGHT = XCharStruct.ascent[some lower case glyph]
    else X_HEIGHT is undefined
```

RELATIVE_SETWIDTH : CARD32

RELATIVE_SETWIDTH is an integer that gives the coded proportionate width of the font, relative to all known fonts of the same typeface family, according to the type designer's or FOUNDRY's judgment.

The possible values are:

Code	English String	Description
0	undefined	Undefined or unknown
10	UltraCondensed	Lowest ratio of average width to height
20	ExtraCondensed	
30	Condensed	Condensed, Narrow, Compressed, ...
40	SemiCondensed	
50	Medium	Medium, Normal, Regular, ...
60	SemiExpanded	SemiExpanded, DemiExpanded, ...
70	Expanded	
80	ExtraExpanded	ExtraExpanded, Wide, ...
90	UltraExpanded	Highest ratio of average width to height

RELATIVE_SETWIDTH can be defaulted if not provided as a font property, according to the following algorithm:

```
if (RELATIVE_SETWIDTH undefined) then
    RELATIVE_SETWIDTH = 50
```

X clients that wish to obtain a calculated proportionate width of the font (i.e., a font-independent way of identifying the proportionate width across all fonts and all font vendors) can use the following algorithm:

```
SETWIDTH = AVG_CAPITAL_WIDTH / (CAP_HEIGHT * 10)
```

Note that SETWIDTH is a real with 0 being the "narrowest" calculated setwidth.

RELATIVE_WEIGHT : CARD32

RELATIVE_WEIGHT is an integer that gives the coded weight of the font, relative to all known fonts of the same typeface family, according to the type designer's or FOUNDRY's judgment.

The possible values are:

Code	English String	Description
0	undefined	Undefined or unknown
10	UltraLight	Lowest ratio of stem width to height
20	ExtraLight	
30	Light	
40	SemiLight	SemiLight, Book, ...
50	Medium	Medium, Normal, Regular, ...
60	SemiBold	SemiBold, DemiBold, ...
70	Bold	
80	ExtraBold	ExtraBold, Heavy, ...
90	UltraBold	UltraBold, Black, ..., the highest ratio of stem width to height

RELATIVE_WEIGHT can be defaulted if not provided as a font property, according to the following algorithm:

```
if (RELATIVE_WEIGHT undefined) then
    RELATIVE_WEIGHT = 50
```

WEIGHT : CARD32

Calculated WEIGHT is an unsigned integer, the calculated weight of the font, computed as the ratio of capital stem width to CAP_HEIGHT, in the range 0 to 1000, where zero is the "lightest" weight.

WEIGHT can be calculated if not supplied as a font property, according to the following algorithm:

```
CapStemWidth = average width of the stems of capitals
if (WEIGHT undefined) then
    WEIGHT = ROUND ((CapStemWidth * 1000) / CAP_HEIGHT)
```

A calculated value for weight is necessary when matching fonts from different families because both the `RELATIVE_WEIGHT` and the `WEIGHT_NAME` are assigned by the typeface supplier, according to its tradition and practice, and are therefore somewhat subjective. Calculated WEIGHT provides a font-independent way of identifying the weight across all fonts and all font vendors.

RESOLUTION : CARD32 (DEPRECATED)

Independent horizontal and vertical design resolution components are required to accommodate displays with nonsquare aspect ratios and are given by the `RESOLUTION_X` and `RESOLUTION_Y` font name fields/properties. The units of the original definition of RESOLUTION are also in conflict with these new properties. X clients are encouraged to discontinue usage of RESOLUTION and to use the appropriate X,Y resolution properties as required.

FACE_NAME : ATOM

`FACE_NAME` is a human-understandable string that gives the full device-independent typeface name, including the owner, weight, slant, set, etc., but not the resolution, size, etc. Normally used as feedback during font selection.

`FACE_NAME` cannot be calculated or approximated if not provided as a font property.

COPYRIGHT : ATOM

COPYRIGHT is a human-understandable string that gives the copyright information of the legal owner of the digital font data.

This information is a required component of a font but is independent of the particular format used to represent it (i.e., it cannot be captured as a comment that could later be "thrown away" for efficiency reasons).

COPYRIGHT cannot be calculated or approximated if not provided as a font property.

NOTICE : ATOM

NOTICE is a human-understandable string that gives the copyright information of the legal owner of the font design or, if not applicable, the trademark information for the typeface `FAMILY_NAME`.

Typeface design and trademark protection laws vary from country to country, the U.S. having no design copyright protection currently, while various countries in Europe offer both design and typeface family name trademark protection. As with COPYRIGHT, this information is a required component of a font but is independent of the particular format used to represent it.

NOTICE cannot be calculated or approximated if not provided as a font property.

DESTINATION : CARD32

DESTINATION is an unsigned integer code that gives the font design destination, i.e., whether it was designed as a screen proofing font to match printer font glyph widths (WYSIWYG), as an optimal video font (possibly with corresponding printer font) for extended screen viewing (VideoText), etc.

The font design considerations are very different, and at current display resolutions, the readability and legibility of these two kinds of screen fonts are very different. DESTINATION allows publishing clients that use X to model the printed page and Video Text clients, such as on-line documentation browsers, to query for X screen fonts that suit their particular requirements.

The encoding is as follows:

Code	English String	Description
0	WYSIWYG	A font optimized to match the typographic design and metrics of an equivalent printer font.
1	Video Text	A font optimized for screen legibility and readability.

M.2.3 Built-in Font Property Atoms

The following font property atom definitions were predefined in the initial Version 11 of the X protocol:

Font Property	Property Type
MIN_SPACE	CARD32
NORM_SPACE	CARD32
MAX_SPACE	CARD32
END_SPACE	CARD32
SUPERSCRIPT_X	INT32
SUPERSCRIPT_Y	INT32
SUBSCRIPT_X	INT32
SUBSCRIPT_Y	INT32
UNDERLINE_POSITION	INT32
UNDERLINE_THICKNESS	CARD32
STRIKEOUT_ASCENT	INT32
STRIKEOUT_DESCENT	INT32
FONT_ASCENT	INT32
FONT_DESCENT	INT32
ITALIC_ANGLE	INT32
X_HEIGHT	INT32
QUAD_WIDTH	INT32 — deprecated
WEIGHT	CARD32
POINT_SIZE	CARD32
RESOLUTION	CARD32 — deprecated
COPYRIGHT	ATOM
FACE_NAME	ATOM
FAMILY_NAME	ATOM
DEFAULT_CHAR	CARD32

M.3 Affected Elements of Xlib and the X Protocol

The following X protocol requests must use the font naming conventions:

OpenFont	For the name parameter.
ListFonts	For the pattern parameter.
ListFontsWithInfo	For the pattern parameter.

In addition, the following Xlib functions must use the font naming conventions:

XLoadFont	For the name parameter.
XListFontsWithInfo	For the pattern parameter.
XLoadQueryFont	For the name parameter.
XListFonts	For the pattern parameter.

M.4 BDF Conformance

The bitmap font distribution and interchange format adopted by the X Consortium (BDF V2.1) provides a general mechanism for identifying the font name of an X font and a variable list of font properties but does not mandate the syntax/semantics of the font name or the semantics of the font properties that might be provided in a BDF font. This section identifies the requirements for BDF fonts that conform to XLFD.

M.4.1 XLFD Conformance Requirements

A BDF font conforms to the XLFD V1.3 specification if and only if the following conditions are satisfied:

- The value for the BDF item **FONT** conforms to the syntax and semantic definition of a XLFD FontName string.

- The FontName begins with the X FontNameRegistry prefix: "-".

- All XLFD FontName fields are defined.

- Any FontProperties provided conform in name and semantics to the XLFD FontProperties definitions.

A simple method of testing for conformance would entail first verifying that the FontNameRegistry prefix is the string "-", that the number of field delimiters in the string and coded field values are valid, and that each font property name either matches a standard XLFD property name or follows the definition of a private property.

M.4.2 FONT_ASCENT, FONT_DESCENT, and DEFAULT_CHAR

FONT_ASCENT, FONT_DESCENT, and DEFAULT_CHAR are provided in the BDF specification as properties that are moved to the XFontStruct by the BDF font compiler in generating the X server-specific binary font encoding. If present, these properties shall comply with the following semantic definitions.

FONT_ASCENT : INT32

FONT_ASCENT is an unsigned integer that gives the recommended typographic ascent above the baseline for determining interline spacing. Specific glyphs of the font may extent beyond this. If the current position point for line *n* is at [X,Y], then the origin of the next line *n+1* (allowing for a possible font change) is:

$$[X, Y+FONT\_DESCENT_n+FONT\_ASCENT_{n+1}]$$

FONT_ASCENT can be approximated if not provided as a font property, according to the following algorithm:

```
if (FONT_ASCENT undefined) then
   FONT_ASCENT = max_bounds.ascent
```

FONT_DESCENT : INT32

FONT_DESCENT is an unsigned integer that gives the recommended typographic descent below the baseline for determining interline spacing. Specific glyphs of the font may extent beyond this. If the current position point for line *n* is at [X,Y], then the origin of the next line *n+1* (allowing for a possible font change) is:

$$[X, Y+FONT\_DESCENT_n+FONT\_ASCENT_{n+1}P]$$

The logical extent of the font is inclusive between the Y-coordinate values Y-FONT_ASCENT and Y+FONT_DESCENT+1. FONT_DESCENT can be approximated if not provided as a font property, according to the following algorithm:

```
if (FONT_DESCENT undefined) then
   FONT_DESCENT = max_bounds.descent
```

DEFAULT_CHAR : CARD32

DEFAULT_CHAR is an unsigned integer value that gives the default character to be used by the X server when an attempt is made to display an undefined or nonexistent character in the font.

The DEFAULT_CHAR is a 16-bit character (not a two-byte character). For a font using two-byte matrix format, the DEFAULT_CHAR has byte1 in the most significant byte and byte2 in the least significant byte. If the DEFAULT_CHAR itself is undefined or specifies an undefined or nonexistent character in the font, then no display is performed.

DEFAULT_CHAR cannot be approximated if not provided as a font property.

Glossary

Access control list
    X maintains a list of hosts from which client programs can be run. By default, only programs on the local host and hosts specified in an initial list read by the server can use the display. Clients on the local host can change this access control list. Some server implementations can also implement other authorization mechanisms in addition to or in place of this mechanism. The action of this mechanism can be conditional based on the authorization protocol name and data received by the server at connection setup.

Active grab
    A grab is active when the pointer or keyboard is actually owned by the single grabbing client.

Ancestors
    If W is an inferior of A, then A is an ancestor of W.

Atom
    An atom is a unique ID corresponding to a string name. Atoms are used to identify properties, types, and selections.

Background
    An **InputOutput** window can have a background, which is defined as a pixmap. When regions of the window have their contents lost or invalidated, the server will automatically tile those regions with the background.

Backing store
    When a server maintains the contents of a window, the pixels saved off screen are known as a backing store.

Bit gravity
    When a window is resized, the contents of the window are not necessarily discarded. It is possible to request that the server relocate the previous contents to some region of the window (though no guarantees are made). This attraction of window contents for some location of a window is known as bit gravity.

Bit plane
    When a pixmap or window is thought of as a stack of bitmaps, each bitmap is called a bit plane or plane.

Bitmap
    A bitmap is a pixmap of depth one.

Border
    An **InputOutput** window can have a border of equal thickness on all four sides of the window. A pixmap defines the contents of the border, and the server automatically maintains the

contents of the border. Exposure events are never generated for border regions.

Button grabbing   Buttons on the pointer may be passively grabbed by a client. When the button is pressed, the pointer is then actively grabbed by the client.

Byte order   For image (pixmap/bitmap) data, the server defines the byte order, and clients with different native byte ordering must swap bytes as necessary. For all other parts of the protocol, the client defines the byte order, and the server swaps bytes as necessary.

Children   The children of a window are its first-level subwindows.

Client   An application program connects to the window system server by some interprocess communication (IPC) path, such as a TCP connection or a shared memory buffer. This program is referred to as a client of the window system server. More precisely, the client is the IPC path itself; a program with multiple paths open to the server is viewed as multiple clients by the protocol. Resource lifetimes are controlled by connection lifetimes, not by program lifetimes.

Clipping region   In a graphics context, a bitmap or list of rectangles can be specified to restrict output to a particular region of the window. The image defined by the bitmap or rectangles is called a clipping region.

Colormap   A colormap consists of a set of entries defining color values. The colormap associated with a window is used to display the contents of the window; each pixel value indexes the colormap to produce RGB values that drive the guns of a monitor. Depending on hardware limitations, one or more colormaps may be installed at one time, so that windows associated with those maps display with correct colors.

Connection   The IPC path between the server and client program is known as a connection. A client program typically (but not necessarily) has one connection to the server over which requests and events are sent.

Containment   A window "contains" the pointer if the window is viewable and the hotspot of the cursor is within a visible region of the window or a visible region of one of its inferiors. The border of the window is included as part of the window for containment. The pointer is "in" a window if the window contains the pointer but no inferior contains the pointer.

Coordinate system   The coordinate system has X horizontal and Y vertical, with the origin [0,0] at the upper left. Coordinates are discrete and are in terms of pixels. Each window and pixmap has its own coordinate system. For a window, the origin is inside the border at the inside upper left.

Cursor   A cursor is the visible shape of the pointer on a screen. It consists of a hotspot, a source bitmap, a shape bitmap, and a pair of colors. The cursor defined for a window controls the visible appearance when the pointer is in that window.

Depth   The depth of a window or pixmap is the number of bits per pixel that it has. The depth of a graphics context is the depth of the drawables it can be used in conjunction with for graphics output.

Device   Keyboards, mice, tablets, track-balls, button boxes, and so on are all collectively known as input devices. The core protocol only deals with two devices, "the keyboard" and "the pointer."

DirectColor   **DirectColor** is a class of colormap in which a pixel value is decomposed into three separate subfields for indexing. The first subfield indexes an array to produce red intensity values. The second subfield indexes a second array to produce blue intensity values. The third subfield indexes a third array to produce green intensity values. The RGB values can be changed dynamically.

Display   A server, together with its screens and input devices, is called a display.

Drawable   Both windows and pixmaps can be used as sources and destinations in graphics operations. These windows and pixmaps are collectively known as drawables. However, an **InputOnly** window cannot be used as a source or destination in a graphics operation.

Event   Clients are informed of information asynchronously by means of events. These events can be generated either asynchronously from devices or as side effects of client requests. Events are grouped into types. The server never sends events to a client unless the client has specifically asked to be informed of that type of event. However, other clients can force events to be sent to other clients. Events are typically reported relative to a window.

Event mask   Events are requested relative to a window. The set of event types that a client requests relative to a window is described by using an event mask.

Event propagation   Device-related events propagate from the source window to ancestor windows until some client has expressed interest in handling that type of event or until the event is discarded explicitly.

Event source   The window the pointer is in is the source of a device-related event.

Event synchronization	There are certain race conditions possible when demultiplexing device events to clients (in particular, deciding where pointer and keyboard events should be sent when in the middle of window management operations). The event synchronization mechanism allows synchronous processing of device events.
Exposure event	Servers do not guarantee to preserve the contents of windows when windows are obscured or reconfigured. Exposure events are sent to clients to inform them when contents of regions of windows have been lost.
Extension	Named extensions to the core protocol can be defined to extend the system. Extension to output requests, resources, and event types are all possible and are expected.
Focus window	The focus window is another term for the input focus.
Font	A font is a matrix of glyphs (typically characters). The protocol does no translation or interpretation of character sets. The client simply indicates values used to index the glyph array. A font contains additional metric information to determine interglyph and interline spacing.
GC, GContext	GC and gcontext are abbreviations for graphics context.
Glyph	A glyph is an image, typically of a character, in a font.
Grab	Keyboard keys, the keyboard, pointer buttons, the pointer, and the server can be grabbed for exclusive use by a client. In general, these facilities are not intended to be used by normal applications but are intended for various input and window managers to implement various styles of user interfaces.
Graphics context	Various information for graphics output is stored in a graphics context such as foreground pixel, background pixel, line width, clipping region, and so on. A graphics context can only be used with drawables that have the same root and the same depth as the graphics context.
Gravity	See **bit gravity** and **window gravity**.
GrayScale	**GrayScale** can be viewed as a degenerate case of **Pseudo-Color**, in which the red, green, and blue values in any given colormap entry are equal, thus producing shades of gray. The gray values can be changed dynamically.
Hotspot	A cursor has an associated hotspot that defines the point in the cursor corresponding to the coordinates reported for the pointer.
Identifier	An identifier is a unique value associated with a resource that clients use to name that resource. The identifier can be used over any connection.

Inferiors	The inferiors of a window are all of the subwindows nested below it: the children, the children's children, and so on.
Input focus	The input focus is normally a window defining the scope for processing of keyboard input. If a generated keyboard event would normally be reported to this window or one of its inferiors, the event is reported normally. Otherwise, the event is reported with respect to the focus window. The input focus also can be set such that all keyboard events are discarded and such that the focus window is dynamically taken to be the root window of whatever screen the pointer is on at each keyboard event.
Input manager	Control over keyboard input is typically provided by an input manager client.
InputOnly window	An **InputOnly** window is a window that cannot be used for graphics requests. **InputOnly** windows are invisible and can be used to control such things as cursors, input event generation, and grabbing. **InputOnly** windows cannot have **InputOutput** windows as inferiors.
InputOutput window	An **InputOutput** window is the normal kind of opaque window, used for both input and output. **InputOutput** windows can have both **InputOutput** and **InputOnly** windows as inferiors.
Key grabbing	Keys on the keyboard can be passively grabbed by a client. When the key is pressed, the keyboard is then actively grabbed by the client.
Keyboard grabbing	A client can actively grab control of the keyboard, and key events will be sent to that client rather than the client the events would normally have been sent to.
Keysym	An encoding of a symbol on a keycap on a keyboard.
Mapped	A window is said to be mapped if a map call has been performed on it. Unmapped windows and their inferiors are never viewable or visible.
Modifier keys	Shift, Control, Meta, Super, Hyper, Alt, Compose, Apple, Caps-Lock, ShiftLock, and similar keys are called modifier keys.
Monochrome	Monochrome is a special case of **StaticGray** in which there are only two colormap entries.
Obscure	A window is obscured if some other window obscures it. Window A obscures window B if both are viewable **InputOutput** windows, A is higher in the global stacking order, and the rectangle defined by the outside edges of A intersects the rectangle defined by the outside edges of B. Note the distinction between obscures and occludes. Also note that window borders are included in the calculation and that a window can be obscured and yet still have visible regions.

Glossary

Occlude	A window is occluded if some other window occludes it. Window A occludes window B if both are mapped, A is higher in the global stacking order, and the rectangle defined by the outside edges of A intersects the rectangle defined by the outside edges of B. Note the distinction between occludes and obscures. Also note that window borders are included in the calculation.
Padding	Some padding bytes are inserted in the data stream to maintain alignment of the protocol requests on natural boundaries. This increases ease of portability to some machine architectures.
Parent window	If C is a child of P, then P is the parent of C.
Passive grab	Grabbing a key or button is a passive grab. The grab activates when the key or button is actually pressed.
Pixel value	A pixel is an N-bit value, where N is the number of bit planes used in a particular window or pixmap; that is, N is the depth of the window or pixmap. For a window, a pixel value indexes a colormap to derive an actual color to be displayed.
Pixmap	A pixmap is a three-dimensional array of bits. A pixmap is normally thought of as a two-dimensional array of pixels, where each pixel can be a value from 0 to (2^N-1) and where N is the depth (z axis) of the pixmap. A pixmap can also be thought of as a stack of N bitmaps.
Plane	When a pixmap or window is thought of as a stack of bitmaps, each bitmap is called a plane or bit plane.
Plane mask	Graphics operations can be restricted to only affect a subset of bit planes of a destination. A plane mask is a bit mask describing which planes are to be modified. The plane mask is stored in a graphics context.
Pointer	The pointer is the pointing device attached to the cursor and tracked on the screens.
Pointer grabbing	A client can actively grab control of the pointer. Then button and motion events will be sent to that client rather than the client the events would normally have been sent to.
Pointing device	A pointing device is typically a mouse, tablet, or some other device with effective dimensional motion. There is only one visible cursor defined by the core protocol, and it tracks whatever pointing device is attached as the pointer.
Property	Windows may have associated properties, which consist of a name, a type, a data format, and some data. The protocol places no interpretation on properties. They are intended as a general-purpose naming mechanism for clients. For example, clients might use properties to share information such as resize hints, program names, and icon formats with a window manager.

Property list	The property list of a window is the list of properties that have been defined for the window.
PseudoColor	**PseudoColor** is a class of colormap in which a pixel value indexes the colormap to produce independent red, green, and blue values; that is, the colormap is viewed as an array of triples (RGB values). The RGB values can be changed dynamically.
Redirecting control	Window managers (or client programs) may want to enforce window layout policy in various ways. When a client attempts to change the size or position of a window, the operation may be redirected to a specified client rather than the operation actually being performed.
Reply	Information requested by a client program is sent back to the client with a reply. Both events and replies are multiplexed on the same connection. Most requests do not generate replies, although some requests generate multiple replies.
Request	A command to the server is called a request. It is a single block of data sent over a connection.
Resource	Windows, pixmaps, cursors, fonts, graphics contexts, and colormaps are known as resources. They all have unique identifiers associated with them for naming purposes. The lifetime of a resource usually is bounded by the lifetime of the connection over which the resource was created.
"RGB values"	Red, green, and blue (RGB) intensity values are used to define color. These values are always represented as 16-bit unsigned numbers, with 0 being the minimum intensity and 65535 being the maximum intensity. The server scales the values to match the display hardware.
Root	The root of a pixmap or graphics context is the same as the root of whatever drawable was used when the pixmap or graphics context was created. The root of a window is the root window under which the window was created.
Root window	Each screen has a root window covering it. It cannot be reconfigured or unmapped, but it otherwise acts as a full-fledged window. A root window has no parent.
Save set	The save set of a client is a list of other clients' windows that, if they are inferiors of one of the client's windows at connection close, should not be destroyed and that should be remapped if currently unmapped. Save sets are typically used by window managers to avoid lost windows if the manager terminates abnormally.
Scanline	A scanline is a list of pixel or bit values viewed as a horizontal row (all values having the same y coordinate) of an image, with the values ordered by increasing x coordinate.

Scanline order	An image represented in scanline order contains scanlines ordered by increasing y coordinate.
Screen	A server can provide several independent screens, which typically have physically independent monitors. This would be the expected configuration when there is only a single keyboard and pointer shared among the screens.
Selection	A selection can be thought of as an indirect property with dynamic type; that is, rather than having the property stored in the server, it is maintained by some client (the "owner"). A selection is global in nature and is thought of as belonging to the user (although maintained by clients), rather than as being private to a particular window subhierarchy or a particular set of clients. When a client asks for the contents of a selection, it specifies a selection "target type." This target type can be used to control the transmitted representation of the contents. For example, if the selection is "the last thing the user clicked on" and that is currently an image, then the target type might specify whether the contents of the image should be sent in XY format or Z format. The target type can also be used to control the class of contents transmitted; for example, asking for the "looks" (fonts, line spacing, indentation, and so on) of a paragraph selection rather than the text of the paragraph. The target type can also be used for other purposes. The protocol does not constrain the semantics.
Server	The server provides the basic windowing mechanism. It handles IPC connections from clients, demultiplexes graphics requests onto the screens, and multiplexes input back to the appropriate clients.
Server grabbing	The server can be grabbed by a single client for exclusive use. This prevents processing of any requests from other client connections until the grab is completed. This is typically only a transient state for such things as rubber-banding, pop-up menus, or to execute requests indivisibly.
Sibling	Children of the same parent window are known as sibling windows.
Stacking order	Sibling windows may stack on top of each other. Windows above other windows both obscure and occlude those lower windows. This is similar to paper on a desk. The relationship between sibling windows is known as the stacking order.
StaticColor	**StaticColor** can be viewed as a degenerate case of **Pseudo-Color** in which the RGB values are predefined and read-only.
StaticGray	**StaticGray** can be viewed as a degenerate case of **GrayScale** in which the gray values are predefined and read-only. The values are typically linear or near-linear increasing ramps.

Stipple	A stipple pattern is a bitmap that is used to tile a region that will serve as an additional clip mask for a fill operation with the foreground color.
Tile	A pixmap can be replicated in two dimensions to tile a region. The pixmap itself is also known as a tile.
Timestamp	A timestamp is a time value, expressed in milliseconds. It typically is the time since the last server reset. Timestamp values wrap around (after about 49.7 days). The server, given its current time is represented by timestamp T, always interprets timestamps from clients by treating half of the timestamp space as being earlier in time than T and half of the timestamp space as being later in time than T. One timestamp value (named **CurrentTime**) is never generated by the server. This value is reserved for use in requests to represent the current server time.
TrueColor	**TrueColor** can be viewed as a degenerate case of **DirectColor** in which the subfields in the pixel value directly encode the corresponding RGB values; that is, the colormap has predefined read-only RGB values. The values are typically linear or near-linear increasing ramps.
Type	A type is an arbitrary atom used to identify the interpretation of property data. Types are completely uninterpreted by the server and are solely for the benefit of clients.
Viewable	A window is viewable if it and all of its ancestors are mapped. This does not imply that any portion of the window is actually visible. Graphics requests can be performed on a window when it is not viewable, but output will not be retained unless the server is maintaining backing store.
Visible	A region of a window is visible if someone looking at the screen can actually see it; that is, the window is viewable and the region is not occluded by any other window.
Window gravity	When windows are resized, subwindows may be repositioned automatically relative to some position in the window. This attraction of a subwindow to some part of its parent is known as window gravity.
Window manager	Manipulation of windows on the screen and much of the user interface (policy) is typically provided by a window manager client.
XYFormat	The data for a pixmap is said to be in XY format if it is organized as a set of bitmaps representing individual bit planes, with the planes appearing from most-significant to least-significant in bit order.
ZFormat	The data for a pixmap is said to be in Z format if it is organized as a set of pixel values in scanline order.

Index

backing-pixel window attribute
127
backing-planes window attribute
127
backing-store window attribute
54, 98, 155, 213
  Always value in 127, 136
  glossary definition 455
  NotUseful value in 127
  WhenMapped value in 127, 136
BDF conformance 452 - 453
bell
  duration 77
  pitch 77
  volume 70, 77
Bell request 70
Below stack-mode value 99
bit gravity
  Forget 98
  glossary definition 455
  Static 98
  window attribute 126
bit plane
  glossary definition 455
bit vector 244
bitmap
  glossary definition 455
bitmasks
  chained 49
border
  glossary definition 455
border-pixmap window attribute
  CopyFromParent value in 126
BottomIf stack-mode value 99
bounding box 112, 120, 241
buffering 31 - 33
  mechanism in server 34
  request 31
buffers
  motion history 163
button grabbing
  glossary definition 456
button masks 42, 214
button or key grab
  conventions 418
ButtonMotion event mask
  in MotionNotify event 214
ButtonPress event 22, 67, 71, 85,
    196
ButtonRelease event 67, 72, 196
buttons 280, 332

byte order
  glossary definition 456
byte swapping 19, 42, 49, 52, 258
bytes
  for keysym values 297
  in errors 43, 48
  in events 43
  in replies 43
  in requests 42
  order of, in connection setup 50
  unused 49

C

C language 5
C libraries 5, 7
  Xlib 5, 11
  Xt Intrinsics 5
cap-style GC component 73, 113,
    219
ChangeActivePointerGrab request
    73, 332
ChangeGC request 74, 261
ChangeHosts request 75
ChangeKeyboardControl request
    77
ChangeKeyboardMapping request
    80, 210
ChangePointerControl request 81
ChangeProperty request 82
ChangeSaveSet request 84
ChangeWindowAttributes request
    85, 399
channel descriptors 7
Chaos address family 42, 75
children
  glossary definition 456
circular arcs 219
CirculateNotify event 87, 88, 136
CirculateWindow request 87, 88,
    89
ClearArea request 90
client 5
  and server responsibilities 9, 10
  communication 35
  description of 4
  forcing termination of 194
  glossary definition 456
  information for at connection
    setup 55
  library buffering 32
  messages 410

fonts
  association with resource ID 92
  BDF conformance to 452
  bounding box of 241
  CHARSET syntax 437
  constructed with linear indexing 42
  constructed with matrix indexing 42
  conventions of in book xiii
  defined by linear indexing 229, 247
  defined by matrix indexing 227, 229, 247
  defining search path for 265
  determining 429
  glossary definition 458
  glyph 120
  list of 199
  loading 218
  multiple charsets in 430
  multiple vendors of same 430
  properties of 429
  property atom definitions 451
  property syntax conventions 440
  returning information about 201, 240
  returning search path for 152
  system independent names for 431
  unique names for 430
ForceScreenSaver request 145, 272
foreground GC component 112, 185, 224, 232
foreground pixel *see* foreground GC component
Forget bit gravity 98
formats of property types 382
FreeColor visual type 108
FreeColormap request 127, 146
FreeColors request 147
FreeCursor request 148
FreeGC request 149
FreePixmap request 150
frozen
  event processing 214, 245
  keyboards 67, 179
  pointers 67, 179
function GC component 185

G

GC *see* graphics context (GC)
GC components
  arc-mode 116
  background 112
  cap-style 113, 219
  changing 74
  clip-mask 115, 261
  clip-origin 114, 115
  dashes 115
  dash-offset 264
  default values for 116
  fill-rule 115
  fill-style 106, 114, 185
  foreground 112
  function 185
  graphics-exposure 116, 216
  join-style 114, 219
  line-style 113
  line-width 112
  list of 111
  plane-mask 102, 112, 147, 155
  stipple 114
  subwindow-mode 115
  tile 102, 114
  tile-stipple origin 114
GC values 112
  ClipByChildren 115
  Copy 185
  EvenOdd 115
  IncludeInferior 115
  list of 111
  Solid 185
  Winding 115
GContext error 322
geometry of drawable 153
GetAtomName request 151
GetFontPath request 152
GetGeometry request 153, 406
GetImage request 155
GetInputFocus request 157
GetKeyboardControl request 158
GetKeyboardMapping request 160
GetModifierMapping request 162
GetMotionEvents request 163, 215
GetPointerControl request 165
GetPointerMapping request 166, 270
GetProperty request 167, 231, 375

INSERT_PROPERTY request
382
INSERT_SELECTION request
381
InstallColormap request 127, 188,
205, 285, 409
installing colormaps 146, 188,
205, 285
conventions 402 - 404
interclient communication 35
conventions 367 - 454
International Standards Organization 65
InternAtom request 189, 329
Internet address family 42, 75
interprocess communication channels 7
Intrinsics
description of 5
IPC *see* interprocess communication channels
ISO *see* International Standards
Organization
ISO encoding 65, 189, 199, 207,
218, 238, 277

J

join-style GC component 114, 219

K

key click volume
changing 77
key grabbing
glossary definition 459
key masks *see* modifier key masks
keyboard controls
changing 77
keyboard grabbing
glossary definition 459
keyboard-modes
Asynchronous 177
Synchronous 177
keyboards 331
encoding 333
frozen 67, 179
grabbing 67, 141, 175, 177, 295
handling 9
layout of 298
mapping 80, 160, 210

mapping conventions 421
releasing 282
returning control values for 158
ringing bell on 70
KEYBUTMASK
definition of 42
keycodes 162
description of 331
mapping 332
returning symbols for 80, 160
used as modifiers 268
value of transmitted by server 53
KeymapNotify event 191
KeyPress event 67, 78, 177, 192,
214
KeyRelease event 67, 78, 177,
214
keys
logical 331
releasing 281
used as modifiers 162, 331
keysym
defining with Common approach
299
defining with Engraving
approach 299
description of 331
glossary definition 459
mapping 332
values 297
KillClient request 29, 194
killing programs 27

L

large data transfers 376
layers of server 33
LeaveNotify event 136, 141, 180,
195, 283
LEDs 158
changing 77
Length error 322
length field
in replies 43
in requests 42, 53
libraries
C 5, 7
client-side 5, 13
Lisp 5
Xlib 7

Index

370, 385
PRIMARY 377
requesting 374
requestor 370
SECONDARY 378
side effects of 381
stored as properties 256, 257
target atoms 379
with side effects 381
SendEvent request 91, 256, 257,
   258
separators of property types 382
server 5
  and client responsibilities 9, 10
  buffering mechanism in 34
  closing connection to 28
  description of 4
  glossary definition 462
  grabbing 182
  information for at connection
    setup 52
  layers of 33
  opening connection to 13, 50, 75
  resetting 295
  restarting 284
  sample 33
server grabbing
  glossary definition 462
session manager properties 417
SetAccessControl request 260
SetClipRectangles request 74,
   115, 261
SetCloseDownMode request 29,
   263, 295
SetDashes request 74, 264
SetFontPath request 199, 265
SetInputFocus request 141, 266
SetModifierMapping request 210,
   268
SetPointerMapping request 210,
   270
SetScreenSaver request 272
SetSelectionOwner request 255,
   274, 371 - 376
shared memory 7
shared resources manipulating
   417
Shift modifier key mask 268, 331
sibling
  glossary definition 462
single-tasking systems 5

sockets
  UNIX domain 7
Solid GC value 185
source window 214
SPAN selection properties 385
stacking order 132, 212, 249, 252,
   287
  glossary definition 462
stacking windows 97
stack-mode values
  Above 99
  Below 99
  BottomIf 99
  Opposite 99
  TopIf 99
Static bit gravity 98
StaticColor visual type 108
  glossary definition 462
StaticGray visual type 108, 109
  glossary definition 462
stipple
  GC component 114
  glossary definition 463
  pixmap 114
StoreColors request 275, 277
StoreColors visual type 63
StoreNamedColor request 277
StoreNamedColor visual type 63
streams 7
StructureNotify event 398
StructureNotify event mask
  CirculateNotify event 87, 88
  ConfigureNotify event 94
  DestroyNotify event 131
  GravityNotify event 184
  MapNotify event 209
  ReparentNotify event 251
  UnmapNotify event 286
SubstructureNotify event mask
  CirculateNotify event 87, 88
  ConfigureNotify event 94
  CreateNotify event 122
  DestroyNotify event 131
  GravityNotify event 184
  MapNotify event 209
  ReparentNotify event 251
  UnmapNotify event 286
SubstructureRedirect event mask
   127
  ChangeWindowAttributes
    request 85
  CirculateWindow request 89
  ConfigureRequest event 95

win-gravity window attribute 126
WM_CLASS property 393
WM_CLIENT_MACHINE property 413
WM_COLORMAP_WINDOWS property 395
WM_COMMAND property 413
WM_HINTS property 391
WM_ICON_NAME property 389
WM_ICON_SIZE property 395
WM_NAME property 388
WM_NORMAL_HINTS property 389
WM_PROTOCOLS property 394, 400
WM_STATE property 395, 413
WM_TAKE_FOCUS atom 400
WM_TRANSIENT_FOR property 394

X

X Consortium 35
X protocol 7 - 8
  client and server responsibilities in 9
  data lengths in 14
  description of 7
  implementation of 7, 31
  keyboard handling in 9
  transferring data over network in 8
  types of errors in 29
X Window System
  description of 3
  example of client session in 11
  networking aspects of 4
  security issues in 35
xkill 27
  description of 28
XLFD conventions 429 - 453
Xlib 11
  and request buffering 31
  description of 5
  functions and protocol requests 351, 357
Xt Intrinsics *see* Intrinsics
XYFormat
  glossary definition 463

Z

ZFormat
  glossary definition 463

Index

About the Editor

Adrian Nye is a senior technical writer at O'Reilly and Associates. In addition to the X Window System programming manuals, he has written user's manuals for data acquistion products, and customized UNIX documentation for Sun Microsystems and Prime. Adrian has also worked as a programmer writing educational software in C, and as a mechanical engineer designing offshore oilspill cleanup equipment. He has long-term interests in using his technical writing skills to promote recycling and other environmentally-sound technologies. He graduated from the Massachusetts Institute of Technology in 1984 with a B.S. in Mechanical Engineering.